MEN IS CHEAP

CIVIL WAR AMERICA

*Peter S. Carmichael, Caroline E. Janney,
and Aaron Sheehan-Dean, editors*

This landmark series interprets broadly the history and culture of the Civil War era through the long nineteenth century and beyond. Drawing on diverse approaches and methods, the series publishes historical works that explore all aspects of the war, biographies of leading commanders, and tactical and campaign studies, along with select editions of primary sources. Together, these books shed new light on an era that remains central to our understanding of American and world history.

MEN IS CHEAP

Exposing the Frauds of Free Labor in Civil War America

BRIAN P. LUSKEY

THE UNIVERSITY OF NORTH CAROLINA PRESS

Chapel Hill

© 2020 The University of North Carolina Press

All rights reserved

Designed by Jamison Cockerham
Set in Arno, Scala Sans, Cupboard, and Cutright
by Tseng Information Systems, Inc.

Jacket illustrations: (front) detail from *War Views. No. 2042, Bounty Brokers Looking out for Substitutes*; (back) detail from *War Views. No. 2041, Bounty Brokers Looking out for Substitutes*. Both published by E. & H. T. Anthony, ca. 1865–1869. Library of Congress Prints and Photographs Division.

LIBRARY OF CONGRESS CATALOGING-IN-PUBLICATION DATA
Names: Luskey, Brian P., author.
Title: Men is cheap : exposing the frauds of free labor
in Civil War America / Brian P. Luskey.
Other titles: Civil War America (Series)
Description: Chapel Hill : The University of North Carolina Press, 2020. |
Series: Civil War America | Includes bibliographical references and index.
Identifiers: LCCN 2019032063 | ISBN 9781469654324 (cloth) |
ISBN 9781469688381 (paperback) | ISBN 9781469654331 (ebook) |
ISBN 9798890851277 (pdf)
Subjects: LCSH: Working class—United States—History—19th century. |
Labor—Social aspects—United States. | Employment agencies—Social aspects—
United States—History—19th century. | Capitalism—Social aspects—
United States. | United States—History—Civil War, 1861-1865—Recruiting,
enlistment, etc. | United States—Social conditions—19th century. |
United States—History—Civil War, 1861-1865—Public opinion.
Classification: LCC HD8070 .L79 2020 | DDC 331.10973/09034—dc23
LC record available at https://lccn.loc.gov/2019032063

FOR ASHLEY

with love

CONTENTS

Acknowledgments xi

Introduction *1*

1 Black Republican *11*

2 Bargains Worse than Fraudulent *44*

3 Capital in Self *78*

4 Worthy of His Hire *112*

5 The Draft, Popularized *143*

6 A Great Social Problem *177*

Conclusion *207*

Notes 221

Bibliography 253

Index 271

ILLUSTRATIONS

"The Biddy," *Vanity Fair*   32

"Progress vs. Old Fogeyism," *Vanity Fair*   33

Leadbeater's Renouned Stove Polish   34

"Out of a Situation," *Vanity Fair*   36

"'Sich a Gittin Up Stairs,'" *Vanity Fair*   37

"Mr. S-W-D.," *Vanity Fair*   39

"The Great Southern Peter Funk Shop," *Vanity Fair*   47

The Intelligence Office   57

Another War Declared   69

Attention Volunteers!   72

Volunteers Wanted!   74

"The Pennsylvania Volunteers," *Vanity Fair*   75

"The Highly Intelligent Contraband," *Vanity Fair*   102

Gray Reserves!   110

"What Will He Do with Them?," *Vanity Fair*   121

"Six Months in Arrears," *Vanity Fair*   124

"Victory!," *Album Varieties No. 3*   140

Emancipated Slaves   172

United States Soldiers at Camp "William Penn" Philadelphia, Pa.   174

Idol of Abolitionism   178

ACKNOWLEDGMENTS

IT IS A PLEASURE, after finishing a book about fraud, to write a few words about the abiding goodness of the people who helped me. I worked on this book for ten years and benefited from the assistance of many kind, sincere, and really smart folks. When I first presented a paper about intelligence offices at the annual meeting of the Business History Conference in 2010, my friends Wendy Woloson and Paul Erickson presented with me, and Ed Balleisen provided thoughtful commentary for us to consider. Wendy and I had long been interested in bringing together scholars who worked on the economies that nineteenth-century Americans labeled marginal and illegitimate but that were actually central to capitalism's development. Our panel gave us the push we needed to do so. I treasure my friendship with Wendy and I am grateful to have had the opportunity to collaborate with her on the conference and essay collection that resulted. We had the good fortune to work with Dan Richter, Bob Lockhart, and a wonderful lineup of essay contributors that included Will Mackintosh, Rob Gamble, Josh Greenberg, Adam Mendelsohn, Brendan O'Malley, Corey Goettsch, Craig Hollander, Mike Thompson, Katie Hemphill, Paul Erickson, and Ellen Garvey. The ideas that came out of that experience shaped what I wrote in these pages.

Many thanks to the National Endowment for the Humanities and the Program in Early American Economy and Society at the Library Company of Philadelphia for funding my sabbatical from teaching in 2014–15. My research at the Library Company and the Historical Society of Pennsylvania was crucial to the completion of this book, and I thank Cathy Matson, Jim Green, Tammy Gaskell, Sarah Heim, Krystal Appiah, Connie King, Linda August, Erika Piola, Sarah Weatherwax, Nicole Joniec, and Ann McShane for helping me navigate these institutions' collections. I also thank Jess Roney, Rich Newman, Sarah Gronningsater, Max Mishler, Randy Browne, Nic Wood, Rachel Walker, Aston Gonzalez, Emahunn Campbell, Jess Linker, Emily Owens, Manuel Covo, Kabria Baumgartner, Ben Fagan, Ben Hicklin, Sonia Hazard, Christine Croxall, Brendan Gillis, Dan Richter, Roderick McDonald, Michelle McDonald, Wendy Woloson, and David Miller for the intellectual companionship and camaraderie that made my stint in Philadelphia so productive and fun.

I am particularly obliged to Ellen Hartigan-O'Connor, my friend of more than fifteen years, for her encouragement and critical feedback. Ellen provided incisive commentary on several conference papers and chapter drafts. I could not have written this book in the way I did without her and her inspiring scholarship. I have been friends with Ben Irvin for just as long. He is, as he has always been, a source of strength, support, good ideas, and good laughs when my spirits need lifting. Thank you, Ben. I would also like to express my gratitude to other colleagues who have taken the time to edit my writing, send me research leads, discuss my work, and cheer me along my way: Jonathan Prude, Scott Sandage, Bill Blair, Cathy Kelly, Clay Risen, Carol Lasser, April Haynes, Lorien Foote, Carrie Janney, Katy Shively, Rachel Shelden, Ryan Keating, Drew Bledsoe, Jenny Weber, John Sacher, Rosanne Currarino, Steve Berry, Kathy Hilliard, Andy Lang, Sean Adams, Jim Broomall, Julie Mujic, Dave Thomson, Michael Caires, Katie Fialka, Andrew Fialka, Robby Poister, Heather Wilpone-Welborn, Emma Teitelman, Steve Phan, Emmanuel Dabney, Bert Dunkerly, Mike Gorman, Rob Widell, Paul O'Grady, Frank Towers, Sharon Murphy, Brian Schoen, Jess Lepler, Joanna Cohen, Emily Pawley, Caleb McDaniel, Seth Rockman, Ken Cohen, Seth Cotlar, Ann Little, Brian Jordan, Sarah Weicksel, Michael Woods, James Cornelius, Keith Bohannon, Jim Ogden, Frances Clarke, and Susannah Ural.

I am very lucky to work in the History Department at West Virginia University (WVU). Kate Staples, Kim Welch, Ari Bryen, Josh Arthurs, and Tyler Boulware are great friends and constituted a first-rate writing group that emphasized the beer, wine, and food as much as the history. They read a lot of this book and I profited from their suggestions. I appreciate all that my colleagues have done to make this book possible. Joe Hodge, Liz Fones-Wolf, Ken Fones-Wolf, Krystal Frazier, Melissa Bingmann, Matt Vester, Michele Stephens, Jim Siekmeier, and Jenny Boulware all gave me ideas and reassurance as I researched and wrote, and my student Montana Williamson helped me with research. I would also like to thank the Eberly College of Arts and Sciences at WVU and the West Virginia Humanities Council for providing research travel funding.

I have had the great honor of working with three amazing Civil War historians at WVU. I cannot rule out the possibility that I am the reason the Eberly Chair in Civil War Studies has revolved so many times. Hopefully, I can persuade Jason Phillips to stay. I have had a wonderful time learning from and collaborating with Jason and look forward to future conversations about Civil War historiography over fried food that we should not be eating in such quantities. No offense to anyone else, but Jason's immediate predecessor, Aaron Sheehan-Dean, is the hardest-working historian in the field. He says yes to everything, and that included helping me get this project off the ground and giving me feedback at crucial stages as I completed it. I am as appreciative of his insightful critiques and encouragement as I am inspired by his work ethic. Moreover, Aaron is a phenomenal cook and knows the best restaurants in any conference town. He is a good friend to have. Pete Carmichael was the chair of the search committee that hired me at WVU, and he has been a life coach, editor, and great friend ever since. There are a lot of brilliant historians out there, but Pete has always impressed me for his determination to find new analytical perspectives from which to read evidence. As a result, he has made me a better scholar and writer. More important, Pete, his wife Beth, and their daughters Cameron and Isabel have been like family to me, and I am grateful to have shared with them the many highs and lows that accompany life. I love you guys.

Pete helped me revise my book manuscript and brought it to the attention of Mark Simpson-Vos at UNC Press, and I feel so fortunate to have been able to work with Mark, Lucas Church, Jessica Newman, Jay Mazzocchi, Cate Hodorowicz, Dino Battista, Christi Stanforth, the anonymous readers, and other members of the Press's helpful and knowledgeable staff. Mark gave me a lot of time to figure out what this book was about and what structure the narrative would take. Once I made those decisions, his suggestions and support were instrumental in helping me feel that the work I was doing had value.

My family has always been there for me through thick and thin. Thank you to Barb Luskey, Pat Luskey, Kate Jacobson, Nora Jacobson, Paul Jacobson, Sharon Rossi Majkut, John Majkut, Gail Warner, Tina Luskey Peters, Jack Peters, Pete Luskey, Howard Whitehead, Mary Ellen Whitehead, Meghan Perry, and Chris Perry for your love and support. Ashley Whitehead Luskey, I love you and dedicate this book to you. Studying the Civil War has bound us together. We have promenaded the grounds of the capitol building in Richmond, hiked Gaines Mill and Malvern Hill, got married to the tune of "Ashokan Farewell," and planted roots in Gettysburg. We have taught our three-year-old daughter, Harper Jane, to recognize the faces of the war's politicians, generals, and soldiers. Our life together is filled with blessings. I appreciate everything you do to make it so.

MEN IS CHEAP

INTRODUCTION

THE MEN ON THE FRONT COVER of this book were ruthless. The caption "Bounty brokers looking out for substitutes" fails to convey what they did and what Americans thought about them. Bounty brokers spirited men into the military service of the United States during the Civil War, often by false pretenses. Northerners denounced them for it, and yet their condemnations of brokers' unethical conduct also obscure the significance of these men and the transactions they made. The activities of labor brokers and the broader cultural conversation about them help to illuminate the ways capitalism and the Civil War, the two most important transformative forces of nineteenth-century American life, shaped each other.

In the photograph, the brokers flank their office and a tool of their trade. Appealing and deceiving advertisements like this one promised hundreds of dollars in bounty payments to men who agreed to enlist. Financial inducements had been part of Union recruitment efforts since the beginning of the war, but they became more essential as the conflict continued, the number of volunteers waned, and the government's desperation for soldiers increased. Monetary considerations were central to conscription as well. The March 1863 Enrollment Act included a commutation clause that allowed drafted men either to pay $300 to release them from service or to find a substitute. The authors of the act believed that commutation would keep the price of substitutes at an affordable level for most draftees. No one would pay more than $300 for a substitute when they could pay the fee. But critics believed the legislation favored the rich, because not all drafted men had $300. In September 1863, reeling from a summer of riotous opposition to the draft, President Abraham Lincoln defended commutation in an unpublished memorandum. "Without the money provision," he reasoned, "competition among the more wealthy might, and probably would, raise the price of substitutes above three hundred dollars, thus leaving the man who could raise only three hundred dollars, no escape from personal service." Lincoln's statement proved prescient. In July 1864, bowing to criticism and noting that too many drafted men were paying the fee rather than serving or getting a substitute, Congress repealed commutation. The labor market for soldiers became fiercely competitive as draftees sought to hire men at escalating rates to do the job of killing and dying for them. Brokers managed these transactions and profited from this competition.¹

Civil War historians have long debated whether the phrase "a rich man's war, and a poor man's fight" accurately describes the economic and social status of enlisted men. There is no scholarly consensus on the question. In fact, the debate has obscured the complex economic processes that motivated and shaped the North's war effort. Fought to uphold the ideal of "free labor," the Union war encouraged Northern entrepreneurs, employers, and soldiers to envision their impending success through the accumulation of capital. Often, they sought the independence that capital purchased by employing laborers whom the war had made vulnerable. The war seemed to offer some Northerners opportunities to get rich because it clarified that other Americans were poor.²

Substitute brokers seized on wartime chances to exploit the desperation that had defined transactions occurring in antebellum "intelligence offices," or employment agencies. Americans hated intelligence offices, and yet they needed them so. During the war, these offices served the military and domestic necessities of the Union army and Northern households. Employers schemed as often as brokers did to accrue the benefits that the labor market offered. Labor brokers helped mobilize soldiers for battle, and in turn soldiers sought to employ former slaves who would ease their burden in camp and their wives' burden at home. Northern civilians used intelligence offices to funnel laborers from the South to their households in order to underscore their independence. In this book, I examine the speculations of those who tried to turn wage labor transactions to their benefit in the Civil War era. The debates about those transactions expose an unsettling contradiction: Northerners' devotion to the principles of free labor and the Union produced rampant speculation and coercive labor arrangements that many Americans labeled fraudulent. The concepts of military and domestic necessity were connected in white Northerners' minds and illuminate what they thought this war was over. In the process of winning the war, white Northerners grappled with the frauds of free labor. They used labor brokers as a foil to conceal their own roles in wage labor's coercions even as they depended on labor brokers to do indispensable work that helped the Northern state and Northern employers emerge victorious.³

What was labor brokers' work, and how did they do it? One member of this despised breed, George Northrup, wrote a breathless letter to his employers John Fay and Richard Dalton on January 5, 1865, that gives us a sense of the business:

> Gents I learned last night that the 15 Dist[rict] is filled their Quota with the credits of 3 Years men that comprises Washington & Ranciler counties & I also learn that the 16 Dist[rict] is filled also & I feare that the most of this State is the same way Men is cheep here to Day 3 Years Sub[stitutes]. 700. to 800. Dollars I think that we will get a call for 500.000 Men by the first of March but not but a few men will be wanted this time if I can find any Place for men I will come Down soon & if not wont come Down at all on this call unless you want me [to] come & help you to sell & if you do let me no
>
> yours in haste.[4]

Fay and Dalton were recruitment brokers for the United States military who had an office in Brooklyn, New York, near the naval rendezvous and other points at which men were mustered into the service. Northrup was their agent upstate, writing from Troy. The firm had information about how many men had presented themselves as potential substitutes. Northrup had information about the extent to which congressional districts had filled the quotas stipulated in the latest draft call. Northrup's news was grim for the brokers. The communities of the Hudson River Valley from just south of Albany north to Lake George had filled their quotas, depressing prices in this market. Men *was* cheap because Northrup found it difficult to sell town commissioners the scraps of paper known as credits on which brokers scrawled the names of substitutes who had enlisted in the metropolis but were to be counted toward draft quotas elsewhere. When the demand for substitutes was low in his location, Northrup could only offer his willingness to find other chances to make deals or his labor to sell credits to town commissioners who visited headquarters in Brooklyn. Or he could put stock in rumors that President Lincoln would in short order make a draft call for 500,000 men. Then the brokers would make money again. Their business operated in ways that would not have seemed strange to contemporaries. Northrup's letter resembles the financial quotations page of the nineteenth-century newspaper, citing prices and making prognostications about the market. Northrup's vision of a future in which credits and men would be bought and sold in volume seems a hopeful dream, but dreams, rumors, best guesses, and even facts could move nineteenth-century markets up and down.

We know about Northrup's letter, however, because this business was rife with fraud. In February 1865, War Department detective Lafayette Baker arrested twenty-seven recruitment brokers who operated in and around New York City and confiscated their correspondence. In doing so, he exposed a network of ambitious men engaged in a coordinated effort to forge enlistment documents and pocket the proceeds of enlistment payments. Without the commutation fee to regulate the substitute market, prices had spiraled upward. Brokers smelled profit, positioning themselves as assistants to drafted men looking for substitutes, town and county commissioners tasked with filling local quotas, and ordinary men and their wives who calculated that soldiering, a desperate choice among desperate choices, was a way to earn money. Armed with prices current, access to information along telegraph wires, and money to grease palms, brokers manipulated the movement of men to their benefit. Substitute brokers were excoriated and essential figures because both drafted men and potential substitutes needed information to find each other in an anonymous market for labor. That was the purpose of any intelligence office. Earlier legislation concerning recruitment had promised a finder's fee of two dollars per soldier for anyone who produced men for enlistment. That fee was just a little higher than what intelligence office agents generally made. By the end of 1863, a government desperate to recruit more men had increased those fees to fifteen dollars for nonveterans. Yet these payments hardly factored in brokers' calculations. They speculated that they could make hundreds of dollars per soldier. And they did.[5]

The fraud in this market resembled the dissembling found in other markets. The brokers filled blank credit forms with fake names, evoking the bookkeeping and accounting fraud pervasive among commercial clerks. They mimicked slave auctioneers by hiding evidence of recruits' disease and physical infirmities from doctors. They adopted the tactics of runners of counterfeit currency, taking men who had failed medical examinations in one location from town to town until they found surgeons willing to vouch for their health and provost marshals willing to accept them. Brokers boasted to one another that they "could put anything in" the army "in the shape of man." But they did not just talk a good game. They were brazen thieves, lubricating substitutes with alcohol in taverns that were sometimes adjacent to recruitment rendezvous in order to steal enlistment payments. Many substitutes woke up with headaches and only dim recollections of how they got to camp. Brokers told their marks to wait in another room while they got their payment from the recruiter. They would then give substitutes a part of the money owed to them and explain that they would get the rest in installments. Brokers would then vanish with the lion's share of the proceeds, confident that families of enlisted men would not have the information, the gumption, or the power to apprehend them. Theft could be hidden by money laundering. Fay and Dalton took at least $20,000 of their profits from this lucrative trade and, in a statement of their abiding patriotism, bought U.S. bonds.[6]

Historians who study the relationship between slavery and capitalism have argued that slave markets created value beyond the worth of enslaved people's labor because slaves could be turned into prices from cradle to grave. The coercive languages and practices of the substitute market might suggest a connection between substitute brokering and the process of commodification at the heart of slavery. The blurring of the paper credits and the exchange of labor in this market led Northrup to use words that seem ironic to us because this was an age of emancipation. But "Men is cheep" was a lamentation among brokers who were not getting the return they wanted in a *wage labor* economy. The substitute market was not a slave trade. It was big business — a wage labor market that created value for the men who managed it beyond the transfer of wages for labor.[7]

Americans found substitute brokers reprehensible for the frauds they committed upon the unsuspecting. Baker believed they were a threat to the nation's quest for survival. The exorbitant value that they created and pilfered made the market in substitutes unique. But substitute brokers were also representative figures who exposed the frauds of free labor — the ideology that motivated Northerners in their fight against a confederacy of slaveholders. Free labor ideology was a beguiling line of thought, promising independence both to workers and employers. Laborers were free to achieve economic independence if they worked hard and saved wages, and men who had capital were free to hire wage workers with their savings. Free labor united Northerners around a set of beliefs — at the time called the "harmony of interests" — that valued the character traits and habits that supposedly explained the success of producers and entrepreneurs alike.[8]

The war for Union tested free labor and exposed its contradictions, for this ideology had insidious consequences that spurred competition for survival as much as success. The war demonstrated that all Northerners were dependent on other people's labor and capital, even though employers' and employees' dependence was not equivalent. Civil War Northerners used their wages — money they considered capital in the making — and their ability to employ workers as indices that measured their relative independence. In that way, the Union war seemed to Northerners an opportunity to become more independent rather than an affront to their faith in free labor. Nevertheless, the war for Union unmade the promise of free labor for workers and upheld the promise of free labor for those with capital. *Men Is Cheap* tells the stories of basement-dwelling employment office keepers, ordinary Union soldiers and famous officers, household mistresses, failed-businessmen-turned-recruiters, politicians, and benevolent society agents who fused their interests to those of the state and used the violent circumstances of war to engage in human trafficking in the name of wage labor and free capital.[9]

Their speculations in the wage labor market unfolded in an institution that Northerners loved to hate. Intelligence offices hosted apparently mundane transactions between hirers and workers, but they provoked acrimonious debates about the legitimacy of exchanges that created value out of wage labor beyond work and wages. Labor agents carved an economic niche for themselves as middlemen who made money by providing information and a service. As such, their speculations resembled those made by other entrepreneurs in an economy and culture that valued ambition. Yet labor brokers' ambitions and the means they used to realize them earned criticism from contemporaries because they meddled with the supposedly symbiotic partnership between employers and employees and often defrauded both parties. As a result, they earned condemnation often directed at other commercial middlemen—clerks and pawnbrokers, for instance—who profited by inserting themselves between consumers and the products they desired. Moreover, intelligence office transactions were controversial because they defined wage labor with far greater precision than the hopeful dogmas of free labor. Labor agents, eager employers, and desperate workers all contributed to a material and cultural system that privileged the ability of employers to procure the most desirable workers over laborers' ability to achieve social and economic mobility. They did so by making assertions that justified their speculations for capital, wages, and marketable things. They also made claims about the cultural meanings of race, gender, age, and class that shaped the contours of those speculations and the market in which they occurred.[10]

The Civil War was a pivotal moment in which Americans tried to reconcile their need for intelligence offices with their anxieties about the transactions occurring within them. Despite concerted antebellum efforts to exclude employment agents and agencies from the narrative of appropriate economic exchange, the federal government, benevolent organizations, and entrepreneurs formed intelligence offices during and after the Civil War to manage what bureaucrats, reformers, and citizens considered to be the crises produced by the conflict. The United States, aided by civilian and military agents, enlisted soldiers in recruiting offices and emancipated slaves at army encampments and installations. White Northerners rushed to fight for the

Union, Constitution, and democracy and enslaved people sought the freedom that Union armies seemed to offer. These movements were inextricably linked to each other, and to a certain extent were based on autonomous choices that individuals made.[11]

Yet free labor linked agency and autonomy, competition and coercion. Any idealism about the former pair of concepts cannot obscure the deep inequities caused by the latter. The war for Union constituted a crisis for free labor and a moment in which those ideals could be fulfilled. Free labor supposedly ennobled hard work, perseverance, and the accumulation of capital, and yet the war made all Northerners dependent on the wage labor market in their competition for success and survival, profit and prestige. The war unmade the hopeful calculus of workers' upward mobility because it gave eager employers and entrepreneurial brokers—themselves threatened by economic crisis caused by financial panic, secession, and war—opportunities to exploit men, women, and children who lacked capital and autonomy. The recruitment of white citizen soldiers, the employment of former slaves in the army as laborers and later as soldiers, and these people's movement to Southern battlefields threatened their access to credit and capital. Their movement also produced a chain reaction of events that spurred the creation of intelligence offices whose managers pushed Southern black women and children to white Northerners' homes to serve as domestic servants and pulled some Confederate soldiers to desert their cause and flee to Northern cities in search of work. Changes in the North's draft legislation produced a market in substitutes run by brokers whose access to labor market information allowed them to prey upon ordinary Northerners and send them into the fight. In the aftermath of the conflict, intelligence offices mediated the movement of Union veterans and former slaves searching for work in the North. These migrations from north to south—and back again—were linked causally and constituted the labor movements of the war for Union. Labor brokers fashioned these causal links and the narrative of this book revolves around their speculations. Filtered by and through intelligence offices and their agents, these labor movements established modes of coercion and patterns of dependence that defined wage labor and won the war. Americans may have condemned the intelligence office and its negotiations, but these institutions thrived because the freedoms of wage labor and slave emancipation that employers most cared about were their own—the opportunities to obtain workers of their choice. The economic and cultural processes unfolding in intelligence offices worked alongside industrialization and a coalescing definition of freedom through contract to expand the power of those with capital and make the postbellum United States what historian David Montgomery has called "a nation of employees."[12]

The speculators I examine in *Men Is Cheap* include not only seasoned labor brokers but also down-on-their-luck merchants, clerks, officers, and soldiers who seized upon the prospect of recruiting workers as a means of getting ahead. Thomas Webster, a Philadelphia tobacco merchant whose antislavery principles put him at odds with the Virginians with whom he did business, became a recruiter of African American soldiers who helped destroy the slaveholders' rebellion. John Nelson, a Connecticut machinist and pugilist, became an army officer and recruiter who employed coercive means to enlist African American soldiers under his command and for his benefit. Charles Brewster, a Massachusetts store clerk, and Henry Walker, a New York farmer, tried to parlay their positions in the Union army to advantage in the labor market for themselves and their families. The words and actions of these men, as well as those of famous leaders such as John Andrew, Benjamin Butler, Abraham Lincoln, and William Still, drive the narrative. Their personal quirks, the fluctuating fortunes of their work, and the fluid networks of employers and laborers they connected help us understand how the economy worked in the Civil War era. Consider, for instance, the brightening prospects of George Northrup in January 1865. Five days after writing his remorseful missive to Fay and Dalton, he learned that it was not clear whether upstate congressional districts had enlisted enough men. Things were looking up. If the local provost marshal did not "act . . . like a Damd Fool about the call & the credits," Northrup would "be on hand" in Brooklyn and "want a good many men." In fact, he hoped that Fay and Dalton were already sending him substitutes or the credits that represented them: "I suppose you are shipping me fast by this time." Success was in the offing to those who moved rapidly to exploit information about the wage labor market and people's vulnerability within it, but success was also fleeting and uncertain.[13]

The characters in this book believed in free labor, slave emancipation, and accumulating profits because these things reinforced each other. The wartime doctrines of military and domestic necessity gave them license to realize principles and amass principal. As the war and the process of emancipation unfolded, those with capital tried to use the power of the state to exploit other people's dependence. The Civil War gave human trafficking renewed strength and prominence in regional and national economies, and traffickers acted with ingenuity to develop new practices that allowed them to remain one step ahead of the law, political edict, military authorities, or cultural opinion. The tight relationship between war and human trafficking highlights the importance of examining an analytical spectrum that distinguishes consent and coercion and shows how these concepts worked together to define how people lived and how they understood their labor arrangements. We can appreciate the distinction between slavery and not-slavery and also comprehend the limited field of workers' choice, their enforced movement to faraway locations, and the ways their lives were shaped by the agency of the liberated. Who were they? They were the people who forced others to move during war—labor brokers, military officers, state officials, and families who desperately wanted workers. Each group took advantage of other people's wartime misfortune to get their man, woman, and child cheap. Coerced people were, during war, a most valuable currency that made capital free.[14]

1

BLACK REPUBLICAN

ON JUNE 16, 1854, as the Kansas-Nebraska Act galvanized its opponents into a Republican Party coalition devoted to free labor and free capital, Thomas Webster Jr. of Philadelphia checked into the Exchange Hotel in Richmond. Thirty-six years old, Webster had been in the tobacco wholesaling business for more than fifteen years. He started in the trade as clerk and then junior partner in the firm of Ruddach & Webster. The senior member of the firm, David Ruddach, was related to his mother. Credit reports from after the Civil War claimed that the business "failed in 1837," but city directories and Philadelphia newspaper advertisements show that assertion to be false. The firm remained in business in the late 1830s and early 1840s, and Webster left it to go into business "on his own hook," to use the parlance of the day, in 1846. Advertisements in the *Philadelphia Inquirer* locate his office near the Delaware River wharves, where schooners and steamboats deposited hogsheads and boxes of leaf and manufactured tobacco from Connecticut, Cuba, Kentucky, Ohio, Pennsylvania, and, most of all, Virginia. Like other businessmen, he emphasized his connections to well-known producers—"factories at Richmond, Petersburg, and Lynchburg" that supplied him "warranted brands." He underlined his attention to local consumers, offering tobacco in "extra fine, fine medium, and inferior grades"—with prices to match—that would satisfy the tastes of a variety of chewers and smokers across Philadelphia's social order. By the early 1850s, one credit reporting agent considered Webster a "fair" risk for loans, although he also believed that Webster's financial stability was underwritten by his 1848 marriage to Eliza Ann Richardson, the daughter of a wealthy umbrella manufacturer. He may have been worth $10,000, a substantial sum in these years, but even so the credit reporter believed that Webster sometimes "gets short" on funds and was "not v[ery]. prompt in paying his bills."[1]

Kinship mattered for success in business. Webster's family ties had facilitated his entrance into the commercial world, and marriage opened new conduits to credit and capital. But Webster's reputation in the city's business community, as reflected in credit reports based on current rumor and fact, remained precarious. By 1854, perhaps in an attempt to bolster his credit or hedge against the potential ruin that unflattering credit reports sometimes caused, he had accepted a position as agent for two shipping companies — Hand's Line that operated schooners sailing from Philadelphia to Baltimore and Alexandria, and the Union Steamship Company, which carried passengers and products among Philadelphia, Norfolk, and Richmond. By doing so, he sought to exploit his commercial knowledge of the traffic in goods along the Delaware, Patapsco, Potomac, and James Rivers for steady gain. In advertisements for the Union Steamship line, Webster touted the accommodations on the company's vessels and the speed, economy, and regularity of the transport. Philadelphia businessmen knew that one of the company's ships would leave the wharf every five days, and Webster assured them that the company took the utmost precautions to ensure that goods and people would arrive safely. Webster did his own business by these ships. In October 1854, for instance, the Union Company's steamboat *City of Richmond* carried "8 cases Tingley's superior sweet" for him to sell to retailers. His agency netted him a comfortable salary of some $2,000 per year and space aboard the company's vessels that he used to make further profits in the tobacco trade. His business interests dovetailed to make tidy profits in an uncertain economy.[2]

While in Richmond, Webster could serve both of his interests: he could solicit clients for the Union Steamship Company or meet tobacco manufacturers beneath the Greek Revival columns of the Exchange Hotel. He could take a short walk to the tobacco factories in Shockoe Bottom to inspect the product being packaged for shipment to Philadelphia. If he had done so, he might have walked past the offices and auction houses of slave traders on Franklin, Wall, and Fifteenth Streets, easily identified by the red flags raised over them to announce impending sales. Maybe he heard the patter of an auctioneer attempting to solicit bids for a human being standing on his block. Webster's conscience surely would have been pricked. He hated slavery and the slaveholding aristocracy. Yet to earn a living as a tobacco wholesaler and agent of the carrying trade he had to cater to slaveholders' interests and depend upon the productive capacities of enslaved people and the value of the commodities they made. Webster coped with the instability and uncertainty of the antebellum business world in much the same ways that other commercial men did, hedging against risk. He differed from many of his contemporaries, though, because the ambivalence of his creditors that forced him to seek safety through an agency was largely the result of his public reputation as a "black republican."[3]

During the economic crisis of the late 1850s and early 1860s that made Northerners' individual and household independence seem more precarious, antislavery businessmen engaged in the Southern trade faced an ethical dilemma as they sought to reconcile their ideology and interest. Webster tried to finesse this dilemma and accumulate economic and moral capital from different groups. Opposed to slavery, Webster nevertheless persuaded some Virginians to deal with him because all could profit jointly in a booming national political economy based on it. Webster's cautious hedge was risky and became untenable as Northerners and Southerners debated the promise and peril of free labor and hurtled toward their separation over slavery. By 1860, the financial uncertainty born of the Panic of 1857 and the secession crisis encouraged Webster to illuminate for Republican allies the moral principles that had caused him economic hardship and made him deserving of patronage. Even though he failed to obtain a political post, Webster positioned himself to move goods and people in support of the Union war as it commenced. It was through the work of middlemen like Webster—as much as through the efforts of abolitionists, Republican politicians, Union soldiers, and enslaved people—that slavery ended and free labor's promise for workers was unmade during the Civil War era. Webster and his ilk represented the speculative—many said the fraudulent—impulses and activities in an economy founded on the fact that having capital meant having power. That capital would make these Northerners more independent in a competitive market, and their speculations would shape the contours of war and emancipation.[4]

The want advertisements of nineteenth-century newspapers, beyond their polite entreaties to the public for patronage, are an index of an abstraction we call the market. They represent the competition for credit and capital and for work, workers, and things, and illustrate advertisers' dependence on producers, distributors, and consumers for access to the resources they deemed valuable. In one column of the July 18, 1854, issue of the *Richmond Daily Dispatch*—published one month after Webster visited the city—advertisers puffed the virtues of children's shoes, cheap clothes, gold pens, and cement they had for sale. A slave trader named Benjamin Davis also offered a fifty-dollar reward for help in recapturing his slave, Charles. Having lost this man he called a thing, Davis offered to pay someone to hunt, catch, and return his property. Davis's desperation for the labor and monetary value Charles represented and the desperation of the slave catcher who needed the reward money—a small fraction of what Charles was worth—would be eased when the latter seized a desperate man on the run.⁵

At his office on Wall Street "under City Hotel," Davis sold men, women, and children to be transported by schooner and steamer to other auction houses in the Gulf States, where they would be sold again to work on cotton and sugar plantations. Apparently, when Webster had been in the city, Davis was trying to sell Charles at an auction sale, but the buyers would not meet Davis's estimation of his property's value. Charles Gilbert—for he had a last name—took matters into his own hands to avoid an auction fate, and as a result forced Davis to reckon with the possibility that he would lose the value he represented. Within a few days of his slave's escape, Davis increased the reward from $50 to $100 and guessed that Gilbert was making his way to Old Point Comfort, where his mother lived. Davis informed the slave catchers who would need to identify Gilbert that the runaway was twenty-one years of age, approximately five feet four or five inches tall, and distinguished by the "ginger-bread color" of his skin.⁶

Davis was right about Gilbert's direction. He had chanced to meet a captain of a Boston-bound schooner who agreed to take him to Massachusetts from the Virginia coast. So he fled east. Old Point Comfort had once been his home. It was also the place where, in 1619, the first African slaves had been forced ashore in North America. Gilbert hoped that, with the help of his mother and friends, it would be the place where his enslavement would come to an end. When he arrived home, however, slave hunters tipped off by Davis's advertisement were stalking the neighborhood and making it difficult for Gilbert's kin to come to his aid. They would pay a price if caught harboring a fugitive. Gilbert's knowledge of the area helped him. He knew that the Hygeia Hotel, a seaside resort for the nation's elite adjacent to the prominent military installation Fort Monroe, was built on pillars that allowed a man three or four feet of crawl space. He survived in a hiding place near the hotel's cistern for four weeks, eating discarded food from a "slop tub" in the dead of night. When a young white boy trying to catch chickens under the hotel threatened to blow his cover, Gilbert snarled like a dog to scare him off. The ruse worked, but only temporarily, because he overheard the boy's incensed father resolve to kill the cur who had frightened his son. On the run once again, Gilbert appreciated how precarious his position was in a landscape overseen by slaveholders and their agents. He climbed up an acorn tree one day, then hid under wooden floorboards in a washhouse in which his friends worked. Flushed out by slave catchers, he retreated to a thicket, then to a marsh, then back to his hiding place under the Hygeia. Evading the reach of the hunters made him miss his appointment with the Boston-bound ship. Gilbert's mother, a free woman, was able at the last minute to cobble together thirty dollars for his passage on another ship. He hid aboard that vessel for another four weeks while it docked at Norfolk. Gilbert's long journey out of slavery ended on November 11, 1854, when he set foot on the Delaware River wharves in Philadelphia. Benjamin Davis, unaware of Gilbert's arrival in the City of Brotherly Love, was still desperately advertising his reward in Richmond for the capture and return of his human property.[7]

We know the details of Gilbert's lengthy and harrowing flight from slavery because William Still, a prominent Philadelphia abolitionist, published his notes concerning Gilbert's experience after the Civil War. Gilbert was one of the hundreds of men and women whom Still and other Philadelphians helped to escape from slavery in the 1850s. Gilbert escaped, Still wrote, on a "steamship bound for Philadelphia." Still's compendium of traffic on the Underground Railroad includes several references to runaway slaves becoming "acquainted" with stewards, hiding near boilers, or even booking state rooms on the *Philadelphia* or the *City of Richmond*, vessels in the Union Steamship Company's fleet. Uncomfortable though their passage may have been on these ships, escaping slaves found temporary confinement in their holds worth enduring because opportunities for independent life and labor awaited them in Canada. Still never mentions Webster as a "helper" or "sympathizer" with the activists and activities of the Underground Railroad. Still notes that friendly captains and stewards aboard these vessels—and not distant agents—arranged for enslaved people's passage. Yet Still also called smuggling slaves to Canada a "business" that had to be "transact[ed]" surreptitiously. Unlike in the domestic slave trade that shipped enslaved people from the upper South to the lower South, "[s]tockholders did not expect any dividends" from this underground traffic in people. "The right hand was not to know what the left hand was doing."[8]

Still's metaphors of the financial market were neither coincidental nor poorly chosen. They were at the heart of a struggle for meaning that declared certain economic acts legitimate and illegitimate. The struggle to declare slavery's capital illegitimate was central to Still's life. His father had purchased his freedom from his owner, and his older brother was kidnapped into slavery for much of his life, losing the ability to control the fruits of his labor. William Still was born in Medford, New Jersey, moved to Philadelphia at the age of twenty-three, and took a job as a janitor and clerk for the Pennsylvania Anti-Slavery Society. In the early 1850s, he became the chairman and corresponding secretary of the Vigilance Committee, which managed the Society's efforts to usher Southern slaves from Philadelphia to Canada. Still and his associates worked to undermine the business of slavery by adopting the means that business used to distribute people and value through the American economy. The Underground Railroad siphoned money from the pockets of slaveholders—the financial capital embodied in enslaved laborers—and sent its passengers into independence on Canadian soil. In his book, Still quoted newspaper advertisements like Benjamin Davis's and the testimony of former slaves to articulate the value that slaveholders lost. Still was keen to note the prices that these former slaves would have garnered at auction and the annual fees that they had paid to masters in Richmond, Petersburg, and Norfolk to hire out their time. These prices and fees made plain the injustice of slavery's theft and the justice of the Underground Railroad's stealings. In fact, the enslaved people whose stories Still told often chose the moment they heard about their impending sale—the moment at which their value would be reckoned—to run away. Through this northbound traffic, valuable commodities became invaluable people working together for collective independence in a confrontation with slavery's capital. There were winners and losers in these transactions, much like in every sector of American business. Slaveholders lost thousands of dollars, represented by the present and future labor and the hiring fees and wages of their slaves. Former slaves obtained a foothold on independence in Canada that they could not enjoy in the United States because the 1850 Fugitive Slave Act created a national market in slave catching to bolster the claims of slaveholders and the authority of the men who hunted human property for them. Once safely across the Canadian border, formerly enslaved men and women wrote jubilant letters to Still that emphasized the transformation of their position in market terms. Under the protection of Queen Victoria, they could keep wages they earned from their labor.[9]

As the Union Company's agent, Thomas Webster observed the company's ships dock at wharves on the Delaware River and was aware of all types of licit and illicit cargo aboard them. He was, at the very least, a silent partner in the business of emancipating Virginia slaves. His tobacco wholesaling business depended on the labor of enslaved people who harvested the crop in rural fields and manufactured it in urban factories. His work as agent of a steamship company whose ships slaves used to leave Virginia and its slave economy worked against his bottom line. The labor of slaves made Thomas Webster more capital, and as a result, more independent, even as his antislavery ideology made his fortunes more uncertain. Still unwittingly illuminated Webster's conundrum when he referenced the escape of Jack

Pettifoot, who had been hired out by his master to the tobacco factory of McHenry & McCulloch in Petersburg. Pettifoot "reached Philadelphia by the Richmond line of steamers, stowed away among the pots and cooking utensils," Still explained. The tobacco manufacturers, Pettifoot told Still, were "rather more oppressive than he agreed for." Webster's 1848 advertisement for the "warranted brands" he had for sale included the tobacco McCulloch sold to him. Webster bet that tobacco manufacturers would continue to do business with an antislavery Northerner because the ships that took away a few of their slaves also carried their products to Northern markets.[10]

Webster's gamble on the nation's political economy and the profit and prestige it offered him was a precarious one. So he broadened his labors from the strictly commercial to the benevolent. In August 1855, Clarissa Davis, one of the enslaved women who fled Portsmouth, Virginia, on the *City of Richmond*, wrote to William Still. She had heard that "the yellow fever is very bad down south." Indeed, in her hometown, the fever raged that summer. Early reports in Richmond tried to downplay the outbreak, but soon the suffering was undeniable and costly for Portsmouth's and Norfolk's municipal authorities. The *Richmond Daily Dispatch* implored the charitably inclined to provide succor to the sick even as it debated whether to quarantine ship traffic up the James River to protect the health of people in the state's capital.[11]

Benevolent associations sprang into action in Richmond and around the country to help pay for the expenses associated with care for the dying. In Philadelphia, Webster tried to alleviate the suffering, urging a public meeting at the city's Merchants' Exchange to do something for the "dying and destitute" among their "Southern friends." He offered resolutions that would systematize the collection and distribution of funds to the relevant agencies in Virginia and became the chairman of the committee tasked with implementing his plan. At a time when sectional conflict was rising to a crescendo, he emphasized ties of personal and commercial friendship between the regions. Aiding the sick in their time of trial would cement bonds of friendship. At the end of November, Webster dutifully accounted for Philadelphia's role in mitigating the fever's impact, telling a public meeting in the city that nearly $46,000 of Philadelphians' contributions had been spent for vital medicines and the transportation of doctors and nurses to the affected areas. Other sums were held over to assist with the burial of Philadelphians who had died while treating the sick, aid for their families and Virginia orphans, and the erection of a monument to their memory. Webster was applauded for his "administrative capacity and unwearied efforts in the discharge of the responsible duties which were confided to him." His commercial acumen translated into success in the benevolent sphere. Perhaps the charitable capital he accumulated for the benefit of Southern friends would translate into personal capital for him. The epidemic had temporarily cut off traffic to the afflicted areas, hampering Webster's two means of earning money through the tobacco and carrying trades. The Union Steamship Company's ships would not dock at Norfolk while the fever persisted. Improving health in the Tidewater would promote a resumption of healthy commerce.[12]

If epidemic disease and its treatment could bring the regions together, the sectional conflict over slavery loomed as a more fatal contagion to the Republic and to Webster's bottom line. In 1856, the prospects for the Underground Railroad's traffic from the James River to the Delaware River dimmed. In that year, Virginia tried to stop the drain of valuable commodities from the state's economy by passing a law "providing additional protection for the slave property of citizens of this commonwealth." That broad title obscured the act's specific purpose—to codify and enforce the inspection of vessels owned by non-Virginians that sailed routes from the state to "any port or place north of and beyond the capes of Virginia." The law specifically required that "steamers plying as regular packets between ports in Virginia and those north"—like the Union Steamship Company's—submit to inspection and stipulated that they had to be "inspected at the port of departure nearest to Old Point Comfort." That location, a place of refuge for Charles Gilbert, became a vantage point from which state authorities hoped to stop fugitives' escape. The law empowered official inspectors as well as river and harbor pilots to search these vessels for enslaved persons "concealed on board."[13]

The law sought to stop what legislators considered a fraudulent underground market by invigorating a market in the capture of slaves. It created a "fugitive slave fund" consisting of tax money collected from Virginia's citizens and fees and fines collected from Northern shipping companies in order to pay inspectors and patrollers for their surveillance. The inspection fee for each vessel was $5, and if a captain evaded the required inspection, he or the boat's owner would be forced to pay a penalty of $500 and be subject to arrest, whereby the guilty party would have to post $1,000 as bond to be released on his own recognizance. If an inspector discovered an enslaved person on board a vessel, members of the ship's crew could be arrested and the ship impounded and forfeited. The inspector would receive $100 as reward for the capture of the slave or "one-half of the proceeds arising from the sale" of the ship. Conversely, an inspector who allowed a slave to escape would be fined $100. The theft that enslaved people and their Northern allies perpetrated yielded legal responses to secure slavery by seizing money from the companies that knowingly or unknowingly smuggled slaves out of Virginia. Virginia's law relied on the power of the state's legal system to accumulate the money and the monetary incentives needed to pay inspectors. The law marked Northern commercial vessels as potential conduits for underground trade and as such those vessels and their owners and agents were made to pay the price. By passing this act, Virginia outlawed the ambivalent attitudes and activities of Northern businessmen such as Webster. The law did not seek to proscribe all interregional trade—just the trade perpetuated by men who might seek to mix licit and illicit traffic in things and people.[14]

The dependable movement of steamships between Philadelphia and Richmond was crucial to Webster's financial stability, and when infectious disease or state law delayed and obstructed that traffic, panic loomed. Their regular circuits aside, steamboats were neither safe nor safe investments. The Union Steamship Company's "splendid side wheel steamer" *Norfolk* was the pride of its fleet, "fitted out in a superior style" with "handsome accommodations" for its passengers. In September 1857, the *Norfolk* sunk during a hurricane some ten miles south of Chincoteague Island. Fortunately, the twenty-one members of the crew and twenty-six passengers, though worse for wear, were safely put aboard lifeboats with just minutes to spare. Unfortunately, the "valuable cargo of merchandise" in the *Norfolk*'s hold was lost. The passengers, picked up by nearby vessels and transferred to the *City of Richmond*, returned to Philadelphia in ragged clothing and without their belongings. "Their wants were promptly attended to by Mr. Webster," Philadelphia's *Public Ledger* explained in its coverage of the disaster. As agent for the company, Webster gave the survivors new "tickets for the South and money for expenses." While the Union Steamship Company weathered this financial hit, the same storm had sunk the *Central America*, another side wheel steamer, off the coast of North Carolina. It carried some $1.5 million in gold from California, hard money that New York bankers had hoped would restore economic calm disturbed by New England railroad directors' rash speculations in Western land and bonds. Those speculations had brought the New Englanders into conflict with Southern railroad owners and investors who wanted to build a Western link from Missouri to California's gold mines. The resulting struggle between settlers backed by the competing interests was civil war in Kansas. Both sides fumbled Western gold, and after the loss of the lucre aboard the *Central America* the financial panic of 1857 began, embroiling the Northern economy in tumultuous default and unemployment.[15]

Webster had cultivated a position as a middleman who supplied people with what they wanted and needed. That position was unstable and made even more so by his wager on the nation's fractured political economy. The decline in Webster's commercial fortunes evidently started before the Panic struck. Legal judgments of several hundred dollars rendered against him in 1855 and 1856 suggested to credit reporters that he "will prob[ably]. be oblig[e]d. to give up bus[iness].," although the "energy & activity" he showed in the "Norfolk Contribution" evidently buoyed his prospects. Webster's charitable spirit earned him friends. But by 1856, credit reporters claimed he was out of the tobacco business, and the next year's credit report lists a legal judgment levied against him for over $4,000 in the months after the panic hit. The plaintiff in the case was John Greaner, a Richmond tobacco manufacturer whose family's products Webster had long sold in Philadelphia. This judgment may have been the result of Webster's reported penchant for not being "prompt in paying his bills." Legal proceedings were the clearest indication that Webster's faith in regional reciprocity and charity was not shared by businessmen who wanted what was owed to them. Webster's commercial and benevolent risks were panning out about as well as those who had banked on California gold. Despite what the credit reports said, however, Philadelphia city directories continued to list Webster as a tobacco merchant through the 1850s. His business clearly changed, however. Newspaper shipping columns show that he had become a general commission merchant, accepting a variety of merchandise from tobacco, to roots, to cotton for sale to Philadelphia retailers. He was still a merchant as well as an agent, but his business had become catch as catch can.[16]

Yet even as he panicked along with his contemporaries, Webster wagered again on sectional reconciliation and antislavery ideology. In 1859, an enslaved man from Portsmouth arrived in Philadelphia eager to obtain assistance. Bob Butt, the enslaved sexton who had dug the graves for 1,159 Portsmouth citizens who lost their lives in the yellow fever epidemic more than three years before, was trying to raise money so that he could buy his and his family's release from slavery. To assuage any concerns that his was an abolitionist project, Butt carried with him the praise of white members of the Portsmouth Relief Association, who proclaimed that "[t]his humble negro" had "performed duty beyond all price." Butt and his family clearly had value in the slave market, though, and the Relief Association attested to their owners' generosity by announcing that they would "abate at least *one-half* of the moneyed value they would command." The white citizens of Portsmouth attested to the moral worth Butt had accrued through waged overwork—he had "earned and saved about one-fifth of the sum which will be required"—

and promised to "assist him liberally" with additional funds. Philadelphians just needed to contribute their mite to assure the success of Butt's endeavor. Webster was one of the "gentlemen" who collected "contributions" on Butt's behalf. From his perspective, helping these enslaved people was a coda to his earlier relief efforts for his "Southern friends." White people in Portsmouth joined with those in Philadelphia in a common purpose, willing to contribute to compensated emancipation for one family. While assisting individual slaves to emancipate themselves aboard Union Company ships had been outlawed in Virginia because it threatened the fabric of slave society, Webster's efforts on behalf of meritorious slaves put him in league with white Virginians who considered themselves to be benevolent. Continuing to cultivate charitable connections across the regional divide might help restore his Southern business interests.[17]

Benevolence offered prestige, but it did not pay bills. Thomas Webster was a thoroughly logistical man. What he did best was bringing things and people together with alacrity, economy, and care. With his business interests in decline, he sought to bolster his finances and his social position through partisan politics. He had been involved in and defined himself through politics for a long time. In 1860, Webster struck up a correspondence with the Ohioan John Sherman, the chairman of the Ways and Means Committee in the House of Representatives. Written in the midst of a contentious presidential campaign, Webster's letters reveal a man changing course, steaming away from the snags of interregional commerce and toward placid waters in which partisan loyalty would yield the status, position, and capital that eluded him in commercial affairs.

Webster's correspondence with Sherman was cheery and optimistic, and gave very little indication of the economic uncertainty in which he found himself. Webster sought to cultivate a patron-client relationship with a powerful man. Fostering such relationships was essential for political and economic advancement. Webster had tried the strategy earlier in the spring of 1860, when he informed Thurlow Weed that he, as vice president of Philadelphia's Central Republican Committee, wanted to proclaim his support in the coming presidential campaign for the Senator from New York, William Seward. These overtures were short-lived, because by the end of May, Abraham Lincoln was the party's presidential nominee. Now, Webster wanted Sherman to know about the Illinoisan's "prospects of brilliant success" in Philadelphia. A coalition in the city known as the People's Party, a conglomeration of antislavery and protariff men, had coalesced with those who valued "'Straight' Americanism" in support of Lincoln. Webster thought he saw evidence of defections from the "'Bell & Everett' junto," a development that augured impending triumph for the Republicans. He guffawed at the wishy-washiness of the "silk stocking gentry" and "men who sell principles *and* dry goods" even as he included them in the large majorities he forecast for Lincoln in the Fall election. To "cement the Union" of these various factions, he urged Sherman to visit Philadelphia and give rousing speeches. Eager to cement his ties to Sherman, he praised him as a man of "talent integrity & zeal." Philadelphians "*All* admire you and all classes would strive to show that in a becoming manner."[18]

Webster strived to show Sherman that he was at once a man's man who understood the bruising conflict of partisan politics, a gentleman whose becoming manner would demonstrate his refinement and civic worthiness, and a sycophant eager to curry favor. He enjoyed telling Sherman about the speech that his friend and Republican congressman John Hickman had recently given in which he assailed the ideas of the "little giant" Stephen Douglas, the Northern Democrats' candidate for the presidency. Hickman "punished him without mercy and about as effectually as Tom Hyer thumped Yankee Sullivan," Webster wrote, referencing a celebrated boxing match. He was effusive in equating Sherman's speeches with sporting men's masculinity, telling him that one of his speeches in Philadelphia had "made another 'ten strike' and again won the admiration of our community." Webster, despite saying he was "enthusiastic and sanguine" about the election outcome, rolled up his own sleeves to canvass for votes, telling Sherman in October that he was trying to convince supporters of John Breckinridge and John Bell to vote for Lincoln and convey to the South "the folly of attempting resistance" in the face of a unified North. Surprisingly, more than twenty of his acquaintances with these political sensibilities agreed to do so, exclaiming "it's all up—might as well." If what he said was true, Webster had rolled his own ten strike.[19]

Sherman, a shrewd politician, surely knew that Webster regaled him with these stories for a reason. He could not have been surprised by the October 1860 letter he received in which Webster recalled Sherman's visit to his family's "little house in Delaware County" outside the city of Philadelphia. The Websters, therefore, had two residences—one inside and one outside the city. Clearly, the umbrella manufacturing fortune of Webster's father-in-law had helped him and Eliza Ann weather the financial storms and concerns that credit reporters had about his businesses. But the legal proceedings against him and his quixotic attempt to proclaim antislavery principles and profit in the Southern trade left him exposed. Webster's striving for success was born of his bottomless thirst for other men's respect. How could he achieve that respect if his peers knew that his wealth had been given him by his father-in-law? He needed to earn his economic and cultural capital—with slow and steady profits from his business ventures and the esteem that came from charitable works.[20]

Yet Webster cultivated a personal friendship with Sherman by enclosing, at Eliza Ann's request, a handkerchief that Sherman had left at their house. Eliza Ann's remembrance bespoke the material and emotional bonds her husband hoped existed between him and Sherman. The handkerchief enfolded the request Thomas Webster was about to make in sentimentality as much as in material interest. Webster claimed he had been "busy today collecting funds and engaging speakers" for the campaign in the state of Delaware, reminding Sherman of his tireless efforts for the cause. He then got down to "personal" business: he had been discussing the campaign with a "friend," who called him a "fool" for not "looking after my own interests—in short—that I ought to be getting influences pledged to me for my claims for patronage from the coming administration." Webster did not want to put the cart before the horse—the victory had not yet been achieved and there would be time to press the matter. But upon further inquiry, Webster discovered "*that already* certain influence is promised to others." So he asked Sherman for assistance in procuring for him the collectorship of the port of Philadelphia. Speaking the language of value, economic and political, he declared "[a]s a merchant I am worthy of it and as an active partisan, I think I merit it." He then recalled his tortuous career in the Southern trade to highlight his sacrifice. Finally, he hoped, the complicated relation between his interest and his ideology would profit him in the political realm. Webster explained how his antislavery principles had made his tobacco business go up in smoke. In 1848, "when doing a business of $400,000 per annum with Virginia"—the value of the tobacco he sold, not the profits he accrued from its sale—"I stood out boldly for 'free soil'" as a supporter of the Democrat Martin Van Buren. By the election of 1856, still boldly "active" in political antislavery, his free soil bona fides left him in "reduced circumstances" in the "Southern trade," for everyone in Philadelphia and Virginia knew him to be a "'black' republican." Webster wanted recompense for his "fidelity to principle" and his "zeal, activity, and intelligent and active work" for the Republican Party. His principles were not a currency white Southerners would accept. His silent participation in the Underground Railroad helped to cheat them out of the principal value of their property. Webster contended that he did not, like other Philadelphians, sell his principles when he sold his products. Unable to accumulate capital as he once did in the Southern economy, he hoped Sherman and Lincoln would find him and his principles valuable. "I find my equanimity a little disturbed and I pour out my feelings," he apologized to Sherman, even though the purpose of his letter was to evoke emotion, from the reference to the handkerchief to the unburdening of feelings. He sought Sherman's help to fight an injustice. To combat the efforts of wealthy men representing "miserable 'conservatism'" who were trying to "grasp the substantial fruits of the victory without having contributed an hours effort," Webster asked Sherman to *drop a line to Mr. Lincoln in my behalf*."[21]

It was a bold, forthright request. Webster had spent his career trying to earn economic and cultural capital by fulfilling the wants and needs of others. That is what middlemen did. In this letter, wrapped in a handkerchief representing political alliance, he had honestly and emotionally presented his wants and needs to Sherman. The Ohioan was cagier. While Sherman's reply is not extant, it appears he told Webster that patronage decisions must await Lincoln's election to the presidency. Webster agreed to drop the matter for the time being. He picked up where he left off in their correspondence, giving Sherman insight into the mindset of acquaintances in Norfolk, with whom he had talked while he recently "had been on business" there. They were "Belleverett" supporters, "sound Union men" whom Webster claimed were "at heart against Slavery." These were the men with whom he dealt after gaining a reputation as a black Republican: antislavery white Southerners. It is possible that business with this small constituency would register as no business at all to a credit reporter. These were the men whom Webster might have had in mind when he wagered that antislavery principles and tobacco profits could coexist. They now informed Webster that fire-eating radicalism was gaining the ascendance in Virginia. Any federal attempt to coerce seceding states back into the Union would lead Virginia to secede as well. "I never saw men more alarmed about the future," Webster told Sherman. "They are bewildered and panic struck." He tried to talk them out of their "folly," but he must have seen the writing on the wall, too. By the fall of 1860, as the election of the antislavery candidate whom Webster supported appeared imminent, everyone knew that secession was likely. Webster's opposition to slavery, intersecting in complex and contradictory ways with personal economic interests and a nationalism that would maintain slavery as an institution, could not shape a peaceful national future.[22]

Webster shared in the panic that Southern secession portended, and his quest for the collectorship betrayed his anxiety. As he repeatedly "sojourn[ed] in Virginia" on business in the summer and fall of 1860, he knew from what his acquaintances told him and what he read in the news that if Virginia seceded, his comfortable salary as agent for the Union Steamship Company would vanish. If family money had helped him hold a comfortable position in Philadelphia's society, the secession crisis threatened Webster's sole remaining source of income that he made on his own. The collectorship of the port would be the comfortable landing he needed to survive the secession panic.[23]

To get it, Webster would have to convince the victor in the presidential election. He met with Abraham Lincoln in Springfield, Illinois, on November 14, 1860, ostensibly to emphasize his credentials for the collectorship. Henry C. Carey, Philadelphia's prominent political economist, wrote to Webster to convey his support to both the president-elect and the office seeker. "You, he should certainly receive well," Carey told Webster, "as there is not a man in the State who has laboured longer, more assiduously, or more profitably, in the cause to which, apart from his own merits, he owes his elevation." Webster solicited letters of introduction from leading Philadelphia Republicans such as Hickman, who told Lincoln that Webster "was one of the most active and valuable members of the Republican party in Eastern Penna. His efforts in the campaign . . . have been untiring, and indispensible. . . . There are few persons whom I regard more worthy of confidence and esteem."[24]

Carey's and Hickman's words were ones that any office seeker would want to read. They valued the worthy Webster's political labor for the party's cause. Strangely, though, when Webster had the chance to present his case to Lincoln, he did not. There was a lot riding on this meeting from Webster's point of view, but he did not betray it to Lincoln or to Sherman in the letter he wrote on his way home. Webster knew how to play politics. He informed Sherman that he had met Lincoln in the Senate Chamber of the State House, where the painters George Healy and Jesse Atwood were finishing their "counterfeit presentiment[s]" of the nation's new leader. Webster knew that his usefulness to Sherman was simultaneously to be his eyes and ears, telling him what everyone looked like, what everyone said, and what could be inferred from both. While Lincoln informed Webster that he had "received" and "read" his "letters of introduction," Webster declined to speak further about "my own pretensions for favor" because Lincoln "did not refer pointedly to them. I merely remarked that I should press them home to him at a future day." There were too many people around to be too bold. Deference would be the way to get ahead. He wrote to Lincoln after their meeting while still in Springfield, enclosing reports about his work assisting the unfortunate yellow fever sufferers in Norfolk and addresses he had written about Philadelphia and Pennsylvania politics. They revealed, so Webster said, his "capacity and energy of character" as well as his political understanding. He promised to provide Lincoln with "convincing proofs that as a merchant and a man I am competent to fill" the collectorship, "and as a partizan that I deserve it." He was nothing if not persistent. He thanked Lincoln for his time, congratulated him on his election, and said he was "glad that my personal impressions of you so fully confirm the warmest hopes of our party in Philadelphia." On this evidence, Webster saw a bright future for his city, state, and nation with Lincoln at the helm.[25]

Webster's deference toward Lincoln was a counterfeit presentiment of his own, for he more fully shared his personal impressions of the new president with Sherman. He lampooned Lincoln, proclaiming that "'Old Abe' came in the chamber in his (usual) shotting gawky rollicking manner," relying on contemporary reports as much as his own eyes to describe the behavior of someone he had just met. Lincoln was entertaining, but also inscrutable. "He chatted, told stories laughed at his own wit — and the humor of others — and in one way and another made a couple of hours pass merrily and never once lost his dignity or committed himself to an opinion." Webster wrote that the conversation was nothing more than "gossip," but it was gossip that he avidly shared with Sherman. He was trying to cultivate the Ohioan's regard and political friendship. The way he ingratiated himself was by suggesting common standards of refinement that bound the men and their wives together. He did this by including a long description of what Mary Lincoln, the president's wife, wore. Webster predicted that Mrs. Lincoln would "grace the White House," and thus he knew that what she wore would be of immense importance to Eliza Ann. Webster "venture[d] to a penny that" Sherman's wife "would not be uninterested in the details of the costume of the future mistress of the White House." Refined Republican women needed to know, from a well-placed source, what material they would have to buy to remain in style. Webster, a coy critic of the principled but profiteering drygoodsman, demonstrated a keen eye for the material culture of refined consumption. He was not just a tobacco merchant, but a gentleman. "Mrs. L. was clad in a fine brocade silk — of an oaken or brown color — with figures of flowers and leaves in a grayish white shine out prominently — made full and long sweeping and trailing at just the proper fraction that Fashion governs & propriety dictates — Her bonnet was black silk trimmed with cherry — She wore a mixed dark shawl and carried a dark lavender or mauve colored parasol."

These were the materials that made Mrs. Lincoln's "attractive & winning" appearance, made her seem so "calm self possessed dignified graceful and easy" and in such stark contrast with her husband, whom Webster limned as "slouchy, ungraceful but withall prepossessing. He is round shouldered, leans forward (very much in his walk) [and] is lean and ugly every way." Deportment and appearance were of great importance to Webster: he followed this description of Mary Lincoln's "costume" with textual sketches of Abraham Lincoln and Sherman that emphasized the physiognomic and phrenological, and Lincoln came in second place in the comparison. Webster, wanting to stoke Sherman's ambitions, warned his patron that he thought Lincoln was weak. "Mr. L. wants aid, counsel — advice from experienced able statesmen," Webster explained, hoping that such leaders acted before "[l]ess scrupulous & less able men may in the meantime offer advice and make an impression on Mr. L." Of course, if Sherman "would but call" on Lincoln, Webster hoped that he would put in a good word for him, too.[26]

The election had not turned on political gossip, and Abraham Lincoln had not always been reluctant to give his opinions. He had triumphed in the presidential election because free labor ideology resonated with a majority of Northern voters. He had done as much or more than anyone in the Republican Party to confront white Southerners' belief that slavery was superior to wage labor. Those proslavery ideas had reemerged in the aftermath of the Panic of 1857, which appeared to have deranged Northern economy and society more than that of the cotton South. South Carolina senator James Henry Hammond seized on this regional economic distinction for political purpose in a speech in the U.S. Senate on March 4, 1858. He proclaimed, "In all social systems there must be a class to do the menial duties, to perform the drudgery of life.... Such a class you must have, or you would not have that other class which leads progress, civilization, and refinement. It constitutes the very mud-sill of society and of political government; and you might as well attempt to build a house in the air, as to build either the one or the other, except on this mud-sill." Hammond explained that white Southerners were fortunate to have an "inferior race" of black slaves to serve as this mudsill class, but he was no less adamant that Northern free society had a mudsill class, too. Yankees vehemently disagreed. They had "abolished slavery" in the previous generation. Free workers were not moored to the social floor. Hammond begged to differ. "[T]he man who lives by daily labor, and scarcely lives at that, and who has to put out his labor in the market, and take the best he can get for it; in short, your whole hireling class of manual laborers and 'operatives,' as you call them, are essentially slaves," he thundered. Hammond's purpose in condemning wage labor and free society was to uphold the virtues of the South's social system, in which he claimed there was "no starvation, no begging, no want of employment among our people, and not too much employment either." In the North, where selling labor in the market was called liberty, free labor was a fraud, driving men to beggary. He envisioned a future in which Northern mudsills, feeling "galled by their degradation," would vote in their interests so that, he told the North's humbugging employers, "[y]our society would be reconstructed, your government overthrown, [and] your property divided." Hammond reminded Northern listeners that he believed abolitionists had "been making war upon us to our very hearthstones" and asked whether defenders of free labor would mind Southerners fomenting rebellion against wage labor in the North.[27]

Lincoln declared, in a speech to the Wisconsin Agricultural Society in September 1859, that Hammond's "'mud-sill' theory" was "false." There was a relationship between labor and capital, he acknowledged, but he decried the notion that men only worked because capitalists got their "consent" or because they were enslaved. He contended that labor was the root of capital and that Northern wage workers were not "fatally fixed for life, in the condition of a hired laborer." He argued that Northern wage workers were a small minority of the region's population. "A large majority," he said, stood outside the labor-capital nexus, "neither *hirers* nor *hired.*" In Lincoln's telling, Northern society's quintessential citizens belonged not to a mudsill class but to one that operated outside the market: comfortably, independently expending their own labor to accrue their own capital—"the fruit of labor." Perhaps some of these citizens, Lincoln mused, worked for themselves and hired laborers, but the existence of these Northerners did not hurt his argument, for they "ask[ed] no favors of capital on the one hand, nor hirelings ... on the other."[28]

Northern wage labor also offered opportunities for upward advancement to its hirelings, Lincoln posited. "The prudent, penniless beginner in the world," he said, was not moored to the mudsill forever. He "labors for wages awhile, saves a surplus with which to buy tools or land, for himself; then labors on his own account for another while, and at length hires another new beginner to help him." This system was "*free* labor—the just and generous system, which opens the way for all—gives hope to all, and energy, and progress, and improvement of condition to all." Northern wage labor was not slavery. Men who remained wage laborers were not mudsills, Lincoln contended. If they did not advance, it was "because of either a dependent nature which prefers it, or improvidence, folly, or singular misfortune." Free labor offered social and economic advancement, something that enslaved people could not attain. Free labor was superior to slavery.[29]

In this conflict about political economy, each region's standard-bearer declared the other's institutions and practices to be fraud committed against workers. It was part of the same debate William Still and Thomas Webster indirectly had with slaveholders. In the North, strongly held beliefs in the theft committed by slaveholders encouraged radical abolitionists like John Brown to envision and enact violent retribution against the Slave Power. Interestingly, though, Northerners immersed in a popular culture shaped by businessmen like P. T. Barnum also thought fraud could be fun. The North's popular prints gave space for regional self-criticism as much as they did condemnation of the South. Popular magazines, advertisements, and images gave expression to the ways wage labor did and did not work. These sources' portrayals of Irish and African American servants played with the meanings of gender, race, and class to create submissive and transgressive social types that readers could use to identify ideal and less-than-ideal workers. The cultural production of these types could help employers exert more control over the laborers they hoped would contribute to their households' efficiency and respectability. Yet these cultural expressions were also contested and unstable, illuminating the complex context in which Northerners and Southerners made assertions about the merits and dangers of wage labor and slave labor in the 1850s.[30]

Irish servant women had become more common figures in Northern homes and popular depictions of households in the wake of the famine migration of the 1840s and 1850s. A multicultural domestic servant population in early nineteenth-century New York, historian Christine Stansell has shown, became dominated by Irish women at midcentury, when they accounted for almost three-quarters of the city's domestic servants. Americans constructed a social type—the Irish "Biddy"—to represent the ungovernable domestic servant who supposedly threatened the authority of household mistresses. In 1860, the comic publication *Vanity Fair*, published in New York but led principally by editor Charles Godfrey Leland and artist Henry Louis Stephens of Philadelphia, used the Biddy as a figure of satirical possibility. In cartoons and commentary about Irish servant women, readers might understand both the threatening erosion of class distinction and gendered power within the refined Northern home and the mighty struggle about political economy between North and South.[31]

The editors, contributors, and artists of *Vanity Fair* were denizens of Pfaff's, a Broadway tavern where the hard-working, hard-drinking newspaper journalists and printing journeymen of New York congregated. Despite their proletarian antecedents and their radical ideas about free love, these bohemians helped to shape prevailing standards of refinement. Like the flash press of the previous decade, the authors and artists of *Vanity Fair* flouted conventions of respectability in an effort to cater to ambitious readers who looked to them for laughs. The publication's scribblers and artists encouraged readers to mock social types as a way to gain control over their destabilizing potential, even as these cultural producers openly confronted, blurred, and transgressed the boundaries of social decorum in their own lives.[32]

Northerners risked laughing at transgressive social types that were at once an affirmation of and an affront to "respectable" precepts and practices, bracketing the types just enough so that they were not making fun of themselves. "Counter jumpers," the male retail clerks who appeared to do no manly work, dressed in the height of fashion, and obsequiously catered to female consumers illuminated the ways consumer capitalism and urbanization eroded reputable manhood. The Irish servant Biddy refused to do work, insolently confronted the authority of the refined men and women who employed them, and dressed elegantly—all challenging readers to reassess the meanings of class and respectable womanhood. *Vanity Fair* proposed that the problems caused by these social types were related to each other, and forced readers to consider their destabilizing cultural impact simultaneously.[33]

Readers of the March 3, 1860, issue, for instance, were confronted with *Vanity Fair*'s plan to reform young clerks' masculinity by having them take positions as domestic servants until they could "stand nearly as much labor as a woman." The joke continued on the very next page in a cartoon that illustrated the tensions in a well-to-do home. An Irish servant woman asked the male head of the house to "carry out the ash-barrel." She inquired impertinently, "d'yeez think that a delicate woman'll be afther breaking her back at such work?" Ambitious clerks lacked masculine strength because they sold cloth to female customers at retail, but men who had already succeeded in the business world were inappropriately asked to do heavy lifting because biddies considered themselves to be too "delicate" for such tasks. While changes in the commercial and industrial economy pushed young men, shorn of manly attributes and prerogatives, into what one antebellum clerk called the "servile trade of quill driving," the same transformations permitted Irish servant women to claim a contemptible sort of independence *from* labor that made household masters and mistresses no more than "slave[s]" to "this terrible Queen o' the Kitchin." The purported "slavery" of white male heads of household was a joke, of course. Unlike the white journeymen who feared "wage slavery," white clerks would presumably become businessmen in their own right. By contrast, domestic servants were often impoverished and householders could always discard one servant and find another.[34]

Well-to-do Northerners exerted a great deal of authority in their employment of wage laborers, but this sarcastic humor hit its mark because the Northern economy produced as many frustrations as it did opportunities, making the project of bracketing social types difficult. White clerks did not always graduate to proprietorship or partnership, and many Irish domestic servants earned and saved impressive sums of money in their bank accounts and put the survival and success of their own households first. When *Vanity Fair*'s artists depicted Irish servant women adopting the dress and demeanor of ladies, they were portraying a real—and from their employers' perspective, unsettling—phenomenon. Flummoxed mistresses and masters in *Vanity Fair* were left shaking their heads as female servants bought new dresses, guitars, and novels to underwrite their own claims to gentility. In her "native home," the Biddy cleaned slop buckets. After only "a month's residence" in the United States, she twirled a parasol, wore fine crinoline, and stuck her nose in the air. Northern readers might have interpreted such a rapid transformation as proof positive of the superiority of free labor, a function of the North's democratic, fluid society and immigrants' self-control. But native-born employers did not applaud the efforts of Irish women to achieve respectability. Such cultural work threatened the efficiency and refinement of their households. Northerners refused to voice support for the possibilities that wage labor offered to ambitious workers who sought to better their condition. Instead, this expression of wage labor condemned the Biddy's ambitions and made jokes about her supposedly unladylike nature, which in turn marked her as a subordinate subject for coercion and exploitation in her employer's household. These depictions shaped the relationships between household mistresses and servants, reflecting the frustration that elite women had with independent workingwomen and justifying their expectations about servants' subjection.[35]

Advertisements for household machines in *Vanity Fair* reveal the ways businessmen exploited the contradictions of free labor ideology in attempts to persuade consumers to make purchases. The firm of Sullivan and Hyatt juxtaposed two servant women—Kate, demure and wearing a hoop skirt, and Bridget, bare-armed and bending over a wash bucket—to proclaim the ability of workingwomen to transcend "old fogeyism" in the name of "progress," if only their employers would buy the "Cataract Washing Ma-

"The Biddy," *Vanity Fair*, February 18, 1860, 120.
(The Library Company of Philadelphia)

chine." Bridget complained that she was "nearly dead with this hard work," and Kate, who used the machine to wash her household's clothing in a fraction of the time it took Bridget, proclaimed that she would "give any house the discharge" whose mistress refused to buy the device. Kate's refined appearance and her forthright announcement of the choices wage labor offered her—she would quit one job to find a better one—were the very things that produced Northern employers' angst toward the Biddy. Yet Sullivan and Hyatt argued that servants' haughty complaints and rapid completion of arduous tasks were "progress" in a Northern economy framed by wage work, conspicuous consumption, technological advances, and upward mobility. By purchasing these mechanical wonders, householders might even repair the harmony of interests by lessening servants' burden and creating the circumstances through which workers could buy goods that appeared fashionable. Market purchases would solve the impending crisis of the household, business firms suggested, by making sure housework was done efficiently and that respectability diffused across the social divide between mistresses and servants.[36]

Yet business proprietors understood the Biddy's potential threat to the

"Progress vs. Old Fogeyism," *Vanity Fair*, February 18, 1860, 127.
(The Library Company of Philadelphia)

authority of householders and mistresses. If employers worried that buying new appliances would make their domestic servants more independent and less obedient, some firms hoped that portrayals of more subservient workers would make customers more comfortable and increase their sales. Leadbeater and Company, a Philadelphia dealer in stove polish, tried to sell its wares in a lithographic advertisement depicting two women scrubbing a kitchen stove with their product. The standing white mistress and the kneeling African American servant work together and mass-produced art adorns the wall, as in many Northern homes. Yet the artistic conventions of portraying a mistress with a kneeling servant, the contrast between the finery worn by the white woman and the kerchief and earring of the black woman, and the comparison between the skin color of the servant woman and the color of the stove, all evoke the Southern plantation and depictions of it. Northern sellers of shoe and stove polish routinely used black servant figures to sell their products—in another advertisement, the appearance of a

Leadbeater's Renouned Stove Polish (Philadelphia, 1861).
(The Library Company of Philadelphia)

black cat alongside a black man suggests the proprietor was trying to make light of blackness — of cats, men, and polish — and argue that African Americans were better household workers. These images were doubly ironic, for the Northern states were postslavery societies in which African Americans endured coercive labor arrangements such as apprenticeship and competition from Irish men and women who took their jobs. Black New Yorkers, for instance, only accounted for 3 percent of the domestic servant population in 1855. Images like this one might have seemed attractive to Northern mistresses in the era of the Biddy, representing the benefits of authority enjoyed in the pre-emancipation Northern past, the Southern present, or a future in which Irish servant women would be replaced by people who were more tractable.[37]

Vanity Fair used the sectional crisis as a lens through which readers could think and laugh about slavery, wage labor, and democracy during the presidential campaign of 1860. Stephens's drawings, in particular, described sectional strife as a crisis of the national household. His sketches drew their ironic force from a corresponding concern about the Northern household and the relationships between employers and domestic servants within it. President James Buchanan was a favorite target for *Vanity Fair*'s stinging humor. In little more than a year preceding the Civil War, the publication portrayed Buchanan as a gas fixture, a jack-in-the-box, a comet, a candle, a crab, a meerschaum pipe, a paint brush, an Easter egg, a giant baby, a woman, a toad, a dog (twice), an iceberg, and a cracked bottle of whiskey. In the cartoon "Out of a Situation," Buchanan assumed the role of the Biddy, bedraggled but wearing a hoop skirt and carrying a bundle labeled "J. B. Wheatland," a reference to his Pennsylvania estate. Buchanan, a bachelor, did not wield the patriarchal prerogatives Americans associated with being a head of household. His subservience to Southern political interests made him seem weak, and an increasingly unified Northern public concerned about an ascendant Slave Power condemned him for this "doughfaced" lack of manliness. He rivaled the male retail clerk, another character whom *Vanity Fair* depicted wearing a hoopskirt, in muddling masculine identity. Mrs. Columbia declares her independence of this disappointing and dissembling public servant as of "next March," when a new servant would assume the presidency. The mistress of the national house would now do the sewing work to stitch North to South that Buchanan had refused to do. Biddy Buchanan's parting request for a character reference — so crucial to domestic servants and patronage seekers like Webster — is unanswered and one which readers, dissatisfied with his public service, would have disdained. The cartoon promised that citizens, much like household masters and mistresses, would remain in control of political servants.[38]

Vanity Fair found the disorder of the nation's household to be fertile ground for political and social critique. Stephens developed the theme in his portrayal of Stephen Douglas as a black mammy and John Breckinridge and Abraham Lincoln as black dandies in the weeks before the election. The stock figures that Stephens drew would have been familiar to white theater audiences who encountered them regularly in blackface minstrel performances,

"Out of a Situation," *Vanity Fair*, April 7, 1860, 233.
(The Library Company of Philadelphia)

and readers might have tapped their feet to the tune of the popular song that Stephens evoked in the drawing's caption, "Sich a Gittin Upstairs." Lincoln pitched into Breckinridge and Douglas in the kitchen, his fighting spirit undoubtedly ignited by the bellows labeled "Tribune," a reference to Horace Greeley's Republican newspaper. The portrayal of candidates in blackface suggests that Stephens considered all three men to be inferior politicians who did not deserve to climb to the presidency. They were lamentable alternatives to the respected leaders who had preceded them. Stephens used the cultural filters of respectability and white supremacy to joke that their ascension to power would violate the ideals of good government. While Lincoln had looked to the bible to provide a metaphor for a fractured nation in his 1858 "House Divided" speech, Stephens looked to a more prosaic source, the social disorder of the American household, to illuminate threats of political disorder to the nation as a whole.[39]

John Sherman was not immune to *Vanity Fair*'s cutting engravings, either. After winning reelection to the House, Sherman was a leading candidate for the speakership. The Republican party held a plurality, but not a majority, of seats, and Sherman's candidacy was derailed by Southern repre-

"SICH A GITTIN UP STAIRS."

"Miss Douglas beller out. Den she jump between us
But I guess she no forgit de day wen Abra'm show his genus!
Sich a gittin up stars I neber did see.
Sich a gittin up stars I neber did see!"

"'Sich a Gittin Up Stairs,'" *Vanity Fair*, October 27, 1860, 213.
(The Library Company of Philadelphia)

sentatives' accusations that he was an admirer of Hinton Helper's book *The Impending Crisis*, in which Helper argued that slavery ruined the prospects of nonslaveholding white men in the South. This line of thinking dovetailed nicely with Republicans' critique of slavery, but it upset Sherman's quest for a position of power in the legislature. *Vanity Fair*'s Stephens cracked wise with a clever riposte against those seeking political power and the elite women whose fashionable dresses were expanding to ridiculous width. Depicted as a dainty debutante chaperoned by party elder William Seward, Sherman wore hoop skirts piled with so many layers of crinoline made out of Helper's book that it was impossible for him to fit in the tiny Speaker's chair. Stephens had depicted Buchanan's loss of and Lincoln's scramble for power as an unseemly upstairs-downstairs drama. Here he critiqued the pretensions of Northerners, encouraging *Vanity Fair* readers to ridicule not only the dreams of men like Sherman and Webster but also the demands of women's fashion that these men took very seriously. Even as Webster criticized Abraham Lincoln as round-shouldered — an adjective often used to describe the hunched desk workers of the era — he drew a portrait of an elegant Mary Lincoln in his letter to Sherman to stabilize cultural meanings that were in flux. Soon, her pretensions, frivolous purchases, unfashionable style, Western identity, and political meddling would become subjects for mockery in the press. Much to the dismay of these fashionable men and women, Stephens argued that cutting political and cultural pretenders down to size would help mend tears in the national fabric.[40]

When Webster wrote to Sherman at the end of 1860, he weighed in on these ideological debates with the utmost decorum and seriousness. The result of South Carolina's secession from the Union would not be what Hammond thought. The belief was strong, so Webster said, in "S. Carolina & the Cotton States" that secession would produce economic panic in the North, roiling cities like Philadelphia and New York with class conflict. The "first blood" of war, so this narrative went, would "flow" in "battles *on our streets.*" Webster blamed Northerners of Southern birth and Northerners involved in the Southern trade for propagating this forecast of the future. Of course, he was a Northerner involved in Southern trade, so he wanted Sherman to know that he was a staunch defender of the Union against "Treason and Traitors." He was adamant that secessionists' "delusion be dispelled." He asserted that the "distress — numbers out of employment &c &c are all grossly exaggerated. The panic is nearly over and men are becoming resolute" — men like himself. Yet Webster had to acknowledge that his faction of the People's Party in Philadelphia was outnumbered in committee by conservatives who "counsel prudence caution — a waiting on events." Webster was not concerned about this "temporary defeat," for he believed Pennsylvania's state legislature would soon pass legislation offering "money, arms and men to aid the Federal Government in enforcing the laws." Then city leaders would be "compelled to ... follow the masses." Hammond was wrong about Northern

MR. S-W-D.—Look here, Miss Sherman, you've rather too much crinoline.

"Mr. S-W-D.," *Vanity Fair*, February 4, 1860, 89.
(The Library Company of Philadelphia)

society and its voters. There was no class conflict in the North, but rather a harmony of interests determined to crush secession.[41]

Webster believed Hammond was wrong about free society and agreed with Lincoln that slavery was wrong. He had been at least a silent partner in an effort to defraud slaveholders. Yet his own experience would have taught him that Lincoln's free labor ideology was a theory that did not bear out in practice. Webster, a Northerner who had lost in the Southern trade, postured in his letters to Sherman that he and his city were not panicking. The economy was not reeling from secession. His quest for the collectorship reveals otherwise. Like other speculators, Webster took risks in commercial endeavors to become more independent because he remained dependent on other people's labor and capital. His experience suggested that Lincoln's vision of independent citizens outside the market was chimerical. Producers, distributors, and consumers all depended on a market beyond their households' ability to expend labor to make capital. When they did not have capital at the ready, Northern citizens needed credit—a precarious thing, as Webster knew. Credit reporters' rumors could defraud market actors of their ability to earn credit, no matter what their political principles. Speculators also needed labor. Their own hard work, by head or hand, was essential, but so was the work of hirelings and slaves. The labor of others was a resource to be exploited by those with capital, and Webster had benefited from the work of enslaved Virginians in fields and factories and free Pennsylvanians on the docks. The war that would follow the secession crisis would be prosecuted by Northern men convinced that Southern slaveholders had exploited laborers so successfully that they had too much capital and political power. Their antislavery cause was grounded in an eagerness to benefit from the demise of these wealthy capitalists.

Of course, Webster did not air any doubts about free labor—if they had formed coherently in his mind—with the politicians he cultivated. To do so would cast doubt on his allegiance to the Republican cause and threaten his claim to patronage. He did not hold back, however, when Lincoln solicited his opinions of Pennsylvania's politicians. "Hickman was her best man and Cameron her worst." John Hickman, formerly a Democrat like Webster, was now a congressman representing Delaware County, where Webster sometimes resided. Simon Cameron was also a former Democrat and one of the "less scrupulous" men Webster thought were seeking control over the president-elect. In January 1861, shortly after news began to circulate that Cameron would be appointed to a cabinet position, Webster wrote Sherman *"confidentially"* that "I have never been an admirer, follower or friend of Cameron's," nor had he ever "been his enemy." He hoped that no Pennsylvanian would be named to the cabinet, fearing that doing so would disturb the equilibrium of the People's Party. He knew that his own quest for patronage hinged on how he navigated between the factions led by Cameron and the new Republican governor of Pennsylvania, Andrew Curtin. He could not resist, however, running Cameron down as a way to burnish his own credentials. Cameron "was not an original friend of Mr L's. He did nothing to secure the victory." Webster felt that he had contributed materially to Lincoln's triumph. Cameron "made no speech to convert crowds for he cannot speak, nor did he write any essay or letter for that too is above his ability.... He does not have influence with the intellectual and chivalrous portion of the party, but he has with the sordid and unreflecting." Webster implicitly told Sherman that he was everything Cameron was not. He had done the work that Cameron shunned. He was a gentleman while Cameron was corrupt. The day after writing to Sherman, Webster felt emboldened enough to write to Lincoln that, while "many active ward politicians" supported Cameron, the "soul and heart of the party, who regard its principles, its fame, its consolidation, its future more than office are opposed" to his appointment. Webster continued to obscure the fact that he wanted and needed office, affirming that he was motivated to give Lincoln the gossip on the streets of Philadelphia only because of his "zeal for you and the party."[42]

Webster next talked to Lincoln in Philadelphia in February, as part of the latter's procession to the capital for his inauguration. It seems likely that, as a member of the committee delegated with the responsibility of receiving the president-elect in the city, Webster heard Lincoln speak from the balcony of the Continental Hotel on Chestnut Street. Lincoln announced to the crowd that secessionists had not adequately explained what "substantial difficulty" justified their acts of disunion. He determined, as Webster had done after South Carolina declared its independence, that "the crisis, the panic, the anxiety of the country at this time is artificial." Lincoln did "not mean to say that this artificial panic has not done harm. That it has done much harm I do not deny." He resolved to "restore peace and harmony and prosperity to the country" if he could.[43]

Panic had hurt Webster and spurred him to seek refuge, a port collectorship in the storm. He was not alone. In the early months of 1861 Webster sent at least three letters of reference to Lincoln on behalf of applicants for other government posts. Artificial panics felt real, and because of Cameron's ascendance and the potential infighting it would cause in his own state, Webster worried about the office he wanted and needed to restore his personal prosperity. He needed Sherman's help more than ever. That became increasingly clear when an Ohioan whom Webster did not know, Salmon Chase, was named secretary of the treasury. Chase would have much to say about the distribution of port collectorships. Webster had Philadelphians like Hickman write and meet with the president on his behalf, but he asked Sherman to "remember me when you are with Mr. Chase." It was becoming clear to Webster that his gossip, hard work, and potential political utility had not persuaded Sherman to assist him. But he was desperate. In the middle of March, Webster was at Willard's Hotel in Washington, probably surrounded by other office seekers, when he informed Sherman, "My prospects are excellent," based on his estimates of the support he had garnered from "the duly elected members [of Congress] of our city, a majority of our state delegation, and seventy odd other members of Congress[,] . . . Our Governor—State Control Com[mittee]: Majority Legislature & of City Councils" as well as "a vast array of the mercantile and manufacturing interests of the City & State." He was lauded, so he told Sherman, "for fitness, fidelity and service to the party." But Webster was not convinced it was enough. He needed a friend who knew Chase to be sure, and Sherman was the man: "*You* see him often, *You* can see him at any moment. . . . You can assist me when I most need help." To put a fine point on his epistolary performance of the preceding ten months, he underlined his dependence: "*I have relied and still rely much, very much on you.*"[44]

On the day Confederate artillerists opened fire on Fort Sumter, a delegation of Philadelphia merchants met with Lincoln to support Webster's cause. Lincoln's notes on the meeting reflect their unanimous view that Webster's "appointment will give general satisfaction, while that of no other person will." Webster had served these men's interests as tobacco wholesaler, shipping agent, and even as the chairman of a committee that ensured that the winter ice on the Delaware River was broken up. He was an important figure in Philadelphia's economy. Yet when the Lincoln administration announced who would receive patronage posts in Philadelphia, William B. Thomas, a merchant more closely aligned with Cameron, became collector of the port. Webster had tried to get a job that would replace the ones that his political principles, economic panic, and secession had taken from him. Over the course of the next five years, Thomas would receive more than $25,000 from the government for his work in the post. That was capital Webster would sorely miss.[45]

The patronage system had not been kind to Webster. Perhaps Cameron had pressed his thumb to the scale, tipping it in the direction of his man. Patronage certainly was not a "just and generous system" that rewarded office seekers' exertions or principles. Yet Lincoln's defense of free labor's superiority gave Webster the resolve to carry on. Despite his dependence on his father-in-law's fortune and the ebb and flow of the nation's political economy, he did not have a "dependent nature." Failure was a state of mind. Webster was a speculator, and speculators just kept speculating. Being a commercial middleman, wholesaler, agent, and charitable coordinator had helped him to survive and succeed when credit and capital were scarce. He had not cashed in on a valuable government post, but the commencement of war meant Americans were on the move. Citizens flocked to recruiting offices to enlist as soldiers, and slaves ran away from their owners to army camps. These movements of people needed logistical men to manage and supply them. Webster's ability to move people and things across distance in the least amount of time at the least possible cost made him useful to the Union. The crisis of war would present him and many other Northern speculators with new ways to capitalize on emancipation and free labor.

2

BARGAINS WORSE THAN FRAUDULENT

THOMAS WEBSTER was not alone in his pursuit of patronage during the secession crisis. Many down-on-their-luck Northerners turned to officers of the state when commercial opportunity was scarce. In Massachusetts, for instance, citizens barraged the office of the new Republican governor, John Andrew, with requests for work. Andrew's correspondence in the early months of the war reveal that traditional networks of patronage, the economic panic caused by Southern states' declarations of independence, and the onset of war all motivated and shaped these pleas. Antebellum politicians had developed a system of patronage that helped partisans obtain employment in customshouses and other government posts. Andrew's ascendance to the gubernatorial seat was promising to many who hoped that the new governor would use his "influence" to find them work. They reminded the governor of personal ties built upon "friendly feelings" and family history. They knew that partisanship might figure into the governor's calculations, and they made sure to clarify that Andrew would be finding a job for a fellow Republican. Historian Scott Sandage has written that patronage jobs were "the last refuge of a man without pluck," but applicants and their surrogates wanted Andrew to know that, beyond partisan loyalties, they embodied the character and habits promoted by free labor ideology. Northern men and women, whether they were applicants for positions in the household, countinghouse, or customshouse, believed that a willingness to work hard and persevere in order to get ahead would help them procure "situations." Andrew's correspondents dwelled on the ways they were "worthy & upright," "skilled," "competent," and willing to do anything. These were just the phrases one would read in the want advertisement columns published in newspapers by employers, job seekers, and intelligence office keepers. Like those employment agents, Andrew could not assist all who plied him for help. The governor's office was not an intelligence office, but applicants earnestly turned to it because they hoped a political friend might wield the power of his position to their benefit. That Andrew could not always do so reflected the limits of his office and created disappointment among office seekers not unlike the dissatisfaction and distrust engendered by employment agencies.[1]

Antebellum Americans' experiences in and debates about intelligence offices reflected and shaped the broader debate about Northern and Southern political economy occurring in the years prior to the Civil War. As politicians worried—and comic publications laughed—about the consequences of the nation divided, intelligence offices and the intense conversations swirling around them reveal the ways Americans were confronting the fact that their households were divided between kitchen and parlor, upstairs and downstairs. The secession crisis and the beginning of the Civil War exacerbated these concerns, because respectable men of business as well as impoverished workers desperately sought safe and steady positions as sources of credit and capital ran dry. Intelligence office transactions illuminated what wage labor was in well-to-do households, popular culture, and political economy in critically important ways just as Northerners and Southerners came into conflict about labor—how it was recruited, moved, and exploited—in the Civil War. Even though Americans despised intelligence offices, they nevertheless adopted them as models on which to speed the flow of soldiers and workers throughout the country during the war. Out of crisis, some Northerners imagined opportunity in the movement of people to accrue credit and capital.

Northerners coping with the economic dislocation of the secession crisis did their best to convince each other that the Confederate States of America were to blame for the panic. Free labor did not cause the crisis. Slavery's illgotten capital did. Henry Louis Stephens, the artist who had happily skewered Northern politicians and their foibles, portrayed the Confederate government as masters of fraud in his June 1861 sketch in *Vanity Fair* entitled "The Great Southern Peter Funk Shop." Peter Funk was the bogeyman of the antebellum capitalist order. In urban "mock auction" houses, Funk was the by-bidder who worked in concert with the auctioneer to misrepresent the quality of goods and drive up their price to gull unsuspecting rural visitors into making bad purchases. Stephens cast Confederate president Jefferson Davis as the auctioneer asking for bids on a spurious loan while gullible "J. DUBIOUS" has his pocket picked by knife- and gun-wielding assailants. A Union soldier outside the establishment carries an American flag that warns passersby of mock auctions, but is unable to arrest the fraud within. Stephens condemned Southern secessionists who refused to pay Northerners what they owed after they left the Union and warned foreign nations of the dangers of lending money to these violent disunionists. The image diverts attention from Northern speculations to emphasize the peculiarly egregious Southern frauds that Union soldiers would avenge. Mock auctioneers had largely taken up shop in the antebellum *North*, not the South. It was in New York City, where Stephens drew this image, that the mayor paid young men to walk the sidewalks of the commercial district wearing placards reading "BEWARE OF MOCK AUCTIONS." Here, Stephens engaged in sleight-of-hand. Voicing the panic and incredulity of Unionists, he displaced mock auction fraud onto slavery's capitalists who had stolen from the forces of free labor and would steal again if given the chance.[2]

The South had produced, despite Webster's valiant claims to the contrary, an economic crisis in the North that imperiled clerks' and business proprietors' ability to provide for their families and realize their ambitions. Applicants for Governor Andrew's influence told of firms "being completely prostrated" by the hard times. Their references said that "they are destitute of means of living," and argued that small-town and urban businessmen felt the pinch of hard times in ways that farmers "who can at least gain a subsistence" did not. Yet the commercial classes were not the only ones who endured hardship. One workingman begged Andrew to find him a position at the Navy Yard to keep his wife from applying for assistance at the "poorhouse."[3]

But Andrew did not often hear directly from the laboring classes. The loudest cries for help came from previously prosperous citizens who believed that they should be given opportunities to maintain their way of life. This crisis had not been self-inflicted, they contended. Neither had it been caused by regular fluctuations in the market. Secessionists were to blame for fabricating a recession. "My principal business has been manufacturing Boots and Shoes for the Southern trade," E. S. Beals of North Weymouth told Andrew in May 1861, "but now my 'occupation's gone' together with probably not less than $10,000 that is now due me by the secessionists." A begging letter was not a genre with which Beals was familiar—he had helped other men get jobs before, but had never been in the position of making the case for himself. Now, he hoped the well-worn cliché "occupation's gone" would convince Andrew to help him. Beals declared his motive was "to serve my Country," and felt qualified to accept a position as paymaster. But he was willing to do anything. Beals must have thought that emphasizing service to the "public good" would secure him a post, but he went too far in saying that

THE GREAT SOUTHERN PETER FUNK SHOP.

"The Great Southern Peter Funk Shop," *Vanity Fair*, June 1, 1861, 257.
(The Library Company of Philadelphia)

he had "no mercenary motive in making this application." He could not be both "willing to work during the war, pay, or no pay," and make it clear that he felt himself "worth a moderate competency" that would help him replenish the losses he had suffered in business with the South. Yet applications for work like Beals's, born of anxiety, are replete with these contradictions as men tried to balance an obsequious stance toward a man with significant

Bargains Worse than Fraudulent

political authority and their belief that they did not deserve the hand the secession economy had dealt them. Commercial men were, by trade and necessity, mercenaries in search of the main chance.[4]

White men were not the only applicants for war work. Aaron Bradley, who identified himself as a black member of the Suffolk County Bar, contacted Andrew after Fort Sumter to "tender . . . my service to the United States." Andrew told him to talk to John Murray Forbes, a railroad executive whom Andrew had made recruiting agent in the city. Forbes was fresh from the speculations in land and bonds that had helped initiate the struggle between proslavery and antislavery forces in Kansas, the Panic of 1857, and the war itself. Bradley knew the outcome of the meeting as it began, when Forbes "received me as all Northern-men alwa[y]s receive all Colored men, with an aire of Natural Superiority." When Bradley informed Forbes that, having been a lawyer, he could certainly perform all the tasks "required of a Soldier," Forbes condescended to offer him a position as a cook. The Militia Act of 1792 in force at the outbreak of the war allowed only white men to serve as soldiers, so Forbes followed the letter of the law. Bradley's response to Forbes's offer was to reject it out of hand as beneath his occupational stature. "I would reather call on God to damn you," he told the recruiter, and "join Jefferson Davis & fight to the death." Bradley's threat was of the type that concerned Northern leaders in the spring and summer of 1861, as reports of black slaves being used as laborers on Confederate fortifications revealed the ways white Southerners were mobilizing African Americans' labor to secure their independence. In a war supposedly about white men's freedoms, Northerners considered the use of enslaved people's labor to be part and parcel of slaveholders' fraud.[5]

Elsewhere, Massachusetts men were offering refuge and work to enslaved black men in order to stop Confederates from employing them in support of the rebellion. Nearly a month after Bradley wrote to Andrew to complain about his treatment, three enslaved men fled to Fort Monroe on the Virginia coast. They told the general in command of the post, Benjamin Butler, that they had been digging trenches and building fortifications for the Confederates nearby. Before the war, Butler—a Democratic politician from Lowell, Massachusetts—had navigated partisan politics with aplomb and fought on behalf of textile mill workers for better working conditions and shorter workdays. He now declared that these enslaved men were "contraband of war," materiel used by rebels to prosecute war against the United States. Butler would begin to break up the Confederacy's mock auction fraud: Virginians could not fire on Northerners from trenches dug by enslaved people and expect the return of their valuable human commodities. The Fugitive Slave Act was no longer in force, for Virginia was not part of the United States.[6]

As he put a stop to Confederate fraud, Butler speculated about how to make enslaved people useful as laborers in the war for Union. Butler explained his purpose in a letter to General-in-Chief Winfield Scott. Defining enslaved men who worked for the enemy as "contraband" in an effort to weaken the Confederacy's ability to wage war was only part of the story. Butler told Scott that he had "determined ... [,] as these men were very serviceable and I had great need of labor in my Quartermaster's Department, to avail myself of their services." Butler made it clear that the contraband policy separated slave from master for a military purpose that would benefit his army at Fort Monroe. He needed men to move supplies, dig trenches, and build fortifications. The Underground Railroad had once siphoned valuable commodities from the Slave South. Now Butler repurposed enslaved people's valuable work to use them as the Confederates had done. The doctrine of "military necessity," as historian James Oakes has written, justified Northern men in thinking that enslaved people's "services could be appropriated." Butler's policy punished secessionists by seizing their property, a satisfying outcome for Northerners who had suffered economically during the secession crisis.[7]

Butler's legal and military answer to the question of what to do with runaway slaves became more complicated when women, children, and entire families joined the exodus to Fort Monroe. He asked Scott what he should do with people who had not worked to aid the Confederate war effort. While he waited for his commander's answer, he would respond with "humanity," welcoming them to remain at the fort. Yet if benevolence seemed to be foremost on his mind, Butler also conceived of these people as a "species of property" that was worth, he told his superior, some $60,000. He wanted Scott to appreciate the figure as an approximation of what he had been able to wrest from the Confederacy. This accounting was similar to what William Still did in his compendium of traffic on the Underground Railroad. Butler also hoped to assuage his commander's fears about the costs of this influx of people to the fort. "I have ... determined to employ, as I can do very profitably, the able-bodied persons in the party, issuing proper food for the support of all, and charging against their services the expenses of care and sustenance of the men laborers, keeping a strict and accurate account as well of the services and the cost of the expenditure determined by a Board of Survey hereafter to be detailed."[8]

Butler would resort to the bookkeeping ledger to detail the debts and credits the army and African American laborers accrued. He ordered Colonel John Phelps of the First Vermont, stationed at Newport News, to put "able-bodied negroes within your lines" to work digging trenches. Phelps was to keep an "accurate record" of the work they did, the supplies and food they were given, and their "names, descriptions, and the names of their owners." Butler would adopt the lingua franca of the commercial world — accounting and bookkeeping — for what he called "future use," to provide receipts to slave owners if his policy was rejected by the Lincoln administration. When Secretary of War Cameron approved the contraband policy on May 30, he insisted that Butler and his subordinates continue to keep correct records of the labor former slaves performed and "the value of it." Though army ledgers would still tally the value of labor, it would no longer be due to slave owners, but rather to workers according to the principles of free labor.[9]

Yet Butler's quest to keep an accurate account of wages did not include paying all of those wages to "contrabands." As he waited for the government to determine the status of former slaves and the legality of his policy, Butler created circumstances in which former slaves would remain dependent. John Wool, who succeeded Butler in command at Fort Monroe, determined to weave wage labor and benevolence together in October 1861. Under Wool's guidance, formerly enslaved men would earn between eight and ten dollars — and women four dollars — per month. Yet Wool directed that they only receive a few dollars from their pay in fifty-cent weekly installments and that the rest be withheld in a fund administered by the quartermaster's department to pay for the support of dependent members of their families. The U.S. military would determine how this money was used, mainly in making certain that black men, women, and children remained, according to *Frank Leslie's Illustrated Newspaper*, "comfortable, clean, well fed and well clothed." Union generals reasoned that former slaves, recently dependent on their masters for their livelihood, lacked the habits and values associated with free labor ideology that encouraged the saving of earnings in order to care for families. They treated black Southerners as subjects of charity, much as Northern almshouses did the urban poor, rather than as wage earners who could support themselves.[10]

If the coercion of slavery was eroding, the subtle coercions of free labor were taking hold. Formerly enslaved men and women would earn wages from the military, but would be forced to depend on the government and private benevolent institutions to disburse funds and supplies so that they could survive. General Wool began to pay former slaves their wages directly only when, in early 1862, an investigation determined that fraud was rife in the quartermaster's department, where clerks noted the wages of formerly enslaved people in an account book but then sold supplies earmarked for their support to other parties. Despite Northern politicians' and generals' faith in accounting, sharpers could manipulate the books to their benefit. The wage, that mite of capital, would make enslaved people more independent, but only if it found its way off the page of the account book and into their pockets. The practices of corrupt officers and clerks made former slaves more dependent on the government, and the revolving carousel of commanders at Fort Monroe created further hardship. When Wool was replaced by John Dix, the army stopped regularly paying its workers once again. By the end of 1862, it owed African American laborers at the fort over $33,000. Free labor, as dictated by military necessity, was a fraud. Many enslaved people in Tidewater Virginia had worked for wages in the antebellum period, keeping a portion for their own use while being forced to give the lion's share to their owners. Wage labor was not slavery, though, and black workers at Fort Monroe freely objected to the fraud and dependence they endured at the hands of their liberators. They tried, mostly in vain, to find powerful friends in missionary organizations and the army who could assist them in recovering what was theirs.[11]

In the summer of 1861, when Butler was still in command, he noted that 854 African American men, women, and children were "claiming protection & food" in his Department of Virginia. The men were "throwing up intrenchments" in nearby Hampton, thus saving white Union soldiers "from that labor under the gleam of the mid-day sun." The women in Hampton "were earning substantially their own subsistence in washing, marketing, and taking care of the clothes of the soldiers." When Confederate encroachment forced these people to flee their homes in Hampton to the safety of Fort Monroe at the end of July, Butler wrote to Cameron to ask, "What shall be done with them?" He also sought to clarify their legal status: "Are they free? Is their condition that of men, women, and children, or of property, or is it a mixed relation?" He was asking these questions not only because military necessity demanded it, with more African Americans crowding for safety in the fort, but also because General Irvin McDowell had issued orders forbidding enslaved people from being sheltered by his troops around Washington. If black Virginians were property, Butler reasoned that "they have been left by their masters and owners, deserted, thrown away, abandoned, like the wrecked vessel upon the ocean." In that case, it seemed to Butler that, according to the law of wreck and salvage, they would "become the property of the salvors." But Northern salvors did not hold human property. The stewards, captains, and agents of the Union Steamship Company had transformed human property aboard northbound vessels into persons, seizing the value slaves represented from their owners and restoring it to free people. If the Fugitive Slave Act was a dead letter, so was Virginia's 1856 law that attempted to impound Northern vessels associated with the Underground Railroad. Union soldiers were saviors, Butler contended. As a result, should not black refugees be given "the free enjoyment of life, liberty, and the pursuit of happiness[?]"[12]

Butler was less than one year removed from his support of Jefferson Davis as a nominee for the presidency of the United States. Now he was willing to destroy slavery if doing so would also wreck a rebellion against the Republic funded by and waged for slavery's capital. The questions he asked his superiors about refugee people's legal status lingered, though, and his own approach to answering them was replete with contradictions. He told Cameron that he hoped to offer former slaves the lofty freedoms of the Declaration of Independence and acknowledged that African American women and men earned the subsistence they got by doing work in service of the Union army. Nevertheless, he and his successors accounted for their wages to hedge against the costs of subsistence and then failed to pay them in full. Former slaves' status was not to be the independence offered by Lincoln's interpretation of free labor. Rather, they would remain dependent on the labor market created by the doctrine of military necessity and the army that governed that market.[13]

Many Northerners saw the labor market that Butler and other Union generals helped to create in Virginia as one open for their exploitation. Emancipation in the Northern states had unfolded in stages in the late eighteenth and early nineteenth centuries and included lengthy periods of apprenticeship in which former slaves found it difficult to accumulate and save money. The process of emancipation kept them poor and vulnerable in the labor market. That was useful for white employers who benefited from the cut-rate price of emancipated people's labor. Many white Northerners had argued that black Northerners lacked the habits or character for the "free enjoyment of life, liberty, and the pursuit of happiness." Montgomery Blair, Lincoln's postmaster general, wrote to Butler to praise his policy and encourage refugees to migrate to Haiti, where he believed they could obtain land of their own. "It is want that makes men work," Blair believed, "and neither negroes nor whites work without being obliged." Free labor spurred by military necessity was in this way a self-fulfilling prophecy: former slaves' poverty forced them to work, and the irregular pay of partial wages kept them poor and obliged to toil. Yet Blair also made the argument that wants, as well as want, forced people to labor. "The whites of our country work more because they have more wants," Blair explained, "the wants of civilization superadded to the necessities of subsistence." He argued that the civilizing process would encourage former slaves to work harder in order to buy manufactured goods made in New England. The movement of former slaves to Haiti would start the process whereby producers became consumers, and reinvigorate the North's economy laid low by secession in the bargain. From Blair's perspective, a policy of colonization would follow Butler's contraband order to punish secessionists and lift Yankee commerce at the same time. Free labor would free Northern capital.[14]

Former slaves might be salvaged for the use of the United States and its citizens beyond the ways Butler conceived of saving them. The secession crisis and the Federal rout at Bull Run led some Northerners to think about how the emancipation of enslaved people was both a domestic and military necessity for the preservation of the United States. On July 23, 1861, the Boston philanthropist David Sears wrote a letter to Massachusetts politicians including Governor Andrew and Senator Henry Wilson. In it, he proposed a plan for compensated and gradual emancipation. Sears believed that Southern secession had created the circumstances whereby Northerners could amend the Constitution and repeal the linkages between slavery and congressional representation in Article I, Section 2. He then would begin—in the border slave states and, once they had returned to the Union, the Gulf States—"buying and liberating enslaved young women." The cost of these purchases would be met by indenturing the children of these women in Northern households. Sears believed that Butler's contraband policy should be ratified as soon as possible so that this great transformation could begin. The War Department should issue a general order for Union armies to take runaway slaves as contraband of war and have them "marched to the nearest depot, and thence ... distributed among the free states, in the ratio of their population." Once they arrived in the North, former slaves were "to be billeted, by authority of the State Executive, upon the ... freeholders, as domestic laborers" or farm workers. Each Northern household would take "not more than two" laborers and then "return" them "to the order of the United States at the end of the war," unless the black Southerners agreed to remain with Northern employers who wanted to continue the arrangement.[15]

Despite Sears's reference to consent when the war ended, coercion was at the forefront of his plan. This proposal would not only countermand the

Fugitive Slave Act, as Butler did, but also make the federal government a broker of former slaves' labor. Sears advocated for the state's power to force employers to welcome Southern African Americans into their households, and a policy of apprenticeship would force black mothers to consent to the state's control over the labor of their children. The arrangement would conclude with the laborers being delivered back to the commercial order of the broker-state. The title of the published version of Sears's text, *Contrabands and Vagrants*, illustrates the correlation he made between poor, supposedly "idle" populations in North and South. The movement of former slaves to the North, in his estimation, would not be part of a trajectory toward independence for workers. Rather, this labor movement, defined by considerable coercion, would serve a doctrine of domestic necessity by alleviating the problem of the divided Northern household that *Vanity Fair* had lampooned.

The New York abolitionist Lewis Tappan shied away from the coercive elements of Sears's proposal, instead emphasizing the benevolent aspects of sending black refugees north. In light of the newspaper coverage that described something approaching a humanitarian crisis unfolding at Fort Monroe, Tappan wrote to Butler that "several friends of liberty" had determined to provide assistance to former slaves and the armies that protected them. Tappan knew that black Southerners within Butler's lines were "abundantly able to take care of themselves, and acquire property when they have the opportunity." No civilizing process was necessary, as Blair believed. Tappan proposed the creation of committees in Northern cities that would act as intelligence offices, "provid[ing] for the removal of the self-emancipated negroes to the free States, where they could find employment and receive wages for their labor." Unlike in Sears's model for the movement of workers, Tappan's proposal favored benevolent societies rather than the state as a broker of labor arrangements. Northern employers would benefit from a new source of labor in their "farms and workshops and families," former slaves would receive "a fair remuneration," and commanders like Butler would "be relieved of care and anxiety" in attending to former slaves.[16]

Despite Tappan's depiction of a win-win-win proposition, Butler thought the plan "would not be profitable." He believed these former slaves were "a class of mostly agricultural laborers" who would thrive near their homes in Virginia on land they could till under the protection of the army and the government. "The most of them would not desire to go North if they can be assured . . . of their safety in the South," he explained. Moreover, he believed that a Northern economy reeling after Southern secession would be inhospitable to former slaves. "To send them North, amid the stagnation of business and at a season when all agricultural operations except harvesting are about to be suspended, to fill our towns with a new influx of people when their labor is not wanted," would be "unwise." While Blair thought the movement of black laborers would help improve the Northern economy, Butler sought to protect those laborers from Northern economic instability that lingered after the secession crisis. Butler encouraged Tappan and his benevolent partners to send clothing for distribution to refugees.[17]

Sears's and Tappan's ideas about moving and brokering work for former slaves continued a long debate about the ways employment agencies represented wage labor and mediated the wage labor relations of the Northern household. On August 31, 1859, a front-page headline in James Gordon Bennett's *New York Herald* had announced the penny daily's latest exposé. "Something about Intelligence Offices," it read. Bennett thought it was necessary to introduce these institutions to readers, but he also acknowledged that their scams had been around for awhile. In fact, a casual reader of the *Herald* over the previous two decades would have already encountered them in columns listing want advertisements and police court proceedings. Americans often found work or workers through ties of friendship, family, or neighborhood, but these employment agencies had become ubiquitous urban institutions in the decade before the war. Bennett estimated that there were between thirty and forty such shops doing a "flourishing business" in Manhattan, while another one or two dozen smaller intelligence offices also dotted the city's landscape. Other commentators counted hundreds. In these offices, employment agents sold information about the labor market to prospective employees and employers so that the former could find work and the latter could find workers. Intelligence office keepers collected a fee ranging from fifty cents to a dollar from each party who sought information. In the waiting rooms of these establishments, agents, workers, and employers met face-to-face, asking questions and inspecting appearances to deduce character traits and skills in the hopes of making an agreeable bargain with each other.[18]

The intelligence office "business," Bennett explained to readers new to the topic, "has been growing and spreading, like every other business in this city, for many years." This was a refrain that commentators would repeat about the intelligence office. Its transactions and its purpose resembled those of other commercial venues. "It seems to be absolutely necessary in large cities," Bennett contended, "that labor, like every other merchantable commodity, should have its special marts." Business specialization was happening in every other sector of the economy. Why not the wage labor market? "There is nothing intrinsic in the business itself which should prevent its being conducted honestly and honorably, and at many offices undoubtedly it is so conducted," Bennett concluded.[19]

Yet what made an article on the intelligence office timely was that it was a scourge on the city's inhabitants. If it was necessary in large urban places, it was also an evil in desperate need of reform. "Swindlers and sharpers," often operating in dimly lit basement offices to evade the surveillance of police officers tasked with enforcing urban licensing requirements, gulled workers out of a fee and never found them work. They sent some young girls to houses of ill fame, polluting their fair character. They fleeced employers by charging a fee and supplying them with lazy or fractious employees who would neither do the requisite work nor stay on the job. Readers did not just have to take Bennett's word for it. They could read letters appended to this story from two aggrieved *Herald* readers who were "victims" of these "bogus" businesses. This cultural debate may surprise us if we only had William Henry Burr's 1849 painting to guide us. The crumpled issue of *The Sun*—and its lengthy want ad columns—on the waiting room floor brought the parties together for negotiation. The women who hope to be hired look on passively as the intelligence office keeper beckons to the seated mistress to make her choice beneath a sign on the wall that reads "Agency for Domestics. Warranted Honest." Everything seems to be above board. We have to dig beneath the surface of this image if we are to understand the ambivalence and fear that Americans felt toward the institution.[20]

Bennett's earnest exposé reveals that concerns about intelligence office fraud emerged from anxieties about the labor relations of the city's respectable households and how business was done in the city. Bennett seemed to disapprove of the ways intelligence offices redirected the flow of labor and capital. He especially lamented that the labor market in domestic servants had shifted in favor of workers, and he believed that shift was another one of the frauds the intelligence office had produced. "The supply of labor in this department is far behind the demand." Not only was a middleman skimming money from labor market transactions, but workers were also benefiting from intelligence offices' presence. New York's Commissioners of Emigration, who operated an intelligence office that found immigrants "employment gratis," particularly irked Bennett. Without having to pay the typical fee, workers were able to keep their capital and thus be less vulnerable and have more choices in the labor market. The Commissioners seemed to be exemplars of the traits of honesty and honor that Bennett said he valued, but they made life harder on employers who searched for skilled and obedi-

William Henry Burr, *The Intelligence Office* (1849), oil on canvas.
(Collection of the New-York Historical Society)

ent servants at a low price. The most desirable employees—identified by their ethnicity (English, Scots, and German) or religion (Protestant)—were snapped up quickly. The "impertinent" remainder, often Irish Catholic immigrants, would have to be compensated with higher wages that drained employers' bank accounts. The "airs" which the "ladies below stairs" were taking in their intelligence office negotiations with mistresses shocked Bennett. He railed against the blurring of social position in the household— "the lady would seem to have exchanged places with the servant" when the latter demanded independence in the kitchen, a night off per week, modern appliances, and high wages. The intelligence office, by driving up wages and putting mistresses on a par with immigrant servants, produced dangerous economic and social consequences. These institutions threatened to upset ladies' pretensions to refinement and authority. Like Webster in his activities as wholesaler and shipping agent, intelligence office proprietors had the information and the wherewithal to supply wants and needs. As Webster did in his activities as silent partner in the Underground Railroad, intelligence men threatened to take capital from employers in the labor market. Even

Tappan's proposal that benevolent agencies take charge of these workers might not, from Bennett's perspective, adequately redress the ways intelligence offices challenged the power of employers.[21]

Yet Bennett did not only care about the threats to class hierarchy in the household. He was also concerned about mistresses' weak negotiating position in the intelligence office. Their weakness resulted from their abdication of household responsibilities. In this way, he shared Henry Louis Stephens's perspective on fashionable women. Even though most ladies continued to cook, sew, and clean, Bennett blamed them for not knowing how to do housework properly. They had become "utterly dependent" on servants and were thus unable to manage or negotiate with them. Bennett believed that reforming the intelligence office would be as much about well-to-do women restoring themselves to their proper place as about prosecuting the swindlers who peddled faulty labor market information. "Some of the fashionable ladies up town, we are told, are talking seriously about forming a society and agreeing to do all their housework for a time in order to bring the girls to reason." This combination of household mistresses would stand as a "bold assertion of 'woman's rights,'" Bennett argued, because its negotiating tactics would force domestic servants to resume positions of subservience or starve. Bennett's critique aimed to put refined ladies and immigrant servants in their place for depleting men's capital. But Bennett's logic about status was faulty. The experiment of ladies doing the work of their own households without assistance would serve to blur the class boundaries that he claimed the experiment would uphold.[22]

The newspaper editor's judgment about fraud in the labor market was inaccurate, too. The last letter from a subscriber that he affixed to the essay was from an intelligence office keeper. W. J. Redpath claimed that the *Herald* article had "classed" his business, which specialized in the placement of merchants' clerks, "with thieves and swindlers." If only Bennett and *Herald* readers knew that he had placed many young men in reputable positions and was willing to open his books and distribute his house rules to anyone who inquired, they would come to the conclusion that he was unfairly maligned and that his office was "the only establishment in this city conducted upon honorable principles." Perhaps Bennett had forgotten his own paper's coverage of legal proceedings filed against Redpath a year and a half earlier, in which the proprietor of the clerks' registry had "'done' Mr. Samuel T. Chase, of Illinois, out of $100." Chase had visited Redpath's office to answer an advertisement placed by a businessman in search of a partner. Redpath had "induced" him to buy $100 worth of patent medicines and $35 worth of furniture before he gave Chase the information he desired. Chase complained to the city's mayor, who revoked Redpath's license to operate the intelligence office when he did not return the money he had obtained under false pretenses.[23]

If Bennett had forgotten, his readers reminded him, for they knew Redpath well. The crook was still in business. Two days after publishing the exposé, Bennett announced that angry citizens had deluged his office with letters about how they had been defrauded by intelligence office scams. After reading the incriminating evidence, and without naming Redpath directly, Bennett acknowledged that it appeared "the offices that claim to be conducted on the most honorable principles are those that practice the vilest impositions." Credit reporters were more direct in their assessment: whether in getting "situations for Young men" or in repaying debts, Redpath "is no wise to be relied upon." It had been inappropriate, one of Bennett's subscribers claimed in a letter to the editor, to differentiate between intelligence offices that operated morally and immorally. They were all "bogus institutions." Bennett had been "done" by Redpath, too, accepting the distinction between honorable and dishonorable dealing when in fact fraud was pervasive in all of the city's commercial districts. Bennett refused to believe that he had been had. He congratulated himself for doing a public service by "exposing" a fraudulent institution that mistreated the poor and the rich alike. Then he confronted his duped readers, proclaiming that "[t]hose who now allow themselves to be imposed upon by intelligence offices will have themselves to blame." Fraud stalked the nineteenth-century economy, Bennett admitted. It could not be vanquished. Victims, if innocent, were also ignorant. Readers would protect themselves only if they perused the want ads in the *Herald*, Bennett declared. That was, he asserted, what intelligence office keepers did. They had no special knowledge of the labor market. Caveat emptor.[24]

Bennett's screed against intelligence offices and those who sought labor market information and bargains there forced Northerners to confront free labor's failure to live up to its promise of efficiency, fairness, and merit-based rewards. Employment agencies fostered concerns about urbanization, immigration, anonymity, and the social order of the household. Those concerns leached into politics. Speaking at New Haven, Connecticut, on March 6, 1860, Abraham Lincoln argued that slavery as a political issue was an obstacle that "prevents the adjustment, and the giving of necessary attention to other questions of national house-keeping." He compared slavery to a snake that slithered into the beds of Northern children who would move to the Western territories. Lincoln quickly dropped the metaphorical references to households and families to espouse the honor of free labor as a strike among shoemakers roiled New England. He declared that he supported the workers' right to strike. "I *like* the system which lets a man quit when he wants to" and "leave[s] each man to acquire property as fast as he can." For Lincoln, free labor permitted men to move across space in order to move up occupationally, economically, and socially. "When one starts poor, as most do in the race of life, free society is such that he knows he can better his condition; he knows that there is no fixed condition of labor, for his whole life." To Lincoln, his own experience proved the rule. "I am not ashamed to confess that twenty five years ago I was a hired laborer, mauling rails, at work on a flatboat—just what might happen to any poor man's son! I want every man to have the chance—and I believe a black man is entitled to it—in which he *can* better his condition—when he may look forward and hope to be a hired laborer this year and the next, work for himself afterward, and finally to hire men to work for him! That is the true system."[25]

To understand the limits of Lincoln's "true system" and the coercions of wage labor in the antebellum North, we need look no further than the New England shoemakers' strike of 1860. Lincoln might have deployed his "house-keeping" metaphor to more powerful effect, because many of the strikers were women. Wage labor not only imperiled the refinement of household mistresses; it also threatened workingwomen and their households. The Panic of 1857 had diminished consumer demand for shoes, straining an industrial sector already defined by cutthroat competition. As factory owners slashed wages, they exposed conflict between married male and female workers who sought to establish a breadwinner wage for men and thus preserve the household as a political and economic unit, on the one hand, and single women who sought higher wages and thus more independence for themselves, on the other. Alonzo Draper, the head of the Lynn, Massachusetts, Mechanics' Association and a strike leader, urged women to join the strike by saying, "Remember ladies, . . . especially, you young and blooming ones, that if you want husbands, wages must go up, for no one can get married at present prices." Wage labor, Draper argued, threatened to circumscribe the formation of households and the patriarchal independence on which they were based. Some women joined a chorus of "Shame! Shame!" in support, but another blurted out, "We don't have any sweethearts," illustrating single women's belief that free labor and wages should boost the individual independence of all workers. When the strike resulted in men's wages being raised and women's wages being diminished, single women made fearful comparisons between their plight and that of enslaved people. "Don't let them make niggers of you," one exclaimed. "American ladies will not be slaves," their banners insisted. Even though Lincoln contended that free labor was superior because it allowed workers to strike, the shoemakers' "turn out" demonstrated that low wages resulted in a competitive quest for survival among laboring people who disagreed about how to achieve independence. Although Lincoln believed that the cherished harmony of interests between capital and labor was alive and well, the strike demonstrated workers' concerns about household survival and social status, underscoring James Henry Hammond's insistence that in free society, war between the haves and have-nots was inevitable.[26]

Lincoln also might have reflected on the crisis of his own household to understand the crisis of political economy. In the 1856 presidential campaign, he had done all he could to convince his fellow citizens in Illinois that a vote for American Party candidate Millard Fillmore would pave the way for Democrat James Buchanan's victory over Republican John Frémont in the state. Lincoln proved prophetic, as Frémont lost Illinois to Buchanan by 9,253 votes out of 239,334 cast. Fillmore had received the votes of 37,531 Illinoisans. For Lincoln, the opportunity for white Northern men to achieve property-holding independence in the Western territories would continue to be threatened by a proslavery Democratic administration.[27]

Lincoln's wife, Mary, was just as concerned about the outcome of the election, but for different reasons. She wrote to her half-sister Emilie in the weeks afterward to complain that her Kentucky relatives were wrong to think her husband was an abolitionist because he had supported Frémont. He only hoped to cordon the institution of slavery from the territories. Mary's letter to Emilie was not only defensive; it also exhibited her independence from her husband. She had favored the spoiler and believed that any right-minded Southerner would see things her way. "My weak woman's heart," she demurely explained, "was too Southern in feeling, to sympathize with any but Fillmore." Fillmore was preferable because he "feels the *necessity* of keeping foreigners, within bounds." Southern slaveholders should have understood the danger of unruly laborers who compromised the authority of their masters. "If some of you Kentuckians, had to deal with the 'wild Irish,' as we housekeepers are sometimes called upon to do, the south would certainly elect Mr. Fillmore next time," Mary informed Emilie. The 1850 census recorded that an eighteen-year-old Irish woman named Catharine Gordon lived and worked in the Lincoln household. The historian Jean Baker suggests that Gordon, who regularly invited men to visit her during the eve-

Bargains Worse than Fraudulent

nings, may have exhibited an independent streak that fostered Mary Lincoln's disdain for Irish servants as a group. Her correspondence in the late 1850s and early 1860s praised other domestic servants in her own home who displayed "submissive" qualities and the "*darkies*" who obediently served the families she visited in the slave states. Mary Lincoln was, by reputation, a terror to domestic servants who challenged her authority. One former employee, Margaret Ryan, later recalled that she had escaped Mary Lincoln's wrath but that her employer "often struck other girls." Abraham Lincoln was the kindly influence in the home, telling Ryan to "[k]eep courage" and "not to fuss with Mrs. L." He even went behind his wife's back to offer additional wages to servants who threatened to leave the family's employ. For doing so, he earned Mary's ire. Troubles with a domestic servant likely led her to tell a friend that "if Mr. Lincoln should happen to die, his spirit will never find me living outside the boundaries of a slave State." Her claim to Southern feelings and her political advice to Southerners emerged from her domestic life in Illinois, dealings with obstreperous Irish biddies, a kindly but misguided husband who deigned to invade her prerogatives as household mistress, and memories of the obedient slaves who worked in her family's old Kentucky home.[28]

Mary Lincoln was, like other household mistresses and workingwomen, making claims about class, gender, and independence that shaped the contours of the labor market. Among the Republican Party slogans during the campaign of 1856 was "Free Hearts and Free Homes," infusing gendered ideas about domesticity that would resonate with antislavery citizens. In published campaign literature, John Frémont's wife, Jessie, was a champion of antislavery in the new state of California. She advocated, like James Gordon Bennett, that housewives do their own work rather than relying on the labor of enslaved men and women. Mary Lincoln, like many Northern and Western ladies, did much of her own housework. Yet by the late 1840s and 1850s she typically hired a young woman to help her. For Mary, a "Free Home" was one with a domestic servant whose labor helped to create a lady's independence and illuminate her household's refinement. Her autonomy was based on the labor of others. Abraham knew this. While serving in Congress in 1848, he wrote to Mary in surprise: "You do not intend to do without a girl, because the one you had has left you? Get another as soon as you can to take charge of the dear codgers." His note was not an order so much as an acknowledgment that household servants' labor freed his wife from the rigors of childrearing. Abraham and Mary's political rift opened because of their assumptions about gender and independence. Abraham emphasized the freedom of white Northern men hoping to get ahead in the West. Mary was concerned with the liberty of household mistresses like herself. Their household was divided between the interests of mistress and servant. Abraham sometimes sided with the latter, but he knew full well that his and Mary's interests were united in the concept of the "Free Home." The functioning and status of their household depended on the work of servants and the authority of the mistress. This set them apart both from waged domestic servants and the single women in New England shoe factories who struck for higher wages for themselves in a bid for independence. Free labor, from the perspective of the Lincolns and others who were in a position to use their capital to hire workers, would bolster the class and gender authority of employers while denying independence to household workers.[29]

The Panic of 1857, an event that imperiled the households and livelihoods of Northerners, created new opportunities for women like Mary Lincoln who were desperate for household order and power. The answer for dealing with the consequences of economic despair was a new intelligence office that would operate much like the one Tappan would propose to Butler. In December 1857, forecasting the prospect of cold weather and the suffering of women turned out of work in the aftermath of the financial panic, reformers Elizabeth Phelps and Eliza Farnham formed the Woman's Protective Emigration Society (WPES) and asked for the public's assistance in the pages of the *New-York Tribune*. Their aim was to transport women who had been "honest and honored laborers in workshops and stores" to the West to work as domestic servants and thus be "raised to respectability and independence." Farnham, the Society's secretary, had masterminded a plan earlier in the decade to bring women to California to be married off to gold miners and thus foster domesticity in a place defined by rough masculinity. She had thought a great deal, therefore, about how to move people over long distances for the purpose of constituting households and bolstering their allegiance to the ideal of respectability.[30]

Farnham and Phelps's plea to the public for assistance reveals their conviction, broadly shared among Northerners, that private charity could correct capitalism's inequalities. The Society did not seek to evade those inequalities so much as redirect supply to meet demand. Its "humane, economical, and effectual" plan was a market solution to the problems associated with the wage labor market. Workingwomen, faced with a shortage of jobs in Eastern cities, could be moved to Western locales where ample situations were available. "[D]onations" of some ten or twelve dollars would pay the transportation of each "homeless, friendless, and penniless" woman and help them escape the degradation of poverty which might lead them toward the "dark stream of vice which pollutes our streets." The Society opened its doors on Canal Street next door to the labor exchange of the Commissioners of Emigration, highlighting the benevolent intentions of the society and fixing in the city's geography the charitable efforts to protect foreign-born immigrants coming into the city and poor women leaving it from the depredations of the worst intelligence office men.[31]

Horace Greeley, the editor of the *Tribune*, offered his support to WPES but also forthrightly condemned the circumstances that created the need for it. What had driven New York women to the brink of starvation or prostitution, Greeley believed, was not financial upheaval but employers who had set their low pay. Unsurprisingly, given their history of combat in New York's press, Greeley disagreed with Bennett. "A woman may be defined to be a creature who receives half price for all she does, and pays full price for all she needs," Greeley reported. "She earns as a child—she pays as a man." It was not worth women's time to appeal to the state for redress of these gender inequalities born of wage labor. "Nothing this side of the pauperism of the almshouse is in reserve for her from the government." To be put on par with a child was onerous, but to be a ward of the state would be too much to bear. From this evidence, much as Bennett would have doubted the efficacy of Tappan's benevolent approach to labor brokering, Greeley would have considered Sears's proposal for state intervention to be misguided. To avoid such an ignominious fate, Greeley thought, the only answer was to move these women to the West. Yet benevolent societies, as much as almshouses, needed state support. WPES asked New York City's Board of Councilmen for $3,000, and on finding it worthy the council appropriated half that amount for the cause. Government officials would not countenance paying poor women directly—much as the Union army would refuse to pay former slaves directly—for they could not be trusted with money outside the surveillance of almshouse overseers.[32]

Fifteen hundred dollars could not sustain the Society's efforts, however, and Farnham begged readers of the *Tribune* for money. The needs of capital and capitalists ultimately shaped the direction of the Society's benevolence. Farnham appended letters from eager employers in places such as Elkhart County, Indiana, to demonstrate the willingness of Westerners to do their part to alleviate an impending crisis. Yet their letters also enumerate concerns and desires not fully understood by the Society. One letter writer expressed delight that young women who had been *"operatives"* in New York would be sent to work in *"good homes"* in the West, demonstrating with italics both the novelty of industrial capitalism and the domesticizing goal of the Society. Operatives might need training in domestic work, but Easterners could be assured both that these women's virtue would be protected in rural Indiana households and that the sinister effects of capitalism would be obscured. Good homes would also become Free Homes, households whose members would be liberated by the domestic labor of impoverished New Yorkers. Another letter writer emphasized employers' desires, laying bare the imperatives of the market. Women earned between $1 and $2.50 per week in Indiana, he wrote, wages that perhaps would entice workingwomen to move west as much out of choice as destitution. He also mentioned that "male help of all kinds is very scarce here," relaying a market need at odds with the project of WPES. The Society tried to ameliorate the uncertainties and inequalities of the wage labor market. Nevertheless, its managers' efforts were ensconced in that market because the employers with whom they dealt and the women they helped to transport could not act independently of it.[33]

The *Tribune* reported in February 1858 that WPES was ready to send one hundred young women by "express train" to Decatur, Illinois, some forty miles east of Springfield. There is evidence that a few of these women ended up in the households of the Lincolns' neighbors and relatives. Moreover, the WPES's agent in the West, Vere Foster, claimed decades later that he had spoken to the Lincolns when he visited Springfield. They allegedly told him that they would "promise to treat any girl we direct to them as one of the family, and to give her a home certain for a month, so as to give her time to settle in a place." Whether Foster delivered such a girl to the Lincolns is not clear. From the perspective of household mistresses in Illinois, WPES provided an opportunity to counteract the circumstances of the Western labor market—defined by high wages and rapid turnover as domestic workers sought better pay and conditions—while also couching these labor arrangements in terms of benevolence. The hire of poor Eastern women thus fit into Illinois's labor market. Mary Lincoln's sister Elizabeth Edwards and her husband Ninian had a few black children indentured to them as "apprentices" in the 1830s and 1840s. The state's laws countenanced lengthy apprenticeship arrangements for African Americans, and many white Illinoisans likely considered them to be forms of benevolent protection and necessarily gradual steps toward freedom, much as white Northerners did in other states that adopted gradual emancipation laws in the early Republic and as Union generals attempted to do at Fort Monroe.[34]

By the 1840s, coercive labor arrangements garnered more criticism in the state. In 1841, Abraham Lincoln served as a lawyer for a white man who refused to pay a promissory note for the purchase of an African American woman, Nance Legins-Cox, arguing that proof of her enslaved condition had to be given first. The seller never gave such proof, and Legins-Cox would not work unless she was paid wages. The appeals court ruling in the case stated that, in light of the absence of legal proof of enslavement, "the sale of a free person is illegal" in Illinois. In practice, however, enslaved people moved into and out of the state in these years. In 1847, Lincoln agreed to defend a Kentucky slaveholder named Robert Matson who frequently brought enslaved people to work on land he owned in Coles County. An Illinois court sided with the abolitionists who had brought suit against him, arguing that the slaves had resided on free soil for more than a "temporary" period and thus were free. In attempting to surmount the challenges and costs of workers' transportation over long distances, WPES offered a service that fit into the context of American laborers' movements during this period and the ways employers sought to traffic in that movement. While the law in Illinois was increasingly turning against slavery, employers sought advantage and were able to harness capital funneled into benevolent societies in order to make wage workers more available to them.[35]

In the context of Hammond's mudsill speech, some observers were quick to consider the ways WPES trains illustrated the hypocrisy of free society. This was not just trafficking in humans' movement but rather human trafficking that broke down household bonds and illuminated the rapaciousness of Northern and Western employers. Southern newspapers reported the case of a WPES train arriving in Bloomington, Illinois—a town about sixty-five miles northeast of Springfield. A married man in search of a domestic servant entered the office where workingwomen waited and spoke with the WPES agent. One woman said that she would go with him, because she recognized him as her husband who had absconded years before. Southerners used this case—representative of Northern wage earners' suffering during the Panic of 1857 and WPES's attempt to alleviate it—to confront abolitionists' assertions about what slave auctions did to black families. They argued that Northern men were apt to leave their wives to suffer in poverty. An article in a Pickens County, South Carolina, paper even twisted the evidence to announce that the ten-dollar transportation cost quoted by WPES was actually the going sales price for New York workingwomen in the West. The movement of these women constituted a "Northern Slave Trade."[36]

Indeed, Western customers were saving capital when they relied on WPES benevolence and New York councilmen's support for transportation, but they were offering the women who worked for them higher wages than most domestic servants could earn in Eastern cities. This was not a slave trade. Yet these women had been industrial operatives or store clerks who likely had earned more wages than domestic servants in any region of the country. The movement of women from New York to the West reveals the ways intelligence offices and employers managed workers' movement by preying on their want. If Montgomery Blair hoped that "want" would make former slaves work to consume Northern products, Northern employers of domestic servants had a history of making "want" work for them in the labor market, since needy workers who had nowhere else to turn would be cheaper and more obedient.

Butler's contraband policy pushed the Lincoln administration and Congress toward passing the first Confiscation Act, which declared the labor of fugitives from rebel owners to be available for appropriation by Union forces. The wage policies initiated by Northern generals at Fort Monroe in these circumstances merged with Northern employers' ideas of wage labor and their interests. Yet the white Northerners who speculated about salvaging former slaves in the summer of 1861 were not alone when they made reference to the secession crisis. Southerners had caused that crisis by not paying their debts, roiling financial markets and unsettling the financial footing of many Northern businesses. The threat to creditors created concerns that the value of bank paper and consumer goods was not what it seemed. For some commercial actors, the response was panic, as they "ran" on banks in order to exchange paper for specie.[37]

Other merchants sought to turn the unsettled value of things to their profit, proclaiming that the secession crisis was a financial panic that would force merchants to offload goods quickly in order to balance their accounts and thus benefit customers looking for bargains. As secession turned to war, Northern businessmen evoked both the promise and peril of free labor, for they offered visions of what consumers could do with their capital just as the state began to mobilize soldiers to do the work of defending the nation. Their pitches to consumers were so persuasive that the state borrowed them to recruit men. Barlow Espy, for instance, advertised the opening of his "cheap store" in Shelbyville, Illinois, in the spring of 1861. By marrying Rebecca Cutler in 1848 and going into business with in-laws in Fort Madison, Iowa, he had, according to the 1860 census, already amassed a fortune of $11,400 in real estate and $6,500 in personal estate. He sought to build a platform for greater wealth by moving to his wife's birthplace in Shelbyville and using family and friendship connections to garner patronage. In an advertisement measuring some three feet by two feet meant to be affixed to walls along main thoroughfares to attract the attention of passersby, Espy touted his connections to the "Fountain Head of the Goods Trade" and his "facilities for purchasing Goods in the East." That center of trade was Philadelphia. He had purchased this advertisement from Duross Brothers, a printing firm in that city. Espy aimed to show the citizens of central Illinois that they could obtain the most fashionable goods from the capitals of manufacturing and retailing in Europe and the Eastern United States. Espy's ad, therefore, promised access to goods across long distances in ways similar to WPES advertisements that offered central Illinois households access to the labor of destitute Eastern women.[38]

The visual culture of advertising reveals how the impending crisis of Union seemed to offer new opportunities for profit. Barlow Espy, already a successful storekeeper, believed he could make a killing in Shelbyville. He registered that belief by envisioning, in his advertisement's header, soldiers in battle array. He also spoke freely in the language of war, adopting the type of questionable puns found in comic publications like *Vanity Fair* to make his customers grin and persuade them to peruse his wares. In this advertisement, dated April 1, 1861—eleven days before Confederates fired on Fort Sumter—Espy advertised that "another war" had been "declared." It was his own war on dishonest dealers and on behalf of the local consumer, and he was going to wage it against the backdrop of the forthcoming struggle between North and South. And he would win it: "Great Slaughter Anticipated! 'WATCHWORD Give nor ask any Quarters!'" The images that Duross Brothers offered to Espy for the advertisement dovetail with the militaristic language of the text. The image of soldiers in column situated beside an army camp scene dominated by the billowing United States flag suggests, as historian Joanna Cohen has written, that advertisements like these portrayed consumption as an act of citizenship. Consumers were encouraged to buy in order to protect the nation's economy in its time of peril.[39]

These troops were spurred on by a commander—perhaps, in Espy's mind, himself—gesturing toward an unseen commercial enemy. In the text, Espy contended that his crusade would be fought under a "banner" reading "*Extermination against all high prices and Undue Profits.*" In a lengthy "Proclamation," Espy repeated a time-honored critique found in antebellum advertisements that credit was too easily available and debtors' unwillingness to pay what they owed was the cause of increasing costs. Southerners' secession-crisis defaults threatened Northern creditors and consumers alike. Espy explained that duplicitous merchants often charged higher prices of "Honest, industrious, frugal prompt paying men" as a way of protecting

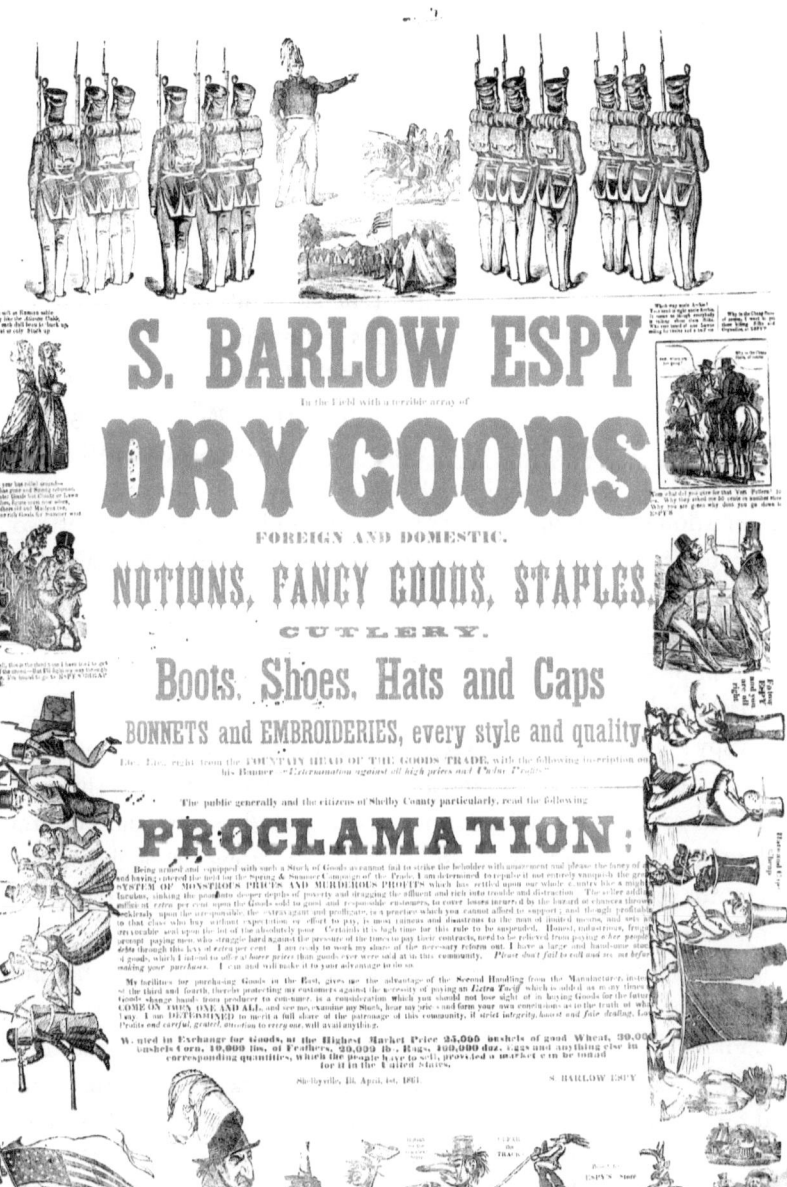

S. Barlow Espy, *Another War Declared* (Philadelphia: Duross Bros., 1861).
(The Library Company of Philadelphia)

themselves from loss at the hands of absconding debtors who failed to pay for the goods they got on credit. These practices hurt all consumers, regardless of class status, but it particularly injured "the man of limited means, and sets an irrevocable seal upon the lot of the absolutely poor." Unable to pay higher prices set by merchants to recoup their losses from "the irresponsible, the extravagant and profligate," poorer Americans could not sample from the bounty of goods merchants offered. Moreover, Espy implied that his competitors charged "an *Extra Tariff*" because they bought goods from middlemen who exacted a fee for moving goods from large cities in the East. Espy contended that his ability to purchase goods directly from Eastern suppliers set him apart from his competitors. He would sell cheap—"at *lower prices* than goods ever were sold at in this community"—while his competitors would sell dear. He would exhibit "*strict integrity, honest and fair dealing,* Low Profits *and careful, genteel, attention to every one,*" protecting his customers from the "SYSTEM OF MONSTROUS PRICES AND MURDEROUS PROFITS" that was stalking the land. By announcing his sincerity, he planted the question in the minds of Illinoisans who read the advertisement: would other storekeepers have their interests in mind when they transacted business? Espy suggested that they would not. Keen to assist local customers whose access to money might have been tight in these hard times, he offered to accept produce instead of cash, knowing he could find a market for agricultural goods.[40]

Espy's attempt to blame fraud on the elaboration of credit was not new, and it illuminated a tension in American commercial culture, since credit networks made it possible for merchants to do business and consumers to buy products. Credit was absolutely necessary, even though consumers might not pay their debts and merchants might raise prices in response. So Espy was not entirely sincere, and his advertisement was an outright fraud in another respect: the advertising copy was not his. Joanna Cohen has shown that it was at least as old as an 1859 advertisement printed by Duross Brothers. The Philadelphia firm printed similar advertisements in 1861 for storekeeping clients around the country who mixed and matched artistic vignettes and text in an attempt to convince customers to shop at their stores. The partnerships of Spruance & Megear of Smyrna, Delaware, P. & C. Templeton of Brady's Bend, Pennsylvania, and S. C. and L. Fox of Sandy Creek, North Carolina, all adopted the "Proclamation" of Espy's advertisement for their own. The text's author is not clear—it may have been supplied by Duross Brothers or culled from advertising screeds of the antebellum decades. Firms might be excused for borrowing the text, for proposing to eliminate fraud sounded so good. It was a pervasive concern in nineteenth-century American commercial culture. The story juxtaposing fairness and injustice sounded especially relevant to storekeepers during a secession crisis that highlighted citizens' and states' loyalty. The firm of S. C. & L. Fox appealed to "Union Men" near their North Carolina establishment some three weeks before the state seceded, revealing that its principals must have thought linking loyalty and commercial fair play was a good bet even as their neighbors were about to exchange their loyalties to a new nation. It seems likely that such appeals worked more effectively north of the Mason-Dixon line.[41]

These advertisers knew that finding a bargain meant even more than loyalty and honesty to many consumers. They told customers, "Secession has produced a wonderful change in the price of goods." Ultimately, the ways credit and debt increased prices and redirected the flow of capital to bad businessmen meant less to Northern consumers than the possibility that firms might be willing to part with their goods for less in order to remain solvent through the crisis. Advertising appeals kept pace with the drumbeat of war. After Confederates attacked Fort Sumter and President Lincoln called out troops, Benjamin Ramage solicited Duross Brothers for an advertisement that would entice customers to buy at his store in Enon, Pennsylvania. He offered western Pennsylvanians goods at "war prices" and touted the high quality and low cost of his stock. This phrase worked precisely as "panic" and "secession" had done before the conflict began. Ramage's argument was that customers should make purchases immediately, before their advantage disappeared. Now that war had officially started, however, the visual culture of advertising took on new potential meanings. Ramage used the same images of the soldiers, commanding officer, and flag, but he also headed the image with the phrase "Attention Volunteers!" This phrase would soon title recruitment posters calling for enlistment. Previously, storekeepers had asked Union sympathizers to take advantage of the prices that panic and secession produced. Now Ramage hoped to gather the custom of men volunteering for enlistment. The headline "Fort Sumter Re-taken" might have been, a month after its surrender to Confederates, a wishful thought or an exhortation to these volunteers to whip the rebels after making purchases at his store on their way to the front.[42]

The visual culture of advertising intersected with the visual culture of recruitment in Philadelphia, and firms such as Duross Brothers were at the forefront of this process. By the summer of 1861, recruiters aiming to fill companies and regiments adopted the images of the printing firm's commercial advertisements. These recruitment posters turned on a transaction as well.

Benjamin Ramage, *Attention Volunteers!* (Philadelphia: Duross Bros., May [1861]). (The Library Company of Philadelphia)

The images of soldiers, their commander, and the flag now represented real men filing toward the training camp and battlefield. "March On! Brave Volunteers," called a recruitment poster with these images for Company H of the Sixty-Sixth Pennsylvania Infantry. Captain H. W. Ducker and Lieutenant A. W. Lyman told men who would enlist that they would receive $2 cash "in hand"—the finder's fee due recruiters—and $100 federal bounty when the war concluded. "Pay, rations and clothes" would be received "at once."

Recruiters expected that volunteers would be courageous and willing to fight for their country's flag. Yet in a competitive urban environment in which potential recruits could choose which regiment to join, company commanders would have been foolish to think that loyalty and civic virtue alone would bring them men. Two dollars in hand would pale in comparison to later local, state, and federal bounty payments to volunteers, but for workingmen living in an uncertain economic climate, it likely represented a way to help their families survive until their monthly pay started. Another recruiting poster for a different company in the regiment, depicting the same images of soldiers and commanding officer, locates the regimental headquarters at the Girard House. This poster highlights the clothing allowance that would be offered to volunteers. At the very moment this poster was printed at the end of June 1861, the Girard House was becoming embroiled in scandal. It was allegedly the site where army contractors produced "shoddy" clothing that unraveled after exposure to the rough conditions of soldiering. Contractors pocketed, as Espy would have said, "undue profits" at the expense of soldiers' comfort and health. Under these circumstances, soldiers filing into the recruiting office in the Girard House to volunteer for the Sixty-Sixth Pennsylvania may have wondered whether the clothing allowance could procure them quality garments. Indeed, many Americans inside and outside the army condemned the activities of the contractors as base frauds.[43]

The shoddy scandal erupted across the Union, and nowhere more palpably than in Pennsylvania. In August, the commission that Pennsylvania governor Andrew Curtin assembled to "investigate the alleged army frauds" issued its report. The commissioners remembered that Pennsylvanians had rallied quickly to the nation's colors. By April 23, ten thousand enlisted men were camped in the state's capital, Harrisburg. Within a month, "the cry went abroad" that the recruits "had been supplied with worthless and insufficient clothing, and with food wholly unfit, and that the Government had been treated worst by those who should have served her best." Yet the commissioners were satisfied with the management of the production process at the Girard House, which strictly followed the protocols observed by the quartermaster at the Schuylkill Arsenal. They did not find fraud in the ways goods were distributed to and made at the Girard House. They had to explain, however, "the stubborn fact that the soldiers were in rags." Henry Louis Stephens, in the pages of *Vanity Fair*, drew the public's attention to the flagrant negligence of shoddy contractors who had produced clothing that literally came apart at the seams, such that soldiers had to cover their bare behinds to shield themselves from the view of female visitors. Stephens cas-

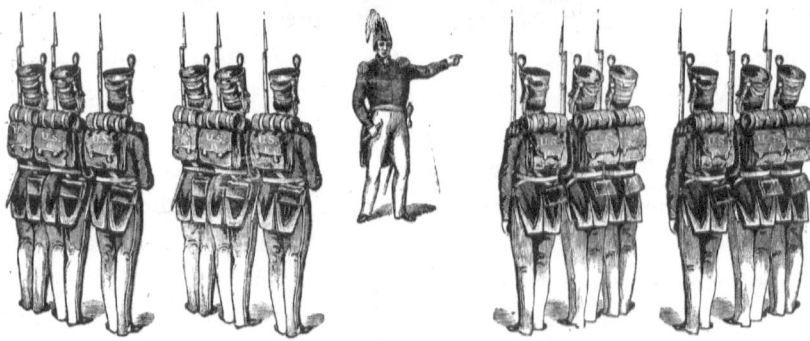

Volunteers Wanted! Company C, Col. Chantry's Regiment (Philadelphia: Duross Bros., 1861). (The Library Company of Philadelphia)

tigated this fraudulent affront to the soldiers who sacrificed for the nation while also lampooning the dictates of gender and class respectability.[44]

The commissioners attributed blame not to fraudulent contractors but to the poor choices government agents had made about materials. They discovered that "satinets, and especially those at 35 to 55 cents, are totally unfit for army pantaloons." If there was blame to go around, it should be shouldered by the hasty purchasers of this cloth when, the commissioners averred, a supply of quality cloth would soon have been available. These purchasers could be excused, though, because they had made their decisions in

"The Pennsylvania Volunteers," *Vanity Fair*, July 6, 1861, 1.
(The Library Company of Philadelphia)

"an hour of the greatest alarm." The commission also attached blame to "incompetent" regimental quartermasters and the agents to whom they delegated their responsibilities. While troops in the regular army received two suits of clothes, volunteers received only one uniform that could not withstand the rigors of soldiering.[45]

The commissioners' report hemmed and hawed about fraud in these transactions. A few merchants may have bribed the state's agents to obtain contracts, and a few other firms may have charged "exorbitant" prices for goods that fell apart or whose colors faded. The commission was pleased to note, however, that there was "abundant evidence presented of the honorable dealing of all the merchants of Philadelphia" who sold their wares to the Girard House operation. State officials did not know the price of quality goods, so they bought cheap things in insufficient quantities to provide for the soldiers. While the state saved its money, the health of the men who rallied to protect it was put at risk. Some merchants received significant profits from their contracts with the government, but the commission hesitated to call these deals "strictly a fraud." It needed a new vocabulary, so that it could "utterly condemn . . . the self-interest which, in an hour of national peril, forgetting all patriotism, seek[s] . . . only how it may turn its country's sufferings to its own greatest pecuniary advantage." The commissioners knew they were drawing a fine line between profit and patriotism, between interest and ideology, at a time of commercial panic and national distress. Business must go on. Merchants and manufacturers could certainly expect that "commissions and profits . . . of an ordinary amount" would be "paid." Yet the commissioners labeled a fearful new category of commercial transaction when they acknowledged that what a man of business "has a right to do" was not what he should do. He should "remember that in cases where the Commonwealth is concerned, there may be bargains worse than fraudulent." Commissioners who strained and failed to find fault with most of the buyers and sellers in the market for soldiers' things nevertheless put commercial men on notice that legitimate commerce would be defined in a time of war by the benefit it offered to the state. Union men could prosper, but not at the expense of their government.[46]

The commissioners reasoned that "positive pecuniary advantage [would] accrue to the State" if, among other things, "the practice of purchasing from second hands [was] abandoned." Middlemen and agents were the cause of added costs, of "speculation" that supposedly "would cease" in their absence. Clothing contracting was a speculation that was hard to pass up, though, for men who had nothing else to do. One of the men who testified to the commissioners in their investigation was Thomas Webster, who identified himself as a "merchant." While a few newspaper advertisements announced the continued traffic of Union Steamship Company vessels to Richmond in the week after Virginia seceded, Webster knew that his days as an agent of the carrying trade were numbered. So when the state of Pennsylvania announced in May that it needed contractors to supply soldiers with overcoats, Webster volunteered. He won a contract to supply fifteen regiments — 11,100 men — with coats, and then obtained the right to supply them with pants, too. Webster did not volunteer to the commissioners an accounting of the profits he accrued from these contracts. Rather, he emphasized that his overcoats "were the only ones offered that conformed in color...—sky blue—to the army regulations." By the time Webster got the contract, Governor Curtin had already named him assistant commissary and charged him with purchasing other things soldiers needed on behalf of the state and assessing the legitimacy of purchases made by other contractors. He bought $50,000 worth of "pork, bacon, beef, bread, flour, coffee, sugar, &c." As commissary, he instructed those who bid for contracts about the rules of engagement. Merchants must "deliver the goods of the best quality at the market price." He informed the commissioners that no merchant had attempted to bribe him to obtain a contract. When the quality of a coffee purchase came into question, Webster insisted that two pots be brewed from "the two poorest bags we found." He and the other commissaries "partook" of it and found it was "good but strong." Webster cared about officers' and soldiers' tastes, too, soliciting testimony among the men in camp to validate his determination that this was "invariably, good, sound, wholesome coffee."[47]

The governor's panel of commissioners did not want to see the state taken advantage of by profiteers. Henry Louis Stephens, former slaves working for the army at Fort Monroe, James Gordon Bennett, and Barlow Espy wholeheartedly agreed in their condemnations of Confederate Peter Funks, thieves in the Union quartermaster's department, intelligence office keepers, and easy-credit merchants. Middlemen's speculations must be mitigated, if not abrogated. But free labor ideology, it turned out, was a fraud. Labor was not superior to capital. The Northern economy depended on middlemen. The state, employers, workers, and consumers needed men like Webster who knew how to get things, how to value things, and how to gather information about things. Webster was an organization man in need of an organization. He was adept at ingratiating himself into a new commercial climate in which he could make money, appear to follow the regulations, and attain power as an arbiter who determined whether the bargains made under his purview were fraudulent—or worse. Webster, the man who had lost the port collectorship he thought his partisanship and commercial ability deserved, tried to make money in war through means that would not trouble his contemporaries. As soldiers mustered for war and encountered the dependence of wage labor in army ranks, they endeavored to speculate in goods, people, and services and make bargains out of the conflict. Like Webster, the frauds of free labor helped them discover that the wrong thing was also the right thing. Being a middleman was good because accumulating capital was good—it was the only way to be more independent in an economy in which everyone was dependent.

3

CAPITAL IN SELF

MAKING MONEY OUT OF WAR has always provoked Americans' condemnation. That is why the shoddy scandal resonated so powerfully with Northern citizens and forced speculators like Webster to get right with the interests of the state through professions of patriotism. Doing so was just as necessary for recruiters as they gathered soldiers to do the state's work and for soldiers as they volunteered for public service. Kings and queens had long employed mercenaries and kept standing armies, but republican citizenship called on Americans to defend their imperiled nation and the ideals for which it stood. Historians have chronicled the ideological rationale for Northern men to go to war in 1861. Defending the Constitution, the Union, democracy, and maybe participating in a process of emancipation were all ideological motivations that encouraged men to enlist. These issues allowed soldiers to highlight their civic virtue by demonstrating their willingness to sacrifice for the common good rather than gain at the public's expense. Recruiters and soldiers wrote about these ideological reasons because they believed in them. They did not fight for money.[1]

Yet Americans' concerns about those who did fight for money—the bounty men who craved enlistment payments rather than the honor of soldiering—reveals that their political culture's expectations for independent citizens existed within an economic context of wage labor that made citizens dependent. For "mercenary" also meant "hireling," a term that carried connotations of dependence even as proponents of free labor ideology sought to rehabilitate it by valorizing wage labor in comparison with slavery. Soldiering was wage labor, and citizens weighed the obligation to sacrifice for the common good against their and their families' economic need. Northerners believed that, by killing and dying, Union soldiers would do the work of destroying an aristocracy—a disloyal slaveholding class that threatened the world's last bastion of liberalism, an ideology that emphasized not only individual political rights but also individuals' economic freedom to compete in the market. The ideological principles that inspired Northerners to go to war—to validate their notions of republican citizenship—coexisted uneasily with the fact that becoming soldiers meant becoming hirelings, mudsills dependent on state and federal governments for survival.²

President Lincoln saw value in the work he called Northern men to do. His messages that called out seventy-five thousand of the nation's militia in the aftermath of Fort Sumter's surrender and more than forty-two thousand volunteers in May 1861 were answered by men eager and willing to serve in the nation's army or navy to crush the rebellion. In his message to Congress on July 4, 1861, Lincoln not only justified his recruitment policies but also asked representatives and senators to volunteer their support: "[P]lace at the control of the government, for the work" of war, he requested, "at least four hundred thousand men, and four hundred millions of dollars." Explaining that these totals were mere fractions of the male population and wealth of the country, he claimed that a "right result, at this time, will be worth more to the world, than ten times the men, and ten times the money." The war's capital costs would be awesome, but the preservation of the Union would be priceless because its form of government best served "to elevate the condition of men—to lift artificial weights from all shoulders—to clear the paths of laudable pursuit for all—to afford all, an unfettered start, and a fair chance, in the race of life." If the nation dedicated to republican ideals spent its capital now, it would help its citizens earn capital for generations to come.³

Lincoln tried to untangle the conundrum that soldiers faced. The war would, he argued, contribute to the triumph of free labor. Soldiers would be dependent for a time but would do the work necessary to save the nation and its principles, bolstered by the North's considerable capital. Northern citizen soldiers, however, often found that their place in the war's economy forced them to scramble for the credit and capital that would ensure their own survival while they fought for the nation's. Free labor's rhetoric of free competition, represented by Lincoln's hopeful reference to the race of life, seemed right to many soldiers. It was part of an ideology that venerated hard work and perseverance and defined wages as capital in the making. Soldiers' wage work put this rhetoric to the test, exposing contradictions between ideology and experience and forcing soldiers to explain what the war was about when they did not have the language to explain away those contradictions. Some accepted Lincoln's bon mots and moved on with their lives. Some blamed middlemen, slaveholders, and the government for the challenges they endured.

Others desperately sought to work harder in an effort to earn more independence. They knew what Lincoln refused to acknowledge: independence was not a status earned outside the market, isolated from other people's capital and labor. All were dependent on the market for these things, and soldiers tried to become more independent within it by accumulating credit and capital through speculation and by employing other people. Soldiers' recruitment, experienced and understood through the prism of consumer capitalism and narratives about fraud, forced American families to create new circulations of credit and capital that connected army camps and distant homes. All Northern soldiers, after the passage of a May 1861 law providing volunteers with a $100 federal bounty at the end of their term of service, were bounty men who hoped that those promises to pay would open lines of credit for family members back home. Some soldiers sought to build on this source of credit to speculate for more individual and family income. Others' struggles with accumulating credit and capital led them to speak of their desire for black laborers as a means to increase their personal autonomy as employers and heads of household. Union soldiers could not take advantage of the "chattel principle," which served as the foundation for human commodification in Southern slavery. In the context of their other speculations about credit and wages, though, soldiers believed that becoming an employer meant earning economic and cultural capital and the independence it conferred. To many Union soldiers, personal autonomy could only be earned—and validated by peers—through the control of workers' labor. American men arrived at recruiting offices driven by a variety of ideological and material forces. Their decisions to enlist and the government's efforts to recruit them cannot be understood apart from the culture of capitalism from which Northerners hailed and the flows of capital that the war would produce.[4]

Recruiting posters reflected the commercial culture of antebellum America. Competition was as close to the heart of recruiting soldiers in the Civil War as it was to the business world that Thomas Webster knew. One of the most intense struggles in Civil War recruiting pitted Governor John Andrew against General Benjamin Butler. After being replaced as commander in Tidewater Virginia in August 1861, Butler returned home to Lowell. He worried that the war effort was becoming an exclusively partisan one in which Republican governors put their friends in command positions. The answer was not to do away with partisan distinctions but, he later remembered, to raise "a New England division of Democrats, and I wanted them of the most pronounced and well-known type." Butler desired his own sphere of influence, and he got

Lincoln to create a new Department of New England in which to recruit five thousand soldiers for an impending expedition. Those orders to recruit in the New England states put him in conflict with Andrew, who believed recruiting in Massachusetts was his sphere of influence. The state's quartermaster general, John Reed, and Andrew's military secretary, Albert Browne Jr., met with Lincoln in September 1861 to register Andrew's concern and convince the president to agree that "no more independent permissions to raise regiments should be granted to individuals." Lincoln explained that other states' governors, namely Edwin Morgan of New York, had "been embarrassed in the same manner as yourself, but to a greater extent," and that orders had been issued by the War Department to clarify that only governors had the authority to recruit soldiers in their states.[5]

Lincoln may have mentioned Morgan's challenges in New York as a way of criticizing Andrew's out-of-state recruiting. Andrew had an agent named Frank Howe in New York City, ostensibly to see to the wants and needs of Massachusetts soldiers traveling south to Washington. Howe was a businessman who sometimes sent Andrew letters on commercial stationery with headers hawking "Howe's Standard Scales" and "Lillie's Safes." While he made sure that Massachusetts soldiers had something to eat and a place to rest while in New York, Howe also solicited New Yorkers to fight in Massachusetts regiments. In doing so, he weighed men's ambitions and safeguarded his state's interests. Howe received two letters on this subject from nineteen-year-old Lewis Parmelee of the Seventh Regiment of the New York Militia. Parmelee had heard "that you propose to raise a Reg't" in Manhattan "for the State of Massachusetts." He believed such an outfit could be recruited in short order and requested the rank of captain in said regiment, "being anxious to obtain a position as a Line Officer." The ambitious Parmelee wrote another letter to Howe the next day with new ideas about how soldiers could be recruited quickly. If Massachusetts paid, like the state of Connecticut, "a much higher rate p[e]r month to their families than they receive from" New York, and if they could receive this state aid "from the date of enlistment, it would be a *double* inducement," Parmelee reasoned. New York's Union Defense Committee withheld relief funds to families until soldiers left for the front. Parmelee knew that soldiers shopped around for the best deal for their households. Perhaps, he continued, enlisted men could also be paid their "first month's wages in advance" to sweeten the deal.[6]

Nothing came of Parmelee's requests, but they were not unique. Months later, Andrew would receive a letter from a captain who had recruited eighty soldiers to serve as cavalrymen. The regiment to which he had originally been assigned was now full. Would Andrew, he pleaded, assign his company to another regiment? "It is perhaps a small matter to which I allude," the man demurred, "but pardon me as it is the turn point in my life & my future success to a certain extent must depend upon it." Wartime recruitment presented a novel means to achieve prosperity and prestige, but it took spending capital to attain them. This officer had "already expended over five hundred doll[ars] in raising" his company and "cannot lose it." His ambitions for status and financial security were in the balance, and Andrew was in a position to determine whether he would succeed or fail.[7]

Andrew's ambitions for recruiting in his state collided with Butler's. The competition between them deepened into animosity because Lincoln's orders obscured which man had the authority to recruit in Massachusetts. Each sought to score political points at the other's expense by sharing letters privately with friends and, in Andrew's case, by preparing to send them to Senators Henry Wilson and Charles Sumner, incoming Secretary of War Edwin Stanton, and a Boston printer for publication. Andrew agreed to help Butler at first, but not at the expense of recruitment for the regiments he had already promised to General Thomas Sherman for an expedition to the Carolina coast. He offered Butler the Twenty-Sixth Massachusetts, led by Butler's friend from Lowell Colonel Edward Jones, and a regiment of Irish troops—making a correlation between ethnicity and political affiliation that he thought would please the Democratic general. Butler "assented" to Andrew's plan but also determined to recruit independently. Andrew would label these soldiers and the officers whom Butler appointed to lead them "irregular."[8]

Andrew and Butler accused each other of turning men into mercenaries. What they could not admit, as Parmelee had done in his letters to Howe, was that financial inducements were the best way to persuade men to join one regiment rather than another. Since both men were angling to make their correspondence public, it behooved Butler and Andrew to portray the other as the sinister recruiter who engaged in inappropriate traffic in free men. A few weeks after Parmelee had suggested it to Howe, Andrew learned that Butler had received permission from Secretary of War Cameron to pay recruits in his division one month's wages in advance. Hardly averse to the practice in theory, Andrew asked Cameron for permission to extend the offer to men he recruited. Cameron refused, arguing that Butler's permission was justified because his troops were "for special service." Vexed by this response, Andrew complained to Cameron that the policy was unfair and disadvantaged his own efforts. In the meantime, Butler told Andrew that he had heard the state's recruiting agents gave soldiers "private bounties" of five or seven dollars. Despite offering his own men immediate financial inducements to join his regiments, Butler described the state recruiters' bounties as "the sale of men" to captains who had "the most money." He recognized that soldiers would "hold off from enlisting for a higher bid" and blamed Andrew for creating circumstances in which "the whole recruitment is demoralized." Butler told Secretary of the Treasury Salmon Chase that he was able to get soldiers, but "it is difficult to get the class of men I desire." This was the lament of the nineteenth-century employer at the intelligence office infiltrating the solemn work of recruiting a national army to put down secessionists. By the fall of 1861, that "class of men" would not be inspired by patriotism alone. Money was the answer, but the republican critique of soldiers for hire weighed on the agents who would pay as much as on the men who would serve. Paying to hire soldiers seemed wrong. So Butler invented a distinction between the footloose mercenary who got a bounty and the employed soldier who received an advance on his wages to send home so that he would not "march leaving his family wholly destitute without knowing when he would get his pay." Soldiering, associated with household welfare rather than personal profit, could thus be understood as the respectable wage labor Lincoln said it was.[9]

Andrew acknowledged that captains with capital were distributing bounties. He did not think it was a good idea, but he also did not think he could tell ambitious recruiters what to do with their own money. Put on the defensive by Butler's aggressive tactics in the recruiting market, Andrew told Adjutant General Lorenzo Thomas in November that he would consider withholding the charitable aid that Massachusetts had legislated to soldiers' families from Butler's men because they had not been recruited "under any authority from the Commonwealth." These payments could be anywhere between four and twelve dollars per month, depending on the "necessities" of each family. In late December, Andrew informed Thomas that he refused to issue commissions to the officers Butler had appointed to the Eastern Bay State Regiment, a unit the general had recruited in Massachusetts. Andrew wanted federal confirmation that it was his responsibility to recruit soldiers and commission officers in Massachusetts regiments. Butler's "insubordinate" recruitment had been to "the detriment and confusion" of enlistments in the state. Andrew's warnings put Butler's recruiting into confusion. One recruiter told Butler that potential soldiers refused his entreaties to enlist unless the state aid was guaranteed. "They say . . . that if they go to war for their Countrys honor, they should not be required to have their little property at home eaten up by wife & children because their pay was but $13 per month, and of course inadequate to the support of a family." In January 1862, soldiers of the Eastern Bay State Regiment boarded the transport steamer *Constitution* in Boston Harbor, still under the command of the officers whom Butler had appointed. As the men awaited the start of their expedition to the Gulf of Mexico, a few of them received letters "by authority of" the governor intimating that Butler's "irregular" recruiting had imperiled their families' ability to collect state aid. Jonas French, whom Butler had placed in command of the regiment, complained of Andrew's treachery, as it made household survival a political issue and threatened a mutiny aboard the ship. French had applied to Andrew for a colonelcy when the war commenced, citing his "eleven years experience in the Militia." An informant told Andrew that French was "more fit for a rebel & traitor than a Patriot" by virtue of his "leading on the rabble" in an anti-abolitionist riot in Boston the previous winter. It took Butler's return to give French an opportunity to lead soldiers. Andrew thwarted French's command ambitions once again when he denied commissions to Butler's slate of officers. Now the governor tried to turn the Democrat's soldiers against him. While Butler could not promise French that he would remain in a position of authority through the coming campaign, he responded to Andrew's threat by offering to pay the aid to the men's families out of his own pocket.[10]

One of the ambitious company commanders attached to the expeditionary force was Captain John Nelson. Nelson had been born in 1834 in Ireland. By 1860, he was a machinist who also ran a sparring school in Hartford. An advertisement published in the *Hartford Daily Courant* at the beginning of the war called him "Prof. Nelson," the proprietor of his own gymnasium. Followers of the pugilistic arts typically distinguished sparring from boxing. Sparring, its denizens proclaimed, constituted the gentlemanly pursuit of the sweet science, perfecting the moves of agility and strength that would help them best their foes, minus the black eyes and bloody noses that would exclude them from respectable society. When Nelson advertised his attention to sparring rather than boxing, he showed how much obtaining people's respect mattered to him. Yet being the proprietor of a gymnasium was not a position guaranteed to enhance one's social status. Despite his claims to a position as master of a genteel pastime, the lion's share of the evidence shows that Nelson was a sporting man who was comfortable in the rough-and-tumble culture of the nineteenth-century city and willing to transport the worldviews and practices of that culture to the seat of war.[11]

In April 1861, he was elected captain of Company E — the Hartford Invincibles—of the Third Connecticut, one of the ninety-day regiments that responded to Lincoln's first call for troops to put down the rebellion. As the Union army marched toward its first battle at Bull Run, Nelson was court-martialed for "conduct to the prejudice of good order & military discipline." Specifically, he was accused of using "profane" language toward Captain George Lewis of Company A and challenging Lewis to a duel. In a letter to the court, Nelson proclaimed that he would meet the accusations like a patriotic man of refined breeding: "[H]aving left a position in Society, in social life, to defend the Flag of our Country, I could not be so far lost to all sense of honor as willingly to forget my manhood." While claiming that his accuser was motivated purely by "malice," Nelson tried to seize higher ground in an act of self-definition that would obscure his status in Hartford. Hundreds of miles away from the high "Society" that probably excluded him, he claimed the honor denied to a humble machinist and gymnasium keeper by wrapping himself in the flag.[12]

Testimony in the case was taken on Independence Day in Falls Church, Virginia. The source of the disagreement was a foot race. A third captain in the regiment, Frederick Fry, had been a contestant, and Lewis accused Nelson of helping Fry during the race—the charge was "carrying" him, perhaps to victory. That night, in the sutler's tent, the officers gathered. Alcohol might, or might not, have been consumed. Nelson asked Lewis whether he had spread the insidious rumor that he had "carried" Fry. Lewis admitted he had. Nelson called Lewis a "God d___d liar" and insinuated that when they got back to Hartford—after this cruel war was over—he wanted a fight to settle the score. Lewis gave as good as he got, threatening that if Nelson ever touched him he would "make daylight shine through you"—that is, he would shoot him. Ultimately, Nelson was found guilty of the type of profanity that upset "good order and discipline," but escaped the more serious charge of challenging Lewis to a duel because Lewis's "provocation" was deemed a cause of Nelson's threats. Nelson proved himself combative, uncouth, and willing to brawl. The "Society" he kept back home must have been of the most suspect kind.[13]

After returning to Hartford at the end of his enlistment, Nelson accepted a captaincy in the Ninth Connecticut, a three-year regiment made up of the most boisterous Irishmen. Governor William Buckingham of Connecticut asked Butler to take charge of this irascible set and bring the regiment up to full strength as part of his division. "They are naturally good men," Buckingham told Butler, but "they are wholly without discipline and without control." On the train trip from Hartford to Lowell to join Butler's force at Camp

Chase, men from the Ninth "managed to tear the roof off of all the cars of the trains" in which they rode and "ransacked" Groton Junction in search of liquor. Butler justified the movement of the Ninth to his command when he told the War Department that the Irishmen's "somewhat exuberantly turbulent character" made it necessary for them to "be taken away from home influences which tend to insubordination." Butler reported to superiors in Washington that the regiment was "doing very well" and envisioned a time when the Ninth would be considered "one of the best of regiments."[14]

Among these men were Captain Nelson's incomplete Company K, which had left Connecticut before it could be officially mustered into the regiment. That fact created problems for its soldiers. A Connecticut recruiter worried, in a letter to Butler at the end of October 1861, that this irregularity in their enlistment would make it difficult for Nelson's men and their families to receive the Connecticut state bounty payments—a substantial sum of $30 per year for the soldier, $6 per month for the soldier's wife, and an additional $2 per month for two children under the age of fourteen—and the $100 federal bounty. These were the same concerns that Massachusetts recruits had as Andrew and Butler dickered over recruiting methods and the responsibility of providing sustenance for soldiers' families. Butler exhibited concern, too, telling another recruiter trying to get men in Bridgeport, Connecticut, for the expeditionary force that "there will be no trouble in regard to the bounty but ... you had better get a Justice of the Peace to administer the oath to your men before you leave Conn[ecticut]." Some soldiers in the Ninth were not convinced that they qualified for their state's aid. In January 1862, a citizen of New Britain, Connecticut, explained to Butler that a number of them had "made over their pay to me to save their families from suffering." Yet completing such paperwork may have been beside the point. None of the men's wages had been received, even though they had enlisted three or four months before. The struggle between politicians and generals for recruiting authority, the absence of paymasters, and the procedural technicalities of enlistment all might jeopardize the welfare of soldiers and their families.[15]

Nelson's purpose in Lowell was to fill his company and prepare to join the rest of the regiment, which had already departed for Ship Island, Mississippi, the staging ground for the expeditionary force's assault on New Orleans. He proved himself capable as a recruiter by using the ambiguous language of the era's commercial culture. "Freemen, Arouse!," he exclaimed in an advertisement in the *Lowell Daily Citizen and News* in December 1861, offering recruits "an extra bounty from the State of ninety dollars and ten dollars when mustered into the service of the United States." Added to the federal bounty of $100, each of Nelson's new soldiers would come away from the muster—in cash or in promises of later payment—of $200 in addition to their monthly wages. But which state was to pay this windfall? Nelson did not clarify. He was recruiting for a Connecticut regiment in Massachusetts on Butler's behalf. Buckingham, in sending the Ninth Connecticut to Butler, did not offer to give Connecticut money to residents of Massachusetts. Nevertheless, that is what Nelson was apparently doing, because he certainly could not expect Andrew to supply such a bounty to Butler's "irregulars"—and Nelson's company was surely recruited irregularly.[16]

Nelson probably did not know from where the money was to come, and he may not have cared. His captain's salary of $115.50 per month was paid by a Connecticut paymaster, even if his soldiers' bounties and state aid might not be. Yet by the time he offered Massachusetts recruits the bounty in a Connecticut regiment, he had probably heard that his superior officer, Colonel Thomas Cahill of the Ninth, had criticized his "inamiable disposition" in the pages of the *Hartford Daily Courant*. Butler acknowledged Cahill's "indisposition to having Capt. Nelson under his command" and asked Governor Buckingham to raise another company in Connecticut to join Cahill's unit. Butler told Buckingham, "I understand that Capt[.] Nelson" and his lieutenant, Henry Finnegas, "will resign their commissions if it is necessary." In reply, Buckingham explained that he could not find officers who would be willing to take command of the company and asked Butler to retain Nelson and Finnegas "unless you can find suitable men to take their places."[17]

Butler had another plan in mind. He tried to solve the conundrum that Nelson's uncertain commission posed by folding it into his power struggle with Andrew. On January 6, 1862, Boston's *Daily Evening Traveller* reported that Nelson's company had been filled and was "now on board the steamship *Constitution*, bound for Ship Island." The newspaper unwittingly reported a surprise: Butler had appointed Nelson captain of Company H of the Eastern Bay State Regiment. Butler and Nelson had double-crossed Colonel Cahill, who wrote his wife from Ship Island that Nelson had "played me that scurvy with reference to Co[.] K." He did not like Nelson, but he wanted and needed Nelson's men. Nelson proved his "inamiable disposition" by engaging in multiple speculations. He recruited in Massachusetts for a Connecticut regiment hoping that the latter state's governor would maintain him in his post. Knowing that Cahill did not like him, he looked to a commission in the Eastern Bay State Regiment, which was also recruiting at Lowell, as a useful position to which he could retreat if he lost his commission in the

Ninth. Incredibly, given Cahill's animosity toward Nelson, it appears that the former had his wife ask the mayor of New Haven to intercede with Buckingham about saving Nelson's Connecticut commission. Cahill was depending on the men whom Nelson recruited and, perhaps fearing that Buckingham's inability to find Nelson's replacement would delay the arrival of those soldiers, decided to overlook his subordinate's disposition to get them. Butler had his own scurvy to play. In February 1862, he wrote to Massachusetts's assistant adjutant general to protest Andrew's opposition to his slate of officers. He tried to justify his appointment of Nelson by asserting falsely that he was from Massachusetts. Butler also claimed disingenuously that he wanted to transfer Nelson to a new company in order to relieve him of having to command enlisted men who were "exceedingly difficult of discipline." Lest anyone think that this decision constituted a critique of Nelson's ability to command, Butler wrote that Nelson deserved praise for "being specially efficient."[18]

Neither Butler nor Nelson got away with these machinations. Cahill's wife heard a rumor in the middle of March that Nelson "never had a commission from Connecticut," but more accurately, he had surrendered it by accepting Butler's offer of command in a Massachusetts outfit. Doing so was a mistake because Governor Andrew won his battle with Butler over the Eastern Bay State Regiment. He appointed Nathan Dudley its colonel and renamed it the Thirtieth Massachusetts. The officers whom Butler had appointed were left without commissions and commands. Cahill told his wife that Nelson "is sorry Enough for his shame in that transaction and would be glad to fall back on the despised Connecticut Commission." Yet Cahill lost by this transaction, too. When Nelson took command of Company H of the Eastern Bay State Regiment, he also took with him at least two dozen soldiers whom he had enlisted in Lowell and other Massachusetts locations for Company K of Cahill's regiment. These men would continue to serve in the Thirtieth Massachusetts after Nelson was replaced. While the recruiting speculations of officers and politicians sometimes endangered the welfare of soldiers and their families, the men who had enlisted in Massachusetts for the Ninth Connecticut had their recruitment legitimated in the eyes of their state. They now served in a Massachusetts regiment that Andrew had cleansed of at least some of its irregularities, making their families eligible for state aid payments. Yet Nelson's theft of soldiers from Cahill meant further delays in filling the Ninth Connecticut's Company K and appointing its new captain. Cahill did "not know how much power the major General may have in the case or how far he may be disposed to back up Nelson." He found out soon enough. Butler's characterization of Nelson as "efficient" clearly stuck in his mind. He appointed Nelson provost marshal of Ship Island, rewarding his subordinate's fraudulent recruiting with a job policing the men they had recruited. Butler and Nelson had proven themselves to be bounty men, like their recruits. Soldiers often needed bounties and state aid for their and their families' survival, and those promises of payment also served their officers' quests for profit or prestige. Sometimes, soldiers' and officers' interests intersected, and at other times they diverged. Butler was impressed by what Nelson had accomplished: the former would highlight the latter's efficiency as a recruiter of soldiers again and again. Given Nelson's inamiable disposition, perhaps Butler saw him as a fighter who could be a useful ally in future speculations.[19]

As these disputes about recruiting unfolded, one of Andrew's regular recruits from Massachusetts was in Washington with his regiment. Charles Brewster of Northampton had enlisted in Company C of the state's Tenth Regiment in April 1861. When the federal census enumerator came to his mother's home in 1860, he had called himself a merchant, but Brewster was actually a twenty-seven-year-old store clerk when he enlisted. His mother, widowed since 1839, told the census taker that she owned $1,200 in real estate and had amassed $500 in personal property. She did not list an occupation, but the presence in the household of a salesman in his fifties, a milliner in her twenties, and a fourteen-year-old African American girl working as a domestic servant suggests she might have made money by taking in boarders. By August, when he wrote to his mother from Camp Brightwood, an installation protecting the nation's capital, Brewster was buoyantly optimistic about the war's result. "[S]esession is certainly going to be licked," he proclaimed. "[T]here aint going to be any more bulls runs on our side." The Union army was too numerous, bountifully fed, and warmly clothed, he explained. For his and his comrades' troubles, they would be paid regularly "in Uncle Sams gold once in two months." Brewster was "eager" to have at the rebels and was convinced that the Union cause was worthy of victory.[20]

That reference to his receiving a regular supply of Uncle Sam's gold was testament to Brewster's faith in the contract he had signed with the government and to his belief that wages were part of soldiers' motivation for fighting. By the end of the month, he had been appointed first sergeant. Yet Brewster received this promotion with frustration rather than glee. It suggested to him that a conspiracy was afoot. He had been wronged. He should have been a contender for a more robust promotion, if for no other reason than "[t]here are great many Lieut[enant]s in this Regiment a great deal bigger fools than I be." A "curse of ill luck" had followed him from the store in which he had clerked to ensure that he never got ahead. It seemed to cast a pall on his future prospects for advancement in the army. "I get a great many compliments for prompt attention to my duties," he groused to his mother, "but so I always did in other business but it never amounts to anything and compliments don't pay." In a letter he sent to his mother in September, he explained that a sergeant made $20 per month, while a second lieutenant made $105.50 for the same period of time. He was not earning the share of Uncle Sam's gold he thought his hard work and proper application to the business of soldiering deserved. Moreover, the men of the Tenth Massachusetts were not paid every two months as promised. At Brightwood and many other camps where Union soldiers were stationed, men were "fast learning to live without money" and beginning to see that the promises of recruiting posters and enlistment contracts were not being kept.[21]

The delays in getting paid were inevitable given the challenges the U.S. government faced with administering a bureaucracy of paymasters and resolving transportation snafus to deliver payments to soldiers on the move. Enlisted men whose supply of money was uncertain also came to understand that they were dependent on a market managed by army contractors and sutlers, the merchants commissioned to sell food and supplies to soldiers in camp. The processes of production and networks of distribution were as murky to soldiers as they were to other Americans experiencing the transformations that industrial capitalism wrought in the nineteenth century. The shoddy scandal of the war's first year did not give soldiers confidence in the products foisted on them. Brewster, once a store clerk, was knowledgeable enough about the quality and price of products to know when he was being cheated. He tried to evade sutlers by venturing into the nation's capital with a pass from a superior officer, a privilege that privates rarely received. He exchanged his government-issue boots for new ones with a Washington merchant because "government shoes are miserable things and cannot be made to last the month." The transaction illuminates the market in which soldiers acted. Brewster had drawn two pairs of boots from the army for $2.10 per pair, and the merchant with whom he dealt offered a 75-cent discount for each pair toward the purchase of goods in his shop. Therefore, Brewster got one pair of new boots that would have gone for the "outrageous" price of $5 for only $3.50. He had exchanged goods he deemed worthless for boots with "soles one inch thick" that would likely last him longer than the two pairs he traded in. In the 1860 New England shoemaker's strike, boot and shoe leather evoked a culture that linked producers in the industry. That same leather, in the material and consumer cultures of soldiering, took on different meanings as it recirculated to soldiers' benefit in a market in which the prices of goods were rising. The merchant collecting the leather made even more capital as a result of that recirculation, but Brewster felt that he made a good deal by using his access to Uncle Sam's goods to speculate for his personal benefit. He knew he was dealing with extortionists. Along with his boots he bought a hairbrush for sixty-two cents that was "no better than I have sold hundreds of for a quarter or less."[22]

Another way for soldiers to escape the market managed by contractors and sutlers was to appeal to the folks at home. Brewster wanted his sister to send him "a couple of dozen of boxes Olmstead Leather Preservative" to care for the boots he just purchased. He had bought a box from a soldier in his regiment even though the man "did not want to sell it," suggesting either that Brewster offered to pay a high price for something he needed immediately or that his authority as sergeant encouraged the man to part with the product as a favor to his superior officer. Since he already had the product he needed, Brewster may have wanted his sister to buy the leather preservative in bulk so that he could speculate in camp. Other men would want to keep their shoes and boots from "cracking out" when the regiment left Washington on the march to meet the rebels. Through his knowledge of brand-name quality, foresight to stock up on goods, and access to those items through his family, he would make a killing in the market at the expense of his comrades. In return, he would make periodic remittances to his sisters and mother to help them survive the war's economic uncertainties.[23]

As soldiers tried to use their commercial knowledge to speculate outside the productive and distributive networks created by the government, Brewster and his comrades considered the ways the war was transforming the labor market. In September, Brewster had written home to explain that an African American man named Juba, who had previously worked in the Brewsters' home in Northampton, was cooking only for the company's commissioned officers and for Brewster. Juba had cooked for the entire company, but its soldiers had not paid him for two months. The officers, thinking that the soldiers' refusal to pay was an unjust decision rather than a reflection of their poverty, declared that Juba should not cook for them any longer. They paid him what the soldiers owed and took his labor all to themselves. The incident reveals that the absence of Uncle Sam's gold widened class and racial inequalities that had existed in the company from the beginning of the conflict. The promise of free labor seems to have eluded officers, soldiers, and cooks alike. Wages were not paid, status could not be attained, and thus the status quo continued to the chagrin of all involved.[24]

While further information about Juba's identity is unavailable, it is clear that the arrival of escaping slaves at Camp Brightwood forced Brewster to reconsider free labor ideology, his own ambitions, and the institution of slavery. In November, he told his mother that nine African Americans came into the Tenth's camp from the Maryland countryside seeking refuge. He affirmed that no member of the Tenth "will . . . send them back." Colonel Henry Briggs, the regiment's commander, "did not come out here to hunt niggers." As Brewster became convinced that the war would end slavery, he continued to despair of achieving advancement and even asked his mother if there was anything she could do in Northampton to obtain an officer's commission for him. He was having no luck doing so in camp. Two orderlies had even received promotion instead of him. "The talk about my being the best" was cheap, he despondently wrote. In the military, being "considered the best is a humbug, and I don't want to hear any more of that stuff." While Brewster thought "this war is playing the Dickens with slavery," he also believed that the Union army perpetuated the frauds inherent in free labor.[25]

The following week, Brewster's interest was piqued by an enslaved man who walked from tent to tent trying to collect $800 from the Tenth's soldiers to purchase his freedom. The Yankees asked why he did not simply "take 'leg bail.'" The slave was cheating himself, when he should be cheating his master. Fraud had a purpose—it should be employed to ruin slaveholders. Brewster wondered whether this plea for charity was a front for more fraud by the slaveholding aristocracy. The man's owner was surely masterminding a scheme to defraud the soldiers by cashing in one last time "before there is no more slavery." His gambit was immoral, taking advantage of men who professed that it was not their duty to "hunt" slaves or give assistance to their hunters. Yet while he reviled the fraudulent slaveholder, Brewster envisioned what it would be like to participate at a slave auction, examining black people's bodies and comparing prices. He acknowledged to his mother that he knew more about the products of the Northern market than about the slave markets of the South, but he reckoned that this enslaved man had to be worth more than $800, "for he was a *right smart* nigger to look at." "Right smart" was an American colloquialism that registered something's impressive—but indeterminate—value. Brewster's experience as a clerk and a soldier had taught him that independence was grounded in the transactions men made. In this time of transition, in a war that seemed to be eroding slavery, maybe $800 would have been a fraud perpetrated on, not by, the slaveholder.[26]

Charles Brewster was neither a trader nor a buyer of slaves. He believed that his and his comrades' actions on the battlefield would topple the slaveholders' regime, "clear our Countrys name of the vile stain and enable us to live in peace hereafter." Yet at the end of 1861, he was crestfallen. The world had conspired against him. Fate had dealt him a cruel hand. It seemed as though everyone was getting a promotion except for him. In April 1861, he had demonstrated his patriotism by jumping at the opportunity to serve. Now, even latecomers from his hometown were winning plum posts in new regiments while he labored as a noncommissioned sergeant, leading the men of Company C through drill at Camp Brightwood. He was convinced that he would never get ahead in life.[27]

President Lincoln's annual message to Congress came to hand early in December, Brewster told his mother. At the end of that address, Lincoln sought to shake men like Brewster out of their doldrums. They were mistaken: the wage laborer's condition was not "fixed." It was in a condition of flux, and with steady application would be defined by upward mobility. "The prudent, penniless beginner in the world," Lincoln wrote, "labors for awhile, saves a surplus with which to buy tools or land for himself; then labors on his own account another while, and at length hires another new beginner to help him." This faith in achievement had long been a hobbyhorse of the railsplitter from Illinois, convinced that he had achieved occupational and social mobility in this very way. In fact, these words should seem familiar. They were the same ones Lincoln had spoken to the Wisconsin Agricultural Society in September 1859, extolling the virtues of free labor to combat James Henry Hammond's mudsill theory. Now, with Hammond's state and ten others having chosen to flee the Union to defend slavery, Lincoln warned that free labor was under threat. The philosophy that proposed capital was equal or superior to labor, rather than labor's "fruit," led to governments like the Confederacy's that would "close the door of advancement" for white men. The "struggle of today" between these two visions of capital's relation to labor, Lincoln argued, "is not altogether for today—it is for a vast future also."[28]

Brewster had agreed to participate in the fight to destroy the insurgent Confederate regime, but he found his commander-in-chief's message disappointing. Brewster's despair at not getting ahead belied Lincoln's claim that "free labor" gave "hope to all" for social mobility. In the context of his own speculations in goods for himself and his comrades and his vision of prices in the slave market, Brewster wondered whether Lincoln was promoting a humbug. Capital—the thing needed to buy the products of work or workers themselves—made people more independent in the market in ways labor alone did not. The president, in Brewster's eyes, did not understand how military victory would be achieved. Lincoln "don't talk nigger enough," Brewster indelicately put it to his mother. "[I]ts no use mincing the matter. Nigger has got to be talked, and thoroughly talked to[o] and I think niggers will come out of this scrape free." The president had, in the previous month, drafted a bill for congressional debate in which the federal government would pay the loyal slave state of Delaware over $700,000 in installments to emancipate approximately 1,800 enslaved people there. In his annual message, the president informed Congress of successful efforts to interdict the transatlantic slave trade and suggested that the federal government should colonize destitute former slaves outside the nation's borders.[29]

To Brewster, gradual, compensated emancipation would enrich slaveholders and colonization would deprive the Union of African Americans' labor. Brewster had come to the conclusion that the war presaged the end of slavery. He also had, through his experience as a junior officer waiting for his chance to get ahead, come to the conclusion that Lincoln's elegy to the promise of free labor was off the mark. Finding no joy in working for others, and unable to work and enjoy capital independently as Lincoln envisioned, he recognized that employing others—the endpoint of the trajectory of free labor that the president described—seemed to be the only thing that made men free. The Brewsters already knew this to be the case. They employed an African American girl, Sarah Washington, in their household. Washington had been born around 1846. In 1850, federal census takers in Northampton listed her and her siblings as "paupers," wards of the local government dependent on taxpayers for their support. By 1860, Washington lived with the Brewsters and did domestic work. As Charles Brewster railed about Lincoln's speech and his failure to "talk nigger enough," he informed his family that Juba was still in camp, presumably cooking for him and the company's officers. He did not "like to interfere with his affairs about sending money. why don't Sarah write to him herself?" Sarah's relationship with Juba remains unclear, but she had evidently asked for Brewster's help to communicate with him. Brewster knew that the war made economic survival difficult. Sarah evidently depended on Juba to make ends meet, illuminating the ways the Brewsters did not provide for her. Charles Brewster considered Sarah Washington a nuisance. His unwillingness to help her by talking to Juba about economic arrangements illuminates how he privileged his own ambitions and how his family's household economy depended on Sarah's dependence.[30]

Charles Brewster believed that he would not get a chance to realize his dreams. Others would. Word came that one of his comrades had been elevated to a position in the brigade quartermaster's department at seventy-five dollars per month. It was nice to see, he remarked sarcastically, that the man's *"patriotism leads him to sacrifice himself for his country."* Fortune had favored the undeserving yet again. It "seems as if everybody got their nests feathered but me, at any rate every body that can't earn thier living any other way," he griped. Fate counted him among the "fools" who were failures. "I wish I had not been so patriotic but had staid where I was well off," he wrote his sister Mary, apparently unwilling to remember that he did not think he was successful in civilian life, either. When he told the census taker in 1860 that he was a "merchant," it was an aspirational designation.[31]

It is always darkest before dawn. Later in December, Brewster was commissioned second lieutenant in Company C. Even before his commission came through, his captain told him to have a new uniform made. As he had done before, Brewster asked for help from his family in getting the things he wanted and needed. His experience as a store clerk helped him envision the uniform he desired. Daniel Kingsley, the merchant tailor whose shop would make the clothing for him, "knows what the regulation uniform is," Brewster told his mother, but he wanted Kingsley to "put a welt of light Blue cloth in the seam" of his trousers rather than a cord, because he had seen the cord unravel from comrades' pants. He said he did not "care to have them very fine" and would trust that Kingsley's "judgment is best." But he wanted the tailor to use "good stout cloth or Cassimere" and to make sure that his apprentices or seamstresses produced "well and strongly sewed" pants, coat, and vest. Next came the officer's accoutrements: he needed a regulation sword, a "scabord without a seam," and a "good sword belt with a plate that will not tarnish easily." These things would be expensive, and so he asked that family members get these for him, too, at an affordable price at the "Manufactury in Chicopee," a town on the Connecticut River some fifteen miles south of Northampton. Prices were just too high in Washington.[32]

These were the material things that represented his rise to power and prestige. He had a clear sense of artisanal value and the geography of prices. He wanted nice things that would not tarnish his aspirations to authority. But he would not pay over the odds for them. In just over two weeks after sending this letter, he wrote to his mother again to let her know that he had heard from Kingsley that his "Uniform was done" and available for him to collect at the "Depot." The pace of production and distribution was astonishing, an example of what Northern industrial capitalism could offer. In the meantime, the soldiers of Company C, despite the unreliability of the paymaster, began to cobble together "a subscription" to buy Brewster his sword and the other symbols of his prominence. Despite Brewster's constant griping about others getting ahead at his expense, the subscription included contributions from "every man in the company"—proof of how much his men loved him. He relished telling his family how much it all cost: "a sword costing $20, a sash costing $20 a belt costing $7 and a cap costing $4.25 a better set of equipments then there is in the Regiment." For enlisted men who were paid $13 per month, contributing to a fund that underwrote the happy realization of their beloved officer's hopes and dreams meant overlooking their own wants and needs. In the weeks after receiving his commission, Brewster ruefully observed to his family that soldiers in the company were "very much in need of New Coats" in winter, shivering in light flannel shirts and left in the lurch by a "Government [that] cannot get uniforms made fast enough." His experience of receiving quality things fast and cheap would not be his men's experience. While he hoped that artisans and manufacturers in Northampton would hurry to pick up the government's slack production, he noted that families had been sending blankets to their soldiers. He mused, too, that his lieutenant's commission allowed him to "carry 80 pounds of Baggage." His increased wages would certainly permit him to purchase several blankets, though he did lament that he would not yet be able to afford the trunk in which to store them.[33]

"I feel quite like a free man once more, now that I am a commissioned Officer," he told his mother. While he claimed that he had trouble explaining why that was—the only difference seemed to be his two shoulder straps—he relied on his mother's understanding of labor and status to clarify. "[B]efore I had lots of work and very little pay and now I have very little work and lots of pay." Indeed, he now had "quite a sum in my pocket, some $85" and a two-month payment of his $105.50 wage on the way. The thing that made him feel free was capital—the money in his pocket. He was about to make the transition that free labor offered—mobility from being a worker at wages to being an employer with capital.[34]

The lieutenancy came with perks. One was David, who had been a slave in Montgomery County, Maryland, just north of Washington. According to Brewster, in January 1862 his "master whipped him in the morning for something or other and he took leg bail in the evening." David walked some thirteen miles and "landed here" in the camp of the Tenth Massachusetts. It is hard to know what David knew about Northern soldiers and what he thought of them once he arrived. He might have heard that the Yankees had adopted the contraband policy of General Butler and that they would protect him from his violent owner. From Brewster's perspective, David could not have arrived at a better time. He, a new lieutenant, was "on the lookout for a servant as I am allowed $13 dollars extra for subsistance and $2[.]50 for clothing per month if I have a servant, and it does not cost half that to keep him." Brewster's considerations turned on his new status as an officer, his concerns about labor, and the economic boon of having a servant. The labor that David would perform would be one of the factors that would diminish Brewster's workload and distinguish him from common soldiers. It is not clear how David's wages would be paid. Because Brewster could support David on only half the allotment provided for his subsistence and clothing, the lieutenant might have considered a plan like the one followed by Union generals at Fort Monroe: pay David a small wage and withhold the rest to pad his own pocket. Brewster wondered if his mother would send some of his old clothes from Northampton for David's use, recirculating more materials to save even more capital from the allotment.[35]

Brewster considered himself David's protector and an overseer of his labor. He also calculated the ways wage labor could create value beyond the labor workers performed, much as slavery did. Possession was the key to unlocking that value. Brewster noted that David's "master paid $400 for him six years ago," registering the former slave's economic value much as he had done for the enslaved man who had asked for help to pay for his discharge from bondage weeks before. Brewster was not making David his slave, yet he clearly thought he was taking possession of him: "[H]e was the only slave his master had and his master never will have him again if I can help it." The end of slavery, in the minds of Northern soldiers like Brewster, meant that slaveholders would no longer be able to possess human beings. Yet white Northerners hoped that the end of slavery would be to their benefit. African Americans would not be slaves any longer, but Northern officers, new to their positions of authority, would control their labor. They would possess young men like David and keep them away from the men who had previously possessed them. Wage labor changed the meaning of slavery's capital. That capital would now benefit the men whom Hammond had derided as the North's mudsill class.[36]

Brewster was not a slaveholder, so he would not be able to possess David forever. The pressure of slaveholders and fellow officers in the Tenth Regiment and the politics of emancipation in the first winter of war doomed Brewster's attempts to maintain control over David's labor. First Brewster played a cat-and-mouse game with David's owner, who came to Camp Brightwood on two occasions to collect his property. Brewster got wind of his arrival and sent David to the woods for safety. When David's owner asked Brewster where David was, the lieutenant claimed not to know. Brewster resolved to rename David "Harry Hastings" to elevate the subterfuge. Brewster also conveyed in his letters home that he was in a position of power as an officer over white soldiers as well as black servants. His men wanted to give the "Nigger hunters . . . such a pounding," but he considered lying and humbug a better strategy, so he refused to encourage them to violence.[37]

When David's owner returned on the same errand and attempted to "bribe" a soldier in a different company for information leading to David's capture, though, Brewster was furious. If that soldier ever came under his command, Brewster told his sister Mary, "he will wish he had never seen a Contraband." Punishing the private would be justified, because "Command Officers have a great deal of Power if they have a mind to use it." That authority was "absolute, and I should not have the least hesitation in using it to the utmost on any man that would be guilty of aiding any master to reclaim any slave." Those shoulder straps may have seemed insignificant, but they gave Brewster the ability to "'let loose the dogs of war'" if one of his men or David's master crossed him. Brewster's power extended to remaking David through free labor. His camp servant was "quite slow but he is willing and I think has improved a good deal since I got him," Brewster told his sister. "I *reckon* he is a *right smart nigger*." For Brewster, "right smart" had once registered value in the slave market. Now these words underscored both a former slave's increasing value in free labor and the power of the person who hired him, kept him, and improved his character. Brewster, despite his frustrations with Lincoln's conception of free labor's promise, supported those ideals when they provided the cultural ties to bind another to his rule. While he was willing to use his "absolute" power as an officer to crush the authority of slaveholders or their proslavery allies in the Union army, he considered himself a benevolent employer. "I reckon he never imagined such an easy life as he has now." Brewster likely never asked David what he thought and appears never to have considered that David's "easy life"—which "only" amounted to cutting wood for Brewster's campfire and tidying his boss's clothing and sword—helped to make the lieutenant's life an easier one of very little work and lots of pay.[38]

Brewster claimed that he acted on his ideological principles rather than self-interest. Colonel Briggs, he felt certain, gave former slaves a choice of whether to return to their masters. The regiment, however, was deeply divided on the legal and moral legitimacy of emancipation. This division became clearer as more Maryland slaveholders arrived in camp to take their slaves back home. On March 1, 1862, six white Marylanders entered the camp and asserted that some black servants were theirs. Several enlisted men of the Tenth encouraged one African American man to make up his own mind about whether to return as a slave. The man said he "belonged to himself now," confronting not only slaveholders' claims of ownership but the power of wage labor employers like Brewster. Soldiers surrounded this man and a white slaveholder named Nolan who claimed to be the man's owner. They asked the former slave to assert the speech rights that had been denied to him in slavery. He recounted that his former master had demonstrated support for the Baltimore mob that had attacked the Sixth Massachusetts the previous April, going so far as to say "that he hoped they would kill every damned Yankee, and that the Massachusetts soldiers were all *released convicts*." Nolan and the other slaveholders, keen to avoid chastisement from angry soldiers, left without accomplishing their task. Not content to let the insult pass, forty-seven men from Company I and perhaps many more members of the Tenth decided to march into the countryside that evening without orders. Absent without leave from their camp, these men, accompanied by Nolan's former slave, descended on the slaveholder's house to "administer the oath of allegiance" to recalcitrant rebels. When they arrived at the Nolan house in Sandy Spring, they were greeted by a woman in her late sixties, the widow Caroline Nolan. In the year before the war, she had informed a census enumerator that she owned $16,265 in personal estate and valued her plantation at $8,000. While the soldiers were there to humble one of her sons, she immediately established that she was in control of her household, telling the soldiers that the black man accompanying them was her property—perhaps one of the six enslaved people she had owned in 1860. The man replied, "Yes, Missus, I was once, but I own myself now." Mrs. Nolan responded by clenching her fist and slugging him in the face. The soldiers at once contested Mrs. Nolan's authority, forcing her sons Thomas and James, both over six feet tall according to the regimental history, to recite the loyalty oath "on bended knees." As they left the premises, the soldiers cleared out Mrs. Nolan's chicken coop. *Sic semper tyrannis.*[39]

If these soldiers were not exactly "*released convicts*," they were absent without leave from their commanding officers, who now were "mounting in hot haste" after their ill-disciplined men. The regimental historian termed the men "runaways," and they were captured and disarmed by the regiment's pickets as they returned to camp. The regiment's impending relocation to the York-James Peninsula in Virginia apparently contributed to the leniency shown these men. Brewster did not mention the rough music some of the Tenth's soldiers administered in Montgomery County, but he did explain in a letter to his mother a few days after the "raid" on the Nolan house that "the whole Regiment is almost in a state of mutiny on the Nigger question." Brewster had based his own willingness to confront slaveholders' claims to property and his own authority over former slaves on his belief that he did Colonel Briggs's bidding. In light of the actions of the mutinous men at the Nolan plantation, Briggs changed his mind. Brewster believed that Orzo Miller, "pro slavery Captain" of Company H, had convinced the regiment's major, William Marsh, to "drive all the Contraband out of camp." Miller and Brewster evidently "had quite a blow up" and Brewster worried that the stance he had taken in favor of allowing the former slaves to remain would lead to his dismissal from the service on the eve of deployment to Virginia.[40]

He may have overstated the case for dramatic effect, though. He explained to his mother that "I have nothing to do with any of the trouble except that I refuse to order off my own servant." The divide among the officers about the politics of emancipation was only one division in the camp. It appears that the actions taken by the runaway soldiers against slaveholders had imperiled the officers' ability to wield authority over them and the African American men who had labored in the camp to the officers' benefit. Brewster's admission that he only cared whether his servant remained illuminates his self-interest in the question. He felt more comfortable arguing the political question. "[T]he men did not come down here to oppress Niggers and they are not quite brutes yet, as some of thier officers are," Brewster explained to his family back home. It was oppression to force black men out of camp into the slaveholders' shackles that awaited them. Some of the Massachusetts men cried, Brewster said, because they refused to "recognize this property in human flesh and blood." The antislavery soldiers and officers risked oppression, too. Captain Miller "has been threatening to have the men sent to the Tortugas for mutiny," even though Brewster considered such a fate improbable. Brewster did not believe that he oppressed David, but losing possession of him would increase his workload and diminish his power as an officer.[41]

Brewster was not a mutineer, at any rate. He would follow Briggs's commands. Yet when his colonel issued an order in "a terrible rage" that banned former slaves from camp, Brewster was not pleased. Briggs had gone "over to the pro Slavery side body and soul. so it seems that the prime object of our being in this country is to return niggers to thier masters." It was galling to Massachusetts men "to submit" to this order. They had never been "so humbled before," said Brewster. As an officer, he could have resigned for this affront against his status and authority. Once again he emphasized the politics of emancipation instead, claiming that going home "would please our slave catching brutes too much." These brutes were not Maryland slaveholders but rather fellow Northern officers. Major Marsh, he claimed, "would go further to return a fugitive slave than he would to save the Union." While Brewster had to "give up my Contraband," he relied on a transitioning political narrative that equated loyalty with antislavery to place him on high moral ground in comparison to other officers. He and the other employers of black men in the regiment sent them north. Two days later, the former slaves came back into camp, having been frightened by white men who "questioned them so closely" on the banks of the Susquehanna, "within ten miles of the Pennsylvania line." Brewster, unable to claim David any longer, now took a dimmer view of black laborers' character and abilities. "I don't know as they are many of them capable of taking care of themselves it don't seem possible that men would get so near to freedom and then turn back." He counseled David "not to be taken alive" and sent him back up the road. As Brewster came to grips with the loss of his power and his identity as a man of capital who prospered through wage labor, he argued that David could only prove himself worthy of self-ownership if he resisted those who sought to make him a slave once again.[42]

Perhaps David's destination was Philadelphia, where William Still had once assisted fugitives on their way to Canada. It may have seemed like a place where he could now own himself. Abolitionists such as Lewis Tappan had asked Benjamin Butler for permission to transport African Americans from Union-occupied areas of Virginia to the North in the summer of 1861. Now, in the spring of 1862, former slaves were arriving in Northern cities like Philadelphia in numbers worth remarking. Henry Louis Stephens seized the opportunity for satire in *Vanity Fair*. He questioned African American refugees' intellect in the same way Brewster did, accused abolitionists of refusing to support black Southerners in the North, and stoked fears among white workers that the influx of these newcomers would lead to a more competitive labor market and lower wages.[43]

The satire was off the mark. There were many Northern employers who craved the labor of former slaves in a time of war. A new publication, the *Continental Monthly*, became their mouthpiece. The *Continental* was edited

THE HIGHLY INTELLIGENT CONTRABAND,

WHO HAS COME ALL THE WAY FROM "DOWN SOUTH" TO VISIT MR. GREELEY, BUT HORACE "DOESN'T SEE IT!"

"The Highly Intelligent Contraband," *Vanity Fair*, April 26, 1862, 203.
(The Library Company of Philadelphia)

by Charles Godfrey Leland, the former editor of *Vanity Fair* who had become disillusioned with the anti-emancipation stance of the comic paper. Leland's new journal argued in January 1862 that it would be a mistake to "export the dark, industrial, productive, proletarian, operative, laboring element from our midst." The *Continental* refused to agree with white Northerners who believed that the "black servants, cooks, barbers, white-washers, carpet-beaters and grooms of Baltimore and Philadelphia" were "idle vagabonds." Every person who could do work held "capital in self." While the *Continental* contended that capital and labor coexisted harmoniously in the North because they coexisted in each individual person, the idea of capital in self certainly benefited the employers who were able to exploit it. Emancipation, by making wage labor national, would create possibilities for Northern employers to profit from the labor, the innate capital, of Southern laborers. That is why, while white Northern workers opposed the migration of former slaves to the North, white Northern employers welcomed it.[44]

Vanity Fair's critique was incorrect in another respect: abolitionists worked avidly to support black refugees in the North. In Philadelphia, the Pennsylvania Abolition Society (PAS) swung into action to develop an institution to house and care for former slaves arriving there and to assist them in finding work. PAS was a good candidate to establish an intelligence office that would connect these people with Northern employers because it had served this function in the early Republic by placing African American youth in relationships of indentured servitude, apprenticeship, and wage work locally in Philadelphia and regionally in the Delaware Valley. The structure of those earlier labor arrangements reflected the limits of Northern emancipation, for legislatures permitted employers to wring further profits from a vulnerable population of former slaves. PAS leaders nominated William Still to serve as their intelligence office's agent. In this role, Still would collect a small fee of one dollar from employers and keep track of their addresses so that Southern families could find their loved ones once the war ended. He would keep a register of the people who were still seeking employment and the wages that they received when they were placed.[45]

No man was better suited for this job, and Still wanted to help. Here was another opportunity for him to assist African Americans to move out of the Slave South and experience greater autonomy in the North. Still professed a willingness to serve, yet before he said yes to PAS, he needed to weigh the desperation of former slaves against his own ambitions. He had just begun to sell stoves—supplementing his already successful trade in other household products like coal and ice—and he knew that processing information about

Southern refugees would take a great deal of time and effort. "I am a poor man & shall be obliged to make exertions to make a living," he explained. He faced a conundrum. He did not want this philanthropic activity to get in the way of his own aspirations for success. Yet he also worried that accepting a salary for benevolent work smacked of self-interest when the fate of enslaved people was in the balance. As in his labors on the Underground Railroad, Still believed that quests for independence could be personal and collective, so he offered to do the work for eight dollars a month. With this generous offer he sold himself short, and PAS quickly assented.⁴⁶

Still tried to defuse opposition to the movement of these refugees to Philadelphia, assuring white readers of the *Public Ledger* that black Southerners were not arriving in numbers large enough to compete with white men for jobs in the city. Only ninety-one of them had arrived by late March, and they would likely, he said, find work in the countryside where farm families needed labor in fields and homes while rural men served as soldiers. Still was soon overwhelmed by requests for help and became dissatisfied with the work. He believed in a systematic approach to bookkeeping as much as any man of business did, but employers and refugees confounded his system. Still was inundated with requests for workers from farmers outside the city, but he had a short supply of laborers. He discovered that he could not get an accurate count of the people who had obtained situations because they made deals outside his office, neglecting to inform him where they had gone and what wages they had negotiated. He also cooperated with agents from freedmen's aid associations in Washington who were trying to make their own deals with employers, so his ledgers remained as inexact as those kept by Union officers accounting for African Americans' work at Fort Monroe. In September, Still told the committee that he could not keep up with the escalating workload. There were simply too many people in search of work and workers, and the strain on his limited time was evident in his letters as he struggled to reconcile principles and profit.⁴⁷

It is telling that, in the PAS employment ledger, Still appears to have listed refugees' names while the white agents who followed him mostly listed employers' names. This may reflect what these agents thought the purpose of their intelligence office was and who they thought it served. Black Philadelphians wondered, too. Even when Still was the agent in 1862, an "Organized Committee, appointed in behalf of contrabands, by a Public Meeting of the Colored Citizens of Philadelphia" requested that PAS explain to them how the agency would work, how funds would be distributed, and whether the "Old Abolition Society"—that is, PAS—would agree to work with black

Philadelphians to secure support for former slaves. This letter is evidence that the mistrust between PAS and black abolitionists from the early Republic continued to simmer. The purpose of this intelligence office would be hotly contested when the numbers of black refugees increased later in the war.[48]

Charles Brewster, after sending his servant David north to fight his own battles, prepared to embark for Fort Monroe with the rest of General George McClellan's Army of the Potomac to do the same thing. He "sent some money to" Daniel Kingsley, his tailor, with instructions to "pay over the balance" to his mother. He wished, he told her, that he could have sent more, but since he had to pay a number of debts and was "going into a strange country," he needed to withhold some of his pay for himself. As it was, the regiment "has not been paid off yet." The only way he had received his wages was by taking his payment "voucher" to a banker who charged a ten-dollar discount. Being an officer had its privileges, including the ability to turn promises to pay into currency. The banker wielded capital most successfully, of course, collecting payment vouchers from officers for ten dollars apiece and eventually cashing them in at face value.[49]

Other men with capital took advantage of soldiers, too. Brewster particularly condemned sutlers. At Warwick Court House on the York-James Peninsula, he complained that the "suttlers are reaping a great Harvest" among the army, charging "twenty cents a pound for cheese fifty & seventy five for butter one dollar for Tobacco and everything else in proportion." The joke was that these prices were very much out of proportion to what Northern consumers would expect things to cost. Sutlers were "vulture[s]" who preyed upon the misfortune of others in the market. Soldiers could not access goods beyond their rations of food and clothing from any other source except home. But soldiers on the move might miss a package sent to them. Moreover, families who needed soldiers to send them money to buy things might not have extra money to buy things for their soldiers, and express companies and the post office charged fees for their distribution services. Soldiers on the move had few choices in this market. They were dependent on sutlers' determinations about quantity, quality, and cost, and Brewster had not taken that dependence "into my calculations of war." His answer was to fantasize about a violent end for the vulture capitalists. "I should like when the war is over to hang all the suttlers ... and let the soldiers surround them and give them a few volleys of minnie bullets."[50]

In the midst of the violence—actual or envisioned—that the Army of the Potomac and their Confederate antagonists perpetrated in Virginia,

Brewster speculated on the possibilities for personal advancement there. He thought that the Old Dominion had all the agricultural and climatic potential to "be as thickly settled and thriving as any count[r]y on the face of the globe." Yet "the curse of slavery ... has blighted it." As he marched toward Richmond, he linked the progress of the war with his own potential future profit. "Tell Uncle Edward," he bade his mother, "that this is the greatest farming soil he ever saw" and "if the Government confiscates I think I shall try to get one." Other Northerners were considering these possibilities, too. In June 1862, the *Continental Monthly* concluded "that the only certain road to Union-izing the South is, to plant in it colonies of Northern men. Thousands, hundreds of thousands now in the army, would gladly remain in the land of tobacco or of cotton, if Government would only provide them with the land whereon to live." The *Continental* believed that land confiscation and slave emancipation would be linked in free labor's triumph. White Northern men who had not been able to achieve success in their home region would retire from soldiering in the South and reap the rewards of valuable land and the capital in self that former slaves represented. "Give a Yankee a fat farm in Dixie, and we may rely upon it that although a Southern nabob may not know how to get work out of a 'free nigger,' the Northerner will contrive to persuade Cuffy to become industrious." White Northerners would unlock the capital in former slaves' labor for their own benefit before the latter would be "capable of being ... farmer[s] on [their] own account." Confiscation and emancipation were the means of accomplishing a counterrevolution in America that the South's rebellious slaveholding aristocracy had not seen coming. "Labor and capital are bursting their bonds," the *Continental* argued in August, and "the Middle Class of North-America which Southerners and Englishmen equally revile, is becoming all-powerful and seeks to substitute business common-sense for the aristocratic policy which has hitherto guided us."[51]

The *Continental*'s reference to a middle class was rhetorical and aspirational. It did not identify a particular social entity; rather, it captured free labor's broad acceptance in Northern society and its opposition to aristocratic alternatives at home and abroad. Brewster had a lot of business common sense, but he did not feel all-powerful. He wanted to be, but his and his family's circumstances were tenuous. Visions of taking rebels' land as well as their slaves and using them to prove the superiority of free labor were continually interrupted by reality—the war's potential for taking all of what Brewster had and what he dreamed. As he extolled the value of Southern land after slavery, his mother let him know that she was thinking of moving in with Brewster's married sister, Mattie. Brewster did not want her to do that. "[I]f I live through the war I hope we can make some better arrangement," he wrote, and he hoped that another year of his lieutenant's pay would "go a long ways towards paying off the Mortgage, and then if I can get a situation we may do pretty well." Despite the personal and real estate Martha Brewster had listed in the 1860 census, the deed to the family's home was evidently not in her name. Now her son, hundreds of miles distant, tried to assure her that all would be well. But a lot had to go well in order for the family to do well. Brewster had to survive, and no one could be certain that he would. He knew this best of all. Writing on May 31 on the banks of the Chickahominy River, he realized a battle was imminent. He wrote to his mother that "if anything should happen and I should get killed, you will be entitled to my pay" and to a monthly pension of fifteen dollars. He instructed her to find the money due to him in two places. He had allotted almost half of his salary to the Massachusetts state treasury for safekeeping so that his family could draw on it when necessary. Martha would have to file a claim with the U.S. Paymaster General to recover the rest.[52]

Charles Brewster lived through the Battle of Fair Oaks, Virginia, begun in the hours after he wrote his mother about how to get his money. The regiment was exposed to Confederate fire from flank and rear, and retreated and charged several times in confused combat. One hundred twenty-two men of Brewster's regiment were killed or wounded, including Colonel Briggs, shot through both legs. Later in the campaign, at Malvern Hill, the culmination of seven days of attacks by General Robert E. Lee's Confederates against McClellan's retreating army, Brewster regaled his family with a description of the Tenth's repulse of a Confederate cavalry charge. "Glorious!! Glorious!!! to see these, who have boasted themselves for bravery and chivalry and the cream of everything in the United States, to see them break and run like sheep before the Mudsills, we see Mechanics and small fisted farmers of the glorious north, and in numbers they were like as a drove of cattle to the drivers." Union soldiers appropriated the label encompassing Southern derision for free society—one that proponents of free labor had long sought to repel—to glory in what they believed would be the demise of the slaveholders' aristocracy.[53]

Brewster was unhurt, but mudsills like him had to count the costs of arduous campaigning. At Fair Oaks, the Confederates had made off with his "Haversack, Field Glass, Knapsack, Blankets, Rubber O[ver] Coat, and the pretty cap Mary sent me," all worth, he estimated, "over thirty dollars." These were all things that he would have to replace once the campaign was con-

Capital in Self

cluded, and those costs would force him to change his plans regarding payment of the mortgage on the house in Northampton. Perhaps his mother understood the limits of his dreams. By July 9, safely bivouacked at Harrison's Landing on the James River, Brewster wrote home thanking his sister Mary "for the description of Mattie's house." Their mother had made the decision to move, a choice that had not only affected her. "You . . . need [not] to have sent Sarah away on account of wages," Brewster wrote. "I could pay her easy enough." He had not been able to send enough money home to make that possible, however. Now his mother was dependent on a sibling and the family's domestic servant was left without a job. This was not how free labor was supposed to work. Mary evidently had ideas about how the war might work for free labor. She asked her brother to send her something better than money—what the *Continental* called capital in self. Charles laughed. "[A]s for my sending a decent contraband I don't know how I could send one but there is a boat load of them down at the landing, and a funny sight they are indeed." Mary seems to have misunderstood: "[T]hey would have to have wages, as well as anybody else, for they are free now," Charles patiently explained. If the Brewsters could not pay Sarah's wages, they would not be able to unlock the capital in a former slave, either. It was a bad idea, anyway, Charles warned, contradicting the *Continental*: "[M]y experience of contrabands is that they are [the] laziest worst good for nothing, of all Gods created creatures." He also contradicted his former self, who had exhibited great pride at his instruction and possession of David: "[T]hat boy I had at Camp Brightwood could not turn round once a week, he was slower than any snail." They were "idle vagabonds" after all.[54]

Of course, many Northern employers disagreed, or at least hoped that Brewster was wrong. The Brewsters' dream of free labor's triumph had been denied. Charles charted his army's failures alongside his family's: "Three long months, Thousands upon Thousands of lives Millions of Treasure gone, lost and to what end[?]," he asked his mother. "Somebody most certainly has blundered, but nobody is to blame." Like General McClellan, he looked to the Northern government and to its people for more men: "Why in Thunder don't they go to drafting? Where are all the brave ones who were 'coming after us, when they were actually needed'?" Charles would see to it, for he took a furlough home to Massachusetts to become a recruiter of soldiers. Maybe doing so would be a way to get ahead.[55]

In July 1862, as Brewster wrote these words and as William Still worked as an intelligence man, a new Union regiment was being organized in Philadelphia to go to the front. In response to losses the Army of the Potomac sustained in its defeat near Richmond and to laments like Brewster's, President Lincoln issued a call for another 300,000 men to serve as soldiers. If the states did not meet their quotas, they would be subject to a draft that would coerce citizens to fight. An advertisement for this new Philadelphia regiment, the Gray Reserves (which would become the 119th Pennsylvania), offered $169 bounty that came from various local and federal sources. It suggested that this regiment was the only one that offered a $25 advance on the government bounty. That was not the case. Northern governors, who insisted that the new call would "fail without it," got Secretary of War Stanton to agree to its payment. The Gray Reserves also offered $2 per soldier as "hand money" that went to "any man furnishing a recruit." Stanton had reinstituted that payment as part of the federal bounty system under pressure from leaders such as John Andrew, who explained in May that these payments to recruiters and advance payment of first month's wages to recruits were crucial if states were to meet their quotas. Andrew's honest insistence that the speculative impulses of recruiters and soldiers drove enlistment was a stark change from the virtuous stance he assumed in his confrontation with Butler in the fall of 1861.[56]

Yet most Americans remained unwilling to undermine the solemn purpose of a citizen soldiery. Peter C. Ellmaker, the colonel of the Gray Reserves, addressed their concerns at a public meeting. Ellmaker had "heard several gentlemen speak of giving bounty to soldiers as a mercenary rule, and that it should cease, because they should have enough patriotism and love of country to go without any selfish inducement." Love of country must come before private interest. Ellmaker defended the practice of paying bounties because he reasoned that every recruit who "serves his country should be able to know that his family... is amply provided for in every want during his absence." These volunteers were not mercenaries, but citizen soldiers who were responsible for the dependent women and children they left behind. It was a nice thing for people at home to think, even though soldiers like Brewster knew that state aid—as charity to families and as bounties to soldiers—might not help enlisted men or officers ensure their and their families' economic survival.[57]

In the crowd listening to Ellmaker that night was Thomas Webster. By this time, he had evidently given up speculating in soldiers' things on behalf of the state and had become a leader in efforts to recruit soldiers. He was the chairman of Philadelphia's Citizens' Bounty Fund, which collected money to distribute to recruiting officers of Philadelphia regiments to the tune of a $5 premium for each recruit and a $50 bounty given to every sol-

GRAY RESERVES!

$169 BOUNTY

The Only Regiment receiving $25 Government Bounty.

All the Government and City Bounty certain for this Regiment.

COL. P. C. ELLMAKER

DON'T WAIT TO BE DRAFTED

$10 REGIMENTAL BOUNTY
$5 COMPANY BOUNTY.
$2 for any man furnishing a Recruit

Gray Reserves! (Philadelphia, [1862]). (The Library Company of Philadelphia)

dier recruited. In this way, recruiters and soldiers both profited. At Independence Hall, Webster and other members of the Bounty Fund committee collected "Subscriptions" to "aid Recruiting" and thus help the city avoid a draft by meeting its quota through volunteering. Webster well knew that public and private interest could not be pulled apart in the ways that Ellmaker and opponents of the bounty system desired. In the columns of the *Philadelphia Inquirer*, where advertisements encouraging the public to subscribe to the Bounty Fund could be found, other entrepreneurs catalogued wants and needs. Recruiters and regimental commanders offered men bounties for their service, intelligence office keepers offered to broker employment for domestic servants in the city, and watch manufacturers and life insurance companies called attention to products and policies they marketed directly to soldiers. Companies advertising in national periodicals such as *Frank Leslie's Illustrated Newspaper* hoped to find agents to hawk their wares "in every City, Town and Camp." They wanted soldiers to sell as agents and be sold to by agents. The speculations that made American capitalism before the war had changed shape to include the profitmaking possibilities of the war itself. If President Lincoln thought that the consequence of war would be to remove impediments for Northerners to run a fair race of life, Webster understood that the competition at the heart of the race of life had to be stoked in order to save the Union. Northerners fought for speculation as much as liberal democracy: a way of life as well as a race of life. As summer turned to fall in 1862, and President Lincoln issued a preliminary proclamation that emancipated enslaved people in the Confederacy, more opportunities for speculation seemed to be on the horizon.[58]

4

WORTHY OF HIS HIRE

HENRY WALKER, a thirty-seven-year-old laborer from Forestport, New York, north of Utica, enlisted as a private in the 117th New York Infantry on August 15, 1862. By signing his enlistment papers, Walker agreed to "bear true faith and allegiance to the United States of America" and to "serve them honestly and faithfully against all their enemies or opposers whomsoever" for a period of three years or the duration of the war. He also agreed "to accept such bounty, pay, rations, and clothing as are, or may be, established by law for volunteers." Oneida County's Board of Supervisors voted to raise $162,700 "on the credit of the county" in order to pay a $50 local bounty to each soldier recruited for the regiment. Walker and his comrades would also receive $50 from the state of New York, $100 from the federal government (with $25 due upon their enlistment), one month's wages of $13 in advance, and the $2 "hand money" for recruiting a soldier. Before they left their home county, then, these New Yorkers had $140 in cash available to them and their families and a promise of $75 more from the federal bounty after they were mustered out of the service. Nine days later, Walker and his regiment disembarked from a train in a city he spelled "fieledelfy" and received breakfast at the Union Volunteer Refreshment Saloon, a benevolent institution whose purpose was to provide food, supplies, and a place for Northern soldiers to rest on their way to the nation's capital.[1]

In Philadelphia, Mayor Alexander Henry read letters from frustrated soldiers who had not received the money that Thomas Webster's Citizens' Bounty Fund had collected for them. Counties and cities had held subscription drives and taken out loans to entice men to sign contracts that demanded soldiers act honorably, honestly, and faithfully in the service of their country. After soldiers signed enlistment contracts, they worried that they had been "deceived," Colonel A. H. Tippin of the Sixty-Eighth Pennsylvania told Mayor Henry. It appeared clear to them that "the City never intended to pay the bounty and that it was only a bait thrown out for their capture." Tippin's men had told him that "their families are absolutely in a state of starvation" without these funds, the idea of which "maddens them" and made them unfit for reliable service. Philadelphia women sought what was owed to them, paying calls to 425 Chestnut Street, the office of the Citizens' Bounty Fund's disburser, Michael Baker. "[A]lmost hourly I am called upon by a Wife, mother, or some other interested in a recruit for payment of the bounty," Baker wrote. He explained the rules and regulations governing these payments to all who asked. Women needed the paperwork of war to prove their soldier had enlisted before Baker would agree to pay them.[2]

Baker had his own complaints about the process of paying bounties. Soldiers received the city enlistment premium, the city bounty, and the federal bounty advance immediately, before they set off for Washington. This plan "encouraged rascality," Baker told the officer in charge of mustering soldiers in the city. Some enlisted men were absconding from barracks with the money rather than fulfilling the obligations of their contracts. Baker blamed recruiting officers as much as the runaway rascals for this rash of bounty jumping. Instead of submitting receipts and descriptive rolls for the transfer of soldiers from recruiting office to barracks to the front and reporting the absence of soldiers without leave, recruiting officers followed no system at all and tried to keep the scale of bounty jumping out of the papers. In taking aim at the "frauds practised by many enlisting on the United States and this Committee," Baker sought to deflect any blame the managers of the Citizens' Bounty Fund might have earned for offering a large financial inducement to enlist. When he made his concerns known to Stanton, Baker had the gall to assert that "the U S pay a great deal for Bounty which is only a premium for swindling," even though the federal advance was half of the city's bounty payment. Baker told Stanton that, to safeguard the city's subscription fund, he would only disburse bounties to enlisted men who were with their regiments, dressed in army uniform, and equipped with the appropriate forms between the hours of 1 and 3 P.M. at the barracks on the day they boarded a train for Washington. He would, that is, institute bankers' hours to protect the committee's capital. If soldiers ran away after he paid them, their rascality would be someone else's responsibility.[3]

In the second summer of the war, Northern states and localities established committees to raise bounty funds by subscription or loan and petitioned the federal government to add its own resources to sweeten their offers. Otherwise they would not obtain enough volunteers to meet the quotas assigned by the Lincoln administration. The bounties that enticed soldiers to demonstrate their civic virtue were the very things that enticed them to defraud their government. When soldiers did not receive the bounties promised by their contracts, they felt "deceived." It was all a "*Humbug*," Baker declared to Stanton. There were so many opportunities for the unscrupulous to break contracts and make money in the recruiting system, and reformers like Baker tried in vain to stop the fraud. Soldiers who came to distrust the promises of contracts sought other avenues to seize greater autonomy. When President Lincoln proclaimed emancipation to strengthen the Union's war effort in ways that validated free labor's commitment to the rights of those with capital, white Northerners saw their chance. The demise of slavery was initiated by the gumption of enslaved people, the presence of Union armies, congressional legislation, and presidential proclamation, it is true, but white Northerners envisioned a free labor future in which they would benefit from emancipation. Wage labor relations accommodated both consent and coercion. Giving consent could lead to fraud, as soldiers well knew, and coercion lingered as African Americans tried to navigate the changing context of labor. White Northerners envisioned mobilizing these black laborers' capital in self to bolster their own wages and credit their claims to independence through the war for Union.[4]

While Baker blamed recruiters for letting capital go missing, the recruiters blamed enlisted men. In North Cambridge, Massachusetts, in September 1862, Charles Brewster told his mother that he was "hard at work" recruiting soldiers while on furlough from the front. Keeping the recruits in the barracks was a challenge. There "is no adequate force or means to keep them here," he groused, so "if a man wants to run away there is nothing to stop him." Those who stayed, like the Irishmen who had been recruited to fill up one of the regular army regiments, became particularly troublesome when it was time for them to embark for the seat of war. They "refused to budge an inch until they were paid thier $13 advance pay." The Irishmen were owed federal, state, and local bounties, Brewster explained, but there "had not been time to arrange the payroll." The system of bookkeeping that Baker and other accountants swore by often failed those waiting for payment. Brewster chose not to blame the bureaucracy of which he was now part and instead made a comparison between the Irishmen's refusal to move and native-born recruits' willingness to march for Washington without the advance of wages or federal bounty. Both groups included fighters, but the "Yankee" troops were about to fight the rebels in Maryland, while the Irish mercenaries returned to the barracks to fight each other.[5]

Henry Walker of New York enlisted at a time when Northerners debated who was being defrauded the most in the process of recruiting soldiers. It was also a time of economic crisis for Walker and his family, unsettling both the material basis for his family's survival and the ways he thought about independence and success. His household was imperiled by the demands the war placed on it. The 1860 federal census shows that he owned real estate valued at $500. Economic panic early in the war likely played some role in driving him from the rank of "farmer" into that of "laborer," the occupational designation on his enlistment papers. His son Albert had enlisted in the Fourteenth New York in May 1861 after claiming he was twenty-one years of age. The census taker listed him as only sixteen and perhaps doing "day labor" in 1860. Albert might have been swept up in the excitement of Fort Sumter and enlisted without his parents' permission. On the other hand, the *New-York Tribune*'s 1860 survey of wages in the state found that the average wage for an upstate agricultural laborer was twelve to thirteen dollars per month. Albert might have reasoned that soldiering for the latter wage plus a clothing allowance and rations might have been a better situation than the seasonal work he found at home. A surviving letter from Albert to his father demonstrates that, even though he had wagered on soldiering, he could not be sure of the wage it offered. Stationed at Arlington Heights, Virginia, outside the nation's capital in August, Albert wrote that he could not afford stamps to keep up a correspondence with the family because "when we got our pay some one stole mine all from me so that I did not have a cent left but the man that stole it got ca[u]ght and sent to jail for it." The uncertainty of health in the army camp made earning wages unreliable, too. Albert died in September of typhoid fever, further reducing the family's earning power. By August 1862, when Henry Walker went to war, his wife, Persis, and their six daughters (the oldest was fifteen years old and the youngest was six) resided on rented land. As he settled into quarters near Washington, he wrote to Persis to let her know that he was hungry. The "reason," he explained, was that the "quarter master does not tend to his duty" and "is making money out of we poor soldiers." There were other swindlers about, too. His knapsack was gone, pilfered by a comrade in arms. This theft must have reminded Persis and Henry of what had happened to poor Albert.[6]

Surrounded by thieves, Walker might have been forgiven if he had given up. But he took his obligations to heart, writing to his family that his purpose as a soldier was to "defend your rights to the best of my abilities." The nation's political and military crisis would be intertwined with his and his family's economic one. He expected and needed much from his wife and young daughters at home. "[Y]ou must adhere to that counsil of your mother for she is more capable of giving yo[u] good advise," he wrote to his girls.

He suggested that free labor's promise was available to all and among the "rights" he would defend. "I wish you to prosper one and all," he proclaimed; "rem[em]ber your life is just what you make it." Self-reliance was necessary in hard times if the Walkers were going to get ahead as a household.[7]

The odds of them achieving prosperity seemed long. Despite the regimental historian's claims after the war, Henry Walker's letters to Persis reveal that the soldiers were still "expect[ing] our State bounty every day," some two months after they had enlisted. His faith in self-reliance was, in terms of free labor, a vision of the future. Faced with the challenge of alleviating his family's economic struggles, Henry Walker resolved to work harder, dispensed advice to his family, and envisioned a future in which he and his loved ones were in control of their economic destiny. Despite their circumstances, he did not believe that mere survival would be their lot. He was looking to make something of himself and his family. He believed that they controlled their future.[8]

Control yourselves, he counseled. Buy pork—especially near "killing time," when it would be cheapest—instead of frivolous daguerreotype "likenesses" to send to him. Watch that man Hewit—if he was the one to float their hay to market, he "will take the advantage of you if he can[.] ... [H]e may get it wet and spoil it it will be very poor stuff if it is wet." In November, Henry told Persis that he did not expect to be paid before the new year. He asked her to send him two dollars, perhaps from the money she had earned by marketing agricultural produce, so that he could buy a pair of gloves that would warm his hands while he dug rifle pits to strengthen the capital's fortifications. Instead, Persis bought the gloves herself, because she could get them for less than two dollars. Henry received the gloves and a dollar bill in about three weeks. She could sure economize. "[Y]ou must get along as well as you can untill I get some money," Henry wrote Persis in December, almost four months after he had enlisted. But she already was. He told her how he was getting along as best he could, by purchasing "Shoom[a]ker tooles" and going to work repairing his comrades' shoes. "I get 75 cts for tapping shooes I have just begun my lether c[o]st 35 cts per lb in george tow[n] when the men get their pay I shall pick up a good meny dollars a mending for the rigament." Close to the city, he took advantage of his proximity to a supply of leather that he could use to repair the well-worn taps, or soles, of soldiers' shoes. An entrepreneur who had tools and raw materials could make money from soldiers who, out of necessity, needed to repair and reuse old items because they could not buy new ones. Conveying optimism about his endeavors, Henry urged Persis to ask neighbors to envision the Walkers' prosperous future, too. Believing he would be paid around the first of the year, he wanted Persis to "trade on that State bounty" that he had yet to be paid. That is, he wanted her to promise creditors that when she got the bounty she would pay them back. As a line of credit with neighbors, the bounty might help the Walkers create the independent future for which they worked and dreamed. Even though their finances were precarious, they sought financial means to make more independence.[9]

When Charles Brewster returned to the Tenth Massachusetts after the Antietam Campaign, he found his men in need of more than a cobbler. Like Walker's 117th New York, they had not been paid in four months. The Tenth Massachusetts was "in a terrible state without clothes, blankets or shoes." Brewster asked his mother to imagine a "more dirty and ragged set," but he was sure she could not. They were "barefoot," lice-ridden "beggars" who had "[n]o courage, no ambition, [and] no hope," the very attributes and faith that would make the war bearable, the ones that Walker wanted to live by and instill in his family. Brewster heard once-stalwart comrades say, "If I could only get home the Union might go to H-ll." He was not optimistic about the nation's chances, and he blamed the self-interested folks back home. "I reckon that the US is about played out, as they cannot feed clothe or pay us," Brewster wrote, "but it makes no difference if everyone that remains at home can get a political office." As his countrymen scrambled for influence and power, he worried about the nation's values and the value of its promises. "I have in my portemonaie an old continental dollar bill and a United States Dollar Greenback... and I wonder how long before they are of equal value." The Union war was at low ebb, and so was the nation's worth. Without anything of value with which to buy from the swindling sutlers, shivering and choking down "a miserable existence on Pork and hard bread," the men of the Tenth Massachusetts felt dependent on the government, "and all our cry is more, more." Their pleas were answered not by "Uncle Sam" but by benevolent groups from western Massachusetts. Brewster received an allotment of "goodies... for distribution to the most needy" and, amid the cries of desperate men "sticking up thier bare toes" to show that they had no socks, the lieutenant devised the fairest means he could think of to dispense the goods—by lottery. Finally Uncle Sam came through with a "full supply of clothing of all kinds" to diminish their wants. The paymaster arrived. The wages received—though not all that was due—allowed Brewster to pay off debts to Northampton merchants and send a little home to his mother. The men were "joyful" about getting the pay and supplies they needed, but Brewster, at least, was not willing to forget the dependence they had all suffered at the hands of the government and their neighbors at home. He still thought "the government is about played out" and warned his mother that they may feel dependent yet again, for "it may be a matter of doubt whether we ever get any more pay or not." Whether they were optimistic or despondent, soldiers like Walker and Brewster understood that having valuable credit and capital was absolutely necessary for them to escape the dependence they often felt. Sometimes the government provided access to credit through its bounties, and at other times absent paymasters drove men to despair.[10]

Both Walker and Brewster knew that material goods could be turned into capital and credit. Walker tried to stretch shoe leather for as much as it was worth, while Brewster asked his sister to buy and send him a "silver watch by mail, a patent lever or something of that kind worth about $10.00." He wanted it to function accurately and be fashionable, but he seemed most interested, because the Union's fate looked bleak, for a source of capital he could liquidate when necessary by selling it to another man. "I sold the one I had for $15.00," he told Mary, and it had only cost him $3.50 to buy it. As a lieutenant, he earned far higher wages than Walker and could use those wages to access a wider variety of high-quality goods in the home market. Their use of material things to stock up as capital in hard times was similar, yet as an officer Brewster had more opportunities for promotion and the financial stability that accompanied it. By the end of the year, Brewster had been named the regiment's adjutant, a position on the staff of the Tenth's colonel, Henry Eustis. "I never saw a man I have more confidence in," Brewster wrote of Eustis. He had heard a "rumor" that the colonel "cannot fail of being a Brig[adier] General some day," and this meant that if Brewster would "continue to merit" Eustis's "good opinion," he could rise to a position of greater pay and respect by yoking his ambitions to his commanding officer's. Under these circumstances even the curmudgeonly Brewster could envision a more lucrative future. He encouraged his mother to draw on his allotment with the Massachusetts state treasury for her own needs and to buy his sister Mary a dress, for "I reckon my credit is good" at Northampton stores. "I want you should have anything you want," he told them.[11]

While Walker dug fortifications and repaired footwear and Brewster distributed stockings and mittens by lottery, President Lincoln resolved to emancipate slaves in the Confederacy to bolster the war for Union. He had issued the preliminary version of his proclamation on September 22, 1862, five days after the Army of the Potomac's victory at Antietam. In addition to declaring slaves in disloyal states "forever free" as of January 1, 1863, Lincoln promised to encourage Congress at its next session to consider legislation "tendering pecuniary aid" to loyal slave states in order to encourage them to make arrangements both for compensated emancipation—whether "immediate or gradual"—and African Americans' colonization outside the United States. This offer made loyalty potentially valuable to states in which slavery was legal. Compensated emancipation had been initiated in the District of Columbia in April 1862. Lincoln told border state politicians in July that slavery "in your states will be extinguished by mere friction and abrasion—by the mere incidents of war." If they did not emancipate slaves on their own, even gradually, the war would destroy slavery "and you will have nothing valuable in lieu of it." Perhaps this idea would even persuade rebels to lay down their arms in hopes of a payout. Lincoln's announcement created an incentive for slaveholding white Americans' loyalty at the same time it offered emancipation to enslaved Americans. It gave the former the option of liquidating their property in the latter for profit.[12]

Lincoln's offer of compensated emancipation to loyal slaveholders would make an expensive war even costlier. He acknowledged as much in his message to Congress of December 1, 1862. He rued the "suspension of specie payment by the banks" of the previous year and praised Congress's legislation that made federal currency a "uniform circulating medium" for transactions and the payment of debts. Most important, Lincoln said, the printing of greenbacks—whose value Brewster doubted—was vital because in "no other way could the payment of the troops . . . be so economically, or so well provided for." Ignoring the logistical problems that plagued paymasters' delivery of soldiers' wages, Lincoln argued that the government was not "played out." It was changing its financial policies to make paying for the war possible, even if that upset soldiers' notion of value. The stability offered by the currency might be undermined by future expenditures like the ones Lincoln proposed concerning compensated emancipation, yet his proposal also offered a chance to end the war. "Without slavery the rebellion could never have existed," Lincoln told representatives and senators, and "without slavery it could not continue." Lincoln urged Congress to adopt a proposal he had made in July to issue interest-bearing bonds "to an amount equal to the aggregate" value of a state's enslaved population in 1860, to be distributed to each state when abolition had been completed. Lincoln reasoned that the plan would make emancipation more affordable because "it would require no ready cash; nor the bonds even, any faster than the emancipation progresses." He allowed for slow progress in this regard, setting the year 1900 as a deadline and contending that the financial burden of the plan would be eased by population growth in the intervening period. In Lincoln's mind, it was a question of numbers. The abolition of slavery would end the war, thus promoting population and economic increase. The costs of emancipation would be borne more easily over time. The plan would save dollars and lives. Much like the soldiers who wanted to save their lives and make their dollars go as far in the market as they could in order to realize their ambitions, Lincoln envisioned a future for the nation in which the labor and capital of current citizens and Americans yet unborn would help create the economic prosperity necessary to fulfill his promises to the nation's slaves. He ended his address with a flourish: "In *giving* freedom to the *slave*, we assure freedom to the *free*." Lincoln offered Northern citizens assurance and insurance. Printing currency in the present would cover men's killing labor as soldiers, while bond issues would cover the loss of human capital in slavery, eventually paid for by the ever-increasing capital of a prosperous nation. In this way, Northerners would "nobly save" the Union, "the last best hope of earth."[13]

Lincoln's bet to save the Union and its soldiers by promising to pay in the future to emancipate its slaves had no takers. Henry Louis Stephens's comic portrayal of the president in *Vanity Fair* as a peddler unable to persuade customers to purchase his stock of goods hit its mark. No Confederate state returned to the Union to cash in on its enslaved population. The loyal slave states did not warm to the president's plan either, unwilling to heed his warning that the war would erode slavery. Even Lincoln's friend, Illinois senator Orville Browning, declared the plan a "hallucination." "Darn these here Blackbirds!," Stephens had Lincoln say, "[i]f nobody won't buy 'em I'll have to open the cages and let 'em fly!" And so he did. The Emancipation Proclamation, which went into effect on January 1, 1863, ended Lincoln's scheme to emancipate through creative finance.[14]

Lincoln's vision of turning enslaved people's value to the benefit of the Union may not have been shared by his countrymen. But they were thinking along the same lines. Many Northerners wondered how emancipation would affect the value of their own labor. As abolitionists such as William Still understood, it was crucial to let white Northern workers know that black refugees posed no threat to their jobs or current wages. Lincoln wholeheartedly agreed in his message to Congress. He proposed colonization for formerly enslaved people and argued that it would augment the wages of white laborers. Yet "even without deportation," Lincoln asked, "why would emancipation south, send the free people north?" There was no reason for former slaves to leave "congenial climes" and ties of family and friendship when they could work for wages from "old masters." Lincoln again queried, "[C]annot the north decide for itself, whether to receive them?" And "[a]gain, . . . has

WHAT WILL HE DO WITH THEM?

A. L.—"Darn these here blackbirds!—If nobody won't buy 'em I'll have to open the cages and let 'em fly!"

"What Will He Do with Them?," *Vanity Fair*, October 4, 1862, 163.
(The Library Company of Philadelphia)

there been any irruption of colored people northward, because of the abolishment of slavery in this District last spring?" With each question, Lincoln seemed more unsure of himself about the "practice [that] proves more than theory." Indeed, the war had produced other visions of laborers' migration that Lincoln did not recognize. He wanted former slaves to leave the country, but abolitionists such as Lewis Tappan wanted them to come north.

Worthy of His Hire

Brewster's servant David left Maryland for Pennsylvania after being driven out of the Tenth Massachusetts's Washington camp, and dozens of other former slaves arrived in cities like Philadelphia, where Northern employers were quite eager to hire them. In October 1862, General John Dix had asked Governor Andrew whether Massachusetts would receive former slaves working in and around his command at Fort Monroe. Andrew advocated keeping them where they were and arming them to defend the Union. In his address, Lincoln leaned not on his previous formulations of free labor ideology but on what and who could be bought and sold. "Labor is like any other commodity in the market," Lincoln admitted—sounding much like James Gordon Bennett in his article about intelligence offices before the war—and the price for it would fluctuate according to its supply and demand. That was what concerned white Northern workers. In Lincoln's search for the ways labor could be valued and brought to bear in the war for Union, he stumbled away from his certainty that labor was superior to capital. Now capital determined where labor would go by offering wages to workers who could get jobs done. The subject whom Stephens styled the *"Inevitable Contraband"* in *Vanity Fair* at the end of the year, distinguished from his earlier rendering of the "highly intelligent contraband" only by the liberty cap the man wore, passed through the threshold separating slavery from wage labor at the end of 1862 looking for a new "Situmavation"—a job. He "wonder[ed] what sort of pusson new massa's gwine to be," and white Northerners wondered too.[15]

Soldiers like Brewster and Walker already knew that labor was a commodity to be sold on the market and that the employing state did not always fulfill the terms of the contracts it made. Northern workers worried that Lincoln's scheme to dangle finance capital to loyal slave owners was a humbug because it might mortgage the nation's future and imperil their livelihoods. It was no less a swindle than, as Stephens put it in *Vanity Fair* after the new year began, the one keeping soldiers "six months in arrears" while they and their families starved. The juxtaposition of these images of the liberated "contraband" and the suffering soldier in the pages of *Vanity Fair* reflects the conflicts emerging among Northerners about how free labor would win the war for Union. Lincoln had long argued that the mudsill theory promoted by Southerners was wrong. Soldiers appropriated the mudsill label for themselves, both worrying that Southerners were right and endeavoring to prove them wrong. Northerners' experience as soldiers confirmed that access to credit and capital made them more independent. Otherwise they were dependent on the state and nefarious entrepreneurs from recruiters to sutlers for survival. Now the president was speculating on how to make enslaved people's capital in self work for the Union war effort. His first speculation was a failure, but failure was a state of mind. He would try to unlock that capital in self by requesting, in the final version of the Emancipation Proclamation, that black Southerners "labor faithfully for reasonable wages." One means of doing so, Lincoln explained, was by making a clause in Congress's July 1862 revision of the Militia Act operational and allowing African American men to enlist in the "armed service of the United States." Two months later, in March 1863, Congress passed and Lincoln signed the Enrollment Act, which would implement a draft of Northern citizens in July of that year. In the same month, Lincoln wrote to the military governor of occupied Tennessee, Andrew Johnson, to encourage him to enlist black men into the military. "The colored population is the great *available* and yet *unavailed* of, force for restoring the Union. The bare sight of fifty thousand armed, and drilled black soldiers on the banks of the Mississippi, would end the rebellion at once. And who doubts that we can present that sight, if we but take hold in earnest." Reeling from his wild financial speculation in emancipation, Lincoln returned to the cautious optimism of faithful free labor and the coercions of soldiering to save the Union. Through slow and steady means, he would plow the capital embedded in soldiers' selves to take each inch of ground in a war of attrition — marching, digging, killing, and dying. The wage work of the soldier, rather than financial flights of fancy, would assure freedom to the free.[16]

The enlistment of African American soldiers had already begun, far away from Washington in places occupied by the armies of the United States. One of those places was in the vicinity of New Orleans, which the expeditionary force commanded by Benjamin Butler had captured in May 1862. Butler's management of African Americans' recruitment in the Department of the Gulf created conflict with subordinates about how emancipation should unfold in the absence of congressional legislation or executive pronouncement. This conflict shows that Union military commanders were willing to speculate on the transition between slavery and wage labor.[17]

In the months after the Union army arrived, Butler received complaints from local slave owners about the conduct of Brigadier General John Phelps at Camp Parapet, a fort guarding a bend in the Mississippi River above New Orleans. These slave owners proclaimed their loyalty to the United States and insisted that Phelps be stopped from offering safe haven to their human property. Phelps had served under Butler in Virginia and helped him implement his contraband policy there. In a June 16 reply to Butler's inquiry about the state of things at Camp Parapet, Phelps praised the Confiscation Act that

"Six Months in Arrears," *Vanity Fair*, January 1, 1863, n.p. (The Library Company of Philadelphia)

prohibited the return of slaves to disloyal owners, but he hoped that the government would enact a policy to guide emancipation more generally. Such a policy would certainly help Phelps, whose officer of the day informed him that more than 150 enslaved people were crowding the road leading to his camp. He had his own ideas on the matter that he wished to share. Slavery was an abomination "unsuited to the age," he declared. "The relation . . . between capital and labor" in that system "is darkling, suspicious, unkindly, full of reproachful threats, and without concord and peace." Phelps called for "a well-regulated system of apprenticeship . . . for effecting a gradual transition from slavery to freedom." He understood that the task system of slave labor offered wages for additional work to enslaved people who did more than their allotted task. Therefore, the transition to free labor would build on current practice. Much as Butler and Phelps had done in Virginia, Phelps's proposal called for withholding wages from workers to help pay for the costs of subsistence. "At the end of a period of five years of apprenticeship, or of fifteen at farthest, full wages could be paid to the enfranchised negro race to the double advantage of both master and man." Another "means" of apprenticeship in the practices of wage labor and "civilization," Phelps thought, was "military service." He believed that fifty regiments of African Americans could be raised in Butler's department, serve for five years, and then be transported to Africa as part of a colonization venture. Butler forwarded these plans to Stanton, "respect[ing]" Phelps's "honest sincerity of opinion" and asking for advice about how to proceed.[18]

Phelps's ideas were modeled on those governing slave emancipation in the North. Slavery had ended gradually in many Northern states, with apprenticeship deployed to develop former slaves' work ethic and to ease the economic blow of slave owners' loss of property. Apprenticeship offered former slave owners a way to make more capital out of vulnerable laborers. As the *Continental Monthly* proclaimed at the end of 1862, emancipated people needed to be "trained in the proper habits of freedom" under white Northerners' "management." The key question in regard to the transition from slavery to wage labor for the *Continental* was whether the United States could reestablish its preeminence in the cotton market. If it was unable to do so, Northerners would have to pay higher prices for inferior Indian alternatives, hurting Northern industrialists, workers, and consumers. "Thus this question of emancipation to the blacks," the *Continental* argued, "is intimately connected with that of justice to the whites." The publication did not support the enlistment of African Americans as soldiers because former slaves needed to produce agricultural staples like cotton to salvage the nation's political economy. White Northerners must be able to buy high-quality goods cheaply. Stanton agreed with the *Continental* in theory, but took a more expansive view of political economy. In September, he allowed the military commander stationed at Cairo, Illinois, to forward the African American women and children whom General Ulysses Grant had sent him from Tennessee and Mississippi to Chicago, where white women "wish[ed] them for servants." The government could make the nation's economy prosper by putting former slaves to work on plantations and by paying transportation costs that would move them to Northern households. One month later, Stanton countermanded his permission, and the annual report of Quartermaster General Montgomery Meigs explains why. The "large number of refugees" who fled to Grant's army left crops in the fields "ungathered." So Grant "ordered them to be employed in picking the cotton, which is ready for harvest." Meigs stated the obvious, that at "60 cents per pound their labor will not prove unremunerative, and the Government can well afford to secure this much needed staple at the wages — $10 a month and a ration — established by the law of July 17, 1862," the revision to the Militia Act that set the wage rate for African American men working in the army. Sending African American refugees to Northern households seemed to be bad business when the nation could obtain prosperity by harnessing cheap wage labor to produce the South's best-known agricultural staple.[19]

Phelps's ideas did not make the transition to free labor and military recruitment of African Americans in Louisiana mutually exclusive, but Phelps and Butler came into conflict about the relationship between the two. In early July 1862, Lincoln ordered that the "fugitive negroes" outside Camp Parapet "must not be permitted to suffer for want of food, shelter, or other necessaries of life." He demurred from addressing Phelps's criticism of the government or his ideas about ending slavery. He stated merely that "those who are capable of labor should be set to work and paid reasonable wages." Without orders, Phelps began to organize three regiments of black soldiers at Camp Parapet. When Butler asked his subordinate at the end of July to employ African American men to cut down trees between Camp Parapet and Lake Pontchartrain to clear the approaches and defend the position from Confederate attack, Phelps offered his resignation. "[W]hile I am willing to prepare African Regiments for the defence of the Government against its assailants, I am not willing to become the mere slave driver which you propose, having no qualifications that way." Phelps believed in gradual emancipation with a period of apprenticeship, but he declined to provide the "management" that many Northerners believed must govern the transition. Butler tried to make Phelps see that his orders were meant to strengthen his military position and not to coerce him into acting as an overseer of enslaved labor. Yet Phelps's missives illuminated the conundrum in which Butler found himself. To strengthen his department's defenses, he needed soldiers, and the Lincoln administration would not send him any. It demanded, instead, that he enlist loyal white Louisianans, which he did to the extent he could find them. In dire need of more men, and without clear advice from the Lincoln administration, Butler rallied to Phelps's standard while declaring the policy was actually his own. He told Stanton that he was ready to "call on Africa to intervene" and augment his depleted forces. On August 22, at the time General Phelps's resignation was accepted, Butler ordered that free black men who had served in the state's Confederate militia—"the darkest of whom," he assured Stanton, "will be about the complexion of the late Mr. [Daniel] Webster"—could now serve in "Native Guard" units of the U.S. Army.[20]

Treasury Department agent George Denison, in New Orleans to serve as eyes and ears for his boss, Salmon Chase, understood that Butler "wanted the credit of doing the thing himself." Chase already knew about other rumors concerning Butler's conduct in New Orleans. He let the general know that he had heard "you were availing yourself of your military command to engage in mercantile speculation, and had already made considerable shipments North on private account." The focal point of the rumors was Butler's brother, Andrew, who used his proximity to power to speculate freely in everything, from goods confiscated from rebels, to cotton and sugar, to monopolies on necessary items like flour and medicine entering the occupied city from the North. There was even evidence he traded with the enemy. Chase warned Butler that the rumors were damaging his reputation and position as commander in the Gulf. Butler responded by telling Chase that he would send Andrew north but that the suspicions against his brother and him were "unwarranted."[21]

Butler's enlistment of African Americans and the capital he may or may not have received through his brother's speculations were related to each other. They could not be pulled apart because they were both central to the triumph of free labor in Louisiana. Denison knew it. "Col. [Andrew] B[utler]. bought the standing crop of a large plantation for $25,000, hired negroes at a fair rate per day—and will make a thousand hogsheads of sugar this year from this one plantation. I say he deserves credit," Denison explained to Chase, "as being the first man bold and enterprising enough to undertake the raising of a large crop of sugar by free labor." Denison was also impressed by the "energy and industry" of the black men who labored in the fields, although he also clarified the coercions under which they did that work. General Butler had declared them "free forever," Denison wrote, "but he has ordered them . . . back to their plantations to work there for proper compensation." They had no choice but to do wage labor for the likes of Andrew Butler, who poured capital into this venture in free labor in order to make more capital. Benjamin Butler obscured these coercions when he corresponded with his superiors. He had a sample of "the first sugar ever made by *free black labor* in Louisiana"—likely from the plantation managed by his brother—sent to President Lincoln along with a cover letter extolling the productivity of African American workers and the "success" of the "experiment." Personal profits could be national ones and demonstrate the superiority of wage labor over slavery.[22]

The recruitment of African Americans for military purposes was not distinct from the Union's project of validating free labor. The man Butler put in charge of the Third Louisiana Native Guard was John Nelson, formerly the rough-and-tumble recruiter in the Ninth Connecticut and provost marshal of Ship Island. Once the expeditionary force ventured to take New Orleans, Nelson, lacking a commission, needed something to do. Butler apparently recommended "young Mr. Nelson" for a position under Chase in the "revenue cutter service," whose ships tried to capture Confederate vessels attempting to run the Union blockade with contraband goods from abroad. Revenue cutters helped to police the boundaries of legitimate and illegitimate commerce. Chase did not think Nelson would be ready for the requisite examination "without some further study." As Chase bestowed "expressions of good will" upon him, Nelson apparently told the secretary that he would return to the Gulf. "I doubt not," Chase wrote diplomatically to Butler, "he will be very useful to you." Nelson got a commission as lieutenant-colonel in the First Louisiana Native Guard on September 27, 1862, and became colonel of the Third on November 11. A few days later, Denison mentioned to Chase that the third regiment of Native Guards was "full" to its capacity of one thousand men. Butler told Lincoln that he was prepared to "send out my third Regt. of Native Guards (colored), and set them to work preserving the cane and roots for a crop next year." Whether preparing to fight rebels or working in plantation fields, Nelson and his soldiers would demonstrate the legitimacy, primacy, and promise of free labor. They would continue to do so after Butler, dogged by rumors of his and his brother's speculations in New Orleans, was replaced by Nathaniel Banks as commander of the Department of the Gulf. In an exit interview, Butler told Banks that Nelson was "a good soldier."[23]

From his new berth as adjutant in the Tenth Massachusetts in Falmouth, Virginia, Charles Brewster did not see how his ambitions could be realized through free labor in the weeks after the Emancipation Proclamation went into effect. After sending his sister a list of the deranged current prices—"60 cts per lb for butter, 30 cts for cheese, 5 cts each for Apples,

$2.50 for a bushel of Potatoes"—he admitted that it did not much matter what things cost when soldiers had no money to pay for them. "I do wish they would pay us our money when it is due, and then we could make some calculations for the future but we never know whether it will be two months or six before we are paid." Brewster had come to realize that the ethic of saving could not be honored in the soldier's economy, in which men had little money to save and no ability to plan for (much less dream of) a more promising future. Further bloodletting had a way of helping ambitious men move up in the world. After the Second Battle of Fredericksburg and the Battle of Salem Church in May 1863 led to the reshuffling of brigade command, Brewster was proud to tell his mother that he had become acting assistant adjutant general of the Second Brigade, Third Division, Sixth Corps. His new "place . . . is a very pleasant one except during marches or battles when it becomes very arduous as I have often to keep my horse saddled night and day and ride around in the dark with orders." By June, however, he had relinquished the post to return to his position of adjutant in the Tenth Massachusetts. He explained to his sister that he had done so because his "pay is no more and the rank no higher" and he had come to realize that "the cost of messing . . . is more than double owing principally to the quantities of liquor drank" by his fellow staff officers. It had been a lateral move with more work and more spending of money he did not have. Trying to cut costs and looking out for the next chance at fulfilling his ambitions, Brewster also felt that he was stagnating rather than moving toward independence.[24]

That next chance involved managing the labor of others on the battlefield and on the home front. Back in February, while complaining about his lack of funds, he had told his sister about two courts-martial of soldiers in his division who had deserted from the ranks. Family impoverishment likely drove these men to desert, and now commanders wanted to make examples of them. Brewster wanted his superiors to make a still larger example, by executing "about one half of" the two or three hundred men—"bounty men," he called them—who had been arrested for desertion in the division. It did not seem "worth while to pay one and two hundred dollars for men to come out here and then" have them try to "skeedaddle home again." There were even more deserters who had eluded the provost marshal to enjoy freedom at home because their neighbors, according to Brewster, "befriend them and look upon a man after deserters, as a sort of fugitive slave hunter, and they hide these faulters and resist the Officer." To help stop the theft of the government's bounties and teach the bounty jumpers' friends a lesson, he dreamed of being "sent home after deserters" to round them up with a "force of a dozen good muskets to back me." He would give the protectors of men who were in dereliction of duty a "taste of war." Brewster did not know how lucrative Provost Marshal General James Fry was about to make deserter hunting and recruiting, after the provisions of the Enrollment Act scheduled a draft that many thousands would evade. Late in 1863, Fry offered men "deputized by the Provost Marshal General to arrest deserters and procure recruits" $30 for each deserter they captured. The payment for each new soldier recruited would be $15 per soldier, while veterans persuaded to reenlist would garner the recruiter $25, both up from $2 per recruit. While Brewster criticized bounty jumpers and home-front sympathizers for stealing the government's money, the government was prepared to pay out even more for recruiters to repopulate the ranks of regiments diminished by the ravages of war. President Lincoln had resorted to a draft out of necessity. "There can be no army without men," he wrote in an unpublished memorandum in September 1863. "Men can be had only voluntarily, or involuntarily. We have ceased to obtain them voluntarily; and to obtain them involuntarily, is the draft — the conscription." Fry's circular shows the government understood that both voluntary and involuntary enlistment would cost money. The profit motive both unmade the army through bounty jumping and served as the only means, by providing new incentives for recruiters, that a Union based on free labor could reconstitute it.[25]

One of the regiments that needed more bodies was Brewster's Tenth Massachusetts. After the Gettysburg Campaign, Brewster told his sister that it needed 370 men to "fill up . . . to the maximum standard." A guard consisting of three officers and six soldiers was sent after "the conscripts" who would make "a big regiment once more," but it did not include Brewster. He was left in the Tenth's camp in Virginia to muse on the Enrollment Act's commutation clause. While critics believed commutation was an injustice that burdened the poor and liberated the rich, a government in need of men to fight a war for its survival could only mitigate, but not obliterate, inequality. Brewster's criticism of commutation reveals that he preferred the competition among drafted men and brokers that Lincoln forecast. If some Northerners thought it was unfair that men without $300 would have to serve, Brewster rued the fact that the measure "obliges only the poor to go who have less at stake in the contest than any other class."[26]

Who had a stake in the war for Union? Ambitious speculators and competitors did. As Brewster griped about the absence of paymasters and deserters and as the Emancipation Proclamation and Enrollment Act went into effect, he continued to look for ways to accumulate economic and social power. A "place" capturing deserters and recruiting soldiers would put him on the path toward financial solvency much more quickly than his current post would. He also sought advantage as an employer. "While we were lying" in Fredericksburg waiting to attack Marye's Heights as part of General Joseph Hooker's ill-fated Chancellorsville Campaign in May, he had "tried to hire" a man "from Missisippi and a deserter from the Reb Army." The man was not a Confederate soldier but a "contraband," whom Brewster called "a mighty smart looking nigger or rather Mulatto." The man refused. Brewster asked him "to hunt me up after the fight was over," but he had "not seen him since." Employing an African American servant might have once again unburdened Brewster of work and made the status of adjutant seem more exalted. In the very same month that he recounted this episode to his folks at home, the *Continental Monthly* published an essay that built on its earlier assertion that emancipation must do justice to white Americans as well as black Americans. Emancipation must offer former slaves political and social equality, the *Continental* asserted in radical tones, while acknowledging that whites would be loath to accept it. From this radical starting point, the essayist explained that the equality he had in mind was competition that pitted members of the white and black races against each other. This was the competition that white Northern workers feared would lead to their impoverishment. The *Continental* had happy news for them. "Whenever two peoples, one of which is little removed from barbarism, and the other having the full strength of a mature civilization, are placed in juxtaposition with each other, on terms of free labor and free competition, the stronger will always either amalgamate itself with the weaker, or extinguish it." If African Americans had to compete with whites at wage labor, they would lose out on the best jobs, do menial work that did not pay a family wage, and stop having children who survived childhood. As African Americans lost this race of life and their population dwindled to the point of "extinct[ion]," they would serve as the North's mudsill class. "[T]here is in every community a lower stratum of population," the *Continental* reminded readers, appropriating Hammond's theory to validate free labor, "in which wages are sufficient to support the individual laborer in comfort, but not sufficient for the support of a family. This not only always has been so, but it always must be, as long as competition continues to be the test of value." The *Continental*'s revised mudsill theory underscored Brewster's longing for another servant. He and other white Northerners could make themselves "all-powerful" by destroying a slaveholding aristocracy and black families and assuming positions of authority over former slaves as wage labor employers. These were the stakes of the war for Union.[27]

Henry Walker, stationed at Fort Baker near Washington in the days after the Emancipation Proclamation went into effect, was hard at work to make the promise of free labor a reality for his family. He had carved out a competitive niche in the limited market available to soldiers. His "Shoe mending" venture was going very well because he had eager customers who lacked choices. There were rarely new shoes to purchase or money to buy them. Walker was often able to send money to his wife Persis through express companies that guaranteed safe shipment. Henry sent Persis $35 on January 3, 1863, and promised to send another $30 three weeks later. These funds included his wages as a soldier as well as the proceeds from cobbling, which could amount to as much as $2 per day. His business continued to thrive in February and March, but he was unable to send more money home because he would have to buy more leather to keep up his trade and "I have got ... over $25 charged on book to boys in camp" who could not pay him back until payday, whenever that would be. Soldiers' ambitions were tempered by the bottlenecks created by government bureaucracy and logistical delay. He reckoned in March that, if the rumor was correct that the men of the 117th would be paid in a few days, he would be able to send Persis $70 or $80. In the meantime, Walker had capital only in his ledger, and in order to buy more leather in Washington he had to go into debt.[28]

Back home in Forestport, Persis's economic position was precarious. She depended on neighbors for credit so that she could access the goods she needed to ensure her family's survival. Henry instructed Persis to remind the men with whom she dealt that she already had credit because he had formerly done work for them or because he would pay them soon from his wages as a soldier. He encouraged her to "use your money to the best advantage make yourselvs as comfortable as you can," and sought to boost her spirits with pithy sayings extolling the bourgeois virtues. "[O]ur coarse in life depends on our own energy. persevere their is nothing like try try agan." Beyond this encouragement, there seemed little else he could do but rail against the "meaner" men who "refused to trust" her in his absence.[29]

There was something else he could do, Persis evidently suggested in a letter that is not extant — get her a pension for their son Albert's death. Despite Henry's competitive ambition and hard work, she needed more money and had ideas about how to get it. Persis was ambitious, too. Free labor's scripts concerning work ethic and accumulating credit and capital were hers as well as his. At her behest, Henry went to Washington to speak with E. B. French, the Treasury Department's Second Auditor, to get Persis his bounty and a pension as payment of the nation's debt to their dead son. He learned how to get the former—Persis had to mail him the bounty certificate for him to "make out the papers"—but no provision had yet been made by Congress for paying the latter. Henry thought that the bounty windfall would make everything right, hoping that his family would finally be more comfortable, more independent. He saw signs that the nation and all its people would prosper. "[T]heir is a great time acoming when all those that live to se[e] it will enjoy the best government that ever was if I do not enjoy it my family will and thousands of poor soles that never new what freedom was."[30]

Walker would be an exemplar of the manhood demanded of volunteers. He would, through discipline and self-sacrifice, help to save the Republic. Now that President Lincoln had issued the Emancipation Proclamation, Walker incorporated the rights of slaves into the cause of defending the Union. Yet for all of free labor's platitudes about impending advancement and Walker's trust in their efficacy, his anxieties festered in his correspondence as he catalogued his ambitions and vented his frustrations. The Civil War forced men like Henry Walker to confront their dependence on their wives. Soldiers' writings show that men knew their wives were familiar with a variety of economic transactions, practices, and strategies, that they worked very hard to benefit households without being told to do so (and often without the assistance of servants), and that their keen insight into household management had emerged from the experiences of domestic economy they shared with husbands. During the war, men's dependence on women's labor and knowledge of money was magnified. Housewives understood their households' domestic necessities and how to address them in ways that soldiers could not from hundreds of miles away. Phrases in Henry's letters reveal his trust in Persis, even if he was quite fond of telling her what to do. In the summer of 1863, she had apparently asked, in a letter that is not extant, whether he thought she spent money frivolously. He replied, "I do not think that you spend more than just what you nead." That might seem like a backhanded compliment, but in other letters he encouraged her to "use your own jugment" and do as "you think best." Husbands and wives relied on each other to get by.[31]

The partnership that defined the Walkers' domestic economy did not, however, topple patriarchy as the structural foundation of the household. The Walkers' correspondence reveals that the credit relationships on which Persis relied were ones that Henry had forged with other male household heads in their neighborhood. Bonds of credit linked men on the home front with those on the battlefield, and men expected that their wives would draw on these communal ties to help them survive. Persis had to confront the ways those expectations might unravel in Henry's absence. In the one extant letter from her to Henry, she explained that a Mr. Blake had reneged on his promise to pay the family's rent while Henry was away. Blake justified his conduct because he believed that Henry "got larg pay enough." Persis gave as good as she got, telling her husband that "I told [Blake] if I had to pay rent I should try to get another house I will not gratify the old Rebel to pay rent if I can find another house." She questioned her neighbor's loyalties for imperiling the household economy of one of the nation's stalwart defenders. Persis informed her husband that she thought Blake was actually angry because she had "sold the manure" on the Walkers' rented property, a transaction she had made in order "to buy some meal." Henry was furious with Blake when he heard the news. The latter's refusal to abide by his promises represented an affront to the former's understanding of what male household heads owed each other. This episode also shows how Persis persisted: she made independent decisions about buying and selling goods in her husband's absence, choices with which men like Blake found fault.[32]

Henry Walker struggled to ensure his family's comfort. The delivery of his pay was as uncertain as ever, and navigating the process of bounty and pension claims was complicated. Any paymaster would be able to start that process, but the paymaster was rarely where soldiers needed him to be. Persis had to deliver him the paperwork so that they could obtain the capital that would assist in her efforts to buy them a new home. That took precious time. But then, as he surveyed the crumbling society of the Slave South from a new vantage point in Yorktown, Virginia, in July 1863, Henry dreamed of another way he and Persis could achieve independence. After spending a day "garding" the property of a Virginia plantation owner who had recently sworn allegiance to the United States, he contemplated the value of the African American women he called "wenches" who toiled in the planter's berry garden and cabbage patch. "I am a going to . . . bring home one to do the work for you," he told Persis. "[T]hey are so black and shiney that you would like to have one to work for you," he explained. Walker hated this Southern slaveholder for helping to inaugurate the war and then hypocritically claiming the fruits of loyalty to the United States. Walker supported slave emancipation. Yet as Benjamin Butler and his brother, Charles Brewster, the *Continental Monthly*, and Henry Walker all knew, competing and succeeding in the wage labor economy meant taking advantage of people when you could. Workers who could perform arduous tasks like the women in the supposedly repentant farmer's field enticed Northern soldiers like Walker. The rebel's disloyalty disqualified him from deserving these workers anymore. The women's "black and shiney" appearance represented their desirability as workers who would make the Walkers' home respectable and supplement Henry and Persis's efforts to obtain a comfortable living. The way the war had rocked the Walker household—Albert's death, Henry's persevering extra work and struggle to get paid, and Persis's trouble with creditors—made the ideal of domesticity difficult to attain. The capacity of black women to do labor that produced sweat and caused their skin to glisten in the hot sun was, according to the logic of free labor, the very thing that would underwrite the Walkers' ambitious vision of household independence.[33]

Colonel John Nelson of the Third Louisiana Native Guard believed that black men's labor would support his own claims to authority and prestige. They would go into battle together and win the plaudits due to honorable fighting men. A *Philadelphia Inquirer* reporter who accompanied Nathaniel Banks's army toward Baton Rouge proclaimed in February 1863 that Nelson, leading a regiment with white and black officers, "has the greatest confidence in his men, and thinks they will fight with a determination neither to give nor receive any mercy." Mostly, though, the soldiers dug entrenchments— manual labor much like they had done to ready sugarcane fields for planting at Butler's behest. William Lloyd Garrison's *Liberator* republished the dispatches of a *New-York Tribune* correspondent to confront the pervasive assumption that African American soldiers were only suitable for manual drudgery rather than fighting. To persuade his readers, the correspondent praised Nelson's regiment, an "orderly, disciplined, robust and effective set of men." The correspondent also emphasized Nelson's hopes to get out of fortification duty. "Col. Nelson, anxious to have an opportunity of exhibiting to the world what his command is capable of, and thus put their manhood beyond all question, has implored Gen. Banks to put him in the foremost point of danger in the coming struggle, and says that his men are ready as himself to stake their lives upon the result."[34]

Nelson made his appeal to Banks to let his regiment show its fighting mettle less than two months after the free black men who served as company commanders resigned from it, announcing that they had no confidence in their colonel. Nelson had insisted that these officers submit to a board of examination to assess their qualifications for command. The free black officers "did not expect, or demand to be putt on a Perfect equality" with the white officers appointed to lead the regiment, they informed Banks in their resignation letter, but they also had not expected the "scorn and contempt" they received. It was as though "[t]o be Spoken to, by a colord Officer . . . seams an Insult" to white men. That was true of Nelson, whose disposition was presumably still inamiable, most of all. "Even our own Regimental commander has abused us, under cover of his authority." Nelson lorded his power over the African American officers by forcing them to admit their "limited Knoledge of military Discipline." As free men, they expected to be treated just so by Northern officers—certainly to a greater extent than they had been as part of the Confederate militia. Nelson signed off on the resignations in an endorsement directed to General Banks: each officer was "of no use to the Survice And entirely unfit for the position He occupys having no military Knowledge or any controle over His Command." Although he did not have entire command over written English, Nelson asserted that he had the military knowledge the black officers lacked and would exhibit the control that these men did not.[35]

Lauded by the nation's premier abolitionist newspaper and successful in ridding his command of free black officers, Nelson got the opportunity to earn the accolades he craved in the Union's campaign to seize one of the last remaining bastions of Confederate power on the Mississippi River. On May 27, 1863, the First and Third Louisiana Native Guards participated in a frontal assault that failed to breach the rebel stronghold of Port Hudson, Louisiana. The Native Guards suffered 169 casualties in the attack, and although they did not achieve their military objective, many Northern observers hailed their courage under fire. They had indeed put their manhood beyond question, as Nelson had hoped.[36]

As the attack of his regiment failed and Banks's army besieged Port Hudson, Nelson sought not only plaudits for his military leadership but also profits. In late July, a Northern newspaper informed readers that a Southern colonel had, during a "pleasant confab" between the lines separating his men from Nelson's regiment at Port Hudson, agreed to a bet with Nelson that rumors of Confederate general Franklin Gardner's surrender to Banks were not true. "I'm not a betting man," the cavalier Southerner said, "and don't know if you are, but I will bet you an even hundred that this is not so." Nelson, of course, was a betting man. He quickly shouted, "Done." Nelson did not have the money on him, so he surrendered his gold watch "as a stake." After the surrender was confirmed, Nelson's rebel counterpart sent his watch and $100 in Confederate currency across the lines. The newspaper correspondent made light of "this little sporting transaction" among sporting men, declaring that the money was nothing more than "pictorial me-

mentoes of a curious event." Nelson might have been gambling further, with some justification, that local Southerners with whom he dealt would take grayback currency in a pinch in hopes that the Confederates could reestablish their control in Louisiana. A sporting man would know that any speculation deserved another that might pay off.[37]

Yet in another respect, the newspaperman was correct. The bet was insignificant in comparison with the larger speculations that Union officers were making in the Mississippi River Valley. In August, after Port Hudson had fallen, Banks began to receive complaints from white slave owners and African American men and women alike that Northern recruiting agents were coercing black men to serve in the Union army. Impressment gangs, under the pretense of eliminating vagrancy in New Orleans, were seizing men in the streets and in the homes of their owners, taking them to recruiting offices, and forcing them to "touch the pen" to enlistment documents without explaining the significance of the papers. "A Colored Man," the author of an anonymously written sheet discovered on a New Orleans street in early September 1863, claimed "our white officers may be union men but Slave holders at heart the[y] Are allways on hand when theire is money." He asserted that "one half of the recruiting officers is rebles taken the oath to get a living." These profit-minded white men of questionable loyalty made vital contributions to the war for Union in New Orleans. By "haveing negro traders for recruiting officers Drawing his Sword over us like we were dogs[,], . . . you will Soon have the union north."[38]

By the time this public sheet was found by the New Orleans police, Banks had discharged John Nelson from the service—honorably, so the August 14, 1863, special order said. Yet Banks wrote to Lincoln three days later to explain that the "discreditable character" of the Native Guards' officers had led to the regiments being "demoralized" and in need of new commanders. He did not mention Nelson by name. Nelson had recruited 816 African American men for his regiment out of the 7,699 reported to have been recruited by that date, and he had led them to great acclaim at Port Hudson. He had not been implicated in the coercive recruitment schemes that had emerged in New Orleans. An entry in the diary of Colonel Nathan Daniels of the Second Louisiana Native Guard explains that Nelson was "deeply implicated in cotton speculation and was compelled to resign." He was also "accused of using disrespectful language toward The President of the United States." Daniels interpreted the news in light of the partisan divide between Banks and Butler, with the former "determined to get rid of the organization of Native Guards because they were established" by the latter and "of course are opposed to him politically." It is also possible that Banks was trying to cleanse his department of the kind of craven profit seeking that characterized Butler's reign. Banks likely gave Nelson a choice of a court-martial or an honorable discharge, a decision that seems gracious if Daniels's assertion about Banks wanting to punish Democrats is given credence. Nelson obviously chose the discharge with his honor still intact. He returned to the East and basked in the glory his former position conferred upon him. In the middle of September, he turned up in Hartford and Boston, where newspapers, probably depending on Nelson's own information, claimed that he was still in command of the Third Louisiana Native Guard, "was the first white officer who took command of a colored regiment," and had served "for several months [as] Acting Brigadier-General of the colored forces in the Department of the Gulf." "[I]t is largely due to his untiring energy," one editor intoned, "that the experiment" in recruiting African Americans for the army "has proved such a success." Perhaps the only truth Nelson told to these papers was that he was "in fine health." He was now on a furlough of forty days, the papers said, and "is soon to visit Washington on business." His business would be to tell still more self-promoting lies to people he had disparaged in furtherance of his speculations. He had learned well from his experience in Louisiana.[39]

In the East, the prospect of recruiting black men to serve in the Union's military forces still disturbed many Northerners. In June 1863, black Philadelphians rallied to form a company to defend the state of Pennsylvania from the threat of Confederate invasion. They did so in spite of the paltry offer of the Citizens' Bounty Fund to pay them one-fifth the bounty it gave to white soldiers and the refusal of Mayor Henry to give their families assurances that they would be cared for in the event their soldiers were wounded or killed. Governor Andrew Curtin and General Darius Couch refused to accept them into the service. A week after this rebuff, however, the War Department gave permission to the chairman of Philadelphia's Supervisory Committee for Recruiting Colored Regiments to recruit three regiments of African American soldiers in Philadelphia and eastern Pennsylvania. On June 27, 1863, as Pennsylvanians panicked about the Confederate Army of Northern Virginia's presence in their state, the Supervisory Committee solicited donations to fund African Americans' enlistment in the Union army. The committee's chairman was Thomas Webster, the veteran recruiter and speculator who had raised money to entice white men to enlist earlier in the war. Now Webster and his fellow recruiters depended on the "private liberality" of the city to pay estimated costs of $10,000 for the recruitment of each regiment of

United States Colored Troops (USCT). In a circular for donations, Webster's committee emphasized the unequal wages of black and white soldiers and the lack of bounty payments to African American enlisted men in order to highlight the recruiting challenge ahead. Black soldiers would only make $10 per month minus a $3 clothing allowance—the terms allowed by the Militia Act of 1862. Yet Webster also encouraged potential donors by explaining that African American recruits would be "credited to the quota of Pennsylvania under the next draft." Webster hoped, moreover, that Pennsylvania would become "the centre of recruitment for the colored population" in states that continued to prevent their enlistment. Each black recruit would be an "unpurchased substitute for a white man." Not only would the recruitment and enlistment of black men save white men's blood; it would also save their treasure. White men's donations would spare drafted white men from having to spend money to hire a substitute under the provisions of the draft. Webster's committee showed white Northerners that the directives of the Emancipation Proclamation, which offered black men the opportunity to work for wages and serve in the military, and the Enrollment Act, which set state draft quotas and the parameters whereby drafted men could hire substitutes, could both help access black men's labor at low cost. Thus, federal legislation to win the war did justice to white men as well as black men.[40]

In the circular it addressed to "Men of Color" in the city on the same day, the Supervisory Committee could not so transparently advocate the sacrifice of black lives for white ones. Instead, it was patronizing. The government's policies about wages and bounties for black soldiers, the committee suggested to black men, were wrong, and it was only a matter of time before right-thinking politicians changed them in favor of equality. It was not appropriate that men who experienced "equality of hardship and of danger" would suffer "inequality of reward." But Webster and his committee also believed that those inequalities, if they were "rightly considered, should" give African American men "a fresh incentive." Freedom in the labor market was not free, according to the white committee members. Black men should face the economic injustices perpetrated against them with "alacrity" and "noble ambition," not for "love of gain" but rather for love of country. Here Webster showed that he had learned as much from Louisiana as Nelson had. "Another Port Hudson," he and the committee proclaimed, "will carry Congress by storm." By Webster's logic, if black Philadelphians spilled their blood just as black Louisianans had done and were continuing to do in front of the Confederates' Mississippi River redoubts, their "deeds may prove that the laborer was worthy of his hire." The two circulars, distributed to differ-

H. L. Stephens, "Victory!," *Album Varieties No. 3: The Slave in 1863* (Philadelphia: William A. Stephens, 1863). (The Library of Congress)

ent audiences, were knit together ideologically. The committee worked to convince white donors that black men's labor and sacrifice as soldiers could be had on the cheap while it assured prospective black soldiers that their bloody sacrifice would prove they could not be had on the cheap. Henry Louis Stephens clarified Webster's point for Northern consumers by publishing a set of twelve pictorial cards charting an enslaved man's progress from the violence and commodification of slavery to his climactic escape and service as a Union soldier. Stephens, once the artistic director for the now defunct *Vanity Fair*, discarded that paper's anti-emancipation stance in 1863 in favor of speculating in ephemera enshrining enslaved people's transition out of slavery. The penultimate card, labeled "VICTORY!," depicts a worker laboring for wages—a mortally wounded soldier swaddled in the American flag.[41]

On July 6, 1863, Republican congressman William Kelley joined abolitionists Frederick Douglass and Anna Dickinson on the speakers' platform at Philadelphia's National Hall to persuade black men to enlist in the Union army. Kelley asked the African American men in the audience if they were "content to spend your lives as boot-blacks, barbers, waiters, and in other pursuits little, if any better than servile or menial when the profession of arms ... invites you to acknowledge manhood, freedom and honor?" The cries of "[n]o, no" rang out in the hall, even though these were the only trades from which white craftsmen had not excluded the majority of African Americans. Douglass spoke to the realities of the Northern labor market. "Do you get as good wages now as white men get by staying out of the service? Don't you work for less every day than white men get? You know you do." Unequal wages should not keep black men from understanding that their "place is in the Union army," Douglass reasoned. Dickinson explained why she thought addressing those inequalities would have to wait. "Thirteen dollars a month and bounty are good; liberty is better. Ten dollars a month and no bounty are bad; slavery is worse. The two alternatives are put before you; you make your own future."[42]

Dickinson's words reflect, perhaps more than she would have been willing to admit, the challenges faced by white and black men who went for soldiers in the Union war. Most of these men believed in free labor's promise — the ability to "make your own future." They would have disagreed about whether thirteen dollars per month and bounty were "good" when they were not paid regularly. Liberty, they most assuredly would have concurred, was "better," but they would have been quick to assert that liberty was possible only with credit and capital. The wage of ten dollars per month and no bounty were bad, and slavery was worse. But the men to whom Dickinson spoke were not slaves. They were free men, living in a state that had passed an act of gradual emancipation during the Revolutionary War. They had been relegated by whites' racism to the worst-paying jobs in the city. Those who lacked capital knew that their futures were often made by those with it. Now Webster and his committee marshaled capital to shape their futures in a new way — perhaps toward manhood, freedom, and honor, but they would have to run the gauntlet to earn those plaudits.[43]

As summer turned to fall in 1863, two Union soldiers stationed on the islands surrounding Charleston, South Carolina, thought about the distinctions that Dickinson tried, and failed, to make. Henry Walker, who had briefly dreamed of sending a black woman to relieve his wife Persis of her burdens on rented property, now encouraged his wife to buy a "peass" of land with his bounty money and the pension for the death of their son Albert that they had finally obtained. "[T]ake your choise. . . . [I]t will make us a home. . . . I want to spend my dayes where you like the best." Independence — secured through the sacrifice and suffering of father and son, the bureaucracy navigated by husband and wife, and the capital that demanded the respect of selfish neighbors—seemed to be in the offing. But Persis must have written Henry that she needed more money to seal the deal. He did not have it. She would have to wait another couple of months, he told her in November, until the paymaster arrived again. Maybe by then their chance to buy the "plase" she wanted would be gone. Henry asked Persis and their girls to do "the best we can and we will do mutch a home is the thing you all want I may never se[e] you but . . . if I am so lucky as to get home . . . you . . . will make me a home to[o]."⁴⁴

On Morris Island, in September, Corporal James Henry Gooding of the Fifty-Fourth Massachusetts wrote to President Lincoln to complain of the discrepancy in wages between white and black soldiers. Gooding let Lincoln know that he and his comrades had been "Freemen by birth" and therefore their enlistment was not governed by "any 'contraband' act"—the Militia Act that set the wages of former slaves who worked in the military service. He chided the president, who had recently sent his Confederate counterpart Jefferson Davis a stern missive declaring that the "United States, knows, no distinction, in her Soldiers" and promising retaliation if black enlisted men were enslaved after their capture. If Lincoln really thought there was no distinction between white and black Union soldiers, "the main question is. Are we *Soldiers*, or are we LABOURERS[?]" Gooding insisted that, having "done a Soldiers Duty," African American men should "have a Soldiers pay"—the wages of "american SOLDIERS" rather than "menial hierlings." To Gooding, much as to every American soldier, being a wage earner was to be dependent, a hireling. The only thing that would make men more independent was to have access to more wages, more capital. Lincoln never replied to Gooding, but a few weeks before he had received the letter, Lincoln had written a memorandum that touched on why Northerners had gone to war and why conscription was the only answer when volunteer enlistment flagged. The nation needed to hire more men to do the killing and dying necessary to save the Union. That Union was based on the right of laborers to rise beyond the station of hireling, but the imperiled nation would have to spend its capital to hire worthy men and make them dependent on the state or else "relinquish the original object of the contest, together with all the blood and treasure already expended in the effort to secure it." The answer to Gooding's "main question" was yes, for soldiers and laborers were one and the same, vital capital that would save the Union.⁴⁵

5

THE DRAFT, POPULARIZED

EXECUTIVE MANSION

Washington, Sep. 29, 1863

Hon. Sec. of War

Sir:

The bearer of this, John A. Nelson, is represented to me, truly I believe, to be the first, and most efficient work day man, in raising colored troops in Louisiana. He wishes to engage in the same service, but wishes not to go back to that department. Can we not put him to it somewhere? Why not appoint him a Colonel and send him to Gen. [James] Barnes, at Norfolk? Please see & hear him.

Yours truly

A. Lincoln[1]

JOHN NELSON went to Washington with lies in his mouth and fraud in his past, and he did not mind telling the former and obscuring the latter when he met with the Republican president he despised. Banks had warned Lincoln in August of the "discreditable character" of the commanders of Louisiana's Native Guard regiments, but he had not named them. It may not have mattered to Lincoln. He needed men like Nelson. The draft riots that had occurred in New York and other cities in the summer of 1863 revealed the extent of Northern opposition to conscription, and Lincoln responded by encouraging the War Department and state governors to recruit black men as soldiers. Nelson's request for an appointment to a position in which he would recruit black troops coincided with a shakeup in leadership personnel in Tidewater Virginia. Lincoln noted in a memorandum a few days before he wrote his reference for Nelson that both Secretary of War Stanton and General John Foster, in command of the Department of Virginia and North Carolina, had decided concurrently but "independent of each other" to relieve General Henry Naglee of his command in Norfolk because he "was disinclined to raise colored troops." Stanton "wanted some one there who would take to it more heartily." Nelson may have gotten wind of this command restructuring and exploited it, or he may have simply arrived at a propitious time for his ambitions to be realized.[2]

Nelson appeared to be a useful man to Lincoln because of his reputed ability to get a job done. It is probable that Nelson praised himself in this regard, likely repeating the lie that he was the "first" recruiter of black soldiers in the Department of the Gulf. Benjamin Butler knew this to be untrue. He wrote to Stanton in October to introduce Colonel S. H. Stafford, formerly of the First Louisiana Native Guard, and explained that Stafford was the first colonel Butler appointed to command black troops in Louisiana. Butler also sought to counter rumors that Stafford had "ever spoken disrespectfully of the President," a charge levied at Nelson too. Nelson had corresponded with Butler in the time since he left Louisiana, because Butler was the one who "represented" his abilities to Lincoln. That letter of introduction is not extant, but its language must have repeated what Butler had said in the letter justifying Nelson's transfer from the Ninth Connecticut to the Eastern Bay State Regiment. Then, he had called the former sparring master "efficient." Lincoln's gloss on Butler's reference may seem tepid: "work day" is not a glowing compliment. Yet Lincoln, dedicated to the proposition that saving the Union depended on increasing the manpower available to the nation's armed forces, knew that beggars could not be choosers. Recruiters were absolutely necessary, and their character flaws and even opposition to the administration could be overlooked in light of the higher object of quickly marshaling recruits for service.[3]

Stanton approved Lincoln's request, named Nelson colonel of the brand new Tenth USCT, and ordered him to recruit his regiment from the population of African American men living along the James and York Rivers and on Virginia's Eastern Shore. This was just what Republicans and abolitionists thought the War Department should do. "Everybody wants to know why we do not raise more Black soldiers," Massachusetts senator and author of the Enrollment Act Henry Wilson told Lincoln on October 25, 1863. Wilson believed the answer was logistical. "If an organizer like [Benjamin] Butler, [John Murray] Forbes an eminent business man of Boston or some other good organizer had committed to him . . . this great work and had full power to act he could in the border states and in the conquered portions of the rebel states raise men with great rapidity—*fill our armies and distroy slavery*.... I intended that the conscription act should include colored men *free and slave* but I do not see that they are enrolled in the Slave states." On November 2, Lincoln ordered Butler to replace Foster as commander of the Department of Virginia and North Carolina. Butler knew, he had told Salmon Chase in October, that Lincoln's latest draft call for 300,000 more soldiers would "bring no men by volunteering." The only way to get the men requested was through conscription, Butler believed, but the draft "must be *popularized*," he cryptically told Chase. At that juncture, before his reappointment to command at Fort Monroe, Butler told Chase in a more playful tone, "I have determined to offer no more advice where it is not asked or desired." On November 5, Thomas Webster wrote to Lincoln from Philadelphia with his ideas about how to give black men "suitable encouragement" to enlist—eliminate "the inequality of pay and bounty" between white and black troops and explicitly include black men as part of the latest draft call. Doing so would reward African American men worthy of their hire, do justice to white draftees, and ensure that the war for Union would come "to a prosperous end." Butler's ideas about how to popularize certain types of coercion would unfold in the coming weeks on the Virginia coast as he and his subordinates defined the parameters of wage labor in their military department. That was a process dependent on the intersecting imperatives of coercion and consent operating within the army. The ways officers, recruiters, and soldiers experienced and understood wage labor during the war was through the filter of force, obligation, *and* free will. Workday men such as Butler, Nelson, and Webster sought access to the labor of other men and tried to harness them to the nation's—and perhaps their personal—benefit. These men did so in different ways, and they came into conflict with each other because they disagreed about the legitimate balance of consent and coercion in a wage labor economy.[4]

John Nelson spared no time in gilding his reputation for efficiency. His first move was to obtain the paper necessary to legitimate his recruiting efforts—printed blanks on which he and the officers he delegated would keep track of enlistments, troop musters, and the credits due to and debts owed by soldiers. He needed recruiters, so he asked the adjutant general's office in Washington to send him white officers to command recruitment parties and, eventually, the companies of men they recruited. He requested that Colonel

John Holman, the commander of the First USCT, a regiment already stationed in Norfolk, let him borrow several "intelligent non-commissioned officers" to recruit men for the Tenth USCT. Nelson assumed, as he had done when engineering the resignations of black officers in the Third Louisiana Native Guard, that most black men were not intelligent.[5]

Nelson was a font of ideas about how to recruit men, reminding his superiors of "my experience in the Department of the Gulf" to lend weight to his suggestions. He advocated a "new" policy of paying recruits one month's salary up front as a way to entice them to join. In doing so, he showed that he had learned from Butler, who had suggested in the first autumn of the war that this policy would be a boon to recruiting. The policy was new only in the sense that it would now apply to black recruits, even as the bounties for white men had risen to several hundreds of dollars, depending on the state where they resided. Nelson asked for permission to clothe his new recruits in Zouave uniforms in order to inspire enlistment from men whom he presumed would want to wear the natty, imposing getup modeled on uniforms worn by French soldiers. Later regimental returns show that the request was at least partially honored by the War Department — 113 Zouave uniforms were in the regiment's possession early in 1864. Nelson knew that recruits could not be obtained by stylish garments alone. He also realized that he was recruiting within a labor market in which men had other options. In fact, they came to the army from other jobs, such as working on Union fortifications at Fort Monroe. Nelson intervened to help his new recruits obtain wages owed to them for their labor on those earthworks prior to enlisting. He also sought to put the hustle in the army paymaster's step. Until they were paid, Nelson explained, his recruits could not buy the necessities of camp life. The tin cups and plates, not to mention drink and food to supplement meager rations, were out of reach without the paymaster's intervention. Nelson proved himself cognizant of the challenges that soldiers faced in their quest to make sure that they and their families survived.[6]

Nelson also sought to make recruiting and labor management more efficient by advocating to his superiors a policy of organizing men living on government farms and working in government departments into military companies that would become part of his new regiment. His Third Louisiana Native Guard had done work on sugar plantations as well as fatigue and fighting work as soldiers, and he thought his experience in Louisiana showed that "the work in the several Departments" under this method of organization "would be done with less expense to the Government and with at least half the number of men, because 3 efficient Officers would at all times be with every one hundred men to hurry forward & facilitate the work while the men would be taken up regularly on the Company muster rolls." Nelson proposed that, by doing duty as recruiters, officers, and farm overseers simultaneously, captains in his regiment would ensure that agricultural production and military labor continued under military discipline, to the benefit of the various departments of the army as well as the economic and social order. Nelson evidently thought that enlisted men, if paid in advance and regularly, would consent to do these various forms of labor. By early November, one month after he took command, Nelson had filled six companies of the Tenth USCT with four hundred men.[7]

General Butler, on taking command in the Department of Virginia and North Carolina, formulated his own ideas and policies about labor. Lincoln's Emancipation Proclamation had permitted slavery to continue in places like the Tidewater that were occupied by the Union army. Yet Butler stipulated that, because nearly all white residents of Norfolk and Portsmouth were disloyal to the United States, his subordinates should "cease and wholly refrain from interfering with the personal liberty of anybody upon the ground of slavery or involuntary servitude, until further orders." Butler mocked a white citizen of Norfolk for fearing that African Americans would "make war with the helpless [white] women and children" residing in the city by replying, "If you do not die until the negroes hurt you, if you behave yourself, you will live forever." In Butler's opinion, emancipation would not lead to anarchy. He would make sure of it.[8]

Destroying slavery was a military necessity for the Union, and emancipation took the shape it did because of the presence and movement of its armies. Likewise, military necessity and the presence and authority of armed Union soldiers and their commanders shaped the contours of wage labor. While Butler's contraband policy had shifted black laborers from work in Confederate camps to work in Union camps, the Emancipation Proclamation complicated military operations for Northern commanders. If black camp laborers signed up to fight, who would do the crucial work of digging trenches, constructing fortifications, cooking, and washing on which the army also depended? Butler and members of his staff began to answer this question in November 1863. As Butler was settling into his new command position, Captain Charles Wilder, the department's assistant quartermaster in charge of providing subsistence to African Americans on government farms, drafted a memorandum for Butler's perusal. Wilder suggested that if the army's black laborers enlisted to fight, they should be reassigned to their laboring posts until other workers could be found to replace them. The

"African laborers and artisans in Government employ," he proposed, would now be "consigned to the charge" of new officials—"Superintendents and Overseers of Contrabands"—who would "issue them ... in numbers suited to the need" to do work for other military officials "requiring help." Under no circumstances were they to be paid more than black soldiers were. Superintendents would be labor agents within the military, taking black men and distributing them to other officials for employment where they were needed. African American men would be, according to this plan, both soldiers and laborers. This proposal overlapped with Nelson's and confirmed that Corporal Gooding's main question to President Lincoln could only be answered in the affirmative.[9]

On December 5, Butler issued General Order 46 to resolve the conundrums posed by the Emancipation Proclamation, military necessity, and wage labor relations in the Tidewater. He broke with his subordinates' proposals, privileging the government's need for soldiers over the army's and the local economy's need for laborers. He reminded the men of his command and a national audience of readers that the "recruitment of colored soldiers has become the settled purpose of the government." He argued that the relationship between African Americans and the government would be shaped by "new obligations" each owed to the other. Butler framed freedom in terms of wage labor's supposed harmony of interests, the symbiotic support system between capital and labor that would replace the bonds between master and slave. Before issuing the order, Butler got permission from the War Department to give black soldiers a ten-dollar bounty to spur their enlistment for three years or the duration of the war. Earlier in the conflict, Butler had condemned John Andrew for giving bounties because he believed that they encouraged unsatisfactory recruits to enlist. His change of heart resulted from his acknowledgment that white soldiers received bounty payments from local, state, and federal governments as well as financial assistance from aid societies to support their wives and children. Butler's order stipulated that a new bureaucrat, the Superintendent of Negro Affairs, would provide "suitable subsistence" to recruits' wives and children while they remained soldiers and, if soldiers died while under arms, for a period of six months after their deaths.[10]

Wages for black soldiers were set, as Butler noted disapprovingly, at ten dollars per month. He hoped that the government would soon give equal wages to black and white soldiers "as an act of justice." Butler also considered the low wage for black soldiers to be problematic in another way. It "discouraged" enlistment because there were more remunerative occupations within the department that black men could pursue. Butler lamented that "the Government is competing against itself" for black men's labor. Before Congress could provide justice to black soldiers, Butler fixed limits on the wage labor market, prohibiting anyone in his command from hiring black men at a rate higher than ten dollars per month with a ration (the rate earned by a soldier) or fifteen dollars per month without a ration. Butler also forced black men between the ages of eighteen and forty-five who were working as agricultural laborers under the auspices of the government to submit to a medical examination with an army surgeon and receive a "certificate of disability or ability" in return. Artisans whose special skills were absolutely necessary to the government's operations would be exempt from these wage limits and medical examinations. While Nelson and Wilder suggested that African American laborers could be of multiple uses to the government, the army, and the agricultural economy, Butler contended that "[t]he best use during the war for an able-bodied colored man, as well for himself as for the country, is to be a soldier." Through the provisions of General Order 46, Butler created the circumstances in which black men would be funneled by low wage rates toward soldiering, and he would know exactly who among them was healthy enough to enlist. Butler had determined how to serve his own labor needs without the acquiescence of African American men or other employers who offered better wages. His conception of the harmony of interests worked mainly to benefit the army's interest, justified by the doctrine of military necessity. Competition, an important aspect of free labor, would be limited when it seemed to benefit workers or other employers.[11]

The "new rights" Butler believed black men had "acquired" during the war were ones he was now circumscribing. In fact, these rights could only be understood in light of the "new obligations" that Butler "imposed upon them." They were the obligations of free labor. "Political freedom rightly defined," Butler explained, was not the enjoyment of civil rights. It was the "liberty to work." Laborers should "be protected in the full enjoyment of the fruits of labor" to the extent that it did not infringe on the government's ability to hire soldiers. No able-bodied person should be allowed to avoid work and benefit from "the fruits of another's labor." African Americans in the department without jobs, much like poor Northerners accused of idleness during the early Republic, would be forced to work. Under Butler's authority, they would dig fortifications.[12]

Butler understood how his efforts to channel African Americans toward military service — a particular type of productive labor — might suggest he favored the indiscriminate use of force. Nothing could be further from the truth, he assured his audience inside and outside his department. He had heard of recent examples of the impressment of black laborers in the department "for private use," and that was out of bounds. The distinction between slavery and free labor, according to Butler's way of thinking, was that "Negroes have rights so long as they fulfill their duties." They could only be impressed to labor for the army in cases of urgent "military necessity." What the nature of those future cases might be, Butler was reluctant to say. The state of war was the ultimate cover for army officers to shape wage labor to suit them. The same argument that Butler had made to justify his seizure of enslaved "contraband of war" from the secessionist enemy could be repurposed to limit wage laborers' choices. Whether the Union obtained a "soldier or a producer"—and Butler considered these types interchangeable—the process of curtailing African Americans' rights under the coercive rubric of obligation was justifiable because it weakened the Confederacy.[13]

Butler's General Order 46 provoked both heated condemnation and exuberant praise. The opposition to the order came principally from government employers of African American laborers, who heard rumors that Captain Wilder was telling their black workers that they could either choose to enlist or be drafted. Seaforth Stewart, the engineer at Fort Monroe in charge of employing black workers there, found it challenging to hire and maintain a reliable workforce at the fort. He had tried "Irish & German laborers of a very inferior class," and a combination of "the worst laborers at this work"— also evidently white men—had "compelled" a strike in 1862 to increase wages. Stewart dismissed both sets of workers and hired black laborers at "[w]ages less than those given to white laborers" but high enough "to enable an industrious person to support himself & family & not enough to encourage one not accustomed to the use of much money to any wasteful expenditure, or to indulge in intervals of idleness." He believed the African American laborers had proven themselves "industrious, fair workmen, docile, more orderly & cleanly than the white laborers, and work has progressed far more satisfactorily to all concerned and with less cost to Government than heretofore." Competition in the labor market should benefit employers, Stewart believed. When workers tried to take advantage of labor shortages in their locale, they should be fired and replaced by workers who would work for less. Those workers should be obligated to take care of their families' subsistence needs out of wages kept at levels that would ensure persistent labor.[14]

Butler's General Order 46 was objectionable to Stewart because, by directing African Americans toward soldiering, it infringed on his rights as an employer. He gestured toward the supposed promise of free labor when he complained to his superiors that Butler should not "prevent the free negroes from learning as rapidly as possible to take care of themselves & families and prevent emulation by fixing a certain rate of pay as the highest which they shall receive, whether they develop capabilities of earning twice that amount or not." Stewart cared little about free labor's promise for workers. He clearly did not mind paying them low wages. He did believe that he had a "right to employ" African Americans to work at the fort and warned superiors that Butler's plan "would require a cessation of work on all the fortifications in this vicinity." When Stanton informed Butler that the Engineer Department would be exempt from General Order 46, its author responded indignantly. "Immediately upon the issue of my Order," Butler told Stanton, "almost every Officer of the Staff in this Department, who had favorite negro laborers in his employ at very high rates of wages, became alarmed and seemed determined to keep them." He lashed out at the extravagance of those wages and the excessive numbers of black laborers employed in the quartermaster's department, both of which constituted wasteful government expenditures. "Of course you cannot desire that the Engineer Officers of the Department should pay more for labor than the price at which it can be procured," needled Butler. "[A]t the present time there is a great surplus of colored labor which can be procured at $10 per month and rations," he wrote, obscuring the fact that he had set those wages in General Order 46. If another government employer of "skilled" black artisans wished to pay higher wages at a level "which his conscience will permit," Butler pointed out that his order allowed him to do so. Butler's conscience was clean because his employment of African Americans would be governed by the market — a market of his own creation.[15]

General Order 46 became part of national political debate, and Butler did not mind that at all. President Lincoln had, three days after the publication of Butler's order, issued a preliminary proclamation of amnesty to white Southerners and a proposal for the reconstruction of Southern states to speed their reincorporation into the Union. Radical Republicans and abolitionists thought his plan was too lenient to Confederates, since it offered citizenship to white men who took loyalty oaths and readmission to the Union for states if 10 percent of the electorate did so. Lincoln also stated that, while reconstructed states' legislatures should "recognize and declare" African Americans' "permanent freedom," those states could pass laws to regulate "their present condition as a laboring, landless, and homeless class." Butler forwarded copies of his order to abolitionists, soliciting their judgment as to whether "it will be a frame work around which free colored labor may be organized in the future." Butler may have hoped that Republican politicians and abolitionists would find in General Order 46 a reconstruction plan that would make him a rival to Lincoln for the Republican presidential nomination. Butler's order was certainly superior to Lincoln's proposal in the minds of many radicals because it presented a clear path to free labor for African Americans transitioning from slavery. Butler believed, he told the abolitionist Wendell Phillips in an insubordinate letter marked "private," that the president's vague proposal gave white Southerners a path to power and "put the negro, his liberty, his future, into the hands of the Supreme Court." Phillips agreed that Lincoln's amnesty plan "leaves the large landed proprietors of the South still to domineer over its politics, and make the negro's freedom a mere sham. Until a large share of those estates are divided, the aristocracy is not destroyed, neither is any *fair* chance given for the development of a system of free labor." Phillips did not know that Butler's plan superseded the proposals of Wilder and Nelson that would have deployed African Americans' labor both on confiscated farms and in the military. If landed property was the only real path to independence, settlement on the subdivided plantations of the Tidewater might have been a vital step toward achieving that goal.[16]

In the wage labor economy he created in the Tidewater, devoid of competition, Butler was quick to explain in General Order 46 that certain forms of coercion—the impressment of black men into the military, for instance— were prohibited. Yet for black Southerners, coercion was always lurking in the process of emancipation. Almost as soon as Butler had issued his order, he started to receive letters from subordinate commanders and Northern missionaries in his department about accusations concerning the illegal impressment of African American men into the army. On December 11, Butler asked Lieutenant Colonel J. B. Kinsman, the man he had named the Superintendent of Negro Affairs, to investigate the recruiting practices of one man in particular—Colonel John Nelson of the Tenth USCT.[17]

One day after Butler ordered the investigation, Kinsman responded to his commanding general with bombshell revelations. Nelson had a "company of Zouaves" who marauded about urban and rural locations in the Tidewater in search of men to impress into his regiment. The Zouave uniforms that might inspire men to bravery on the battlefield and strike fear into the hearts of enemies were actually part of Nelson's scheme to force black men, uneasily situated on a continuum between slavery and independence, to serve in the Union army. Nelson's gang rowed boats to the "oyster rock" off Craney Island, Nelson's headquarters in the Elizabeth River and, until recently, the location of a "contraband" camp. Zouaves strode onto farms near Yorktown and charged down the streets and onto wharves in Norfolk to get their men. Kinsman was fearful that "volunteering . . . will be entirely discouraged in this section of the Country" if the press gang was not stopped. Kinsman had uncovered damning evidence that Butler had competitors in shaping wage labor in the Tidewater, men who sought to manipulate the language of consent and test the limits of coercion in order to accomplish the goal of recruitment that Butler deemed so crucial. Of course, Butler had narrowed the definition of "volunteering" in General Order 46 by limiting workers' choices in his department, but Kinsman's response to Butler was a means of validating one form of coercion while outlawing another. Butler decided that further investigation was necessary, and Kinsman got to work.[18]

Black women were among the first to testify about the danger of Nelson's press gang. Just as Persis Walker and other white Northern women had done, they framed the problem of recruitment as a problem of household economy. Jane Wallis told a representative of the American Missionary Association that soldiers had "taken" her husband James, a "shoo make[r] by trade," away from his work and inducted him into the army "against his will." She understood soldiering was hard work, and she was convinced that her husband, "verry delicate, and in bad health," was "not competent to bee A Soldier." His impressment would also imperil her and the couple's children. Already in ill health, they would simply try to "[g]et along the best we can." Phillis Bess sought General Butler's assistance in getting her husband Sam back from the press gang. He had been taken while oystering even though "he did not want to enlist." He had already presented himself for induction into the army and was "rejected by [the] examining Sergeant." Now she was left in despair at the considerable challenge of raising eight children without his support. She enumerated her needs—seven dollars per month in house rent, clothing for her little ones, "food and wood & everything"—and calculated that she could not do it alone, praying that "Gen Butler will send him back." It is clear that these women were not looking for government subsistence. They sought their households' independence. Phillis Bess knew money and knew it was the source of autonomy. Both Butler's order modulating the wage labor economy to funnel men into the army and the coercive measures taken by Nelson's Zouaves cut against African Americans' notion of what freedom meant.[19]

The press gang, it is clear from the testimony of black men, did something akin to what Butler did. It intervened in a wage labor economy taking shape in an area in which slaveholders' rights to property were both exempted by the Emancipation Proclamation and made tenuous by Union occupation. David Owens, who testified to an investigator in Portsmouth that he employed young men "hauling wood," spoke to the ways the gang's orders came into conflict with those of employers. When the Zouaves "ordered" Abram Nash, a fifteen-year-old employed by Owens, to "halt," Owens ordered Nash "to drive up to the Woodpile." In a figurative tug-of-war over Nash, Owens "ordered him to move along," and soldiers told him to "stop." It mattered to Owens that Nash was his employee. He "paid his mother" for his services. The soldiers believed their demands had precedence, and they finally seized Nash, whom Owens claimed had "never come back." The process of emancipation emboldened soldiers to take slaves from slaveholders. These Zouaves also felt no compunction in taking wage workers away from their employers to satisfy their labor needs. The uncertainties about which labor system was in force opened up the possibility that men's consent could be compromised, that coercion might be permissible.[20]

America Nash, probably Abram's older brother, told an investigator that the press gang "asked me if I wanted to enlist." When he forthrightly told them no, they changed their tack: "[T]hey asked me if I had'nt better go, than to be made to go," making coercion seem like a decision that he had to make. Nash apparently took the question to mean that a draft call would necessitate his service at a later date. He responded, "O yes, I don't intend to be made to go. when I am obliged to go I shall enlist." The Zouaves meant for him to go right now: "[T]hey said, come along then and see the Lieutenant." They explained that "we are ordered to take all men that are not in the employ of the Goverment," showing the ways Nelson's recruiters evoked the spirit of Butler's General Order 46 through a clever and willful misreading that could be used to justify their actions. Nash accompanied the gang to a wharf, where he encountered the aforementioned lieutenant, drunk. Nash showed "bills" to a sober sergeant on duty that identified him as a self-employed coal hauler. The sergeant tried to confiscate them, but Nash held them tight, understanding their power to act as his freedom papers. He and the sergeant disagreed about which obligations, the ones he supposedly owed to the press gang or the ones he owed by contract to his customers, mattered more. America Nash's independence was in the balance, and he had to act of his own volition to keep it. He walked into a store on the wharf "as though I would get a cigar" and walked out the back door to evade his captors.[21]

Many of the men coerced to serve as soldiers in the Tenth USCT were working on government farms harvesting corn for white overseers, but as the testimony recorded by Kinsman's clerks suggests, some were working for themselves. They dug at oyster beds to earn support for their families. They owned shops and possessed drays and boats that helped them transact business. In fact, some of them pleaded with the Zouaves for time to settle their commercial affairs before they came to the recruiting office. "I am not prepared there is all my crop to be got in and all I have would be destroyed," John Banks informed the soldiers who came for him. These men may have been engaged in humble occupations for which Union commanders did not recognize skill, but they were clearly positions through which African American men were establishing livelihoods that would benefit them and their families. Humble beginnings were where men started the race of life, said the president of the United States. The extent to which the progress of war had provided these men opportunities to realize their aspirations is unclear—some had been free before the war began, and many were merely eking out a bare subsistence. Yet others had seized the chance that the presence of the Union army and the unsettling of slavery in the Tidewater had given them to claim independence.[22]

The Zouaves were the instruments Nelson used to wrest that independence away. The coercions of the past helped them succeed in their work. The existence of a pass system, a holdover from the era of slavery in which free African Americans had to carry papers proving their legal status, created the circumstances for a clever ruse. The Zouaves asked to see the passes on the spot or told black men that they were required to show them to Nelson at headquarters on Craney Island. Nelson's thugs wanted their coercion to be shrouded in the guise of consent. They asked men if they wanted to enlist before they prodded them "at the point of the bayonet" into a waiting boat that would take them to a recruiting office, a surgeon's exam, and induction into the Tenth. If the gang thought the aura of consent should be admired, even in the breach, black men believed that their consent mattered. They believed that signing documents was a momentous event. Putting their "hand to the Pen" or raising their hand were declarative actions that free men performed. They seemed to acknowledge this even while they were also quick to explain that they did not know what they were signing. They sometimes engaged in intense negotiations about consent with people they knew. Moses Reddick, a black resident of Portsmouth, was on sick leave after having served eighteen months in some capacity with the army when he was confronted by a Zouave named John Smith. Reddick told Smith he wanted to rejoin the army on his own terms: "I said John I dont want no man to 'press me, when I get well I am going into the Army any how." Smith believed that neither Reddick's consent nor his health mattered. "I don't care a d__n you have got to go again," he retorted. "I will blow your brains out," Smith told Reddick before the latter, claiming he needed to grab a coat from his house, "made my escape by jumping out a back window."²³

It was hard for most African American men to give the Zouaves the slip, because the boundary between consent and coercion was unclear. George Colden, who was impressed into Company E of the Tenth USCT, admitted under oath that he never "object[ed] to being a soldier." Yet when asked by his interlocutors what his "opinion" of being a soldier was, he explained "My opinion is; as long as it is, it must be so. I think I was obliged to be a soldier." To some extent, this sense of obligation percolated through American culture. It was the obligation of citizenship. White Northerners had come to understand that black Southerners represented the vast majority of Southerners loyal to the Union. Loyal men often considered themselves obliged to serve and sacrifice for their country. One impressed soldier, Beverly Smith, knew that signing enlistment papers meant "[t]o fight for my Country" in order to achieve the aims of the war for Union. In the minds of white Northerners, though, black Southerners' loyalty did not justify claims to citizenship. That fuzziness was captured in the testimony of impressed men. Were their feelings of obligation coming from autonomous choice or the threat of force? The men called before Kinsman — beset by their own feelings and the coercive tactics of the Zouaves — blurred the boundaries between these two sources of obligation. It was not clear to them, in the months after the Emancipation Proclamation gave them the right to serve and the Enrollment Act created a federal draft that forced chosen men to serve, what their obligations were. George Colden's feelings of resignation to his fate would prove fatal. He died on picket duty at Petersburg in June 1864.²⁴

In December 1863, forty-two-year-old William Carney was gathering oysters in the Elizabeth River when soldiers informed him that he would, under orders from Colonel Nelson, have to report to Craney Island to show his pass that allowed him to do so. When Carney's boat touched the island's dock, there stood Colonel Nelson, leering at him. "[Y]ou will do for a soldier," Nelson said. Carney disagreed, although he was willing to submit to an examination by an army doctor. When the doctor determined he was fit to serve, Carney refused to be mustered in. Nelson ordered Carney and thirteen other recalcitrant men to the guardhouse and forced each of them to "tote" a thirty-two-pound cannonball for some nine hours. Carney heard "some gentlemen," perhaps junior officers, tell Nelson that if Carney "dont choose to swear you cant make him," but Nelson replied, "[B]y the time I put him in the guard house and make him go to ball he will be willing enough."[25]

That cannonball, seeming to grow heavier with each passing hour, broke Carney's resistance. The next morning, he raised his right hand, signed an "X" in place of his name, and was mustered into the Tenth USCT. The punishment he was made to endure vexed him. "It hurt me bad thinking I had been a slave all my life and it was ignorant and foolish to go against the government when the government was going for me. I thought it was wrong for me to go against the government and I thought it was hard for me to tote the ball. And I didn't know how to get at it." Carney felt obligated to serve a nation dedicated to ending slavery, but he could not square the Union's support for emancipation with Nelson's coercive treatment. While held in the guardhouse, he had "learned a good deal from the men of my own ... Colour" about military service, "which caused me to be more satisfied," he later acknowledged. When he saw Colonel Nelson again, though, he said he had enlisted because he feared continued "persecution" if he did not. He still believed he was not healthy enough to serve. All things considered, though, he "told the Colonel I would try to do the best I could and I will die trying to do the best I can."[26]

In the printed "Final Statement" that ends Carney's compiled service record, his captain George Torrey filled in the blanks to explain that Carney was "entitled to a discharge by reason of Death" from pneumonia at a hospital in City Point, Virginia, in March 1865. Despite Butler's order offering a ten-dollar bounty to black men who enlisted, Carney's service record does not show that he received it. Captain Torrey was not above nickeling and diming his soldier beyond the grave. He noted that Carney owed twenty cents for lost ordnance and another $1.10 for lost "equipage." Like many of his comrades, he owed the sutler a few bucks. Dead for his country, Carney was still in arrears. Defined by coercion as much as his freedom to choose, Carney's experience illuminates the contradictions inherent in free labor. His widow Mary would face a prolonged struggle to obtain a pension for William's service. She tried to prove that they were married by calling women who had known her for twenty years to vouch for the fact of their "cohabitation" after January 1860, even though as enslaved people their marriage had no legal basis. The clerk of court who examined her case flagged her previous marriage to a man by the name of Meredith (even though this marriage had no legal backing either), calling her witnesses back to proclaim her "high character for truth and virtue." After being dragged through the proverbial mud in public by a white bureaucrat, she finally obtained a monthly pension of eight dollars backdated to the death of her husband.[27]

Some observers, such as Nelson's superior officer General Edward Wild, did not initially think Nelson's recruitment practices were improper. He found little evidence to support the claims of black residents that their husbands were being impressed into the army. Only on one occasion, Wild told Kinsman, did Nelson overstep his authority. After calling in "the boats of the oystering fleet lying off Craney Island," Nelson "canvassed them strongly for recruits" but did not coerce men to join. Wild perhaps based his determination on the evidence that some of the impressed men themselves thought they were acting of their own volition when they decided to follow the press gang to Nelson's post. Soldiering may have been the best occupation available to some of these men, either because competition for jobs had become more intense or because Butler's General Order 46 had reduced options to labor at higher wages. Some of the coercion, therefore, was coming from pressures in the market. Mills Benton, one of the men testifying to Kinsman, explained that he was willing to join the Tenth just as soon as he could obtain the wages owed to him for "working on the fortifications." The impressed men were evidently considering all of their choices, limited though they may have been. Despite his efforts to curtail disobedience, Nelson questioned other men's testimony against him by claiming that they had not put up any resistance to enlisting at the time they "touched the pen." These ideas harked back to the founding ideals of the nation, for they linked independence to a person's willingness to resist in order to retain it. Therefore, black enlisted men who did not resist coercion, like slaves who did not resist their enslavement, were not suited for freedom. Nelson talked out of both sides of his mouth, punishing men for not doing his bidding and criticizing them for not defying his coercive measures.[28]

Some federal officers in the Tidewater were dismayed by Nelson's recruiting methods. Colonel John Holman of the First USCT claimed to have become aware of Nelson's impressment scheme on November 26, probably because the two colonels were fighting over a recruit. In October, Henry Williams had climbed into a boat on the Appomattox River and set sail for Portsmouth. He was "a runaway," he later testified, sailing from slavery in Petersburg to reunite with his parents. On the third night after he began his journey, strong winds and currents forced him to make landfall at Craney Island, just a few miles from his destination. In the dark, he "saw a light and called" out to it, only to be seized by a platoon of black soldiers belonging to the Tenth USCT. The next morning, he requested that the white officer of the guard give him permission to proceed. He refused, telling Williams he would have to await the decision of the regiment's commander, currently away from the post. When Colonel Nelson arrived a few days later, "[h]e asked me to stay until I got a uniform." He "said he wanted to make a soldier of me." The Civil War had loosened slavery's coercions to enable Williams's escape. It provided an opportunity to seize choices and autonomy. The war produced other coercions that anchored him in a place so close to—and so far from—home and greater independence. But Williams did have a choice to make. He made it clear to Kinsman that he had not consented to join the Tenth. Nevertheless, he was given "shoes and overcoat" and dragooned into serving in Nelson's press gang to "recruit"—the word was Williams's—for the Tenth USCT, which included men from Nelson's regiment as well as a "Squad of the 1st" USCT, Holman's outfit. Williams came to like the men of the First, and they him. A corporal in that regiment persuaded his captain to enlist Williams after the former slave proclaimed his "desire" to join the First and professed to have been forced against his will to join the Tenth. Nelson's response to Holman was uncompromising. Williams was a "deserter" from his regiment, and he had the enlistment documents and clothing account to prove it. He accused Holman's men of "enticing" Williams to leave and demanded that Holman return him to Craney Island. General Wild later explained that Holman "courteously gave up the man without dispute." Holman then heard Williams's story and thought the "enlistment paper has rather a bogus look." The dates on which Williams supposedly volunteered and enlisted were some fifty days apart. That showed "unfair play" in Wild's estimation, despite his earlier assertion to Kinsman that Nelson had done little wrong. Nelson's request for blanks at the time of his mustering in as colonel was pro forma, but those pieces of paper could be manipulated for his purposes. Making men sign papers that they could not read, and then using them to keep recruits in the regiment, was Nelson's modus operandi. It helped him compete with others who sought access to black men's labor. Williams remained with the Tenth USCT as a cook, and in August 1864 he was accidentally shot and killed in the regiment's camp outside of Petersburg, the city in which he had been enslaved.[29]

The testimony concerning the case of John Nelson illustrates the ways African American men negotiated the end of slavery, heroically struggling against the regulations of a new regime, press gangs, and military officers who came into conflict with each other about the parameters of the wage labor economy that would replace slavery. As the coercions of slavery phased into the subtle coercions of military passes, labor for wages, and a culture of obligation to the Union and its war, black Southerners made assertions about consent to confront the coercion of soldiers putting bayonets at their backs and to navigate the authority of a military tribunal that inquired about their free will.[30]

After Kinsman's investigation had run its course, Butler found Nelson guilty of impressing soldiers into his regiment and dismissed him from the service, "subject to the approval of the President." Nelson wrote to Lincoln to intercede, and the latter did so in a letter to Butler on January 14, 1864, explaining that "Col. Nelson insists so earnestly that he had not, at any time, authorized, or knowingly permitted the impressment of negro recruits into his regiment, and is so well sustained in his character generally." He refused to approve Butler's action without a "fuller investigation of the facts." Butler held Nelson over for that examination in the Hygeia Hotel, next to Fort Monroe at Old Point Comfort. Before the war, the hotel had been a place of refuge for the elite to enjoy the cool ocean breezes in the hot summer and for runaway slaves like Charles Gilbert, who hid near its cistern while hoping to make his escape on ocean currents. Now it was a ruined hulk shorn of its antebellum splendor, ordered destroyed by Secretary of War Stanton to widen the range of fire for Fort Monroe's artillery. From this inhospitable abode, Nelson wrote to Lincoln once again to help him obtain an early release from his "confinement." He protested his "innocence" of the charges levied against him and accused Butler of changing the rules for determining who among the officer corps would serve on a board of examination in his case. He disavowed any "egotism," but reiterated that he had agreed to command African American troops "the earliest of any" and adopted a trope that Butler and Lincoln had both used to describe him. "I can safely assert that the problem of Negro soldiers efficiency, would not have been solved at Port Hudson, but for myself." He had treated his men with "careful kindness and unresting solicitude" in Louisiana, and he was wounded by the "absurdly preposterous" charge "of cruelty to the negro." He asked Lincoln to shield him from this "persecution."[31]

It was a letter that might have obtained further clemency from the president had not Butler and his board of examination determined that Nelson did not write it. The author was Jared Thompson, formerly a lieutenant in Company K of the Thirteenth Connecticut, a regiment that had been part of Butler's 1862 expedition to the Gulf, where he must have befriended Nelson. Soon after Butler had been reappointed to head the Department of Virginia and North Carolina, Thompson wrote to ask permission to "raise a regiment" of black soldiers. Butler seems to have ignored this request. Thompson came to Nelson "flat broke" and "anxious to go to Washington" to seek a situation for himself. Nelson "lent" him some money to pay his way and to assist him with letter writing and penmanship skills. Thompson wrote the letter and signed it with Nelson's name. He delivered it personally to Lincoln and asked for a speedy resolution of Nelson's case. Thompson also tried to exact revenge on Butler, spreading rumors that Lincoln had declared in their meeting that "General Butler is not fit to have a command" and that he only returned him to a position of authority after "the people at the North held public meetings asking me to do so." Butler was so disturbed by the publicity of the declarations that he had the tribunal investigating Nelson take Thompson's deposition under oath while he asked Lincoln for clarification that he still "possessed the confidence of the President." The discovery of the letter's authorship spelled doom for Nelson. Thompson's letter not only undermined Butler's authority and the army's chain of command; it also brought Nelson's education into question. The board of examination convened to examine Nelson was presided over by Alonzo Draper, colonel of the Thirty-Sixth USCT and leader of the 1860 shoemaker's strike in New England, and focused on Nelson's "capacity, qualifications, propriety of conduct, and efficiency" as well as the impressment charges. This board, made up of Nelson's peers in command of black soldiers, found him "of very limited general education" and "grossly deficient in his knowledge of tactics and regulations." His actions—contacting the president outside of military channels and having Thompson write and sign a letter on his behalf—were deemed "improper." Even his vaunted reputation for efficiency was brought into question by the impressment scandal, for which the board ruled him "grossly and culpably negligent." For all of these reasons, Nelson was "not qualified for his position as Colonel" and was "ordered to be mustered out of the service."[32]

In a response Draper's board allowed him to make before the verdict was read, Nelson rebutted the charges against him. He felt "embarrassed" by the results of his educational examination, claiming he had not been able to "read up, and become thoroughly conversant" with the material on which he was questioned. The black officers of the Third Louisiana Native Guard whose military knowledge Nelson had dismissed must have snickered when they heard of Nelson's failure. Treasury Secretary Chase had been right. Nelson needed to study more for examinations. But Nelson defended himself. He had been appointed directly by the president "without going before an examination board"—why did "my failing to do that particular sum in the Rule of Three" matter for determining "my qualifications as a military man"?

Officers who had passed a board of examination "have complimented me on my abilities," Nelson proclaimed. Butler himself, Nelson told the board, had called him "a good military man," a judgment Butler made by observing Nelson's leadership at the company and regimental levels over a span of two years. Nelson had "intended," so he said, that the letter Thompson wrote be sent not to the president but to his member of Congress, Connecticut representative Henry Deming, for Deming to intercede with his friend Butler. He thought he had a right to do so as a citizen. Nelson admitted that black men had been impressed into service, but he asserted that his orders were for his subordinates to stop doing so and avoid any conduct that gave the "impression" that they were coercing men to join the regiment. As to his forcing William Carney and others to tote cannonballs, Nelson defended his prerogative as a commander to discipline soldiers who "refused to drill." These obstinate men had only "complied with one part of the contract" by enlisting. They had received uniforms and supplies and thus "were in arrears to the government." When they refused to muster in, Nelson considered it his "right to punish them any way I thought proper to keep order in my camp." He had not intended the punishment to last more than thirty minutes and blamed junior officers for their "stupid" decision to let it continue for longer than that.[33]

"If I have not done right it was not because I did'nt mean right," Nelson said as he made a last plea of innocence. He certainly had not engaged in these efforts to recruit men for personal profit. "I drew my pay, as my orders read, . . . to fill up my regiment. So you see," he told the board, "I had no interest, no selfish interest to serve." Butler had received anonymous information that refuted Nelson's claim. A correspondent who signed his name "Detective" told Butler that, when Nelson left Boston for Craney Island to take command of the Tenth USCT, a "notorious Burglar" and brothel keeper named Bob Lucas joined him. Lucas, who had recently "served several terms in the Charlestown State prison" for burglary, was to serve as the regimental sutler. "Detective" asserted that Nelson paid Lucas money to buy goods in Norfolk, load them aboard the tugboat *John E. Mulford* rented by the army for moving recruits to camp, and set up shop. After selling the goods to the men of the Tenth, Lucas and Nelson would "divide the profits equally between them." This detective work puts Nelson's request for his superiors to pay his men more regularly—like his requests for Zouave uniforms and blank forms—in a new light, for he and Lucas would profit from those payments because soldiers could only purchase items from the camp sutler. Perhaps Nelson had saved money from his Mississippi River Valley cotton speculations or his own wages as colonel—$212 per month—to fund this speculation in soldiers' goods that promised a steady income.[34]

Butler could not let the board's decision pass in silence, lest he lose an opportunity to compare a subordinate's treachery with his own righteousness. Butler recounted Nelson's checkered career in the service and acknowledged his own role in helping Nelson get those positions. He challenged Nelson's inaccurate claims about his wartime experience, particularly his repeated claim that he was the first to recruit African American soldiers. Butler also leapt to the defense of African American men and their families who had been harmed by Nelson's impressment tactics. Nelson had engaged in "duplicity" toward black men and demonstrated a "moral obliquity" in his methods of coercing them to serve in his regiment. Butler also defended himself. Nelson had, by enlisting the "rascally adventurer" Thompson in his scheme, perpetrated a "subterfuge and dishonest proceeding" against Butler and Lincoln that the former considered "unbecoming an officer and a gentleman." Nelson's pretensions to respectability had finally been unraveled by his inamiable disposition and dastardly deeds.[35]

Henry Wilson told Butler in December 1863 that he was, "in freeing and elevating the African race in our country" through the "humane" General Order 46, "writing your name in letters of living light." Nelson's removal from command confirmed that Butler's system of wage labor, and not impressment, would shape the transition out of slavery for African Americans in the Tidewater. Yet Butler was not the only Northern gentleman seeking to employ black Virginians as soldiers. As Kinsman's investigation into Nelson's impressment activities commenced, men from New England advocated for the right to enlist black soldiers in the South to count toward their recruitment quotas. Massachusetts's manufacturing and railroad titans wrote to Stanton on December 10, 1863, to explain the rationale behind the plan. Northern industrial production had been compromised by the steady enlistment of white operatives and tradesmen into the military. In occupied areas of the South, "large numbers of men Black and White have been thrown out of their usual occupations" and were dependent on charity to survive. "Sound political economy" dictated filling the military with unemployed men and paying them the bounties offered by the "producing states" in the North and counting their enlistments toward draft quotas.[36]

Butler encountered his own problems with establishing sound political economy in his district. To alleviate them, he wrote to John Murray Forbes, one of the authors of the letter to Stanton. In 1861, Forbes had forbidden black Bostonians from enlisting, but now he was the chairman of the Executive Committee of the Society for the Promotion of Recruiting among Freedmen in Boston and the man whose name Wilson had put forward to Lincoln as a good candidate to provide organization for recruiting in the occupied South. Butler told Forbes that his General Order 46 had contributed to a rush of enlistments, but he did not have enough funds to provide subsistence for the families of those soldiers. He asked Forbes to send clothing—"either new or second-hand"—for the wives and children of the men who had enlisted in his department. "As soon as it is possible to get the matter organized, I think the labor of the negroes, with the savings of their earnings, will be sufficient to meet these expenses, but at present we are not able so to meet them." Butler asked Forbes to send him the materials that would help "fulfill my part of the contract to the negroes, who by their readiness to enlist are fully up on their side." Benevolent aid could, by clothing the poor, help the state honor free labor's promise.[37]

Butler had "popularized" African American men's enlistment in his department by regulating the wage labor economy. Forbes and other Northern industrialists had ideas about making the enlistment of black soldiers even more popular in the North by allowing them to count for draft quotas that would otherwise ensnare white men. In November 1863, he had been in Washington at John Andrew's behest to advocate for equal pay for black soldiers in Massachusetts's pioneering Fifty-Fourth and Fifty-Fifth regiments. At the same time, he was working with a coalition of agents from Northern states to pressure the War Department to allow loyal states to recruit black Southerners to fill their quotas. He believed that other states should take the lead, lest Massachusetts's radicalism—Forbes indelicately told Andrew, "[W]e are looked upon as entirely monomaniac upon the 'everlasting Nigger'"—would lead to the rejection of their pitch. With its high state bounties, Forbes believed that Massachusetts had a competitive advantage over other Northern states and would "get the first pickings" of former slaves in the South. The state offered a $325 bounty, a sum calculated to entice enslaved men from "far within the enemys lines" and eat at the "*vitals* of Rebeldom." In fact, one objection Stanton made to Forbes was that states like Massachusetts had the agents and funds in place to fill their quotas in the South that the loyal Western states lacked. Forbes thought the practical need for men would ultimately overwhelm Stanton's concern about fairness. "Then will come up such a competition for the African as has never been seen outside the Gulf of Guinea!," Forbes bellowed to Andrew. Competition was the very essence of free labor. It was fair, and it would win the day. The "everlasting African," Forbes told Andrew, was soon to "become the most popular" figure "in the country among all classes of Draft." He bid to popularize recruitment by creating a national labor market.[38]

The plan to recruit black men from the Department of Virginia and North Carolina to fill Northern states' quotas threatened the limited, local wage labor economy Butler had created in General Order 46, for his $10 bounty would be eclipsed by the substantially larger sums offered by Northern states. Even as Butler asked Forbes to supply clothing so that he could honor the contracts he had made, he explained that competition with the New England states "would put a stop to my recruiting." More bad news came to undermine Butler's plans. On the same day he wrote to Forbes, he received a $20,000 check from Provost Marshal General Fry to cover the costs of paying the $10 bounties to African Americans already recruited. Yet Fry also told him that Stanton had "revoked" Butler's permission to offer those bounties in the future because Congress was opposed to the practice. Forbes's correspondence gave Butler another idea about how to encourage recruitment. He agreed that if "we get the men into the United States service ... it does not matter much where they come from." He proposed that, instead of the New England bounty money being paid directly to enlisted men, it could be "paid to me to constitute a fund for their families, out of which they might be supported." This fund, filled with Massachusetts's hefty bounty payments, would far exceed the subsistence monies that General Wool had collected out of black refugees' wages at Fort Monroe two years before. The justification for doing so was the same, however. Black Southerners supposedly had not yet learned the habits of saving that came from acclimation to free labor. Laden with a bountiful supply of greenbacks, Butler would not have to rely on Forbes and other New England reformers for the materiel necessary to support black soldiers' families. Despite rumors of his own speculations in New Orleans and the malfeasance that had run rampant in Wool's quartermaster's department earlier in the war, Butler intimated that Forbes could trust him with large sums. He would take care of everything. Forbes followed Butler's reasoning perfectly, asking him if he could "help us by sparing a few of your *light weights*"—African American men of enlistment age—"upon our helping you to take care of the families which prove such *heavy* weights"—the needy women and children those men left behind.[39]

This trade would bolster the interests of white citizens and the federal state simultaneously. Black men would take the place of white men to save the Union. What better way, Butler must have thought, to popularize recruitment? Such a plan would work even more efficiently, Forbes explained, if

Massachusetts could recruit "in the Rebel districts," for sending them north would throw black Virginians into the arms of "Land Sharks"—unscrupulous recruitment brokers—who would "steal them away for their bounties." Forbes urged Butler to use his "influence at Washington" to allow Northern states to recruit in the South, but if that failed, he should use "[m]ilitary necessity" as an excuse to "send us a Transport Load of Negros who have signed on articles before leaving" to Long Island, where Forbes's agents would collect them for transshipment to Boston. Such a smuggling operation would have looked different than the smuggling of enslaved people in the transatlantic or domestic slave trade only by the direction of the compass in which they steamed. Forbes knew this was wrong. "I suppose this might be irregular & need some straining of the letter of the law but perhaps you will take the responsibility," he suggested to Butler. Butler would not do so, informing Forbes three days later that Stanton "has directed that I shall not allow any negroes to enlist outside of my department." Forbes sent word that, until the War Department changed its policy, both would have to be resigned to the shipment of $2,500 worth of clothing for the use of "colored soldiers' families."[40]

Despite Stanton's efforts to clamp down on these expressions of free labor and their attendant coercions, he could not stop the recruitment of black Southerners by Northerners trying to fill their quotas. Days after Butler issued General Order 46, a captain in the office of the Commissary of Subsistence in Portsmouth, Moses Hill, contacted Butler's provost marshal, Charles Whelden, to promote Connecticut's willingness to pay black recruits an additional thirty dollars per year during their enlistment to cover the shortfall between the wages of white and black soldiers. Ten dollars of the additional money would be paid upon enlistment, a payment that Stanton was just about to stop Butler from making. A newspaper clipping that Hill included in his correspondence with Whelden suggested that Congressman James Ashley of Ohio was about to "introduce an important bill ... providing that the free States may recruit all their quotas in the Rebel States, offering bounties as they please." Ashley's impending legislation was probably what encouraged Hill to tell Whelden that his proposal to recruit black Virginians for Connecticut was "perfectly lawful," even though Ashley's bill was not law. Hill knew it, for he also thought his proposal "requires secrecy."[41]

John Andrew, for whom Forbes had been working, wrote to Lincoln to complain. The rights of "freemen and refugees from slavery" to migrate to Massachusetts in order to "better their fortunes and support their families" were being curtailed by government policy. "The industry of Massachusetts imperatively demands every laborer now on her soil or willing to come." He enumerated the production of the state for the benefit of the federal government. Massachusetts regularly filled "her quota of soldiers, [and] manufacture one third of all the woolen goods in the country, without which the army cannot live a day. And notwithstanding the shoe contracts in which she directly participates, many of the shoes contracted for by people of the other States are farmed out at a profit to her shoemakers and stitched by the hands and hammered out on the lapstones of Massachusetts. The earnings of their industry," he concluded, "are invested for the support of the Government, for the[y] hold at least one twelfth of the National Loan." The war had eliminated the need for shoemakers to strike. Andrew argued that his state exemplified free labor as Lincoln understood it, whereby labor produced capital that would bolster the war for Union. Limiting the mobility of laborers threatened this profitable system.[42]

Lincoln understood that this expression of free labor was a fraud. He knew exactly who the laborers were whom Andrew—like his agent Forbes—was trying to entice to Massachusetts. "Coming down to what I suppose to be the real facts," Lincoln lectured Andrew, "you are engaged in trying to raise colored troops for the U.S. and wish to take recruits from Virginia, through Washington, to Massachusetts for that object." The obstacle Andrew faced, Lincoln knew, was the "loyal Governor of Virginia," Francis Harrison Pierpont, who was also trying to recruit black soldiers and "objects to your taking his material away." Lincoln applauded Andrew's professed desire to foster immigration to Massachusetts, but he doubted that Andrew really meant it. Rather, Andrew's letter was meant to tip the scales of recruitment competition between loyal states.[43]

Lincoln told Andrew that his administration had to play fair between governors, although he knew that "abuses" had taken place whereby men in one place were spirited away to another to fill distant communities' quotas. The Enrollment Act had created recruitment districts along lines of congressional representation and stipulated that local communities make lists of the different classes of their citizens eligible for the draft. It assumed that communities would encourage and pressure local men to fill their quotas to avoid drafts, but it said little about how localities and states could fill their quotas. The War Department determined in 1863, over the opposition of radical Republicans like Wilson, that black men could not serve as substitutes for white men because of the differential between their wages. Yet the absence of clear language in the law explaining which recruits could count toward local draft quotas allowed middlemen to cash in. In December 1863,

Aaron Willett, a forty-two-year-old black laborer, met Joseph Peck, who had an office on Lombard Street in Philadelphia's African American neighborhood. Peck told Willett that he was from New Haven and a lieutenant recruiting black men to serve in his regiment, the Twenty-Ninth Connecticut (Colored) Infantry. Willett thought he was negotiating a contract when Peck offered him a $400 bounty and monthly relief payments of $6 for his wife and $2 for each of their children. Willett was incredulous—would Connecticut pay relief to recruits who did not live there? It was a question that white men must have asked Nelson when they enlisted in the Ninth Connecticut at Lowell in the fall of 1861. Peck assured Willett it would. Such a large sum, over and above the wage for black soldiers, would help Willett's family survive and even thrive in his absence. So he boarded an overnight train from Philadelphia to New Haven. On arriving, he was first "taken to a Cellar kept ... by Peck" and then to "a large store-room, where we found a short, thick-set man" named Benjamin Pardee, who introduced himself as the regiment's colonel. Pardee sent Willett and several other recruits to the provost marshal's office, where they were "stripped and examined by a Surgeon and ... passed" for enlistment.[44]

Located underground and in places that looked like businesses, recruitment brokers cheated men like Willett. Having passed the surgeon's examination, Willett was ready for a financial reckoning. There was bad news. Peck told him that each recruit had cost him $20 to transport, and that fee would come out of his bounty. Pardee then gave Willett $200, explaining that was all he would get. Willett refused to enlist at that price, half of what he had bargained for. Pardee was not fazed by Willett's opposition and simply tried to keep the con going. He persuaded Willett that he would be paid $75 more once he was in camp. He also warned him of thieves there and asked, would Willett care to have Pardee put his money in a bank for safekeeping? "Supposing his story to be true," Willett later testified, he gave the man he thought was his commanding officer $170. But Pardee's and Peck's stories were not true. Neither was an officer in the Twenty-Ninth Connecticut. Pardee was the superintendent of Connecticut's recruitment for colored regiments. Peck worked for Pardee, one of several white and black men who recruited for Connecticut in Philadelphia and occupied Alexandria, Virginia. These agents made $3 per day, had their travel expenses paid, and wore army uniforms to give credence to the stories they told to unsuspecting recruits. Pardee's scheme made further profits possible for them. Connecticut law offered $300 bounties to all recruits. Pardee and his agents were offering what they calculated the market would bear in each location. In Alexandria, they offered $150 and pocketed the remainder for themselves. In Philadelphia, they offered more than the allotted inducement and sought other means to defraud men like Willett.[45]

Willett lost nearly all of the money promised to him. The community of Bristol, Connecticut, got to count him toward its quota, but the state of Connecticut paid nothing toward the relief of his family. General John Dix, now commanding the Department of the East in New York City, investigated Pardee and his cohort and ordered that bounty payments in his department must be paid directly to the recruit. Connecticut governor Buckingham, Provost Marshal General Fry, and Secretary of War Stanton presented a united front in disapproving Dix's order. Buckingham argued that Dix had interfered with a state's right to recruit its soldiers as it saw fit. Pardee sensed Buckingham's support for his work, and when Dix hauled him in to answer the charges, he refused to testify, arguing that Dix had no authority over him. Fry contended that there could be "no material success" in "recruiting without the intervention of recruiting agents." If the payments did not go through the hands of brokers, the government would fail in its efforts to staff armies. Some soldiers "may be swindled," Fry acknowledged, but if Dix's "order is enforced we will not get the men, which is the point to be looked to." While Stanton thanked Dix for his attempt to stop recruitment fraud, he revoked the general's order. To get men, the government would condemn brokers' fraud but permit them to continue perpetrating it. Dix lamented the War Department's decision. Pardee and other "swindlers" were "filling the ranks of the Army with a class of men exasperated by the deception practised upon them and ready to desert the first opportunity." One of those men was Aaron Willett, who deserted his regiment in February 1864 even before it was deployed to the theater of war. Court-martialed upon his capture, Willett was sentenced to lose ten dollars per month from his salary for six months, and his term of service was lengthened to account for the time of his absence. The war had linked independence with the wage, capital in the making. Pardee and Peck had become independent at Willett's expense, while the defrauded soldier lost capital promised by a contract and would be forced to abide by that contract despite the hirers' fraud. The court-martial sentence took still more capital away from him. By the time he returned to his regiment in November, Congress had passed legislation to pay black soldiers the same wages as white soldiers, but more than three-quarters of Willett's pay was withheld by the government. Impoverished by fraud and government discipline, Willett died of disease in December 1864.[46]

John Nelson had lost capital, too. A postmortem on his removal from command, published in a Connecticut newspaper, underscored his loss of cultural capital. "He was a professional pugilist before the war"—in other words, the paper claimed, a common boxer, a fact he had tried to obscure with his "sparring school." On April 16, 1864, he wrote a letter noted for its halting prose and idiosyncratic spelling to a "Mr. Read," probably quartermaster general of the state of Massachusetts, John Reed, to recoup economic capital. It was a report of expenses entailed while he commanded the Tenth USCT. "I Enclose my Recepts for Comutation of Quarters whitch I am justly Entitled to I thought I could colect it in Washington But the Quarter master General says the Quartermaster of Butlers Dept must Pay me so I wish you would Colect it for me and send me the Ballence." Having once enjoyed a position of power as a colonel and speculator, Nelson was now in need of cash and navigated the federal bureaucracy with as much knowledge as an enlisted man. "If you carrey it to Gen Butler I think he will order it Payed at once Pleas answer as Quick as Possable I send you the Origenal order Puting me on detatched service all Officers on detatched service are alowed this Comutation. I never Colected eny suposeing I Could get it in Washington Eney time," he explained. Anytime had become this time. He needed money immediately to survive the crisis created by his dismissal and, perhaps, to fund new speculations.[47]

During his confinement at the Hygeia Hotel, Nelson had written to Butler in hopes of flattering his commander and obtaining his release and return to command. "I have always thought of you with the most profound respect and admiration," Nelson wrote, evidently with the assistance of someone else. "I have laboured hard to raise the Tenth Regiment under many disadvantages and hoped by next Spring to bring into the field a well disciplined Regiment which would reflect credit on their down-trodden race." His efforts produced a regiment, according to the official sent to inspect it in February 1864, that was "composed [of] ... many men that to my judgement should never have been enlisted, and should now be gotten rid of as a demoralizing element." The regiment's officers and soldiers lacked respectability, self-control, and education—like colonel, like regiment—and as a result, the inspector believed that "selections should be made from other regiments enlisted farther North" to improve its quality.[48]

Farther north, Thomas Webster and Philadelphia's Supervisory Committee for Recruiting Colored Regiments were also enlisting black troops. They were doing so, they believed, according to principles of honesty and integrity. At the committee's headquarters on Chestnut Street and at Camp William Penn just north of the city, Webster led efforts to recruit the Third,

Sixth, and Eighth USCT regiments in 1863 and was filling up the Twenty-Second and Twenty-Fifth USCT regiments as the investigation of Nelson concluded in early 1864. To achieve his recruitment goals, Webster depended on a culture of persuasion — resonant of the commercial world in which he had the most experience — rather than one of coercion. Webster sought to perpetuate the idea that Southern slavery operated by force, while the North liberated labor and capital. He also had the merchant's and promoter's sense that representations of slavery's coercion would sell in northern popular culture, especially if they were used to produce the capital necessary to vanquish slavery. In December 1863, he wrote to John Phelps about an upcoming meeting he was organizing in Philadelphia to raise money to fund schools for African American children in Louisiana. Phelps was the antislavery general who had run afoul of Butler in the Department of the Gulf for attempting to enlist black men in the Union army before Butler was ready to do so. He had returned to Vermont and struck up a correspondence with Webster, perhaps through his family connections to Representative John Hickman, Webster's Republican political patron in Philadelphia. Webster kept Phelps abreast of the efforts of Philip Bacon, one of the general's former subordinates in the Gulf who now sought charitable support for "free colored schools" there. Bacon disseminated photographs of the former slaves he tried to assist. These photographs depicted phenotypically white children and black men wearing what Webster called "instruments of torture." The way these photographs — and the public display of these people — worked in the North was to highlight the sexual and physical violence of slavery, a violence that violated Northern ideals of family and free labor. Webster informed Phelps that the *"white slaves from Louisiana"* would be presented onstage at Philadelphia's Concert Hall alongside *"Wilson Chinn*, a griff negro, branded on forehead ... and wearing Iron Collar." These staged representations of the *"patriarchal institution! of the South"* would open Northern pocketbooks to support the war for Union and the free society Northerners hoped to build in slavery's place. Webster suggested that the photographic representations of slavery's violence be sold for twenty-five cents apiece to members of the audience primed to believe that purchases could promote politics. He hoped that Phelps would consider making the journey south to Philadelphia to give a lecture about his experiences in the Gulf and his ideas about emancipation to keep the issue in the public eye. If he did, Webster wrote cryptically that he hoped he would have a chance to "talk negro" with Phelps during his visit. The general declined the invitation, but Webster later informed him that the meeting "was a great success, not so much in the way of proceeds as in the

M. H. Kimball, *Emancipated Slaves* (New York, 1863).
(The Library Company of Philadelphia)

making of sentiment, although the pecuniary returns from sale of Photographs & Lecture are respectable." Philadelphians poured out their sympathy in dollars and cents to win the war for Union.[49]

For Webster, this attempt to support the education of former slaves was intertwined with his recruitment of black soldiers. The means he took to succeed in the two spheres were similar. By December 1863 Philadelphia had increased its bounty offers to white and black recruits to $250. Beyond the monetary inducements, Webster urged that "extensive advertising" in the form of handbills and "huge posters" be used to stoke interest in recruitment events in Philadelphia and neighboring Delaware and Maryland for the Supervisory Committee's black regiments. The lithographic print produced by the Philadelphia firm of P. S. Duval & Son evokes Duross Brothers' advertisements for retailers and military recruiters at the beginning of the war by portraying a commander and soldiers under an American flag. Emancipation modified the premise of those earlier images. Webster and his committee used this depiction of African American soldiers to encourage black men to serve their nation and the cause of "FREEDOM!" Webster underscored this call for civic virtue by arranging for recruiting events to be accompanied by enlisted black soldiers marching in martial splendor and music from a military band to provide an inspiring backdrop for speakers exhorting still more black men to enlist. Webster believed that pomp and circumstance, coupled with access to bounty funds and a willingness to "canvass" as if in a political campaign, would cause a *"furore"* of "excitement among the colored people" and ensure large enlistments. Once they were mustered in, these men must not be imposed on by middlemen. When a sutler at Camp William Penn "speculated freely" at the expense of African American recruits who had just been paid their bounties, he was dismissed, and Webster wrote to the War Department to ask that it not appoint a replacement immediately. The committee hoped to "select a perfectly reliable person to recommend" for the post. In 1864, the committee recommended William Still for the position, and the War Department appointed him. Still's business speculations, Webster and other antislavery Philadelphians knew, would be constrained by his desire to treat black soldiers fairly in their transactions in order to promote collective independence.[50]

Webster and the Supervisory Committee also opened the Free Military School for Applicants for Commands of Colored Troops in Philadelphia to train white men seeking commissions in USCT regiments. Webster sent Phelps money to place advertisements for the academy in Vermont newspapers and encouraged the general to write a training "text book" for the students at the school. In correspondence with Major C. W. Foster of the War Department's Colored Troops Division, Webster contrasted the existence of the committee's school and the importance of its work with the "accounts in the papers of the conduct of . . . certain officers in command of colored Troops in Genl Butlers department." These officers were, he told Phelps, "disgraced" for their "cruelty, Drunkenness, and other vices," grouping them with slaveholders and their violence. He told the War Department that he and the Free Military School's instructors "resolved to teach correct ethics" in their course of instruction "as well as Infantry Tactics and Army Regulations." Because the *"necessity for officers of the proper tone is obvious,"* Webster asked Foster for help in identifying and providing furloughs for white enlisted men and junior officers who wished to advance in the ranks by taking command of black troops. Unlike Nelson, they would have to temper their own ambitions to ensure the success of the common project—the "Colored

P. S. Duval & Son, *United States Soldiers at Camp "William Penn" Philadelphia, Pa.* (Philadelphia: Supervisory Committee for Recruiting Colored Regiments, [1863]). (The Library Company of Philadelphia)

movement"—in which Webster thought he was engaged. Webster even sent Butler a circular advertising the Free Military School, believing that Butler needed the type of men the school would produce.[51]

In April 1864, Webster and other members of the Supervisory Committee visited Washington to lobby Stanton to increase black soldiers' pay to an equality with white soldiers' wages both as a matter of justice and a stimulus to recruitment. From the nation's capital, Webster traveled south to visit Yorktown, where the Sixth and Twenty-Second USCT regiments had been sent, to assess the "welfare" of the men and observe a camp of formerly enslaved refugees. Yorktown was in the Department of Virginia and North Carolina, and in preparation for the trip, Webster asked allies to send letters of introduction to Butler on his behalf. John Murray Forbes described Webster as "the heart & hand of the Committee" in Philadelphia "for raising colored troops. He & they have *done* what we in Massachusetts *hoped* to do in the way of stimulating the recruiting of Colored Regiments." Forbes also asked Butler "to *weigh & examine* his plans for I know you will help any which commend themselves to your judgement." Those plans remain unclear, although Butler gave Webster a pass to travel from Fort Monroe to Yorktown and back on April 15. When Webster returned to Philadelphia, he learned that the Supervisory Committee had, in his absence, passed resolutions prohibiting any member of the committee from incurring expenses without first getting permission from the committee as a whole. In response, Webster drafted an indignant resignation letter. He had done "much to revolutionize public sentiment in our city, our state and beyond them, and to make the grand policy of the Government in summoning the colored race to arms, understood and popular." He had, as Butler and Forbes tried to do, popularized the employment of black men as soldiers, mainly through persuasion rather than coercion. Having been so important in this regard, he was insulted by the committee's resolution. It suggested he was a "mere machine" doing a job that could be done by a "clerk of the most limited capacity." He had "called the committee into existence and done so much of its work," and he could neither accept its "censure" nor maintain his membership "without the loss of self respect." The logistical man, so willing to simper when encountering the powerful, was feeling his oats.[52]

His resignation was not accepted by the committee, and he continued in the work of recruiting black regiments in Philadelphia and surrounding states. It remains a mystery as to which of Webster's expenses the committee wanted to regulate. In May 1864, Webster collected new letters of introduction to carry with him to Butler, and they give us a potential clue. Though recruiting black men made him feel strong, Webster still had to approach powerful men with hat in hand. J. W. Forney, the Philadelphia politician and newspaperman, informed Butler that Webster "was an old Democrat like yourself, but is now, and for years has been, one of the leading Anti Slavery writers and organizers in Pennsylvania." He "possesses a thorough knowledge of Norfolk and Richmond" from his commercial activities before the war and could "prove to be of immense value in the great operations soon to be opened by you." As Butler started his military campaign toward Richmond in the spring of 1864, Webster's personal understanding of Virginia's people and ports might be of some public use. Webster was engaged in a campaign for his private interest as well. He had learned that John Sherman might not advocate effectively on his behalf, so he turned to his senatorial colleague from Ohio, Benjamin Wade, to tout Webster's knowledge of Virginia's principal cities as a potential help to Butler. Wade clarified what Webster wanted. The Philadelphian had "lost twenty years of earnings in Trade by Richmond People and naturally wants to attempt to recover his losses in that city." Webster hoped that Butler would take Richmond. He offered local knowledge of waterways, people, and places in return for "a permit to trade" in the conquered Confederate capital. Webster sought to be among the first Northern merchants to collect old debts, seize control over the renewed carrying trade, and get in on the ground floor of the reconstructed tobacco economy. Accompanying Butler and his soldiers—some of whom Webster had recruited—might be the best way to recover from antebellum business failure. Webster's efforts to recruit black men to prosecute the war for Union were never far removed from his efforts to restore the capital he had lost to slaveholders. Even though Butler assisted speculators in areas under his command and most likely profited himself from doing so, there is no evidence that he took Webster up on his offer.[53]

Webster may not have received immediate reward for making the war for Union more popular by recruiting African American soldiers. Yet he, Butler, Nelson, and Forbes, by utilizing the concept of consent at the heart of free labor, the commercial culture of persuasion, and the coercive practices that "military necessity" and discipline made available, had played important roles in augmenting the enlistment rolls of the Union army. The recruitment of soldiers encouraged by the Emancipation Proclamation and the conscription regulations of the Enrollment Act filled army regiments depleted by disease and costly military campaigns. The larger Union forces that renewed the assault against Confederate foes in 1864 would produce a chain reaction whereby refugees and deserters moved to the North. These labor movements would illuminate how the war for Union freed white Northern farmers and household mistresses most of all.

6

A GREAT SOCIAL PROBLEM

ON JULY 18, 1864, President Lincoln issued a call for 500,000 new volunteers to serve in the nation's military forces. A draft would take place later in the year if state and local quotas were not met. With the upcoming presidential election surely on his mind, the artist Henry Louis Stephens portrayed Lincoln as the "Idol of Abolitionism," a grotesque giant who swallowed Northern citizen soldiers whole to feed his unseemly and insatiable hunger for racial equality. Formerly the artistic director of the anti-emancipation publication *Vanity Fair*, Stephens had tried to profit from publishing pro-emancipation cards depicting the transition of African Americans out of slavery. Now he returned to a critique of emancipation that *Vanity Fair* had helped to make: Lincoln was wrong. The war for Union threatened individual profits and national prosperity. It fed the federal government's monstrous maw. Soldiers were chewed up, their corpses spit out, and hungry widows and orphans were left to count the human cost.[1]

Yet Lincoln won reelection. He did so because of the struggle and sacrifice — not to mention the votes — of military commanders and enlisted men in Virginia, Georgia, and beyond. He also did so by not forsaking the pervasive and popular free labor ideology that had put him in the presidency in the first place. Tacking between the consent and coercion of wage labor, black and white soldiers fought to preserve the Union because they believed, despite the clear limits to independence they encountered, that they could succeed in the race of life that Lincoln celebrated. Political allies beseeched the president to revoke the Emancipation Proclamation to boost his electoral prospects, but he refused. "Any different policy in regard to the colored man," he told a correspondent in September 1864, "deprives us of his help, and this is more than we can bear. We can not spare the hundred and forty or fifty thousand now serving us as soldiers, seamen, and laborers. This is not a question of sentiment or taste," he continued, "but one of physical force which may be measured and estimated as horse-power and Steam-power are measured and estimated. Keep it and you can save the Union. Throw it away, and the Union goes with it." The war for Union, Lincoln reasoned,

Henry Louis Stephens, *Idol of Abolitionism* (Philadelphia: L. H. Stephens, [1864]). (The Library Company of Philadelphia)

would be won on its balance sheet as much as in the hearts and minds of its citizens. This was true from the perspective of both the War Department and individual Northern households. Mudsill soldiers—volunteers, draftees, and substitutes—poured from the North toward the South to vanquish the slaveholders' aristocracy. The manpower that went into their killing and dying work produced the movement of thousands of white and black Southern refugees to the households of white Northerners. Recruiters, brokers, benevolent societies, and Northern families—all believers that free labor could emancipate them—would try to seize the power, the capital, embedded in the labor of the men, women, and children fleeing to them. Doing so would help them win the war for Union.[2]

On June 15, 1864, a division of African American soldiers under the command of Brigadier General Edward Hinks, part of the Eighteenth Corps of the Army of the Potomac commanded by Major General William "Baldy" Smith, participated in an attack against the Confederate defenses at Petersburg, Virginia. Hinks's division included the Sixth and Twenty-Second USCT regiments that Thomas Webster's Supervisory Committee had organized in and around Philadelphia and the Tenth USCT formerly commanded by John Nelson. In firefights at Baylor's Farm and at the batteries lining the Confederates' Dimmock Line that protected the approaches to the city, observers noted black troops' bravery and, in the words of Smith, their "splendid conduct."[3]

The attacks were only partially successful. Smith's men pushed Confederates out of their defenses, but their commander did not press the attack vigorously. General Robert E. Lee's Army of Northern Virginia reinforced the Petersburg defenses, and the two armies dug in for a siege. The attack on the Dimmock Line was a culmination of the efforts of men such as Benjamin Butler, Thomas Webster, and John Nelson to deploy black men as soldiers and laborers in service to the war for Union in this theater of combat. As Butler and his subordinate commanders had prepared for the Bermuda Hundred campaign along the James River earlier that spring, they did not hesitate to force black men to work for the army. Assistant Superintendent of Negro Affairs Orlando Brown, stationed in Norfolk, told his superior J. B. Kinsman that he had heard complaints from "a large number of colored women and children" that black men had been "transported up the James River to work for the Government." The "order for their impressment" had been issued by Brigadier General George Shepley, who argued that "urgent military necessity compelled" him to proceed as he did. Shepley informed Brown that he would have followed Butler's guidance in General Order 46 to impress white workers as well, but black laborers were the only Southerners of reliable loyalty. Military necessity was the reason that Butler initiated his contraband policy and published General Order 46. Military necessity and claims about allegiance also helped confirm the rationale for eroding the independence of African American men when it suited the army.[4]

Under orders from Shepley to secure the laborers required, Brown tried to convince black men "of the urgency of the case" and promised to accompany them to assure that "Muster Rolls should be properly made out" so that they would be paid correctly. These promises worked wonders. From Brown's perspective, the men happily became "[v]olunteers," a term that justified his exhortations and obscured the coercive means—forced transportation and speeches about obligation—accompanying the consent they gave him. When Brown discovered that sixty men were not sufficient to complete the work the army needed done, he told Kinsman that he had "noticed several negroes on the banks of the river as we were passing up" to Bermuda Hundred. Butler ordered Brown to "collect all of the able bodied negroes that can be found on the banks of the James River, and turn them over to the Q. M. Dept." The quartermaster's department would pay for their transportation to the site because it benefited from their labor. After Brown succeeded in impressing forty-five black men for the job, Butler issued a subsequent order for him to return to Norfolk and Fort Monroe in search of two hundred more African American workers to ship to his front. Still this was not enough. Brown asked Captain Charles Wilder to have another hundred workers ready for him at the fort the following morning. Brown repeated what he had heard "on good authority that hundreds can be procured in Hampton and vicinity." Brown also let Kinsman know that these men would be paid twenty dollars a month, perhaps expecting that the offer of wages double what black soldiers made might diminish the concerns of wives and mothers about their impressment. That Butler allowed the payment of these high wages in contravention of General Order 46 suggests that the "urgency" of "military necessity" was not the concept that persuaded workers to volunteer to do the hard work that the army expected of them. These men wanted more wages in order to make impressment palatable. As in Nelson's impressment case, consent and coercion were defined by the terms of the labor market and military discipline.[5]

The impressment efforts for the Bermuda Hundred campaign disrupted African Americans' households. Scouring the countryside for black men to serve the army as laborers, Brown also picked up 150 black women and children who lacked "shelter of any kind" and sent them on a steamer plying the same channels of the James River to Norfolk that Webster's Union Steamship Company boats once did. By the middle of June, Brown reported that he could not provide for the families that soldiers and laborers had left behind, many of whom now resided in the coastal cities of Norfolk and Portsmouth "without employment." He informed Kinsman that he had stopped issuing "rations to the families of soldiers unless they will remove to Govt. Farms" and asked whether he had Kinsman's support in doing so. He also asked for guidance about whether he could force the people he moved to government farms to do "such labour as they are capable of doing." Brown's questions reveal that the army was unable to live up to Butler's promises to soldiers' families in General Order 46. Brown wished to respond by curtailing the independence of the destitute. Kinsman's reply to the overcrowding, unemployment, and threat of disease circulating among these refugee populations was to initiate contact with benevolent institutions to take black women and children to Northern cities and alleviate the army's burden. Kinsman tried to identify women and children "not belonging to the families of soldiers" who did not have a job and were subsisting on the supplies of the government as suitable candidates for relocation. They were not the people to whom promises had been made. Brown reported to Kinsman that these people—like soldiers' wives and children—had "strong objections to leaving," so he asked for "permission to compel them to go of course using as little severity as possible towards them." As was standard operating procedure in Butler's department, white officers advocated coercion so long as no one else thought it was too coercive.[6]

Kinsman assured Butler in July 1864 that "the demand" in the North "for these servants is very great." Northern soldiers like Charles Brewster and Henry Walker and civilians eager for workers to support their claims to respectability would gladly pay wages to former slaves and thus allow them to support themselves. Butler had broached the subject of moving black families to Philadelphia in April with Charles Wilder. Wilder replied with bad news. "I can scarcely find one willing to go," he said. "A few have returned" to Virginia after having refugeed to the City of Brotherly Love earlier in the war, Wilder explained. They "reported among their associates, that they were not well used, which makes them hesitate about going." Kinsman did not hesitate. In July, as he was making arrangements to take "fifty orphans to the Philadelphia friends" and one hundred more to New York and Boston, he used African Americans' reluctance against them, telling Butler that some "prefer to stay here in idleness." He asked Butler for the authority to force black women and children to accompany him. Butler refused, but he was willing to employ coercion when necessary to help black women understand what emancipation was. "I would not send any negro woman North who does not wish to go," he admonished his subordinate, "but if one has agreed to go and then refuses she should be put to hard labor in the field." No one would be allowed to change her mind. African Americans' emancipation would be shaped not only by military necessity but also by domestic necessity, as an alliance among Union soldiers, officers, politicians, and households used consent and coercion in order to move black Southerners northward.[7]

Henry Walker, who had wanted to send a "black and shiney" woman home to Forestport to help his wife Persis complete domestic tasks, took part in the Eighteenth Corps's first attacks on Petersburg with his regiment, the 117th New York. Early in 1864, Persis Walker had tried to accumulate the capital necessary to buy the land on which to make the family a home. Those efforts were dealt a crippling blow not only by the irregularity of Henry's pay and the sporadic nature of his shoe repair business but also by the theft perpetrated by other men. A comrade by the name of William Paasch — a twenty-year-old Prussian immigrant from Boonville, a town northwest of Forestport — stole forty dollars out of a letter Henry was getting ready to mail to Persis. Henry suggested that his wife have a friendly neighbor nose around to see if William's mother, Mrs. Paasch, was all of a sudden flush with cash.[8]

No matter, the Walkers would just have to do without. Persis had chosen a "plase" and Henry thought the "contract" she had made was "great." They just had to "try hard to pay for it and then it will make us a home." The purchase would buy them independence. "I will try to do the best I can for you all," Henry assured Persis. "I have earned a bout $30 sins I had my m[o]n[e]y stolen," and once the paymaster came, he would get his wages and the men would get theirs. Then they could pay him their shoe-mending debts. He could make even more money, he told Persis, if she sent him leather to patch soles that were wearing thin. He told her to contact a Forestport wagonmaker, Cephas Weeks, for a supply. He wanted polish and pegs, thread and sewing awls to expand his operations. With sixteen-year-old daughter Olive now teaching school and Henry increasing his tapping fee to $1, the Walkers once more envisioned independence for themselves through hard work. Walker tallied up the proceeds of his labor for Persis in March 1864. "I earn from $1 to $3 per day when I am off duty":

I have $33.35 cents on book. I have sent you $10 since pay day I have sold my Watch for $6 so that will make $39.35 if I get it all next pay day and our pay $26 to

39.35
26
$65.35

the $10 that I sent you maide the $75 that I spoke of but I said if we got 4 months pay I would send $75 but we got 2 months pay so you se[e] I am a head of what I told I would do we shal get our pay now soon I think this is the money that I speak of now that I want you to save $25 of to pay on the contract 65 or $70 in all yet to come to save from so yo[u] see that shoe mending yet has some money.

Henry and Persis counted the dollars and cents because accounting—even in this primitive form—was the language of ambitious people. In itemized inventories of tools, supplies, and personal items being turned into profit margins on the page, Henry Walker made a market legible and tried to live up to the cultural narratives of self-making and try, try, again. He was not alone in doing so, for Henry's letters reveal that Persis was asking questions and making statements about their shared economic destiny. Even though he advised her what to do, Persis's activities at home as purchaser of land, a house, and supplies for his business venture and her market savvy as a negotiator with neighbors about access to credit, capital, and land made her a vital participant in navigating the market.[9]

Persis informed Henry that reenlistment bounties at home had risen to $900. It was a sum that would surely make their dream of independence a reality. "I could make a pile in a short time as to re enlist ment if the war is not closed," he exclaimed, and he resolved to "enlist as soon as their is a chance." Excited by the prospect of earning hundreds of dollars by touching the pen—in a way that the black men with whom he fought at Petersburg could not—Walker sent his cobbling tools home from his regiment's camp in Yorktown in April 1864. Unfortunately, the Walkers would once again discover that life was as precarious for soldiers as economic survival was. Henry was wounded in the trenches at Petersburg in the first days of the Army of the Potomac's siege of the city. He was transported to Philadelphia, where he died in a hospital of gangrene on July 24, 1864. A U.S. Army chaplain wrote Persis to say that Henry had been "well cared for, but no efforts could save." Henry died on the cusp of getting ahead in the race of life. Persis's quest for survival was not over. She spent almost three years petitioning for a widow's pension from the federal government to support her and their children. She succeeded in her application and earned eight dollars per month, plus two dollars per month for each of her five children under the age of sixteen until they turned that age. Her lawyer won, too, collecting $18.68 for his services, taking more than one month of the pension funds that Persis would put toward the management of her household. It is not clear whether she was able to buy that "plase" for a home for her family. Henry's final resting place is Philadelphia's National Cemetery, one mile from the site of Camp William Penn, where African American men recruited by Webster's Supervisory Committee were readied for combat.[10]

On the day the Eighteenth Corps attacked Petersburg, Charles Brewster was with the Army of the Potomac's Sixth Corps, north of the James River near Charles City Court House. His term as a soldier was coming to an end, and rather than think of the battle his black and white comrades were fighting, he wondered "what I am to do for a living when I come home." The best idea he could think of was "to come out again as a substitute" for a drafted Northampton neighbor. Although his comrades "declare they would not enlist again for all the wealth of the United States," Brewster contended that at home, people would "be ready to do" veterans "any injury for the sake of a dollar." Speculators all, citizens would be happy to take former soldiers' capital from them. As he told his sister Mary a few months before, the "Military ... pays better than anything else." Indeed, that was true for junior officers. Remaining in the army was the only way Brewster believed he could "take care of you after I get the house paid for." So he would stay.[11]

His state's need to recruit more soldiers, his own experience with doing so over the course of the conflict, and changes in recruitment patterns soon gave him an opportunity. In July 1864, three weeks after his discharge from the Tenth Massachusetts, Brewster was commissioned a captain by Governor Andrew and sent to Norfolk to recruit black soldiers for the state. On Independence Day, Congress had made the practice of recruiting black Southern men to fill Northern states' quotas legitimate. Norfolk was, as a result, plagued with agents from many other Northern states. "I presume," Brewster told his mother upon his arrival, "that before a week there will be 500 or more here more than there is niggers in the whole Dept." Brewster tried to scout for untapped markets but unwittingly traveled across landscapes—from Fort Monroe to Norfolk to Virginia's Eastern Shore—that had been picked clean by recruiters like Nelson. Other Northern states offered recruits bounties of $500 or $1,000, inflated by funds coming from towns and villages aiming to avoid a draft by paying over the odds for men they did not know to serve in place of their citizens. Massachusetts only offered its state bounty of $325. Hirelings had choices in this market, and that made it difficult for Brewster to do Andrew's bidding and swell Massachusetts's ranks with black Southern men.[12]

Brewster's male family members and friends in Northampton hoped that he could be the middleman they needed to give them some control in the substitute market. Before he left for the Tidewater, Brewster had evidently suggested that he might be able to provide substitutes to those who needed them back home. Once he arrived, though, he realized that doing so would be beyond his station and means. "I might possibly get" substitutes, he told his sister, "but I should have to come home with them, and run the risk of losing them on the way for the country is full of substitute runners, and they are paying $1000.00 for them in New York and I might not be able to run them through." Butler's declaration that "no colored man shall be taken away from this Dep't" meant that Brewster would have to get white men to agree to make the perilous journey north through the gauntlet of substitute brokers aiming to seize them for their own profit. Brewster assured his family, "I am on the trail of some white men and if possible I will get a couple and bring them in." He also told them to expect he would "fail," for this was a market in which "nobody seems to think it all necessary to fulfil promises."[13]

Brewster condemned substitute brokers who were doing precisely what he aimed to do. His condemnation served as a way to consider the possibilities that speculation offered and cleanse himself of any suspicion that he was a runner of men. He wanted to keep his search for substitutes on behalf of his friends a secret from "the state house" because "they discourage the procuring of substitutes and would not like it if they knew I got them." He knew he needed the influence of the powerful. The assistant adjutant general in the military department was from Massachusetts, and Brewster hoped that his superior would steer potential recruits his way instead of toward agents from someplace else. That was the only way to combat the higher bounties being offered by other states. He also knew that the substitute market offered opportunities to make money fast. He had once thought about serving as a substitute for a drafted man. Now, with the business of recruiting black men into the army "dull," he wished he "had 500. dollars." If he did, "I would leave the state service and go into the substitute business where I think I could make some money as from 1000 to 1200 dollars is freely offered for substitutes, and if I was out of this and could stay here and look round I think I could get some." The idea of helping family and friends get substitutes suggested to him the wider possibilities offered by markets in men. Unfortunately for him, he lacked the capital and autonomy necessary to exploit it. Instead, he satisfied himself with procuring the services of a domestic servant for his sister Mattie's family while in either Northampton or Virginia. "I am glad the Scotch woman proved such a valuable acquisition to your household, and did such justice to my faith in *her honesty*." This white immigrant woman replaced Sarah Washington, the African American servant who had worked for his family. Brewster announced to his mother in October that he also "was thinking of bringing in a contraband when I come" home to add to the family's small household staff. Brewster had the mind of a middleman and, like other brokers, relished thinking about ways to exploit labor transactions that would accrue economic and cultural capital to him and his family. That middleman's mind, aiming for power and prestige, would be evident more generally in Northern society as Southern refugees, made vulnerable by war, moved to the region's cities.[14]

In the fall of 1864, the authors of essays entitled "Our Domestic Affairs" and "A Great Social Problem" attempted to persuade readers of the *Continental Monthly*—the journal that declared the war for Union should do justice to whites and serve the interests of a Northern middle class—that one of the nation's highest priorities should be the reformation of the "evils which attend our domestic service." Never mind that sickening casualty figures from the summer's military campaigns and the stalemate of siege operations around Petersburg threatened the Republicans' policy of slave emancipation (which the *Continental* supported) if Democrats won majorities in the upcoming election. "Each house is divided against itself," the *Continental* mused, adopting the phrase that Lincoln had used in 1858 to describe the crisis of American political economy arraying Southern slavery against Northern wage labor. The "two camps" in Union households were "hostile, though perhaps not in open war with each other: and Camp Kitchen has the advantage of position." These essayists were earnest. Contemporaries, they said, only discussed the topic "flippantly, and with unworthy levity." The joke was on author and reader alike. There were "no good servants" anymore, and very soon there might be "no servants at all."[15]

How had it come to this? Irish domestic workers, the obstinate "Biddies," knowing that the demand for their services was intense, exhibited too much "independence" and sought other positions at the slightest provocation, the *Continental* contended. Poor native-born women could not be convinced that household service was respectable labor. Instead they chose to be seamstresses and loom tenders and thus suffered a "dwarfing, degrading, wretched slavery." The Civil War had produced other dislocations. Soldiers had gone off to fight, so employers in search of male workers inevitably encountered "*labor famine.*" Moreover, as Union armies marched through the South, they "destroyed the last lingering type of the servant post: the faithful black." The slaveholding aristocracy, while an impediment to the triumph of a Northern middle class the *Continental* had called into being, had provided the discipline that promoted the faithfulness every employer wanted.[16]

All was not lost, however. These concerned authors also believed that slave emancipation would alleviate the impending crisis of domestic labor in Northern households. Slavery, the *Continental*'s authors averred, had fostered a class of slaveholders who believed labor and capital were at odds with each other. The Irish servant women in Northern cities who shared these ideas were impediments to free labor's harmony of interests between employer and employee. The *Continental* favored equality of opportunity and equality before the law for all Americans, but its contributors also believed that the "subordination" of workers should define wage labor relations. The end of slavery, they hoped, would force white Southern women to do more work in their homes. The result would be "a swarming out from the kitchens of the South of Dinah and Phillis *et als.*, and many of these superfluous servants will find their way North" to be employed in Yankee domiciles. "The trained house-servants of the South are the best in the world," the *Continental* informed readers, sidestepping its concerns that the war and emancipation had compromised their fidelity. "They are docile, cleanly, quickwitted, and respectful to humbleness." Competition from formerly enslaved women might bring intractable Irish domestics to heel. Slave emancipation promised to liberate white Northern employers.[17]

White Northerners fought the Civil War to promote and vindicate free labor. White Northern workers opposed the influx of Southerners to their region during the war, fearing that competition would depress wages, lead to rampant unemployment, and impede their quest for independence. As the *Continental*'s take on the region's "great social problem" reveals, this competition was precisely what Northern employers wanted, and they took advantage of black and white Southerners' indeterminate and vulnerable status as outsiders. The records of the Pennsylvania Abolition Society (PAS) and the Union Volunteer Refreshment Saloon (UVRS) show that Northern employers believed that emancipation and war justified their appropriation of Southern refugees' and Confederate deserters' labor. The labor scarcity that the *Continental* mentioned may have existed in some occupations typically filled by the men who had gone for soldiers, and Confederate deserters and black male refugees may have fit the bill. In the Northern household, however, the problem was not a scarcity of workers. Rather, a lack of obedient domestic servants threatened to invalidate white Northerners' claims to authority and refinement. The *Continental*'s cultural work fostered fantasies that war and emancipation would be the means by which Northern employers would become able — by engineering a glut in the labor market — to exert more control over the workers they hoped would contribute to their households' efficiency and respectability. Agents of these benevolent societies tried to temper white Northern workers' fears and steadfastly believed in the charitable purpose of their mission. Southerners would, according to PAS, "have an opportunity of becoming acquainted with Northern habits & Customs" associated with free labor before returning home to reshape Southern society in the North's image. Employers believed that what they were doing was charitable, too. They would provide Southerners working for them with wages, shelter, clothing, and, in some cases, education. Yet they emphasized what this migration might do for them. They hoped the war would unshackle capital, their logic grounded in the nation's history of slave trading, the North's antebellum experience of gradual emancipation, and employers' reliance on social typing in their efforts to obtain ideal wage workers. According to this logic, the independence of white Northern employers would be augmented by Southerners who moved north and worked in their households. Slavery's "chattel principle" would give way to wage labor's already established coercions.[18]

In July 1864, Joseph Truman, the chairman of PAS's Committee on Employment, advertised in the Quaker publication *Friends' Intelligencer* that a group of fifty "colored orphans" would soon arrive in the city. Quaker readers "and others ... in want" could be supplied, stating their requirements as to the "age and character" of the laborers they desired. These children were part of the group of people Kinsman was preparing to transport from Fort Monroe. The prospect of their arrival excited Northern employers. Two years earlier, the president of Haverford College, William Mitchell, had predicted it would be so, telling Truman that people of his acquaintance were asking whether he knew how to obtain the services of "'good half grown girls,' and men & boys."[19]

Jane Cary, the wife of an Albany, New York, flour merchant, wrote to Truman immediately because his advertisement offered hope for solving the great social problem of her household. "The Irish have a complete monopoly here and take recently great advantage of it." Cary did not want a child. "I should like a woman," she explained, "who understood cooking washing and ironing and would be obliging and willing." Jane Cary's ideas about the Irish stranglehold over domestic positions had likely coalesced in her relationships with Bridget Fitzpatrick, Hannah Conway, Ann Fox, Mary McGinty, Mary Reuben, and Rosanna Barney, all Irish-born servants who were listed as living with her in federal and state census records between 1850 and 1865. When Cary referred to these women's alleged power in the domestic labor market, she identified her own desire for "advantage." She assured Truman that if she could only get an obedient woman from the South, she "would appreciate her greatly and treat her accordingly." Cary also hoped to tip the scales of power in her community, promising Truman that if this experiment worked in her household, she would try to find places for black Southerners among her friends. This letter folded a claim about Cary's benevolence—to both former slaves and her neighbors—into an ambitious assertion about her economic opportunity and social authority. It therefore was a clear statement of what emancipation meant to her. She would be the instrument of breaking an unjust conspiracy among laborers that limited the authority of household mistresses, and she would accrue respect for doing so. Her efforts would make all domestic servants—Irish and African American—more "obliging" and augment the prestige of other aspiring women in Albany.[20]

The African American refugees from Butler's military department about whom Jane Cary inquired set off from Norfolk aboard the steamer *George Leary* in August 1864. An unidentified Union sailor aboard the vessel deployed the ironic sensibility of *Vanity Fair* to play with the blurry identities of black Southerners making their way to the North. He joked about the potential for profit in his journal, knowing full well that he would not earn a cent. "Now we are put in a glorious business surely! In the nigger trade!" The sailor taunted the ship's cargo, which included, he said, "[t]he Miss Phyllis, and Miss Lucy dee-ahs," the social types that the *Continental* used to reference African American women who would allegedly obey the orders of Northern mistresses. The sailor also called them "apes," commented on the color of their skin ("black, blacker, and molasses colored"), and speculated openly about what they would "fetch" in the slave markets of Cuba, where he "proposed going" to his fellow sailors for a laugh. The white Northern missionaries accompanying the refugees were not amused by the sailors' banter. The instability of former slaves' status in this moment before the passage of the Thirteenth Amendment to the Constitution only served to fuel rumors that black Southerners might be funneled to Cuba for sale by white profiteers. The sailor aboard the *George Leary* ogled black women just as Southern slave traders had done, calculating the value of their skin color and bodies within a wage labor network that he thought resembled a slave trade.[21]

This ship would supply employers of wage labor in and near the ports of Philadelphia, New York, and Boston. Nevertheless, Ezekiel Jenkins of Camden, Delaware, adopted the language of the domestic slave trade when he wrote to Truman about his household's labor needs. "I have concluded to try one or two" of the children, he said, "if any of suitable age and Sex remain on your hands to dispose of. If not," he reasoned, "probably another invoice may arive seeking homes." He hoped Truman had a "likely boy" of twelve or fourteen years, "compactly built, well grown to age, healthy and sound" who had a "lively cheerful good disposition." He also wanted a "lively active girl" with similar characteristics. "Likely" and "lively" were the descriptors that peppered the auctioneering chatter of the slave trader. For Jenkins, the language of the slave trade was the most direct way to convey what he considered desirable in prospective workers. If no individuals in this shipment suited him, there would soon be, available for his perusal, another "invoice" of people with the characteristics he desired, even though these people could not be bought and sold.[22]

The adult women who moved within this transportation network often earned wages of $1.00 to $1.25 per week as domestic servants, much as their Northern counterparts did. Yet the language of the slave trade might have seemed appropriate to Jenkins because of the Delaware Valley's history of gradual emancipation and because of the ambiguities of slavery and freedom in this moment of Southern emancipation. Indeed, slavery had not ended in the state of Delaware, a fact suggesting that the legal status of any transient black Southerners whom Truman sent to Jenkins might be unclear. Other correspondents believed that the movement of African American children into their households offered opportunities to renew the process of apprenticeship that had shaped how white and black Northerners experienced slave emancipation in their region. In the Delaware Valley, those experiences had long been brokered by organizations such as PAS. Elisha Bassett of Salem, New Jersey, told Truman that Joseph Noland, the African American youth whom PAS had sent, did not "want to go back no more to the south." Bassett might not have relayed Noland's words so much as his own dreams for control over his new employee's movements. Bassett acknowledged that he appreciated Noland's intelligence, even though the boy was "smaller than I would have liked." Bassett complained to Truman that "I have no security to enable me to hold him after he grows a little older if through bad advice by servants he should be inclined to leave. I wish so to use him that he may like his home," Bassett explained, "yet boys often get notions in their heads not best for them." Because other workers might poison Noland's mind with the opportunities mobility offered to wage laborers, Bassett wanted Truman to bind Noland, either by word or law. "Something from thee assuring him that he was placed under me till . . . his twenty first year might have a good effect," Bassett believed. As they had done in the early Republic, Northern employers sought to limit the freedom and prolong the coercion of former slaves through apprenticeship. Although the process of wartime emancipation did not permit Bassett to make Noland his "apprentice for life," as New Jersey's 1846 abolition law had done for slaveholders in the state, binding Noland out until his majority seemed like just recompense for the government's outlay for transportation and Bassett's payment for his upkeep.[23]

Bassett's letter reveals his concerns about competition with other employers in the labor market. The PAS employment ledger most clearly shows that the agency intensified competition among laborers for work rather than contributing to the ennobling progress of wage workers toward independence. White workers worried that the arrival of black refugees would depress wages and displace them from their jobs. Yet given that white Philadelphians had relegated African Americans to the lowest-paying menial work before the war, white workers who remained in Philadelphia enjoyed higher wages and less competition while soldiers fought for the nation's survival (although inflation ate up additional earnings). The ledger illustrates, rather, that black workers in Philadelphia were most threatened by the arrival of former slaves from the South. Black men who worked as day laborers did not experience diminished competition for work on the home front before African American enlistment was legal in 1863, and black women who worked as domestic servants were already competing for places with Irish women in the city. The ledger makes this competition between black Northerners and Southerners clear, for the penciled notations for employers "supplied" with laborers include generic references to a "Boy from the South" on the one hand and full names with street addresses on Rodman, Gaskill, and Addison Streets — alleys located in Philadelphia's African American neighborhood — on the other. The latter group included permanent, not temporary, residents who might have been further disadvantaged in this labor market by the arrival of competitors. Yet William Still had argued in 1862 that PAS could help all black laborers. He told the Society then that, at times when the supply of Southern refugees in the city had dwindled, "[t]hose living here in want of employment . . . call quite often." He asked the Society to encourage black

Philadelphians' efforts to find work through PAS by advertising "in the various Halls & places where the societies among the colored people generally meet." Black Philadelphians who ventured to the PAS office might have considered it a vital clearinghouse of information wherein any worker could find a job. Some employers were open to hiring anyone.[24]

But many of them were particular. Truman's correspondents relied on social typing—especially references to race and "character"—as a means of explaining how black Southern workers would contribute to the refinement of their households. They did so in ways reminiscent of the cultural construction of the Biddy in the antebellum period. In a letter to Truman, Benjamin Chase, a wealthy farmer and produce dealer in Macedon, New York, wrote, "I would like to have for myself, a coulered Girl from 12 to 14 years of age." He specified that he wanted her to be "of rather dark couler of sprightly appearance" and also hoped that she "would be well calculated for general house work in the country ... and not brawny." It would be "decidedly preferable," he said, if she was noted for her "quick Motion." He informed Truman that his neighbors also wanted young girls of "prepossessing appearance" who knew how to do housework or were the sort of person Truman "calculated" would be eager to learn how to do it properly. Chase's reasons for emphasizing race and physiognomy were likely bound up in his assumptions about the respectability of his and his neighbors' households and the work performed within them. Contemporaries agreed that appearance mattered, even if they disagreed about what that appearance should be. One applicant to PAS wanted a "light complexted girl," another hoped to find a "yeller girl," while yet another told Truman, "I don't want a yellow boy, but as black as he can be." These employers hoped that the attractive faces and lithe figures of young, black Southerners would ornament Northern households and perform the domestic tasks necessary for their refinement. They would, that is, solve the problem created by the unladylike—because she was relentlessly striving—Biddy. These references to skin color show the multiple ways white Northerners tried to shape and intertwine the meanings of race and respectability within the labor market. It is unclear whether Truman was able to suit Chase or any of the other applicants. A few years after the war, Chase hired an Englishwoman to serve in his household.[25]

Even as they applied different meanings to race and respectability as it suited them, white Northerners deployed old types in new circumstances. The "good half grown girl" whom William Mitchell had mentioned—and bracketed in quotation marks—in his 1862 letter to PAS was a very desirable type of worker. One letter, from Mary Smith of Medford, New Jersey—William Still's hometown—can stand in for the rest. She wanted a girl "of ten years" who exhibited "a sprightly and active dispo[si]tion" and was "susceptiable of instruction." But she also wanted something more. "I expect her permanently and if I can make her useful it will open a door for many more in the Neighborhood." PAS wanted their charges to learn the customs of wage labor, but there seems to have been some confusion on Smith's part. Wage labor, based in contract, was always temporary, a proposition that limited the exposure of both employers and laborers. Slavery was based on the permanence of places. But Smith was not confused. She asked Truman to "let me know the terms." She knew she would have to pay this girl wages. She wanted control, and the PAS intelligence office seemed to offer it to her. She would be a labor broker, too, like Jane Cary. If, as an employer, she could show her neighbors that former slaves were not lazy as was feared, she could arrange for the arrival of more black refugees to benefit neighboring women. Smith was not describing the conspicuous consumption of laborers in a state of slavery. She was demonstrating that wage labor could accrue employers cultural capital among neighbors who also wanted to do business in a new and conspicuously national labor market.[26]

The intelligence office, the institution that defined wage labor in the nineteenth century, created value for the middleman or middlewoman. That is what contemporaries found objectionable about it. Intelligence agents' dollar fees paled in comparison to the commission profits of slave traders, but their slow and steady gains skimmed value from labor brokering to the outrage of Northern employers and workers who felt cheated by their transactions. The benevolent intelligence office was supposed to mitigate these concerns. PAS charged a fee to employers, but not to workers, and used the proceeds to care for the refugees waiting to find jobs. Yet the employers who corresponded with the PAS office also tried to accrue value beyond the labor these refugees would do.

In the antebellum period, as they fretted over the destabilizing potential of the Biddy, Philadelphians did nothing less than create a market out of the value inherent in the label and person of the half-grown girl. Embedded in that designation were meanings of age and gender that allowed housewives who could only dream of employing an adult servant to get someone to do more work for less wages. In the want ads of city newspapers in the 1840s and 1850s, Philadelphia employment agents listed half-grown girls to entice employers to their waiting rooms, eager employers called for half-grown girls, and young women searching for work described themselves as half-grown girls. Often the ads simply read "WANTED—A half grown GIRL," because

A Great Social Problem

everyone knew who this was and what she did. The label referred to age and bodily size, but it also stood in for the value of the work she did. The half-grown girl was the servant for the housewife who still did the bulk of her own household labor and who could not afford an adult servant at full price. She was a young girl who could play with or monitor children and help around the house, all for cheap. In 1854, a self-described "half-grown girl" offered to work without wages for one year, suggesting how ideas and practices of apprenticeship shaped the labor market for young people in and around Philadelphia. Other sources reveal that half-grown girls worked for half wages and that they could be as old as twenty years of age, meaning that it might be difficult for a young woman to shed the label and assume a place in the ranks of adult domestic servants who deserved full wages. The "terms" that Mary Smith asked for were elastic, and that was by design. The arrival of Southern refugees permitted white employers to dream of the more perfect subjection of African American girls, no longer slaves, to their control. The presence of black, Southern, half-grown girls in the North was evidence of the ongoing destruction of the slaveholders' aristocracy and the rise to prominence of Northern employers whose respectability was based on the considerable coercions — Smith might have referred obliquely to permanence — of wage labor. In this way, half-grown girls symbolized what this cruel war was over. As the *Continental Monthly* had once prophesied, they represented a means by which the Northern middle class might become all-powerful.[27]

This incipient national labor market, however, was also conspicuous for its failure to get employers the workers they wanted. Mary Smith wrote back to PAS two months after her first letter, and she did not feel all-powerful. She was disappointed. "This may inform Thee that I was not suited with the little colored girl Sophrona in as much as she could not understand nor hear what I said neither could I understand what she said therefore after keeping her ten days I procured for her a very good home I went to sea her not Long sinc she appeared cheerful & happy had improved much in her looks & they incline to keep her." Smith tried to evade the criticism that she was the lazy one — she had not tried very hard or for very long to fulfill the permanent bargain she wanted to make. Instead she blamed a failure to communicate and bathed in self-praise for being useful to the community of white women who wanted domestic servants. Smith could report her success in placing Sophrona, cheerful and happy Sophrona, in a very good home that would be made even better by the labor of a half-grown girl.[28]

The potential power embedded in these labor arrangements was fleeting, but even as employers came to realize that emancipation would not make them as independent as they had hoped, they continued to craft a language of class that would help them mitigate their disappointment. In May 1865, Ann Cope wrote to Jane Boustead, a PAS employment agent, about Matilda and Lydia Berry, two young African American women from Maryland who had left their mother and sister in Washington because there was no employment for them there. Once they were ensconced in the Cope household in Chester County, Pennsylvania, the Berrys talked incessantly about returning to Washington or Philadelphia. They told Mrs. Cope "that they did not intend to stay but a month when they came." They, and not their mistress, would decide how temporary or permanent their employment would be as they assessed what would be best for them and their family. The Berrys "seem to think it an indignity to do many parts of my work," Cope complained. It "would seem from their talk as if they had never known what it was to be active in business, neither are they disposed to improve," she lamented. "I believe they think it is the duty of the whites to maintain them in ease." African American refugees did not solve the problem of the Biddy. They exacerbated it.[29]

Yet the process of shaping the meanings of age, gender, race, and household gave Northern employers such as Ann Cope the tools they needed to solve the "great social problem" and maintain their authoritative economic and social positions. Cope invested great meaning in the harmony of interests, but only as a concept to be proclaimed and rejected when it suited her efforts to seize power and social standing. She believed that her charity should have begotten gratitude, emulation, and obedience from her workers, but the Berrys were not the eager-to-serve social types the *Continental* had promised would "swarm" from the South. As a result, Cope told Boustead, "they are of very little use to me." They could walk to Philadelphia for all she cared, "and they may undertake it, for most certainly they will do as they please." She discarded charity in favor of wielding her wage labor prerogatives: "I have engaged a person who I expect will suit me better than they both do." This movement of laborers had gathered momentum because Northern employers believed that the ideal worker was available in the South, but perhaps Cope calculated that the emancipation of black Southerners had succeeded in making Northern laborers less recalcitrant. Faced with the reality of emancipated slaves who seized the opportunities of geographical and social mobility open to them, Northern employers like Cope relied on their wartime cultural work to pivot to a position of even greater strength over white and black workers in the political economy of wage labor.[30]

By the end of the Civil War, PAS was pleading for help to fund its venture to find employment for former slaves in the city. Fees paid by expectant employers had run dry, leaving the Society without money to house black refugees before they were placed. So it asked the city's House of Industry to do so. In the end, former slaves would encounter not the Northern habits and customs that illuminated the promise of free labor but, rather, the competitive customs of nineteenth-century capitalism, which drove some poor souls to the almshouse.[31]

While loyal Southerners were drawn into the labor arrangements for which the Union war was fought, Northern employers also hired Southern laborers of questionable loyalty. When President Lincoln came to Philadelphia to visit the city's Great Central Sanitary Fair in June 1864 — escorted by a committee chaired by Thomas Webster — he gave a speech in which he praised the "Cooper-Shop and Union Volunteer Refreshment Saloons" for having "contributed to the comfort and relief" of Union troops who passed through the city on their way to Washington and points south. Henry Walker had eaten at the latter with his comrades of the 117th New York in 1862. By 1864, UVRS had accepted a new purpose. It created an employment agency to assist Southern refugees and deserters from the Army of Northern Virginia — unable to return to their Dixie homes — who began to trickle northward in search of work and sustenance. In February 1864, the War Department sought to regulate the movement of white Southern refugees and deserters in General Order 64. Civilians and soldiers coming into Union army lines would be read Lincoln's amnesty proclamation of December 1863 and offered the chance to take a loyalty oath to the United States "if they so desire." They were to be informed that they could not be forced to join the Union army and that they could obtain "employment from the United States." Confederate soldiers who deserted to the Army of the Potomac would be sent to Washington or "as far north as Philadelphia" to find jobs. The migration of Southern deserters and refugees turned into a steady stream when the Army of the Potomac tightened its siege of Petersburg in the fall of 1864, choking off vital supplies to Confederate troops. The men and women who operated UVRS, supported by contributions from wealthy commercial, industrial, and financial men, agreed to help these Southerners find homes and jobs in and near the city. UVRS records reveal a presumption that all refugees and deserters had taken a loyalty oath, and some Southerners wrote about their fondness for the United States. A deserter from the Second Georgia wanted the officers of UVRS to know that "if *there was a spark of prejudice* or *disloyalty to the glorious Star Spangled Banner* left in my bosom upon arriving in this city, it has been totally and *forever* extinguished by the unprecedented generosity" of their "noble institution."[32]

The letters addressed by prospective employers to Joseph Wade, the institution's employment agent, show that Northerners only rarely referenced deserters' and refugees' oaths. They appeared to care less about loyalty and more about whether their demands for labor would be met in a time of war when many local men were in the army. Household heads' requests for workers were alternately particular and nonspecific. Lancaster County farmer Jacob Rupp wanted two young men to work on his farm until the winter months and another who could run a cooperage. As an afterthought, perhaps remembering the labor needs of his wife, he implored Wade, "[I]f the girls are plenty send us one." A Delaware farmer hoped to "leave an order" for "5 or 6 farm hands," not appearing to care whether they were white "refugees or Colored Contrabands." A Gloucester County, New Jersey, farmer told Wade about a neighbor named Joseph Cahaley who needed an agricultural "hand" on his place "as soon as possible." While the letter offered a "permanent position" to one of the "deserting 'rebs,'" the "fair wages" it promised were not enumerated. Cahaley's neighbor explained that the employer would decide what was "fair" once the laborer arrived on his farm. Wade endorsed the letter with the names and biographical information of two soldiers who had served as privates in the Sixty-First North Carolina and had worked on farms before the war.[33]

Other employers mentioned wages because they understood that they were competing in a national labor market. One offered "$16 to 20 Dollars per mounth and their Boarding washing & mending" to "men of good habits," and another offered $20 each month without those additional services. Both were generous offers that demonstrate the ways the labor market in the countryside near Philadelphia was shaped by the absence of Northern soldiers and the other job opportunities Southerners might find elsewhere in the North. Employers found that many deserters and refugees were hardly passive or merely grateful for employment. Southern whites sought opportunities for advancement outside Northern employment agents' auspices. Employers who had been jilted by the deserters vented their frustration to Wade. One soldier sent to North Wales, Pennsylvania, to work for Maxwell and William Rowland on the North Pennsylvania Railroad was there for a "short time," but "thought he would try at something that he could make more wages" and left. Workers' freedom of mobility, a constituent element of free labor, was inconvenient for employers, who responded by plying Wade for more men. Maxwell planned to send William to the city to fetch another "good stout boy or man." Sure enough, Wade had another teamster, late of the Thirty-Fourth North Carolina, to fill the position. Whether employees deserted employers' homes in search of better arrangements or were dismissed for heavy drinking, employers simply wrote back to Wade, "Pleas send me some more soon."[34]

Refugees could take advantage of these labor market realities to find a new home for themselves. Louisa Rosson took to the roads of Madison County, Virginia, in 1864 and arrived at UVRS on April 25. Her husband William, who served in the Twelfth Battalion Virginia Light Artillery, had been court-martialed and docked one month's pay in June 1863 and deserted to the Army of the Potomac on March 9, 1864, before the Overland Campaign began. William must have coordinated his desertion with Louisa, for she told UVRS when she arrived in Philadelphia with her three children that he had "left home" on March 6. Louisa and the children were sent to live in a household in Roxborough, just northwest of Philadelphia. By June, William's comrades from the Twelfth Battalion, Churchill Weakley and Bumbery Back (the latter was related to William by marriage), had arrived in Philadelphia to inquire about the locations of their wives and children. UVRS had no information for them, but William Rosson reunited with his family and settled in Philadelphia after the war. In 1870, he managed a farm and owned $900 in personal and real estate, compared to the $100 in personal estate he owned in Virginia before the state seceded. Deserters found opportunities for advancement in the North.[35]

Yet a few former Confederate soldiers communicated with Wade after being placed about the tensions between consent and coercion in wage labor. Twenty-one-year-old Alex Cabaniss arrived at UVRS on August 24, 1864. A private in Company A of the Forty-First Alabama, he had deserted from the Army of Northern Virginia with his corporal, thirty-three-year-old Jacob Neighbors, three days before. This was not the first time he had been absent without leave from a Confederate army, having deserted in June 1863 from General Joseph Johnston's army cobbled together to relieve Vicksburg, Mississippi. Cabaniss's first desertion was a short affair—he returned to his regiment in October. His second would be permanent. He and Neighbors agreed to work for Owen Trainer in a Wilmington, Delaware, livery stable. Yet Trainer lied to the Alabamians. He procured them from the Saloon in order to coerce them into enlisting in the Union army as substitutes for Northern draftees. The market for substitutes was a thriving one, but Cabaniss was a savvy economic actor—or so he proudly told Wade. "[I]t Want Not Him that was Smart a Nuf to Fool me that way Nor Never Will," he wrote four days after leaving Philadelphia. Trainer clearly eased his demands, for Cabaniss informed Wade that "Hee Treeted us Very will and Ses Now He Dont Want us to Go if it ant Hour on Free Will." Caught in the act of trying to push Cabaniss and Neighbors to do something they did not want to do, Trainer evoked the language of the "free" market. Wage workers, he said, could decide for themselves where to work. Cabaniss and Neighbors secured jobs at "the foundry" in Wilmington. Cabaniss's difficulties with Trainer had unnerved him some. He claimed to be "Better Reconsild Sence I Got Employment." Despite this encounter with a scoundrel, Cabaniss believed in the promise of free labor. "I thinke I Wil Bee Satsfide after a While Wee git $8 per Weeke and Wee Have to Pay 4 Dollars per Weeke For Board But I think that I can do Better than that after a whil." Neighbors, in his own letter a few weeks later, told Wade that he had earned twelve dollars in the preceding week, although a hand injury was limiting how many days he could work. Both men envisioned advancement for themselves through wages. Their purpose in writing to Wade was to locate two other privates from the Forty-First Alabama who had been sent to a farm in Delaware County, Pennsylvania, so that they could share their good fortune and reconstitute the community they had known at home and in their regiment. Cabaniss begged Wade to send word to his "Pardner[s]" that they could find plentiful and lucrative work in Wilmington. In fact, Neighbors told Wade that they had obtained positions for their comrades "if [they] are not other wise engaged." Appreciative of Wade's help in finding work, the Alabamians tried to cut out middlemen and rely on friendly networks of intelligence gathering to help their friends obtain jobs.³⁶

Confederate deserters and white civilian refugees valued their autonomy and their freedom to move as much as black refugees in the Philadelphia area did. They moved over long distances to find better jobs, reunite with friends and family, or keep body and soul together. From Cressona, Pennsylvania, almost a hundred miles northwest of Philadelphia, Anna Shippen wrote to her son Edward about the same time Cabaniss wrote to Wade. "We had a deserted confederate I presume, at the door, to ask for bread & water. . . . He seemed too much frightened almost to eat & drink & with a quick step hurried" to a neighbor's "to seek employment." The episode, so at odds with Shippen's daily experience, haunted her. "This horrid war when will it be over!," she cried. "I cannot help saying that I think it kept up by fraud & speculation."³⁷

Alex Cabaniss may have been grateful for what Joseph Wade had done, but he should not have trusted him. Employers asked Wade to give the refugees and deserters "instructions to Keep out of the hands of sharpers," but it appears that the man many employers and deserters called "Uncle Josey" was one of them. In July 1864, weeks after Congress repealed the $300 commutation clause from the Enrollment Act and President Lincoln called for 500,000 more men to serve as soldiers, Samuel Price wrote to his "dear cousin" Wade from Wilmington, Delaware. The evidence suggests that these men, unlike those who used the word "uncle" to foster fictive kinship ties, actually were related. Price recounted a conversation the pair had recently had, in which Wade urged Price "not to pay extravagantly for a substitute." The repeal of commutation made finding a reasonable price difficult. Price had negotiated an $800 deal with a Philadelphia substitute broker, but then the draftee had second thoughts. Maybe his dear cousin could help him. "Can you get any of the numerous arrivals from Rebellious states to accept or go into the Army for the year Bl[ac]k or White[?]," he asked Wade. On the day before Cabaniss and his comrades arrived in the city, Wade received another letter from Price. He had evidently tried to get his own substitute in Wilmington, but that man had "backed out," Price communicated. "Now I want you to stir me up a good man. One that will pass. I want to be rid of the matter & you may go as high as Six Hundred & fifty $650. & as much less as you can get one for. but get one & send him down. I'm tired of fooling about it here." Price's calculation was that a Confederate deserter or a black Southerner who had escaped Butler's clutches would be substantially cheaper than a white Northern substitute because they had been made vulnerable by the dislocations the war had produced. Price was in earnest, hoping to put a "Young Rebel" in as a substitute for himself. It is possible that Cabaniss and Neighbors factored into Wade's calculations. Perhaps he had hoped that the Alabamians could be persuaded to replace Price in the Union ranks for the right price. They refused to be taken so cheaply, preferring autonomy and the slow and steady gains of work among the crashing machines at the foundry to the whistling shells and bullets of the battlefields they had just fled.[38]

The probability that Wade had tried to run a few grayback deserters from Philadelphia back south in Union blue in order to help a family member could be overlooked for all the good work that UVRS was doing. The institution "furnished to passing soldiers 500,000 meals, to soldiers from the Hospitals & camps near the City 165,000 [meals], to Refugees Freedmen & Rebel Deserters 135,000 [meals] making in all 800,000 meals." Wade had a steady supply of deserters at the ready for Northern employers—the Army of the Potomac and the "Association to Procure Employment for Rebel Deserters" in Philadelphia worked hand in glove. On March 23, 1865, the Union army circulated thirty thousand copies of the *Philadelphia Inquirer* among Confederate troops at Petersburg, which included an article detailing the association's purpose and the opportunities UVRS offered to deserters. The association claimed that some six hundred Southerners—starving, poorly clothed, and despairing of victory—came into Northern lines the next night. Within two weeks, Petersburg and Richmond had fallen. The association's leaders tried to take credit for the "important effects" the circulation of the *Inquirer* had on the willingness of General Lee's men to stay in the trenches. The happy result for Northern employers was to enhance their opportunities to find the workers they wanted.[39]

Yet earlier in the spring of 1865, victory in the war for Union did not seem assured, and substitute brokers plagued Northern cities. Brewster obviously knew that their business was lucrative, and Wade dabbled in it to help his cousin. Everyone, it seemed, had heard a story of a young man who had been swindled out of the rich payments purportedly available to men who went for substitutes. The agent of the Philadelphia Branch of the U.S. Sanitary Commission sent a note to Wade to ask if he could let a New York mother stay at UVRS for a night while she did rounds at "the Hospitals in this city in search of her son... [who] it is thought was sold as a substitute by one of the numerous swindlers Known as Substitute brokers." The frauds of substitute brokers—also called recruitment brokers or bounty brokers—became so pervasive that the War Department sent Colonel Lafayette Baker to Manhattan to investigate. In February 1865, Baker arrested many of the men who managed and manipulated a speculative wage labor market in which they created value and lamented when "Men is cheep."[40]

They were not the only speculators Baker encountered. The other participants in that market—substitutes and their wives—hoped it could create value for them. That is what they gambled on. Substitutes were often victimized by bold, brazen fraud. The social types created at the time—the intrepid soldier and the virtuous soldier's wife in opposition to a cabal of nefarious swindlers—sought to distinguish the latter who speculated from the former who sacrificed and were sacrificed. The swindlers were real, but Northerners—much as they did with "Biddy" and "half-grown girl"—created social types because it helped them manage capitalism's culture in a time of war. The testimony that Baker heard reveals the strategies, preparation, and hard work of ordinary people who speculated in the substitute market as much as it illuminates their suffering at the hands of brokers. Substitutes and their families thought they had a friend in Baker, and they hoped the state might help them claw their way to survival in an economy that limited their access to resources. They potentially had leverage in ways that Sophrona, the Berry sisters, and Alex Cabaniss did not. The testimony that Baker heard clarifies people's ambitions for a better life as they struggled to survive the Civil War.[41]

The development of a labor market in substitutes managed by brokers illustrates why commutation failed as a policy. Before July 1864, drafted men could not find enough substitutes who would serve in their stead for $300 or less. The government also failed to spend the funds accumulated from commutation fees because men expected more capital to do the work of killing and dying. Town supervisors felt the pressure of commutation's failure—with each call of the federal government, they had to fill quotas or risk a draft. The substitute market was expensive, adding to the costs of war for citizens who paid higher taxes to fund local bounties and contributed to draft insurance funds to protect themselves if their names were called. Town commissioners tried to lessen these burdens on their citizens, communicating with each other before visiting city brokers' depots to share information that would help them secure the services of men on the cheap. When streetwise brokers compelled them to pay higher prices, supervisors complained to Baker, trying to cover up the fact that they had been speculating in this market in order to lower costs for their communities.[42]

The spiraling rates for substitutes after commutation was repealed obviously hurt laboring men who could not pay a high-priced substitute. Yet the escalating rates for hire provided opportunities to working people who chose to go to war. Baker repeatedly heard from men who had tried to bend this market to their benefit but who had come away chastened by the experience. Their assertions that they had been cheated should be understood as a crucial aspect of the economic crisis the war produced, a crisis that was as much about cultural meaning as material distress. Their narratives obscured ambitious motive, justified conduct, and sought second chances. One soldier named Michael Lawrance wrote to Baker in March 1865 from the camp of the Fifth Rhode Island Artillery in New Bern, North Carolina, asking for help in bringing a broker to justice. The broker had promised him, if he went from New York to Providence to enlist, that he would get $300, half of which would go to "get[ting] me clear." What Lawrance called a "swindle" by a broker was a bounty-jumping scheme. He was asking Baker to collect the other half of this bounty, because he could not find the broker himself "without deserting," and he "scorn[ed] that idea," even though that idea was the whole point of bounty jumping. It bears saying that, even though bounty jumping offered pecuniary success over and above mere survival as men enlisted, obtained a bounty, and enlisted again, Baker's records show that jumpers were often the agents of a broker who allowed them to keep only part of the stealings.[43]

More often, speculations by substitutes were not so obviously fraudulent. Substitute hire was a new opportunity to make households more solvent and their members less dependent. Some substitutes directed recruiters to pay their hire to third parties to whom they owed money. Sometimes that third party put the man up to it—that is, he acted as a broker—but these instances show the ways men used this market to alleviate financial pressure on their households when they would not have been able to do so otherwise. Soldiers' wives and mothers called on paternalistic aid from Baker and the government, relying on cultural scripts that they hoped would create sentimental ties with the clerks and officers listening to their testimony. They lived on what their husbands and sons could earn, and without their support they had nowhere else to turn.[44]

The testimony that Baker's clerks copied shows that women struggled for survival against a variety of men—brokers, army officers, and relatives—who had the ability to make their lives difficult. Women and their allies coupled stories of "destitute circumstances" and appeals for help with tales about male relatives who withheld husbands' substitute hire from them. One woman feared that the $500 her husband had been paid was lost forever, drowned at the bottom of her brother-in-law's whiskey bottle. Brokers challenged women to prove that they were married to soldiers who were owed payments and hid behind vague assertions about what army regulations said they owed. Both were tactics that imperiled the welfare of wives and children in the absence of breadwinning husbands and fathers. Ambitious sons might do the same, their heads turned by the prospect of earning a sum of money that vastly exceeded their yearly wages. Struggling to make ends meet, these men were as susceptible to the call from substitute brokers as they were to pitches made by employers who offered high wages. Making decisions about their careers without the knowledge or permission of parents could separate young men from their protectors and devastate the family economy all at once.[45]

Women did not always play the role of shrinking violet. They were central figures in family economies: they found out what was theirs and demanded it. Some appear to have learned about the substitute market by surprise, after receiving a letter from a husband or son informing them that they had enlisted or been duped into enlisting. This news was especially hard to hear because family survival was often predicated on men's, women's, and children's combined earning power, and now women not only lost their men's wages but also work time of their own as they retraced the steps of husbands and sons back through the market in order for the family to benefit from the payment owed to them. Jane Wilsey's husband Jacob telegraphed to ask her to venture from the family home in Brooklyn to Trenton, New Jersey, where he had been sent after joining the army in Newark as a substitute. He hoped she would "get my money, for I can't draw it myself" after being sent to Virginia three days after enlisting. On arriving in Trenton and speaking to an officer there, Jane Wilsey discovered that the army would not let her have the money either, since her husband "could draw it in the army himself." Undeterred by the conflicting information, she returned to Newark and tracked down the man who had paid $900 to a broker named Mead to hire a substitute—Jacob—for him and confronted Mead's brother-in-law, who claimed not to "know who it was that brought her ... Husband to that office." She suspected that "some foul play and great wrong [had been] committed," though, and after further sleuthing put the argument to Baker that Mead had pocketed $400 that should be her family's. Baker's investigations into the fraudulent system potentially provided Jane Wilsey with the muscle that could obtain restitution, but she had done the detective work herself to determine how this market operated and how her household had been cheated.[46]

After Baker arrested substitute brokers and bounty jumpers in February and March 1865, he began to receive letters from family members proclaiming that their men were innocent and that they should be released from their confinement in Washington's Old Capitol Prison. They had been at the wrong place at the wrong time. They had temporarily fallen in with bad men. Local worthies attested to their honesty and integrity. It was probably just as well for Baker that the end of the war absolved him of adjudicating what fraud was and who perpetrated it in each and every case. By the war's end, a few brokers had even started to impersonate Baker's detectives, accusing citizens of bounty jumping and demanding that they empty their pockets of money to make the accusations go away. Everyone agreed that fraud was everywhere and eminently adaptable. In Baker's records, everyone was saying that they did not do it.[47]

Northerners condemned the substitute business as fraud even as they failed to appreciate the ways it represented the wage labor market of their region in the nineteenth century. We may think that workingmen were gullible when they fell for brokers' stories about future payments in installments, but working people were not paid for jobs up front in this era. They also risked losing back pay if they did not give employers two to four weeks' notice that they were quitting. This new market in substitutes seemed lucrative, but it was opaque in its operation. So they trusted people who claimed they had insider knowledge about how it worked. Asymmetries of information in the labor market had spawned a class of intelligence office keepers in the antebellum period who were often accused of cheating workers looking for jobs. No amount of local government licensing and regulation could put an end to it. The monetary value of that theft paled in comparison to what substitute brokers cleared off during the Civil War. When substitutes discovered they had been cheated, they thought that Baker, a representative of the federal government, would assist them in reclaiming the windfall that was supposed to be the legitimate fruits of speculating in free labor—the money that might have led to a more stable economic outlook. Unfortunately, in only a few cases was Baker able to recover money stolen from substitutes. He was as weak an instrument as local mayors' offices had been before the war. Drafted men were dependent on the broker and his extortion, too, but after they paid the brokers, their responsibilities ended. For women like Jane Wilsey, the con went on and on. No matter for the drafted man whom Wilsey encountered in Newark. He could rightly say that he did not cheat her. She should blame the broker.[48]

Northern employers reaped the reward when the Union army's pressure on Confederate forces and its inability to provide subsistence to former slaves generated migrations of Southern refugees in the last months of the war. Employers gained access to workers through the auspices of benevolent institutions and used social typing, references to the domestic slave trade and the constraints of apprenticeship from the era of Northern emancipation, and the cultural assumptions of free labor to strengthen their control over workers and resolve the "great social problem" in their households. The market in substitutes after commutation seemed to offer the men being hired a competitive advantage, as bounties and hiring fees mounted for Northern draftees and taxpayers. In the end, substitute brokers engaged in fraud that both negated substitutes' competitive advantage and provided an opportunity for Northern employers to obscure their own exploitative practices. They, as well as the substitutes, could blame brokers for the ills of free labor. The efforts of employers to accumulate capital through the labor of displaced Southern refugees, exploitative though they were, looked positively benevolent when compared to the reprehensible acts of substitute brokers. Those brokers, of course, were vital figures who sent men into the Union army to constitute a part of the physical force that Lincoln believed necessary to win the war for Union. Brokers' impropriety helped to obscure Northern employers' victories in the war as well.

CONCLUSION

AFTER PRESIDENT LINCOLN was felled by an assassin's bullet, Ralph Waldo Emerson declared that when the Illinoisan had won the presidency, "[t]his middle-class country had got a middle-class President at last." Emerson deployed "middle class" as a rhetorical device to identify the "manners" and "sympathies" that public servant and citizens shared. Lincoln had, Emerson believed, "what farmers call a long head; [he] was excellent in working out the sum for himself." He also "was a great worker; had prodigious faculty of performance; worked easily." "A good worker is so rare," Emerson explained, for "everybody has some disabling quality." Lincoln "liked nothing so well" as his work. He calculated the superiority of labor over capital, he figured how the nation could finance emancipation at low cost, and he accounted for the manpower the United States needed to survive. The war for Union, embodied in these ideological, financial, and material speculations, had vanquished a slaveholding aristocracy that did no labor for itself. That war had cleared opportunities for other Northern speculators to work for their own success in the race of life. They would often do so by using "middle class" in the same way that Emerson did, validating one's own hard work and exploiting the labor of others while casting that exploitation as justice, a result of others' "disabling qualities."[1]

In Virginia City, Montana Territory, one man obscured an exploitative past that might have been disabling. In November 1864, Governor Sidney Edgerton ordered all citizens to meet later in the month to be organized into militia companies by the territory's acting assistant adjutant general, John Nelson. Edgerton's order identified Nelson as "Colonel." Nelson's move from Virginia to Virginia City seems to have been as lateral as his move from New Orleans to Norfolk. He was pushed out of Virginia, but he was also pulled to Montana to realize his ambitions for advancement. In October 1864, he sought election as representative to the territorial legislature. He lost, but standing for political election had made him look sober, even if Virginia City was a place to get drunk and strike it rich in gold and quartz mining. Nelson tried to profit either way, leaning on his experience as a machinist and denizen of sporting culture. In the newspaper he advertised his wholesale liquor store, boasting of "A CHOICE LOT OF OLD RYE" that "makes up splendidly in Hot Drinks." At his "Leviathan Hall," he scheduled boxing and wrestling matches for the miners. He also convinced Connecticut manufacturers of his acquaintance to invest in his proposal for a quartz mining company that would operate hydraulic machines by steam power to realize *"big things"* — to turn their capital into more capital. The investors told Nelson they had "no doubt of your success, honesty, integrity, energy, determination & ability." But they should have had doubts. The enterprise was, in the estimation of historian Jeffrey Safford, "a complete failure," ending in recriminations and lawsuits between Nelson and his investors. By 1870, he had moved two hundred miles with his wife, Eliza, and three children to new diggings at Missoula. By 1880, he and his wife had four more children, and they had moved to Park City, Utah, where he continued in the mining business. When he died that October of pneumonia at the age of forty-five, the *Salt Lake Herald* called him one of the "most prominent and public spirited citizens." As he finished running the race of life, the soldier of fortune had finally gotten the respect he craved.[2]

Other former recruiters and brokers sought their fortunes after the war, too. Charles Brewster returned home to Northampton, Massachusetts, and turned businessman, prospering in the sale of goods respectable people needed to decorate their homes — sashes, paint, and flowers — instead of labor brokering for domestic servants to work in them. Joseph Wade went to western Pennsylvania's oil fields to find capital in crude. He may have been part of an "Oil concern" which several leaders of UVRS had cobbled together on shares. He wrote back to his Philadelphia friends in May 1865 from Venango County, imploring them to tell him how things were going back east. He had heard that "Old Jeff Davis had been captured," and he hoped the government would "[h]ang him and try him afterwards." As for his prospects in oil country, Wade thought he was working in "a mighty temperate place my Habits have undergone a Considerable Change I only get a drink on Sunday." He could be sober when he needed to be. "I have Worked pretty hard since I have been up here," he wanted them to know. "This Oil Business is not what it is Cracked up to be some men make a great deal of Money at it by Rascality & I have had a good opportunity of learning some things of them." Not enough to succeed, however. He returned to Philadelphia, and in 1866 he was working as a secretary for the agent of a national insurance company capitalized at $200,000. Wade had secured a comfortable commercial berth, but precious little of that capital was his.[3]

The men who succeeded in the oil business did not do so only through rascality. They tried to access the labor of men who might be looking for a new start, and they did this by taking advantage of intelligence offices created by benevolent organizations. The Soldiers Aid Society of Cleveland, Ohio, for instance, helped unemployed veterans find work and kept careful records of former soldiers' names, units, national origin, trades before the war, and physical disabilities received from military service. The Society's matrons also operated under certain assumptions about soldiers' willingness and ability to work. Among the articles they cut and pasted into their records was one titled "Disabled Soldiers," published in the *Army and Navy Journal* in January 1865. Citizens would surely "sympathize" with men who had sacrificed a limb in service to the nation, the journal explained. But disabled men must not wallow in sorrow. The "public cannot furnish disabled men with energy, honesty or self-respect, and will not forever help men who are unwilling to help themselves." The essay's author warned that Americans assumed soldiering had "unfitted" them "for active or laborious employments in civil life." Veterans must — by their own conduct, hard work, and perseverance — prove them wrong. "The public have no prejudice against a soldier," the author explained, now potentially talking to all veterans, both disabled and able-bodied. They did, however, "have strong prejudices against a dirty loafer 'who has been in the Army.'" Conversely, "soldiers from well-disciplined regiments come back better employees than they were before they went away." Veterans were thus caught in a bind created by the contradictions of free labor. They needed to demonstrate the ambitious endeavor and persistence that would suggest their fitness for upward advancement, even if their war-ravaged bodies — disabling qualities — would not let them. If they faltered, they would be accused of lazy "sogering" — another label in the labor market that had long been used to describe the malingering of a variety of workers, from sailors to slaves. Frederick Winslow Taylor, who would develop time-motion studies at the end of the nineteenth century to speed production, referred to this behavior as "soldiering." The only answer to the problem of the dirty loafer was for veterans to prove themselves eager and obedient workers who could be disciplined and directed by those with capital.[4]

Businessmen who funneled their capital into the oil business, for instance, were eager to employ tractable laborers. The men sent to work at the oil refinery of Morehouse, Merriam & Co. in Cleveland included workers who had been teamsters before the war, but also George Burdett, a twenty-five-year-old veteran of the 102nd Ohio who told the Society that he wanted a "[s]ituation in a Store, not so particular about salary, as having some position where he will have an opportunity of being advanced." Undifferentiated from the former teamsters, it appears that Burdett would work with his hands rather than with his head. Burdett's dreams for advancement in the race of life — like those of many other veterans who believed in free labor — were clearly less important to the Society than his new employer's interest in getting workers. Presumably, the Society would have had little sympathy for Burdett if he did not advance from his job as a laborer in an oil refinery. His character would determine how far he would rise in the world. Applicants knew that capital, not character, was the desideratum in the market. One entry in the Society's ledger, for a nineteen-year-old veteran of the 103rd Ohio, George Ford, read, "Good looking, common school education, will do anything." But then the Society's employment agent noted that Ford got tired of waiting for a place. "Gone to Oil City. Gone to Oil City," the agent repeated. If the Society did not find these men jobs quickly, they would take matters in their own hands and venture to the heart of the latest speculation. Fifteen miles north of Oil City in Titusville, Pennsylvania, J. T. Briggs, an agent for Wood & Mann, a company that sold "Portable Engines and Cleveland Pit Pipe," declared to the Society that "[w]e are in want of a Colored Boy about 20 years of Age, capable of taking care of Horses and making himself generally useful around the house. If I can find a good one I will pay him good liberal Wages." The Society sent James Young, formerly a servant for an officer in the 197th Ohio. In the employment ledger, under "disability," the Society's agent had written "none. but lazy." When Young arrived in Titusville, Briggs's partner L. H. Severance agreed with the Society's appraisal and sounded much like Charles Brewster did when he talked about his former camp servant, David. "He is a genuine specimen of the Southern *nigger* & says he can 'shuffle' with the best of them on the dance." Severance was not impressed. "He is hardly steady enough for me & I am inclined to let him try some hotel work where he may find the 'complexion' & Society to suit his taste." It is not clear from the records whether Young was able to find another job, much less the "Society," to suit him.[5]

On March 5, 1865, the *New-York Tribune* reported that the "appointment of a Chief of the Freedmen's Bureau is now engaging the attention of public men. Gen. Butler, Judge Birney and Thomas Webster, jr., are mentioned in this connection." The Bureau of Refugees, Freedmen, and Abandoned Lands, commonly known as the Freedmen's Bureau, had been created by an act of Congress just days before. Its purpose would be to protect the civil rights and ensure the social and economic welfare of newly freed slaves. The three rumored nominees had all contributed mightily to the effort of recruiting African American men into the Union army and advocating for racial equality of pay among soldiers. William Birney had commanded the

Twenty-Second USCT, a regiment organized by Thomas Webster's Supervisory Committee in Philadelphia, and had returned to Maryland at the end of the war to lead the recruiting of black soldiers there. Benjamin Butler had played an important role in shaping Union policies on emancipation and wage labor in various theaters of war and occupation.[6]

None of these men were named to the post. Webster would have been flattered by such public recognition but probably took the rejection in stride. He had always been a "nearly" man in American politics and patronage. Postbellum city directories listed him as a "shipping agent," but it does not appear that he resumed business with much alacrity. It would have been difficult for him to return to tobacco wholesaling immediately after the war. Black soldiers of the Army of the Potomac's Twenty-Fifth Corps, some of whom Webster had helped to recruit, were among the first to enter Richmond on April 3, 1865. In the captured rebel capital, one of their first tasks was to contend with fires that retreating Confederates had set to tobacco warehouses in the city so that the capital those crops represented did not fall into Yankee hands. A postbellum assessment of Webster's credit among Philadelphia businessmen declared that he was "not thought reliable for his contracts." Prognostications about his commercial viability remained uncertain, just as they had been before the war. Webster was not destitute. He and Eliza Ann could still call on "her fathers estate" for sustenance. The credit reporter had heard something else, though, something more troubling. Webster had "made some money during the war, in claims & Bounty." During the conflict, Webster never gave up his speculations about how to make the public good benefit his private balance sheet. As he devoted his considerable logistical skills to army contracting and recruiting in the war for Union, Webster gained access to information about how soldiers and their families could navigate the federal bureaucracy to get what was owed them, and he charged for it. The records of this side hustle are not extant, so the extent of his bounty and claim operation is not clear. But he had no qualms about making money out of the war. If he had received the offer of the Freedmen's Bureau post, he might have wondered whether rumors of his war profiteering would have caused a scandal. More likely, he realized that thanks to his capital resources, he did not need a political post now like he did in 1860. By 1871, a credit reporter pronounced Webster "[o]ut of bus[iness]," whether because he lacked credit among his peers or had access to capital from family and wartime wealth. He died in 1894 at the age of seventy-six.[7]

Butler had been removed from command by President Lincoln and General Grant in January 1865 after he bungled an attack against Fort Fisher in Wilmington, North Carolina. After Butler's removal, an investigation revealed evidence of rampant speculation by Northern businessmen in the Department of Virginia and North Carolina, including trade with the enemy. Butler emerged from the investigation relatively unscathed and launched an impassioned defense of his military rule. He had "established," so he told a friendly audience at home in Lowell at the end of January, "system, order, and organization of labor, so that the freedman who would work could work; and those who would not work might find means whereby they should work." He took credit for the wage labor policies that netted five thousand black recruits to the military "without bounty" and the unknown number of African American men recruited by Northern states to fill their draft quotas. He provided "food and raiment, and protection from the inclemency of the weather" to black women and children in his department and "demonstrated that the former slave population of the South can be self-supporting, even without a large proportion of the able-bodied men." Butler seemed to be auditioning for the leadership of a government agency that would ensure workers' right to contract, provide supplies and shelter to the poor, and do it all at low cost to the citizens of the United States.[8]

If winning the Freedmen's Bureau post was his aim—and it was—he did not succeed. Because we know of his efforts to give black soldiers bounties and move black refugees northward, it is clear that Butler was not telling his audience the complete truth. The problem for his contemporaries was neither his dishonesty nor his willingness to turn a blind eye to fellow citizens' speculations. It was his radicalism. He reiterated his supposed opposition to bounties, arguing that they placed "a load of taxation upon every laboring man" that would prove a burden for future generations. Soldiers and former slaves should be rewarded for their loyalty and sacrifice in the war for Union with land confiscated from disloyal white Southerners. Brewster and other Union soldiers had dreamed of the independence that Southern land represented. Butler thought his proposal would shift the financial burdens of the war from Northern citizens to Southern traitors.[9]

This proposal for confiscation was rarely tried in the years after the war, although many Northern soldiers did move to the South, buy land, and start agricultural ventures that became profitable through the wage labor of former slaves. Even Butler could not reconcile his radicalism with a much less radical belief that the black Southerner was, as he told another Lowell audience in February 1865, "by our wrongs untaught, uncultivated, and without the habit of self-dependence, fitted thus to take care of himself." African Americans were not yet educated in the Northern habits and customs, as

PAS would have it, that would teach them what to do with capital and independence. Butler suggested that white Americans should "simply ... let the negro alone," but only alone to "enjoy the right of selecting his own place of labor; the person for whom he will labor, if not for himself; to make his contract for his labor; to determine its length and its value." On the one hand, soldiers — mainly although not exclusively white soldiers — might have access to the land of traitors in order to accumulate capital, but former slaves' sole right would be to work. Self-dependence, grounded in former slaves' right to work, would remain separate from independence, grounded in white men's right to earn capital from other people's work. Butler's iconoclasm would be the marker of his long career near the center of postbellum politics.[10]

After the war ended, the Freedmen's Bureau, under the direction of General Oliver Howard, played a crucial role in establishing wage labor relations in the South and negotiating labor contracts between landowners and former slaves. Some of the bureau's officers were initially reluctant to create intelligence offices. "The system of agencies," one officer told a rural Maryland landowner who had inquired about obtaining African Americans to work for him, "is felt to be an evil as usually conducted." The bureau should help "idle" black Southerners to find jobs and be an advocate for them in contract negotiations with employers, but antebellum and wartime experience had shown that "the interference of a third party is not desirable."[11]

Yet at the same time, other Freedmen's Bureau officers supported the creation of and justified the need for employment agencies, seeking to head off what they considered an impending social crisis. In the summer of 1865 in Memphis, Tennessee, for instance, local bureau superintendent Nathan Dudley, the man whom John Andrew had once put in command of an "irregular" regiment recruited by Butler, witnessed former slaves congregating in urban communities without the means to make a living, even as rural white landholders clamored for their services. Black men and women, not wanting to live under whites' surveillance any longer, refused to go to work in the country. Dudley, believing that he knew former slaves' interests better than they did, asked bureau commissioners for the authority to move them onto rural plantations. "Planters are sending Agents through the City to secure hands and promise these Agents as high as five and ten dollars per hand," he told his superiors in Nashville. Such agencies were "perfectly legitimate," he said, reminding them that "Intelligence Offices for the purpose of obtaining situations and servants exist in every City in the North." Intelligence offices represented the essence of wage labor to Northerners like Dudley. What better way to highlight slavery's demise, given that the bureau had a federal mandate to broker contractual arrangements between employers and employees, than by managing wage labor transactions in intelligence offices?[12]

Americans had long tarnished the legitimacy of these transactions, yet Dudley's declaration about them represented a sort of ideological alchemy whereby intelligence offices could be made to shine as emancipation unfolded in the South. His argument soon held sway in the nation's capital, where, at the corner of Fourteenth and M Streets, the Freedmen's Bureau opened a labor agency of national scope. The purpose for establishing the labor brokerage was clear: to help some twenty thousand impoverished African Americans in Washington get on their feet economically by finding them work, alleviate "sanitary and social peril" in the city, and reduce the financial burden this destitute population placed on the federal government. The bureau would achieve this goal by sending black workers to farms, towns, and cities where landholders and business owners needed them. In February 1866, the bureau sweetened the deal for employers, agreeing to pay transportation costs for laborers who had already been engaged to work. Employers would pay the bureau one dollar for every male laborer and fifty cents for every female laborer before the negotiation of wage contracts commenced. As historian Robert Harrison has shown, some eleven thousand black workers obtained jobs through the auspices of the bureau between 1865 and 1868. Charles Howard, assistant commissioner for the District of Columbia and younger brother of the bureau's superintendent, sought to create a network of intelligence offices to shepherd laborers to employers by writing to ministers and members of Northern benevolent societies who had experience with running employment agencies. In explaining his purpose to them, though, he was forced to confront the conflicting imperatives of the benevolent intelligence office. "My object," he said, "was not to find good help at a cheap rate for Northern employers but to benefit the poor freedpeople here."[13]

Bureau commissioners, while making the claim that their intelligence office was legitimate due to prevailing Northern practice and its benevolent purpose, were ambivalent about their role in brokering labor deals. Prospective employers certainly hoped to get good help cheap, and their interest conflicted with bureau officials' responsibilities. Charles Howard and his deputies acted as canny labor negotiators, telling some employers that the wages they proposed to give workers were too low and criticizing them for taking office fees out of their employees' wages. They tried to maintain oversight over branch office agents and keep them from gouging workers and employers with extra fees. The bureau sought to protect laborers' interests, hearing depositions from people who had contracted with landholders under the auspices of the bureau's intelligence office only to encounter employers who refused to pay them or who treated them violently.[14]

Simultaneously, bureaucrats, prospective employers, and concerned observers slipped easily into the language of class that emphasized the opportunities intelligence offices offered to employers. Charles Howard gave citizens hoping to hire black workers a choice: either come to Washington themselves and "select just the persons you desire" or hope that a portion of "the next lot" wending its way to the nearest benevolent society office would suit their needs. A former captain in the 127th Illinois who had recently purchased a Mississippi plantation wrote to the bureau offering to pay wages of "15$ pr month for 1st Class men & 10$ pr month for same class women," borrowing the labels used in antebellum slave markets. President Andrew Johnson, an observer who cared little for the plight of former slaves, asserted that the bureau's agency "was little better than another form of slavery." The editor of the Washington *Evening Star* explained that an accusation made by New York newspapers—that the bureau was "trafficking in negroes" and "running them off to the Southern States"—seemed credible because of the reputation of intelligence offices. This employment agency, the paper wryly observed, was "doing good, . . . [by] saving" African Americans "from the hands of many so-called 'philanthropists,' who will collect claims, write letters and perform other services for the black man for pure love of the race and—a *small consideration.*"[15]

Many of these "philanthropists"—entrepreneurs looking for the main chance—were among the bureau's most avid correspondents, hoping to realize their ambitions through labor brokerage, giving voice to their frustrations, and sharing their ideas about local and national labor markets. The bureau heard from many citizens who wanted to be employment agents, perhaps hoping to obtain monetary fees and the social benefits of having helped neighbors hire laborers in a distant market. If the bureau sent "four or five" black laborers to Cortland County, New York, John Holbrook announced, "I will undertake to find them good situations in families." Marylander F. A. Tschiffely claimed that four hundred men, two or three hundred women, and two hundred boys could find remunerative work in Montgomery County. After doing their own research, however, bureau officials demurred, believing the demand for labor was not sufficient to warrant sending so many workers there. While it is unclear why Tschiffely would have made such claims, he may have hoped to portray a sluggish labor market in the hopes of creating a glutted one that would drive wages down.[16]

Just as some of the bureau's correspondents angled for the rewards that labor agents could earn, some employers hoped to use the bureau's scheme to create competition in their neighborhoods between black and Irish domestic servants. "There is general disgust with Irish help," C. L. Woodworth of Boston told Oliver Howard, and it was native-born Bostonians' "desire that colored girls could be secured to take their places" in order to break Irish women of "their conceit & importance." These tractable "colored girls" would hopefully serve the forces of cultural production and cement the social and economic authority of the city's best families. Republican, pro-emancipation, anti-Irish, and staunchly respectable, Brahmins believed that hiring black domestic servants offered opportunities to cultivate regard for the poor, raise them in the estimation of the world, and drive Irish women into poverty in order to make them less obstinate.[17]

Employers and agents could become belligerent when they felt that transactions with the government's intelligence office curtailed their ambitions. J. O. Bloss of Rochester, New York, was furious that he had only been able to get ten workers after sending "orders upon orders" to the government. Bloss surmised that federal bureaucrats denied hundreds of white New Yorkers access to laborers because they had a vested interest in creating "red tape regulations," impeding the flow of laborers to the North "lest their occupation should cease." The emancipated workers whom Bloss and others desired sometimes disappointed their employers when they decided to return to their family and friends in Washington after a brief sojourn in the North. Charles Howard tried to stop his agents from encouraging this mobility, but to no avail.[18]

While ordinary citizens tried to use the government's free transportation policy to become employment agents on their own hook and as the bureau's agents tried to collect fees on the sly, other intelligence office keepers competed avidly with the bureau for the capital that laborers represented. Oliver Wood, a Baltimore intelligence agent, made a brokering business out of false pretenses. In 1865, he had his employees tell African American laborers in the Washington intelligence office that he would negotiate contracts on their behalf with Maryland employers, only to force them to board ships at Baltimore to sail to the Caribbean to harvest guano. Unabashedly, Wood wrote to Charles Howard the next year, asking to partner with the bureau to move black workers to Northern employers and illuminating his efforts to drum up employer demand in the region. "I have worked hard for Twelve months and spent considerable money to induce the Farmers to seek out this idle labor," he wrote, claiming that he "had enough to contend with to keep off the Sharks ... and Sharpers who are stealing my men." The bureau's assistant commissioner for Baltimore accused Wood of being one of those "Sharpers" for making false representations to twelve black men from Richmond. These former slaves claimed that Wood's agent had told them they would earn fifteen dollars per month in Baltimore. When they arrived at Wood's office there, he sent them to the village of Fairhaven in Anne Arundel County to work for six dollars per month, minus the "expenses incurred in our getting there." A few of these workers walked from southern Maryland to the bureau's intelligence office in Washington, hoping to adjudicate their complaint. These men found a friend in W. F. Spurgin, the superintendent of the Washington intelligence office, who had served as captain in the One Hundredth USCT during the war. Spurgin condemned Wood's "rascality" and argued that he should be "arrested and prosecuted for deceiving and swindling freedmen."[19]

Needless to say, Wood thought such a punishment would be unjust. He contended that his agent in Richmond had hired the men for ten dollars per month—a wage Maryland farmers would have been willing to pay until the black Virginians informed Wood that they were "Machanics and did not wish to Farm." Wood was the aggrieved party in his own mind: "[T]hey put me to all the expense they could from Richmond to Fairhaven and I had every dollar to pay and did not receive one cent in return." These were the dangers of being a middleman in the market, forwarding funds to clients in the hope of accumulating larger profits. Sometimes even the intelligence office keeper could be duped—or could claim to have been duped. Wood protested too much. He had been a substitute broker during the war and should have known better.[20]

William Still had been a middleman during the war, too. He brokered labor arrangements for black Philadelphians and Southern refugees, served as sutler at Camp William Penn for black recruits, and pursued avenues for private gain in groceries and household goods that also benefited African American consumers in his city. In the generation after slavery's capital had stolen value from his father and older brother, Still worked hard on behalf of himself and African Americans to recoup that value in personal and collective quests for more independence. His race of life had hardly been run on a level track, and in the postbellum years Still made public his struggles to control his capital in self and declare his independence. He recalled a cold December day in 1863, when he paid streetcar fare for himself and a white employee to ride from Camp William Penn to downtown Philadelphia after a day of sutlering for African American soldiers. The conductor, following the law segregating streetcars, forced him to ride outside on the frigid platform while his white employee enjoyed a warm berth inside the car. Still, surely fuming about the supposed freedom of those with capital, decided to walk home from Germantown rather than suffer the indignity. The episode anchored Still's argument for desegregation of the city's public transportation in order to make the capital of all Philadelphians equal. He published *The Underground Railroad* in 1872 to underscore this point. His personal quest for value in the market for books was made through the aggregated stories of African Americans who stole from the slaveholders' aristocracy and helped to initiate a war against it.[21]

Most African Americans searching for independence in the labor market through the Freedmen's Bureau found that it was difficult to control the value of their labor. Spurgin's accusation of guilt and Wood's plea of innocence show that the practices of and ideas about the bureau's intelligence office did little to resolve Americans' ambivalence toward an institution that played a crucially important role in shaping wage labor and emancipation in the Civil War era. As abolitionists and historians of slavery's capital have understood, auctions that turned enslaved people into commodities represented the quest for value inherent in Southern slavery. In similar ways, intelligence offices — and not free labor assumptions that a harmony of interests bound employer to employee on the shop floor, in the farm field, or in the home — represented the quest for value at the heart of wage labor relations. Intelligence offices revealed that the cornerstone of free labor ideology — that hard work, good character, and saving would help workers get ahead — had crumbled. This was disconcerting to Americans, but it was also delightful, for the intelligence office could fulfill employers' desires to staff agricultural and manufacturing enterprises with laborers possessing particular skills and fashion respectable domestic spaces with obedient and knowledgeable servants. Employers' independence was made in intelligence offices, where they could accrue wealth and respect through the labor of workers they encountered there.[22]

Yet white Northern employers contrived to define the end of slavery, a transition to wage labor managed in part through intelligence offices, as a frightful moment in which they might lose independence. The *Continental Monthly* prophesied a grim future during the final months of the war. Until inventors created a "housekeeping Utopia" serviced by machines — perhaps operating by the steam power that Lincoln used as metaphor — Northern employers would always be disappointed with their household staff, whether they were Irish immigrants or African Americans. Without servants, there would be no "civilization" and no "refinements of life." Respectable people would move to hotels, "huge gilded pens" in which they would pay ever-escalating rates to workers "who will have a share of the profits" and begin to tip the economic and social order in their favor. Middle-class Americans, surely not all-powerful, would be forced to move to "hovel[s]" or socialist communities in which there was no inequality and thus no prestige. This was, surely, the end of the refined household and the end of class distinction, if not the end of days. Beyond hoping in vain for improved "machinery" or "automaton flunkies" to take workers' places, the *Continental* identified a reformed "model intelligence office" as the only place to which employers might apply for "aid." Intelligence offices represented the problem at the heart of—and the solution to—the labor question in Civil War America. Confronted by untrustworthy middlemen and recalcitrant workers, Northern employers were faced with the terrifying prospect that they just could not get good help anymore.[23]

In reality, employers had won the war for Union, and they had won it with the assistance of intelligence offices managed by the state, benevolent institutions, and entrepreneurs. The concerns exhibited in the *Continental* masked the ways war and emancipation had increased the power and prestige of Northern employers of wage labor. This book has chronicled the speculations of a variety of Northerners—from the common soldier and household mistress to the more powerful businessman, officer, and politician—who do not always get credit for being among abolition's agents. They believed wholeheartedly in free labor, because the trajectory that ideology mapped for Northerners showed that the only way to more independence in a market in which all were dependent was through the accumulation of capital and the opportunity to exploit others' labor. They fought the war for Union against slaveholders to bolster their own authority. The movement of workers created by soldier recruitment, emancipation, and what Lincoln called the "friction and abrasion" of war gave them opportunities to do so. Intelligence offices served this war for Union by marshaling workers whose capital in self the state and employers could access for their benefit. These institutions could also take the blame for the inequalities and disappointments of wage labor, obscuring the fact that the war's labor movements had unmade the promise of free labor for working people. That promise had long been a problem for white, middle-class northerners. In the 1870s, in a bid to consolidate the power that intelligence offices had helped them attain, they spurned the radical reconstruction of southern society and confronted laborers' strikes in their own region with state-sponsored violence.[24]

NOTES

ABBREVIATIONS

BL Baker Library, Harvard Business School
BRFAL-DC Records of the Assistant Commissioner for the District of Columbia, Bureau of Refugees, Freedmen, and Abandoned Lands
CW Basler, *Collected Works of Abraham Lincoln*
HSP Historical Society of Pennsylvania
KL Letters, Orders, and Telegrams Received by Lt. Col. J. B. Kinsman
LCP Library Company of Philadelphia
LOC Library of Congress
MHS Massachusetts Historical Society
NA National Archives
NYH *New York Herald*
OR *War of the Rebellion: A Compilation of the Official Records of the Union and Confederate Armies*
PAS Pennsylvania Abolition Society
PI *Philadelphia Inquirer*
PL *Public Ledger*
RDD *Richmond Daily Dispatch*
RG Record Group
WRHS Western Reserve Historical Society
WTCWIO Blight, *When This Cruel War Is Over*

INTRODUCTION

1. War views. No. 2042, *Bounty brokers looking out for substitutes*, LOC; Lincoln, "Opinion on the Draft," *CW*, 6:447–48; Shannon, *Organization and Administration*, 2:14, 32; Murdock, *One Million Men*, 197–207; Marvel, *Lincoln's Mercenaries*. For more on the opposition to the draft, see Bernstein, *New York City Draft Riots*.

2. For recent interventions in the debate about "a rich man's war, and a poor man's fight," see Glatthaar, "A Tale of Two Armies"; Marvel, *Lincoln's Mercenaries*; Robertson, "Rich Man's War, Poor Man's Opportunity?" Seth Rockman's argument that the "early republic's economy opened up new possibilities for some Americans precisely because it closed down opportunities for others" is exactly right. The Civil War clarified this fact about class and capitalism in America and expanded the opportunities for capital on a national scale. In this book, I build on Rockman's insights by examining the ways a moment of slave emancipation—as opposed to intersecting wage and slave labor systems—helped to bolster employers' choices and autonomy. See Rockman, *Scraping By*, 3.

3. *War views. No. 2041, Bounty brokers looking out for substitutes,* LOC. For recent work that emphasizes the ways the concept of "military necessity" shaped the experience of emancipation during the war, see Taylor, *Embattled Freedom*; Manning, *Troubled Refuge*; Oakes, *Freedom National*. By examining the links between military and domestic necessity, I build on the insights of historians who have asserted the importance of assessing the connections between homefront and battlefield. See Attie, *Patriotic Toil*; Giesberg, *Army at Home*; Silber, *Daughters of the Union*; Clarke, *War Stories*, 21–22.

4. George Northrup to Fay & Dalton, January 5, 1865, box 1, Baker Papers, NA.

5. "Astounding Frauds on Government," *New York Times*, February 8, 1865; Shannon, *Organization and Administration*, 2:43–44, 55–56; Murdock, *One Million Men*, 255–304; Murdock, *Patriotism Limited*, 107–48; Michael Thomas Smith, *Enemy Within*, 127–53; Marvel, *Lincoln's Mercenaries*, 192; *Circular of James B. Fry, Provost Marshal General, 1863*, box 2, folder 6, Alexander Henry Papers, HSP.

6. Testimony of George H. Sitterley, April 1, 1865, and Mackenzie & Mitchell to Richard Dalton, January 24, 1865, box 1, Baker Papers, NA; Carmichael, *War for the Common Soldier*, 190; Luskey, "Dishonest Clerks and the Culture of Capitalism"; Walter Johnson, *Soul by Soul*; Mihm, *Nation of Counterfeiters*; Kamensky, *Exchange Artist*; Mackintosh, "Loomis Gang's Market Revolution"; Luskey, "Men Is Cheap"; Thomson, "'Like a Cord through the Whole Country.'"

7. For the creation of value in "slavery's capitalism," consult Baptist, "Toxic Debt, Liar Loans"; Berry, *Price for Their Pound of Flesh*; Rosenthal, *Accounting for Slavery*; Schermerhorn, *Business of Slavery*; Hilliard, *Masters, Slaves, and Exchange*; Hilliard, "Bonds Burst Asunder"; Murphy, *Investing in Life*, 184–206; Stanley, "Slave Breeding and Free Love"; Beckert and Rockman, "Introduction," 14; Martin, "Neighbor-to-Neighbor Capitalism"; Rothman, "Contours of Cotton Capitalism"; Boodry, "August Belmont and the World the Slaves Made." On the need for more scholarship that "blurs the line between slavery and freedom" and illuminates "the historical process by which the boundaries between slavery and 'freedom' were drawn," see Stanley, "Wages, Sin, and Slavery," 284; Walter Johnson, "Pedestal and the Veil," 306; Smallwood, "Commodified Freedom," 298.

8. Eric Foner, *Free Soil, Free Labor, Free Men*; Burke, *Conundrum of Class*, 108–32; Richardson, *Greatest Nation on Earth*, 2–5; Huston, *Calculating the Value of the Union*, 67–103; Tuchinsky, *Horace Greeley's* New-York Tribune, 12–13, 167–68; Glickstein, *Concepts of Free Labor*, 11–16; Lears, "Concept of Cultural Hegemony," 575–76.

9. John Clegg has written that "widespread and systematic market dependence" is a "unique feature of capitalist society." See Clegg, "Capitalism and Slavery," 282, 300; Zakim and Kornblith, "Introduction." For more on capitalism's coercions, see Mishler, "Myth of Modern Slavery." For the ways nineteenth-century Americans created hedges against risk that illustrated their market dependence, see Levy, *Freaks of Fortune*. I have benefited greatly from Jeffrey Sklansky's observation that, in order to understand the contours of class in nineteenth-century America, we must acknowledge that "control over the means of payment . . . has been comparable to control over the means of production." See Sklansky, "Labor, Money, and the Financial Turn in the History of Capitalism," 43–44. See also Sklansky, "Elusive Sovereign"; Sklansky, *Sovereign of the Market*, 93–165. For the ways free labor ideology united white Northerners across class lines, did not lead to workers' advancement, and embodied an employers' "creed," see Paludan, *People's Contest*, 178; Rodgers, *Work Ethic in Industrial America*, 32–37, 153. For the ways the Civil War unshackled Northern corporations, see Adams, "Soulless Monsters and Iron Horses."

10. Luskey, "Special Marts," 360. For more on intelligence offices in the antebellum and Civil War eras, see Urban, *Brokering Servitude*, 7–15, 29–98; Dudden, *Serving Women*, 79–87; Licht, *Getting Work*, 98–140. For more on the nineteenth-century debates concerning commercial transactions, financial instruments, and commodity circulations that produced contested definitions of economic legitimacy and illegitimacy, consult the essays in Luskey and Woloson, *Capitalism by Gaslight*. For more on the problem of middlemen in this period, see Luskey, *On the Make*; Woloson, *In Hock*. For reassessments of social categories as ideological and cultural processes that shaped experience, see Currarino, "Toward a History of Cultural Economy"; Hartigan-O'Connor, "Gender's Value in the History of Capitalism"; O'Malley, *Face Value*.

11. Luskey, "Special Marts," 360–61; Ayers and Nesbit, "Seeing Emancipation"; Gallagher, *Union War*.

12. Montgomery, *Beyond Equality*, 28; Stanley, *From Bondage to Contract*; Steinfeld, *Coercion, Contract, and Free Labor*, 10; Eric Foner, *Reconstruction*, 18–34, 124–75; Beckert, *Monied Metropolis*, 176–77, 280–81; Richardson, *Death of Reconstruction*; Paludan, *People's Contest*, xxv–xxx. Scott Sandage defines the Civil War as a "war for ambition" in *Born Losers*, 189–225. On the need for "causal stories" that illustrate the material, financial, and cultural "connections" in the history of capitalism, see Lipartito, "Reassembling the Economic," 138. I use "labor movements" here to suggest that the dependence of laborers was just as important a marker of class as consciousness and formation. For more on class formation and consciousness during the war, see Lause, *Free Labor*; Russell L. Johnson, *Warriors into Workers*; Mahoney, *From Hometown to Battlefield*. For my ideas about the ways we define class—a "struggle for power and prestige among Americans who had unequal access to wealth and the trappings of refinement"—and the ways it operated in nineteenth-century America, see Luskey, *On the Make*, 17; Luskey, "Ambiguities of Class." For recent scholarship about the movement of African Americans to Northern places during and after the Civil War, see Urban, *Brokering Servitude*, 64–95; Schwalm, *Emancipation's Diaspora*; Greenwood, *First Fruits of Freedom*; William Cohen, *At Freedom's Edge*, 44–108; Faulkner, *Women's Radical Reconstruction*, 117–31; Harrison, *Washington during Civil War and Reconstruction*, 60–108.

13. George Northrup to Fay & Dalton, January 10, 1865, box 1, Baker Papers, NA. On the problem of anonymity in the history of capitalism, see Agnew, "Afterword." By focusing in detail on the ebb and flow of fortune and failure in these men's lives, I draw on the narrative strategies employed in Carmichael, *War for the Common Soldier*.

14. James Oakes has contended that Republicans opposed slavery as much as they supported free labor, using the concept of military necessity as a justification to achieve their goal of freeing enslaved people. He laments that "the broad appeal of principled antislavery politics goes unexplained" in the historical literature. I take Oakes's point but also take a different tack, focusing on the motives and actions of Northerners who were rapaciously self-interested in slavery's dissolution. In this way, my book builds on the work of Scott Reynolds Nelson, who has explained how Northerners with capital—represented most clearly by the railroad directors who exploited political connections and used shady financial practices in an attempt to establish an empire of wheat to confront King Cotton in the late 1850s—helped to inaugurate the sectional conflict in Kansas, the Panic of 1857, and the war itself. See Oakes, *Freedom National*, xv; Nelson, *Nation of Deadbeats*, 126–58. Recent scholarship has begun to examine the complex, contradictory, and contingent meanings of consent, coercion, and mobility during eras of war, emancipation,

and state-building in nineteenth-century America. Examples of that literature include Stacey L. Smith, *Freedom's Frontier*; Taylor, *Embattled Freedom*; Manning, *Troubled Refuge*; Foote, *Yankee Plague*; Jim Downs, *Sick from Freedom*; Emberton, "Unwriting the Freedom Narrative"; Gregory P. Downs and Masur, "Echoes of War"; Stanley, "Instead of Waiting"; Sternhell, *Routes of War*; Reidy, *Illusions of Emancipation*; Silkenat, *Driven from Home*; Pryor, *Colored Travelers*; O'Brassill-Kulfan, *Vagrants and Vagabonds*; Levine-Gronningsater, "Delivering Freedom."

CHAPTER 1

1. "Arrivals at the Principal Hotels Yesterday," *RDD*, June 17, 1854; *McElroy's Philadelphia City Directory* for the years 1839–46 chart Webster's entry into the business world from clerk to merchant. His partnership with Ruddach dissolved sometime in 1846: an advertisement for the firm in *PL*, March 14, 1846, shows the firm still intact, and an advertisement in *PI* for July 23, 1846, reveals Webster to be in business alone. Ruddach started the firm of Ruddach and Sons in 1847, suggesting that his sons had come of age and perhaps, at the age of twenty-eight, it was the right time for Webster to become the proprietor of his own firm. See also Wimmers, Agnew, Blanchard, and Paterno Family Tree, https://www.ancestrylibrary.com/family-tree/person/tree/110700724/person/320083086924/facts?ssrc, accessed March 23, 2018; Thomas Webster, Jr., Tobacco M[er]ch[an]t, Pennsylvania, vol. 131, p. 364, Thomas Webster, Shipping Agent, Pennsylvania, vol. 144, p. 208, R. G. Dun & Co. Credit Report Volumes, BL; *PI*, April 27, 1848, September 29, 1849. For the marketing strategies of tobacco producers and distributors, see Hahn, *Making Tobacco Bright*, 45–47. On the role of the Kansas-Nebraska Act in the formation of the Republican Party, see Eric Foner, *Free Soil, Free Labor, Free Men*, 125–26.

2. *PI*, September 13, October 7 and 16, November 23, 1854; *McElroy's Philadelphia City Directory* for 1855. For the importance of marriage in accumulating wealth and credit, see Luskey, *On the Make*, 200, 219. For the rise of credit reporting as a means of weighing risk in antebellum commercial transactions and the ways rumors often shaped credit reports, see Sandage, *Born Losers*, 99–188. For the cautious strategies young businessmen employed to achieve commercial stability in this volatile era, see Balleisen, *Navigating Failure*, 203–19.

3. For the geography of the slave trade in antebellum Richmond, see McInnis, *Slaves Waiting for Sale*, 55–83. For an example of Northerners whose Southern business interests collided with their antislavery principles, see Lasser, "Conscience and Contradiction."

4. My argument that speculation, "wrecking," and Barnumesque humbug were key features of the antebellum economy depends on the insights of Sandage, *Born Losers*, 70–98; Cook, *Arts of Deception*; Balleisen, *Navigating Failure*, 135–62; Balleisen, *Fraud*, 43–104. For more on the contradictory "business ethics" adopted by Northerners involved in the Southern trade, see Rockman, "Northern Manufacturers, Southern Slavery."

5. *RDD*, July 18, 1854.

6. *RDD*, July 20, 1854.

7. *RDD*, November 13, 1854. For the beginnings of African slavery in Virginia, see Oakes, *Freedom National*, 93. For the "carceral landscape" of American slavery, see Walter Johnson, *River of Dark Dreams*, 209–43. For more on the antebellum Hygeia Hotel, see Engs, *Freedom's First Generation*, 6.

8. Still, *Underground Railroad*, 4, 54, 57, 60, 63–64, 192, 201, 235–40, 309, 584.

9. Still, *Underground Railroad*, 56–58, 64–65, 67, 74–78, 141, 158, 163, 191. For more on Still's life and antislavery career, see Hall, "To Render the Private Public," 36–37; Diemer, *Politics of Black Citizenship*, 151, 154, 157–59, 167–69, 171–72; Varon, "'Beautiful Providences.'" For more on the underground railroad, see Blackett, *Making Freedom*; Eric Foner, *Gateway to Freedom*. For the business of the domestic slave trade, consult Schermerhorn, *Business of Slavery*. Julie Winch and Richard Bell have examined a competing market wherein free black Philadelphians were kidnapped into the domestic slave trade. See Winch, "Philadelphia and the Other Underground Railroad"; Bell, "Counterfeit Kin."

10. Still, *Underground Railroad*, 153–54; *PI*, April 27, 1848, October 16, 1854.

11. Still, *Underground Railroad*, 61; "Portsmouth," *RDD*, August 10, 1855; "Want Money," *RDD*, August 13, 1855; "The Health of the City," and "Quarantine," *RDD*, August 15, 1855.

12. "Meeting in Aid of the Sufferers at Norfolk, Portsmouth, and Gosport," *PI*, August 17, 1855; "Town Meeting," *PL*, August 17, 1855; "Norfolk and Portsmouth Sufferers," *PL*, August 22, 1855; *PI*, October 4, 1855; "The Virginia Sufferers," *PI*, November 30, 1855.

13. "Chap. 47. An ACT providing additional protection for the slave property of citizens of this commonwealth, passed March 17, 1856," *Acts of the General Assembly of Virginia*, 38–41.

14. "Chap. 47. An ACT providing additional protection for the slave property of citizens of this commonwealth." For more on the passage and implementation of this law, and some of the legal proceedings that resulted, see Schwarz, *Slave Laws of Virginia*, 140–44.

15. "Grand Excursion by Sea to Virginia," *PL*, May 9, 1857; "The Particulars of the Sinking of the Steamer Norfolk," *PL*, September 18, 1857; "Storm on the Southern Coast," *PI*, September 17, 1857. Forty-eight ships were lost in the storm. See "Extent of the Gale," *NYH*, September 21, 1857. For more on the Panic of 1857, see Nelson, *Nation of Deadbeats*, 126–58; Huston, *Panic of 1857*.

16. Thomas Webster, Jr., Tobacco M[er]ch[an]t, Pennsylvania, v. 131, p. 364, R. G. Dun & Co. Credit Report Volumes, BL. For more on Greaner and his firm's commercial relationship to Webster, see *RDD*, January 19, 1853, and *PI*, July 23, 1846. See *McElroy's Philadelphia City Directory* for the years 1856–59 for references to Webster continuing in the tobacco trade. *McElroy's* for 1860 was the first that lists him as only an agent of the Union Steamship Company, and *McElroy's* for 1861 was the first to describe him as a "shipping and commission merchant." For references to Webster receiving merchandise on Union Steamship Company vessels, see *Press*, September 11 and 15, October 8, 1857; *PI*, January 11, 1858, October 5, December 7, 22, and 29, 1860, January 11, April 3, 1861.

17. "To the Philanthropic," *PI*, January 24, 1859.

18. Webster to Sherman, May 28, July 13, 1860, vol. 14, John Sherman Papers, LOC; McCorison, "Impressions of the President Elect," 293. For more on politics in Civil War–era Philadelphia, see Dusinberre, *Civil War Issues in Philadelphia*.

19. Webster to Sherman, July 26, 1860, vol. 15; December 31, 1860, vol. 19; and October 12, 1860, vol. 16, Sherman Papers, LOC. For the "sporting culture" of antebellum America, see Gorn, *Manly Art*.

20. Webster to Sherman, October 15, 1860, vol. 16, Sherman Papers, LOC.

21. Webster to Sherman, October 15, 1860, vol. 16, Sherman Papers, LOC; Rockman, "Northern Manufacturers, Southern Slavery." For the importance of material and emotional appeals and registers in partisan politics of this era, see Woods, "Tracing the 'Sacred Relicts'"; Woods, *Emotional and Sectional Conflict*.

22. Webster to Sherman, October 26, 1860, vol. 16, Sherman Papers, LOC.

23. Webster to Sherman, July 26, 1860, vol. 15, Sherman Papers, LOC.

24. Carey to Webster, November 9, 1860, and Hickman to Lincoln, November 8, 1860, Abraham Lincoln Papers, LOC.

25. Webster to Sherman, November 15, 1860, vol. 17, Sherman Papers, LOC; McCorison, "Impressions of the President Elect," 297; Webster to Lincoln, November 14, 1860, Applications for Appointments as Customs Service Officers, RG 56, Entry 247, Records of the Division of Appointments, Records Relating to Customs Service Appointments, NA, https://s3.us-east-2.amazonaws.com/papersofabrahamlincoln/PAL_Images/PAL_PubMan/1860/11/257185.pdf, accessed May 3, 2018.

26. Webster to Sherman, November 15, 1860, vol. 17, Sherman Papers, LOC; McCorison, "Impressions of the President Elect," 297–99, 301. Mary Lincoln wore the same ensemble on her first shopping trip to New York City in spring 1861, and the newspapers' glowing description mimicked Webster's. See Fleischner, *Mrs. Lincoln and Mrs. Keckly*, 197.

27. Hammond, "Speech on the Admission of Kansas," in *Selections from the Letters and Speeches of the Hon. James H. Hammond*, 318–20. For more on the proslavery critique of free society and Republicans' response, see Eric Foner, *Free Soil, Free Labor, Free Men*, 62–69; Lause, *Free Labor*, 27; Walter Johnson, *River of Dark Dreams*, 380–81.

28. Lincoln, "Address before the Wisconsin Agricultural Society, Milwaukee, Wisconsin," September 30, 1859, *CW*, 3:477–78; Eric Foner, *Free Soil, Free Labor, Free Men*, 30; Boritt, *Lincoln and the Economics of the American Dream*, 176–80.

29. Lincoln, "Address before the Wisconsin Agricultural Society, Milwaukee, Wisconsin," *CW*, 3:478–79.

30. Luskey, "Special Marts," 365; Luskey, "Houses Divided," 644; Cook, *Arts of Deception*.

31. Dudden, *Serving Women*, 65–72; Stansell, *City of Women*, 155–68; Anbinder, *Five Points*, 128; Urban, *Brokering Servitude*, 29–63; Luskey, "Houses Divided," 644.

32. Leland, *Memoirs*, 19–20; Stansell, "Whitman at Pfaff's"; Lause, *Antebellum Crisis and America's First Bohemians*, 86; Sentilles, *Performing Menken*, 138–65; Cohen, Gilfoyle, and Horowitz, *Flash Press*; Roberts, *American Alchemy*; Halttunen, *Confidence Men and Painted Women*; Gallman, *Defining Duty in the Civil War*, 15, 25; Luskey, "Houses Divided," 644–45. For more on the cultural sensibilities of Civil War Americans, see Carmichael, "Soldier-Speak"; Carmichael, *War for the Common Soldier*, 230–65.

33. Luskey, "Houses Divided," 645.

34. "The Advertising of the Future," *Vanity Fair*, March 3, 1860, 156; "Biddyism," *Vanity Fair*, March 3, 1860, 158; Luskey, *On the Make*, 69, 83–118; Roediger, *Wages of Whiteness*, 65–92; Luskey, "Houses Divided," 645–46.

35. "The Biddy," *Vanity Fair*, February 18, 1860, 120; "Shopman," *Vanity Fair*, July 7, 1860, 15; Luskey, *On the Make*, 211–27; Stansell, *City of Women*, 157; Diner, *Erin's Daughters in America*, 103; Anbinder, "Moving beyond 'Rags to Riches,'" 753–57, 768; Anbinder, *Five Points*, 126–27; Urban, *Brokering Servitude*, 31–32; Rockman, *Scraping By*, 192–93; Enstad, *Ladies of Labor, Girls of Adventure*; Luskey, "Houses Divided," 646–47. Matthew Gallman has shown that this critique of Irish domestic servants' ambition continued during the war in *Defining Duty in the Civil War*, 106.

36. "Progress vs. Old Fogeyism," *Vanity Fair*, February 18, 1860, 127; Woloson, "Rise of the Consumer"; Luskey, "Houses Divided," 648.

37. *Leadbeater's Renouned Stove Polish*, LCP. For similar advertisements, see Sinclair,

Wootten's Excelsior Stove Lustre or Pure Black Lead, LCP; advertisement for Japanese Polish Co., *Vanity Fair*, March 24, 1860, 207. White Northern artists had mocked African Americans' consumption habits and presentation of self in the early Republic. See Bushman, *Refinement of America*, 434–40. For the domestic servant population in midcentury New York City, see Stansell, *City of Women*, 156–57. For apprenticeship in postemancipation New York, see Levine-Gronningsater, "Delivering Freedom," chaps. 1–2.

38. "Out of a Situation," *Vanity Fair*, April 7, 1860, 233; Luskey, *On the Make*, 85; Pierson, *Free Hearts and Free Homes*, 122–27; Lynn, "Half-Baked Men," 35–52; Luskey, "Houses Divided," 649–51.

39. "'Sich a Gittin Up Stairs,'" *Vanity Fair*, October 27, 1860, 213; Bunker, *From Rail-Splitter to Icon*, 53; Lott, *Love and Theft*. For other instances in which blackface minstrelsy connected politics and the household, see Neely, *Boundaries of American Political Culture*, 103–5.

40. "Mr. S-W-D.," *Vanity Fair*, February 4, 1860, 89. Just weeks before, *Vanity Fair* had portrayed Helper as a bedraggled and bearded house servant carrying a broom and wearing a bonnet and a dress that did not reach his ankles. The caption read, "THE GREATEST PLAGUE IN LIFE. An Unsatisfactory Helper in the House." See *Vanity Fair*, January 21, 1860, 61. See also Fleischner, *Mrs. Lincoln and Mrs. Keckly*, 210–30; Luskey, *On the Make*, 150–51.

41. Webster to Sherman, December 31, 1860, vol. 19, Sherman Papers, LOC. As Matthew Gallman has shown, there was panic in Philadelphia's business community. Southern secessionists owed some $24 million in unpaid debts to Philadelphia businessmen, which was surely one of the reasons that 533 of the city's firms failed in 1860 and 1861. See Gallman, *Mastering Wartime*, 268–69, 312–16; Sandage, *Born Losers*, 190, 199.

42. Webster to Sherman, January 7, 1861, vol. 19, Sherman Papers, LOC; Webster to Lincoln, January 8, 1861, Lincoln Papers, LOC.

43. Telegraph from Webster to Lincoln, February 11, 1861, Lincoln Papers, LOC; "Reply to Mayor Alexander Henry at Philadelphia, Pennsylvania," February 21, 1861, *CW*, 4:238.

44. Webster to Sherman, March 7, 1861, vol. 24, Webster to Sherman, March 16, [1861], vol. 25, Sherman Papers, LOC. See also *Press*, March 16, 1861, quoted in McCorison, "Impressions of the President Elect," 294. For a few of the reference letters Webster wrote to Lincoln, see Webster to Lincoln, January 1, April 2, 1861, RG 59, Entry 760: Appointment Records, Applications and Recommendations for Office, Applications and Recommendations for Public Office, 1797–1901, NA, https://s3.us-east-2.amazonaws.com/papersofabrahamlincoln/PAL_Images/PAL_PubMan/1861/01/260968.pdf and https://s3.us-east-2.amazonaws.com/papersofabrahamlincoln/PAL_Images/PAL_PubMan/1861/04/261482.pdf, accessed May 3, 2018. For the cultural processes that made financial panics, see Lepler, *Many Panics of 1837*.

45. "Philadelphia Merchant Delegation," April 12, 1861, Lincoln Papers, LOC. See also "Memorandum on Philadelphia Patronage, Edward Joy Morris," dated April 1861, in Lincoln Papers, LOC. Morris, another Republican congressman from Philadelphia, believed Webster should be the collector of the port. For Thomas's "compensation as collector," see House of Representatives, *Report on William B. Thomas*, 1. For Webster's work as representative of the trustees of the Delaware River ice boat, see *PI*, December 30, 1856. For more on Lincoln's choice of Thomas, see Carman and Luthin, *Lincoln and the Patronage*, 65–66.

CHAPTER 2

1. For a selection of the letters that job seekers sent to Andrew, see William A. Moorhead to Andrew, April 12, 1861, box 3, folder 17; J. E. Dawley to Andrew, May 1, 1861, box 4, folder 1; Wilson Flagg to Andrew, May 20, 1861, and George Perkins to John A. Andrew, May 20, 1861, box 4, folder 7; George E. Ellis to Andrew, July 13, 1861, and Charles Blanchard to Andrew, July 13, 1861, box 5, folder 5, Andrew Papers, MHS. For more on patronage posts and party politics, see Sandage, *Born Losers*, 139; Formisano, "'Party Period' Revisited."

2. "The Great Southern Peter Funk Shop," *Vanity Fair*, June 1, 1861, 257. See also Goettsch, "'The World Is But One Vast Mock Auction'"; Rockman, "Northern Manufacturers, Southern Slavery."

3. Leonard Wisson to Andrew, May 16, 1861, box 4, folder 5; Wilson Flagg to Andrew, May 20, 1861, box 4, folder 7; Edw[ard] Southworth Jr. to Andrew, May 23, 1861, box 4, folder 9; John Lawton to Andrew, June 10, [1861], box 4, folder 17; and Charles Blanchard to Andrew, July 13, 1861, box 5, folder 5, Andrew Papers, MHS.

4. E. S. Beals to Andrew, May 24, 1861, box 4, folder 9, Andrew Papers, MHS. For more on begging letters, see Sandage, *Born Losers*, 226–57.

5. Aaron A. Bradley to Andrew, April 30, 1861, box 3, folder 20, Andrew Papers, MHS. On Forbes, see Nelson, *Nation of Deadbeats*, 126–58; Larson, *Bonds of Enterprise*. On the Militia Act's prohibition against black soldiers, see Luke and Smith, *Soldiering for Freedom*, 6. For black men who volunteered for military service in Massachusetts during the first months of the war, see Kantrowitz, *More Than Freedom*, 275–77. On Confederates' use of enslaved laborers on fortifications, see Martinez, *Confederate Slave Impressment*.

6. Pierson, "'He Helped the Poor and Snubbed the Rich,'" 40, 45–49; Trefousse, *Ben Butler*, 27–28; Manning, *Troubled Refuge*, 32, 172–73; Oakes, *Freedom National*, 91–96.

7. Butler to Scott, May 24–25, 1861, *Private and Official Correspondence of Gen. Benjamin F. Butler*, 1:106; Oakes, *Freedom National*, 97; Manning, *Troubled Refuge*, 38, 173; Siddali, *From Property to Person*, 35.

8. Butler to Scott, May 27, 1861, *Private and Official Correspondence of Gen. Benjamin F. Butler*, 1:113; Oakes, *Freedom National*, 98–100; Manning, *Troubled Refuge*, 174–76.

9. Butler to Phelps, May 28, 1861, and Cameron to Butler, May 30, 1861, *Private and Official Correspondence of Gen. Benjamin F. Butler*, 1:114, 119; Taylor, *Embattled Freedom*, 25–26.

10. "A Census of the Contrabands," *Frank Leslie's Illustrated Newspaper*, March 8, 1862, 246; Berlin et al., *Freedom: . . . Series I*, vol. 2, *The Wartime Genesis of Free Labor*, 86–88; Gerteis, *From Contraband to Freedman*, 19–20; Lause, *Free Labor*, 59; Urban, *Brokering Servitude*, 74; Taylor, *Embattled Freedom*, 40; Reidy, *Illusions of Emancipation*, 238–43; Brasher, *Peninsula Campaign and the Necessity of Emancipation*, 32–80; Rockman, *Scraping By*, 194–230.

11. Manning, *Troubled Refuge*, 54–56; Taylor, *Embattled Freedom*, 41–46; Newby-Alexander, *African American History of the Civil War in Hampton Roads*, 16, 32–37; Berlin et al., *Freedom: . . . Series I*, vol. 2, *The Wartime Genesis of Free Labor*, 93. For the ways bookkeeping created and shaped how Americans understood the market, see Zakim, "Bookkeeping as Ideology."

12. "List of Negroes claiming protection & food, July 29, 1861," Butler to Cameron, July 30, 1861, *Private and Official Correspondence of Gen. Benjamin F. Butler*, 1:183–88. Andrew

Cohen contextualizes Butler's contraband policy by examining the experience of Butler's father as a privateer and Butler's references to secessionist "piracy" at the 1860 Democratic convention in *Contraband*, 66–68. Kate Masur illuminates the multitude of meanings given to the word "contraband" in this moment of emancipation—and thus demonstrates the term's usefulness for Northerners—in "'Rare Phenomenon of Philological Vegetation.'"

13. Pierson, "'He Helped the Poor and Snubbed the Rich,'" 50.

14. Blair to Butler, June 8, 1861, *Private and Official Correspondence of Gen. Benjamin F. Butler*, 1:130. For the Blairs' and other Republicans' ideas about colonization, see Eric Foner, *Free Soil, Free Labor, Free Men*, 267–80; May, *Slavery, Race, and Conquest in the Tropics*, 182–84. See also Manning, *Troubled Refuge*, 177; Abbott, *Cotton and Capital*, 95–98.

15. [Sears] to Andrew, July 23, 1861, box 5, folder 8, Andrew Papers, MHS. The letter to Andrew is identical to the published version of Sears, *Contrabands and Vagrants*, which is addressed to Wilson. See also Winthrop, *Memoir of the Hon. David Sears*, 17; O'Brassill-Kulfan, *Vagrants and Vagabonds*.

16. Tappan to Butler, August 8, 1861, *Private and Official Correspondence of Gen. Benjamin F. Butler*, 1:199–200.

17. Butler to Tappan, August 10, 1861, *Private and Official Correspondence of Gen. Benjamin F. Butler*, 1:200–201.

18. "Something about Intelligence Offices," *NYH*, August 31, 1859, 1; "Intelligence Offices," *National Police Gazette*, November 7, 1846, 68; *New York Times*, July 26, 1855, 3; Luskey, "Special Marts," 360.

19. "Something about Intelligence Offices"; Luskey, "Special Marts," 360, 363.

20. "Something about Intelligence Offices"; William Henry Burr, *The Intelligence Office* (1849), Collection of the New-York Historical Society.

21. "Something about Intelligence Offices." One of the purposes of the intelligence office operated by the Commissioners of Emigration was to protect immigrants from a group of nefarious entrepreneurs dubbed "land sharks" who exploited newcomers' ignorance of markets in transportation, housing, and labor. See O'Malley, "Lickspittles and Land Sharks."

22. "Something about Intelligence Offices."

23. "Something about Intelligence Offices"; *NYH*, February 16 and 18, 1858.

24. "The Intelligence Offices—Complaints of Scores of Victims," *NYH*, September 2, 1859, 4; W. J. Redpath, Com[mercial]. Agency, 78 Broadway, September 8, 1859, New York, vol. 377, p. 1, R. G. Dun & Co. Credit Report Volumes, BL. For the ways entrepreneurs tried to exploit the blurry boundaries between respectable and disreputable business in nineteenth-century America, see Hemphill, "Selling Sex and Intimacy"; Erickson, "Economies of Print."

25. Luskey, "Special Marts," 360; Lincoln, "Speech at New Haven, Connecticut," March 6, 1860, *CW*, 4:14, 18, 24–25.

26. Lincoln, "Speech at New Haven, Connecticut," *CW*, 4:24; Blewett, *Men, Women, and Work*, 120–22, 128; Lause, *Free Labor*, 16–17; Roediger, *Wages of Whiteness*, 65–92.

27. "Form Letter to Fillmore Men," September 8, 1856, *CW*, 2:374. For state returns for the 1856 election, see "The American Presidency Project," http://www.presidency.ucsb.edu/showelection.php?year=1856, accessed March 31, 2017.

28. Mary Lincoln to Emilie Helm, November 23, 1856, Mary Lincoln to Hannah Shearer, October 2, [1859], and Mary Lincoln to Hannah Shearer, January 1, [1860], in Turner and

Turner, *Mary Todd Lincoln*, 46, 59, 61; 1850 Federal Census, Springfield, Sangamon County, Illinois, M432_127, p. 120A, image 247, ancestry.com, accessed June 23, 2017; Margaret Ryan interview with Jesse Weik, October 27, 1886, Elizabeth Edwards interview with William Herndon, 1865–66 [January 10, 1866], John S. Bradford interview with Jesse Weik, 1883–89, in Wilson and Davis, *Herndon's Informants*, 596–97, 445, 729. See also Baker, *Mary Todd Lincoln*, 105–8, 122; Urban, *Brokering Servitude*, 42, 52.

29. Abraham Lincoln to Mary Lincoln, July 2, 1848, *CW*, 1:496. For the ways gender shaped the market, consult Hartigan-O'Connor, "Gender's Value in the History of Capitalism." For more on the ways these gendered ideas worked in antislavery political culture, see Pierson, *Free Hearts and Free Homes*, 131–33. For the ways unfree and free labor coexisted in the early Republic and Civil War era and increased the power of employers, see Rockman, *Scraping By*; Stacey L. Smith, *Freedom's Frontier*.

30. "Appeal of the Woman's Protective Emigration Society," *New-York Tribune*, December 14, 1857; "Woman's Protective Emigration Society," *New-York Tribune*, January 19, 1858; Roberts, *American Alchemy*, 221–42.

31. "Appeal of the Woman's Protective Emigration Society"; "Woman's Protective Emigration Society"; Urban, *Brokering Servitude*, 50.

32. *New-York Tribune*, December 14, 1857; *Proceedings of the Board of Councilmen of the City of New York from October 5th to December 31st, 1857*, 1149–50. For Greeley's radical ideas about alleviating the "crisis of free labor," see Tuchinsky, *Horace Greeley's* New-York Tribune.

33. "Woman's Protective Emigration Society"; Urban, *Brokering Servitude*, 51.

34. "Girls for the West," *New-York Tribune*, February 17, 1858; Baker, *Mary Todd Lincoln*, 105. Andrew Urban quotes Vere Foster quoting the Lincolns in *Brokering Servitude*, 52. For apprenticeships in the Edwards household, see Cicero, *Creating the Land of Lincoln*, 83–84; Cornelius, "Introduction," xvii.

35. Eric Foner, *Fiery Trial*, 47–49; Heerman, "'Reducing Free Men to Slavery.'"

36. "A Case of Unexpected Recognition," *Wilmington Journal*, February 26, 1858; "Singular Story," *Memphis Daily Appeal*, February 12, 1858. Both of these articles claim that the story was first published in the *Bloomington Pantograph*, a newspaper started by Abraham Lincoln's friend Jesse W. Fell. See also "The Northern Slave Trade," *Keowee Courier*, March 20, 1858.

37. For more on the financial dislocation and retail strategies of the secession crisis, see Philip S. Foner, *Business and Slavery*, 208–23; Zakim, "Dialectics of Merchant Capital," 71–74.

38. 1860 Federal Census, Washington Township, Lee County, Iowa, roll M653_330, p. 634, image 642, Family History Library Film 803330, ancestry.com, accessed June 13, 2016; Espy, *Another War Declared*, LCP.

39. Joanna Cohen, *Luxurious Citizens*, 182, 194–95, 200–201.

40. For discussions of antebellum merchants' attempts to navigate discussions of credit and cash purchases with their customers, see Bruegel, *Farm, Shop, Landing*, 27–28, 58–59; Clark, *Roots of Rural Capitalism*, 162–63, 220.

41. Spruance & Megear, *Secession Has Produced a Wonderful Change in the Price of Goods*, P. & C. Templeton, *Attention Union Men!*, and S. C. & L. Fox, *Attention Union Men!*, LCP; Joanna Cohen, *Luxurious Citizens*, 195.

42. Ramage, *Attention Volunteers!*, LCP; Joanna Cohen, *Luxurious Citizens*, 181–82.

43. *March On, Brave Volunteers*, and *Volunteers Wanted!*, LCP.

44. "Report of the Commission Appointed by the Governor of Pennsylvania to Investigate the Alleged Army Frauds, August, 1861," *PI*, October 12, 1861.

45. "Report of the Commission Appointed by the Governor of Pennsylvania."

46. "Report of the Commission Appointed by the Governor of Pennsylvania." For more on the Girard House scandal and the debates about shoddy in the Civil War North, see Wilson, *Business of Civil War*, 12–13, 24–25, 148–90; Michael Thomas Smith, *Enemy Within*, 15–36; Gallman, *Defining Duty in the Civil War*, 14–16, 91–122, 251–52; Gallman, *Mastering Wartime*, 287–88. For other nineteenth-century debates about the values embedded in clothing, see Mendelsohn, "Rag Race"; Weicksel, "Dress of the Enemy."

47. *PI*, October 12, 1861. For advertisements for the Union Steamship Company after Virginia seceded, see *PI*, April 23, 25, and 27, 1861. The company's stockholders met at least one more time, on February 4, 1862, and listed Webster as "general agent." See *PI*, February 5, 1862.

CHAPTER 3

1. McPherson, *For Cause and Comrades*; Gallagher, *Union War*; Manning, *What This Cruel War Was Over*. For ideas about virtue and citizenship in nineteenth-century America, see Furstenberg, "Beyond Freedom and Slavery."

2. For the ways antebellum Northerners hoped the destruction of slave society would ennoble free society, see Eric Foner, *Free Soil, Free Labor, Free Men*, 58–65. For the changing meanings of "hireling" in antebellum America, see Roediger, *Wages of Whiteness*, 44–47. Michael Smith examines the public outcry over bounty men in *Enemy Within*, 127–53. For more on soldiers as wage workers, consult Way, "Class and the Common Soldier in the Seven Years' War"; McGrath, "'A Slave in Uncle Sam's Service'"; Marvel, *Lincoln's Mercenaries*. For the ways republican ideology shaped soldiers' and officers' definitions of citizenship, see Lang, *In the Wake of War*; Bledsoe, *Citizen-Officers*.

3. Lincoln, "Message to Congress in Special Session," July 4, 1861, *CW*, 4:431–32, 438; Sandage, *Born Losers*, 221.

4. For slavery's "chattel principle," see Walter Johnson, *Soul by Soul*. For examinations of Northern recruiting practices and processes, see Gallman, *Mastering Wartime*, 11–53; Blair, "We Are Coming, Father Abraham — Eventually."

5. Butler, *Autobiography and Personal Reminiscences of Major-General Benj. F. Butler*, 295, 307 (quotation); Reed and Browne to Andrew, September 6, 1861, *OR*, Series 3, 1:813–14. See also War Department General Order 78, *OR*, Series 3, 1:817; Shannon, *Organization and Administration*, 1:261.

6. Parmelee to Howe, September 17 and 18, 1861, box 6, folder 5, Andrew Papers, MHS. For Howe's business stationery, see Howe to Andrew, October 11, 1861, box 6, folder 11, Andrew Papers, MHS.

7. E. A. Andrews to Andrew, January 28, 1862, box 8, folder 7, Andrew Papers, MHS.

8. Andrew to Simon Cameron, September 23, 1861, Browne to Sherman, September 23, 1861, *OR*, Series 3, 1:818–19. For Andrew's reference to Butler's "irregular" troops, see Andrew to Lorenzo Thomas, November 27, 1861, *OR*, Series 3, 1:840. The pretense of civility in the correspondence between Butler and Andrew was first breached when Butler wrote a letter to Andrew on October 12, 1861, in which he addressed the governor as "His Excellency" in quotation marks throughout, painstakingly mocking what he saw as the recipient's empty pretensions to authority. When Butler returned a later communication

from Andrew's military secretary A. G. Browne Jr. because Butler deemed it "of improper address and signature," Andrew and Browne wrote Butler to condemn his hypocrisy in light of the October 12 letter. Recriminations bore further recriminations—when Andrew refused to commission the officers Butler had named for his regiments, Butler accused Andrew of appointing a known seducer and adulterer as colonel of the Sixteenth Massachusetts. See Butler to Andrew, October 12, 1861; George C. Strong to Browne, December 18, 1861; Andrew to Butler, December 18, 1861; Strong to Andrew, December 19, 1861; Browne to Strong, December 20, 1861; Butler to Andrew, December 28, 1861; Andrew to Butler, December 30, 1861; and Butler to Andrew, January 1, 1862, *OR*, Series 3, 1:831–32, 846–49, 854–56. For the increasing publicity of the conflict between the two men, see Andrew to Stanton, January 25, 1862, and Andrew to Sumner and Wilson, December 21, 1861, *OR*, Series 3, 1:810–11, 865; Howe to Andrew, January 21, 1862, box 8, folder 5, Howe to Andrew, January 23, 1862, box 8, folder 6, and Howe to Andrew, January 27, 1862, box 8, folder 7, Andrew Papers, MHS. See also Trefousse, *Ben Butler*, 89–95; Engle, *Gathering to Save a Nation*, 105–6, 147–48.

 9. Cameron to Benjamin F. Larned, October 2, 1861, Butler to Andrew, October 5, 1861, Andrew to Cameron, October 5, 1861, Cameron to Andrew, October 5, 1861, and Andrew to Cameron, October 6, 1861, *OR*, Series 3, 1:822, 824, 827, 828–29.

 10. Andrew to Thomas, November 27, 1861, *OR*, Series 3, 1:841; Andrew to Thomas, December 27, 1861, and Samuel F. Bradlee to Butler, December 1, 1861, box 9, Butler Papers, LOC. The letters to Butler's soldiers were signed by Thomas Drew, Andrew's assistant military secretary. See Butler to Charles M. Whelden, January 7, 1862, Drew to George Downing, January 6, 1862, Drew to Joseph Hardy, January 6, 1862, French to G. F. Shepley, January 8, 1862, and Shepley to Butler, January 8, 1862, *Private and Official Correspondence of Gen. Benjamin F. Butler*, 1:314–18. See also French to Andrew, May 28, 1861, box 4, folder 11, and Thomas H. Dunham to Andrew, September 3, 1861, box 6, folder 1, Andrew Papers, MHS; Butler, *Autobiography and Personal Reminiscences of Major-General Benj. F. Butler*, 309–10; Shannon, *Organization and Administration*, 2:50–52; Marvel, *Lincoln's Mercenaries*, 58.

 11. Strong to Nelson, October 18, 1861, Department of the Gulf, Letters Sent, vol. 1, NA; *1860 Federal Census*, Hartford, Connecticut, roll M653_78, p. 156, image 50, Family History Library Film 803078, *Geer's Hartford City Directory for 1860–61*, 189, ancestry.com, accessed May 14, 2018; *Hartford Daily Courant*, April 23, 1861; Gorn, *Manly Art*, 47–56; Foote, *Gentlemen and the Roughs*, 73–75.

 12. *Hartford Daily Courant*, April 26, 1861; Court Martial of J. A. Nelson, NA. For more on this case in the context of the contested meanings of masculinity in the Union army, see Foote, *Gentlemen and the Roughs*, 106–7.

 13. Court Martial of J. A. Nelson, NA.

 14. Butler, *Autobiography and Personal Reminiscences of Major-General Benj. F. Butler*, 311–14; J. D. Williams to Nelson, October 29, 1861, and "Draft of Report to the War Department on the Condition of the Department of New England," November 18, 1861, box 8, Butler Papers, LOC.

 15. Joseph Thompson to Butler, October 30, 1861, box 8, Butler Papers, LOC; Strong to Thomas Millington, October 22, 1861, Department of the Gulf, Letters Sent, vol. 1, NA; J. A. Pickett to Butler, January 21, 1862, box 10, Butler Papers, LOC; Keating, *Greatest Trials I Ever Had*, 22; Marvel, *Lincoln's Mercenaries*, 100.

 16. "Freemen, Arouse!," *Lowell Daily Citizen and News*, December 14, 1861.

17. John A. Nelson, Compiled Service Record, Thirtieth Massachusetts, https://www-fold3-com.www.libproxy.wvu.edu/image/272/525421542, accessed June 21, 2019. Butler to Buckingham [draft], December 9, 1861, and Buckingham to Butler, December 21, 1861, box 9, Butler Papers, LOC; *Hartford Daily Courant*, October 18, 1861; Keating, *Shades of Green*, 115.

18. *Daily Evening Traveller*, January 6, 1862; Nelson to Butler, January 4, 1862, and Butler to Assistant Adjutant General of the State of Massachusetts [draft], February 13, 1862, box 10, Butler Papers, LOC; Margaret Cahill to Thomas Cahill, [March 16, 1862], in Keating, *Greatest Trials I Ever Had*, 59, 61.

19. Margaret Cahill to Thomas Cahill, [March 16, 1862], Thomas Cahill to Margaret Cahill, March 22, 1862, in Keating, *Greatest Trials I Ever Had*, 61–62; *Farmer's Cabinet*, May 1, 1862. Determining the exact number of soldiers whom Nelson recruited for the Ninth Connecticut and took into the Thirtieth Massachusetts is difficult. The roster for the Eastern Bay State Regiment, attached to Andrew's refusal to commission Butler's officers in the latter's papers, lists Nelson's "Company belonging to 9th Conn Regt.," suggesting the entire company was transferred. J. M. Ingersoll's postbellum list of men transferred is a fraction of the total number of soldiers and officers mustered into Company K of the Ninth at this juncture of the war and has influenced my estimate in the text. See Andrew to Thomas, December 27, 1861, box 9, Butler Papers, LOC, Murray, *History of the Ninth Regiment*, 53; Ingersoll, *Catalogue of Connecticut Voluntary Organizations*, 420–21. The *Hartford Daily Courant* noted on September 6, 1862, that a new captain had just been appointed to Company K of the Ninth Connecticut because Nelson had been "dropped from the roll of Conn. volunteers." For more on Nelson, Cahill, and the Ninth Connecticut, see Keating, *Shades of Green*, 43–67, 115; Keating, *Greatest Trials I Ever Had*, 62n19.

20. Brewster to Dear Mother, August 24, 1861, *WTCWIO*, 30; Blight, introduction to *WTCWIO*, 5, 8; 1860 Federal Census Manuscripts, Northampton, Hampshire, Massachusetts, roll M653_505, p. 918, Family History Library Film 803505, ancestry.com, accessed May 16, 2018.

21. Brewster to Dear Mother, August 29, September 22, 1861, and Brewster to Aunt Lu, September 3, 1861, *WTCWIO*, 33, 36, 40. For northern soldiers who chafed at the limits imposed on their independence by the military's chain of command, see Foote, *Gentlemen and the Roughs*, 147. For the coalescing belief in this era that contract rights defined freedom, see Orr, "'We Are No Grumblers'"; Stanley, *From Bondage to Contract*.

22. Brewster to Dear Mattie, October 23, 1861, *WTCWIO*, 51–53. For the ways goods were conduits between cultures of production and consumption in nineteenth-century America, see Jaffee, *New Nation of Goods*. For the ways soldiers created economies in camp, see Carmichael, *War for the Common Soldier*, 184; Lang, *In the Wake of War*, 82–104.

23. Brewster to Dear Mattie, October 23, 1861, *WTCWIO*, 51–53. See also Brewster to Dear Mary, November 21, 1861, and Brewster to Dear Mother, November 24, 1861, *WTCWIO*, 59, 62.

24. Brewster to Dear Mary, September 25, 1861, *WTCWIO*, 43, 353n17.

25. Brewster to Dear Mother, November 17, 1861, *WTCWIO*, 57–58.

26. Brewster to Dear Mother, November 24, 1861, *WTCWIO*, 61–62, 354n32. For "right smart," see http://www.oed.com.www.libproxy.wvu.edu/view/Entry/317963?redirectedFrom=right+smart#eid, accessed May 16, 2018.

27. Brewster to Dear Mother, November 17, 1861, *WTCWIO*, 57.

28. Lincoln, "Annual Message to Congress," December 3, 1861, *CW*, 5:51–53.

29. Brewster to Dear Mother, December 4, 1861, *WTCWIO*, 64; Lincoln, "Drafts of a Bill for Compensated Emancipation in Delaware," November 26[?], 1861, "Annual Message to Congress," December 3, 1861, *CW*, 5:30, 48–49.

30. For information on Sarah Washington, see 1850 Federal Census Manuscripts, Northampton, Hampshire, Massachusetts, roll M432_320, p. 135A, image 271, and 1860 Federal Census Manuscripts, Northampton, Hampshire, Massachusetts, roll M653_505, p. 919, Family History Library Film 803505, ancestry.com, accessed May 16, 2018.

31. Brewster to Dear Mary, December 8, 1861, *WTCWIO*, 65–66.

32. Brewster to Dear Mother, December 14, 1861, *WTCWIO*, 67–68, 354n35.

33. Brewster to Dear Mother, December 14, 1861, and Brewster to Dear Mother and Mary, January 9, 1862, *WTCWIO*, 67–69, 75.

34. Brewster to Dear Mother, January 15, 1862, *WTCWIO*, 78.

35. Brewster to Dear Mother, January 15, 1862, *WTCWIO*, 78. David A. Cecere has written about Brewster's hiring of David in his essay about the changing meanings New England soldiers gave to race during the war. For Brewster, a means of achieving social and economic advancement "was to acquire the services of a black hireling, which perhaps alleviated [Brewster's] anxiety over being a white hireling himself." See Cecere, "Carrying the Home Front to War," 309. See also Urban, *Brokering Servitude*, 75; Oakes, *Freedom National*, 171; Carmichael, *War for the Common Soldier*, 42; Teters, *Practical Liberators*, 83–105.

36. Brewster to Dear Mother, January 15, 1862, *WTCWIO*, 78.

37. Brewster to Dear Mary, January 23, [1862], Brewster to Dear Mother, February 22, 1862, and Brewster to Dear Mary, February 26, 1862, *WTCWIO*, 81, 87–88.

38. Brewster to Dear Mother, February 9, [1862], and Brewster to Dear Mary, February 26, 1862, *WTCWIO*, 82, 89–90. On some officers' belief in their absolute power over soldiers, see Foote, *Gentlemen and the Roughs*, 123.

39. Newell, *"Ours,"* 69–72; 1860 Federal Census Manuscripts, Sandy Spring, District 5, Montgomery, Maryland, roll M653_478, p. 67, image 67, Family History Library Film 803478, 1860 Federal Census Slave Schedules, Entry for John C. Jones, "overseer Mrs Nowlen owner," District 4, Montgomery County, Maryland, p. 4, ancestry.com, accessed June 17, 2016.

40. Brewster to Dear Mother, March 4, 1862, *WTCWIO*, 92–93.

41. Brewster to Dear Mother, March 4, 1862, *WTCWIO*, 92–93. For the divide within the Union army about setting policy on "stealing" and "catching" enslaved people in 1861, see Oakes, *Freedom National*, 176–91.

42. Brewster to Dear Mattie, March 5, 1862, Brewster to Dear Mother, March 8, 1862, *WTCWIO*, 93–94, 96, 355n15; Cecere, "Carrying the Home Front to War," 309–10; Furstenberg, "Beyond Freedom and Slavery."

43. "The Highly Intelligent Contraband," *Vanity Fair*, April 26, 1862, 203. For white northern opposition to former slaves moving to the North, see Schwalm, *Emancipation's Diaspora*, 81, 95–100; Manning, *What This Cruel War Was Over*, 94; Gallman, *Mastering Wartime*, 223; Gigantino, *Ragged Road to Abolition*, 243–44; Voegeli, "Rejected Alternative"; Masur, "'Rare Phenomenon of Philological Vegetation,'" 1063.

44. Masur, "'Rare Phenomenon of Philological Vegetation,'" 1065; Leland, *Memoirs*, 22, 27–32; Fahs, *Imagined Civil War*, 159; "What to Do with the Darkies," *Continental Monthly* 1, no. 1 (January 1862): 84; "Our War and Our Want," *Continental Monthly* 1, no. 2 (February

1862): 116; "The True Basis," *Continental Monthly* 1, no. 2 (February 1862): 136–38. See also Richardson, *Greatest Nation on Earth*, 219–20.

45. For the work of PAS's Committee on Employment in the early Republic, see Dunbar, *Fragile Freedom*, 33–34; Nash, *Forging Freedom*, 145. Sarah Gronningsater argues that New York politicians adopted the precepts and practices of the English Poor Law to help white slaveholders navigate the end of slavery in their state. Keen on identifying the distinctions between early Republic and postbellum emancipations, Gronningsater also writes that, while "pauper apprenticeship was not racialized, hereditary slavery, . . . its logic and laws found nourishment in the same ideological soil." See Levine-Gronningsater, "Delivering Freedom," chaps. 1–2 (quotation on 39). See also Rockman, *Scraping By*; Harris, *In the Shadow of Slavery*; Gigantino, *Ragged Road to Abolition*, 234–38; Diemer, *Politics of Black Citizenship*, 187.

46. William F. Mitchell to Joseph M. Truman, February 20, 1862, Still to Dillwyn Parrish, March 11, 1862, Still to Joseph M. Truman, March 13, 1862, Correspondence Incoming, folder 19, 1862, "Agreement between Committee of the Board of Education of the PAS and W. Still," undated, Board of Education, Committee on Employment, Minutes, 1864–1865, and undated, folder 28, PAS Papers, HSP.

47. Still, "Contrabands in Philadelphia," *PL*, April 7, 1862; Still to Educational Committee of the Abolition Society, May 8, 1862, Still to Joseph Truman Jr., May 8, 1862, Still, Report, May 22, 1862, Thomas Garrett to Still, 7 mo 10th 1862, and Still to Truman, September 15, 1862, Correspondence Incoming, folder 19, 1862, PAS Papers, HSP. For other reformers who grappled with the contradiction inherent in doing "good while doing well," see Lasser, "Conscience and Contradiction," 2. For African Americans who argued that personal thriving and commonweal could coexist, see Rael, "African Americans, Slavery, and Thrift," 189; Hall, "To Render the Private Public," 47.

48. William James Fuller, A. M. Green, and John A. Williams to the Executive Board or the Officiary of the Old Abolition Society of Penn., April 1, 1862, Incoming Correspondence, folder 19, 1862, PAS Papers, HSP. For the Union Contraband Relief Committee's public meetings at Rev. John A. Williams's "Methodist Church in Lombard street, near Sixth" in support of black southerners in Philadelphia, see "Contraband Meeting," *PI*, April 1, 1862. For Williams's letter thanking the Union Volunteer Refreshment Saloon for feeding black Southern refugees at its establishment, see John A. Williams et al. to Arad Barrows et al., May 14, 1862, box 1, folder 3, Samuel Fales Collection, HSP. For the conflict between PAS and African American abolitionists before the Civil War, see Newman, "Pennsylvania Abolition Society."

49. Brewster to Dear Mother, March 26, April 3, 1862, *WTCWIO*, 103, 105.

50. Brewster to Dear Mother, April 23, 1862, *WTCWIO*, 118. For vulture capitalists, see Balleisen, *Navigating Failure*, 135–62.

51. Brewster to Dear Mother, April 23, May 14, 1862, *WTCWIO*, 120, 128, 356n18; "Desperation and Colonization," *Continental Monthly* 1, no. 6 (June 1862): 660; "Rewarding the Army," *Continental Monthly* 2, no. 2 (August 1862): 163. See also Paludan, *People's Contest*, 200.

52. Brewster to [Dear Mother], May 15, May 31, 1862, *WTCWIO*, 130, 141–42.

53. Brewster to unnamed recipient, undated (but probably around July 4, 1862), *WTCWIO*, 343; Newell, "Ours," 98–115; Broadwater, *Battle of Fair Oaks*, 100–101.

54. Brewster to Dear Mother, June 2, 1862, and Brewster to Dear Mary, July 9, 1862, *WTCWIO*, 144, 165. For an examination of the significance of enslaved and free African

Americans to the Peninsula and Seven Days Campaigns, see Brasher, *The Peninsula Campaign and the Necessity of Emancipation*, 102–228.

55. Brewster to Dear Mother, July 12, 1862, *WTCWIO*, 167.

56. *Gray Reserves!*, LCP; Seward to Stanton, July 1, 1862, Stanton to Seward, July 1, 1862, and Andrew to Stanton, May 30, 1862, *OR*, Series 3, 2:183, 100.

57. *PI*, July 30, 1862; Brewster to Dear Mother, September 1, 1862, *WTCWIO*, 181–82.

58. *PI*, July 30, August 2, September 3, 1862; *Frank Leslie's Illustrated Newspaper*, April 12, 1862, 368. For the marketing of goods to Civil War soldiers, see Woloson, "Wishful Thinking," 802–5; Murphy, *Investing in Life*, 262–83. For the recruiting efforts of the Citizens' Bounty Fund, see Gallman, *Mastering Wartime*, 28–31; Blair, "We Are Coming, Father Abraham—Eventually," 195.

CHAPTER 4

1. Henry Walker Volunteer Enlistment, http://contentdm6.hamilton.edu/cdm/compoundobject/collection/civ-117/id/332/rec/1, accessed October 26, 2016; Mowris, *History of the One Hundred and Seventeenth Regiment, N.Y. Volunteers*, 19–20, 33–34; Henry Walker to Persis Walker, August 26, 1862, Henry Walker Correspondence, LOC.

2. Tippin to Henry, September 9, 1862, box 1, folder 10, Alexander Henry Papers, HSP; Baker to John A. Smith, August 21, 1862, Michael V. Baker Letterbook, Citizens' Bounty Fund Committee Records, HSP. Soldiers often gave their wives instructions about how to obtain bounty payments: see the muster forms of Mathew Cahill of the Eleventh U.S. Infantry, Edward Barrett of the Thirty-First Pennsylvania, Muster Forms for $50 Bounty (January 1863), Series 2, box 11, folder 10, Citizens' Bounty Fund Committee Records, HSP.

3. Baker to Charles Ruff, September 30, 1862, Baker to Stanton, October 3, 1862, and Baker to Stanton, November 7, 1862, Baker Letterbook, Citizens' Bounty Fund Committee Records, HSP.

4. Baker to Stanton, November 14, 1862, Baker Letterbook, Citizens' Bounty Fund Committee Records, HSP.

5. Brewster to Dear Mother, September 1, September 19, 1862, *WTCWIO*, 181–83.

6. Albert Walker to Henry Walker, August 8, 1861, Henry Walker to Persis Walker, September 3, 1862, Henry Walker Correspondence, LOC. For Albert Walker's enlistment in the Fourteenth New York and his death, see New York Civil War Muster Roll Abstracts, New York State Archives, https://www-fold3-com.www.libproxy.wvu.edu/image/31589 3660?terms=albert%20walker&pqsid=CjIsVcR9CWKDRhm85SpVyA:63000:935946663, accessed May 21, 2018. For the Walker household, see 1860 Federal Census Manuscripts, Remsen, Oneida County, New York, roll M653_825, p. 755, image 680, ancestry.com, accessed May 21, 2018. See also Carmichael, *War for the Common Soldier*, 62; Paludan, *People's Contest*, 154–55; Osterud, *Bonds of Community*, 205, and "Wages of Farm Laborers," *New-York Tribune*, February 18, 1860, 5, which states that farmers in a few areas of the state offered board as well as wages to their agricultural workers. As a point of comparison, the *Tribune*'s examination of Manhattan's labor market found higher wage rates for urban craftsmen and clerks. For instance, bakers averaged $6 per week, coopers earned $7.50 per week, and retail dry goods clerks took home $10.50 per week. See "Labor and Wages," *Tribune*, March 31, 1860.

7. Henry Walker to Persis Walker, September 3, 1862, Henry Walker Correspondence, LOC. See also Reid Mitchell, *Vacant Chair*, 3–18, 155, 158, 166.

8. Henry Walker to Persis Walker, October 17, 1862, Henry Walker Correspondence, LOC. Beyond visions of future economic prosperity, the Civil War forced Americans to reconsider their ability to shape the future, sparking divergent forecasts of the conflict and its results. See Phillips, *Looming Civil War*.

9. Henry Walker to Persis Walker, October 6 and 17, November 13, December 7 and 14, 1862, Henry Walker Correspondence, LOC. For the ways American entrepreneurs circulated goods in "secondhand" markets in nineteenth-century America, see Gamble, "Promiscuous Economy"; Mendelsohn, "Rag Race"; Thompson, "'Some Rascally Business'"; Garvey, "Back Number Budd."

10. Brewster to Dear Mother, November 1, 5, and 25, December 1, 1862, *WTCWIO*, 187, 189–93. On the slow movement of Union paymasters in the winter of 1863, see Marvel, *Lincoln's Mercenaries*, 167. For compelling analyses of the ways Americans valued various forms of currency in the nineteenth century, see Mihm, *Nation of Counterfeiters*; Greenberg, "Era of Shinplasters."

11. Brewster to Dear Mary, December 10, 1862, Brewster to Mother, December 23, 1862, *WTCWIO*, 196, 202–4; Marvel, *Lincoln's Mercenaries*, 63.

12. Lincoln, "Appeal to Border State Representatives to Favor Compensated Emancipation," July 12, 1862, and "Preliminary Emancipation Proclamation," September 22, 1862, *CW*, 5:318, 434. For the process of emancipation in the nation's capital, see Masur, *Example for All the Land*; Oakes, *Freedom National*, 288–93.

13. Lincoln, "Annual Message to Congress," December 1, 1862, *CW*, 5:522–23, 530–33, 537. See also Lincoln, "To the Senate and House of Representatives," July 14, 1862, *CW*, 5:324–25. For more on Lincoln's annual message, see Donald, *Lincoln*, 395–98; Boritt, *Lincoln and the Economics of the American Dream*, 235–41.

14. "What Will He Do with Them?," *Vanity Fair*, October 4, 1862, 163. Browning is quoted in Donald, *Lincoln*, 397.

15. Lincoln, "Annual Message to Congress," December 1, 1862, *CW*, 5:535–36; "The New Place," *Vanity Fair*, December 27, 1862, 307. For more on Lincoln's colonization plans, see Magness and Page, *Colonization after Emancipation*. See also Andrew to Dix, October 16, 1862, in Berlin et al., *Freedom: . . . Series II, The Black Military Experience*, 127–28; Taylor, *Embattled Freedom*, 94–95. For other Republicans' opposition to colonization for the reason that it "will deprive the country of what it most needs, which is labor," see Eric Foner, *Free Soil, Free Labor, Free Men*, 278.

16. "Six Months in Arrears," *Vanity Fair*, January 1, 1863, n.p.; Lincoln, "Emancipation Proclamation," January 1, 1863, and Lincoln to Johnson, March 26, 1863, *CW*, 6:30, 149–50; Luke and Smith, *Soldiering for Freedom*, 14.

17. For another instance in which Union army commanders and treasury department officials resolved these issues, see Rose, *Rehearsal for Reconstruction*.

18. Frank H. Peck to Phelps, June 15, 1862, Phelps to R. S. Davis, June 16, 1862, and Butler to Stanton, June 18, 1862, *OR*, Series 1, 15:485–91.

19. "The Freed Men of the South," *Continental Monthly* 2, no. 6 (December 1862): 730–33; J. M. Tuttle to Stanton, September 18, 1862, Stanton to Tuttle, September 18, 1862, Stanton to Tuttle, October 13, 1862, and Annual Report of the Quartermaster-General, November 18, 1862, *OR*, Series 3, 2:569, 663, 808. See also Schwalm, *Emancipation's Diaspora*, 76–78; Manning, *Troubled Refuge*, 110–14; Taylor, *Embattled Freedom*, 94.

20. Stanton to Butler, July 3, 1862, *OR*, Series 3, 2:200; Phelps to Davis, July 30, 1862, Butler to Phelps, July 31, 1862, Phelps to Davis, July 31, 1862, Henry Deming to Butler,

August 4, 1862, Butler to Phelps, August 5, 1862, Butler to Stanton, August 14, 1862, and General Orders No. 63, August 22, 1862, *Private and Official Correspondence of Gen. Benjamin F. Butler*, 2:125–27, 151, 154–55, 191–92, 209–11; Butler to Stanton, [September] 1862, *OR*, Series 1, 15:559. For more on Butler, Phelps, the employment of former slaves as laborers, and African American military recruitment in and around New Orleans, see Oakes, *Freedom National*, 245–55; Trefousse, *Ben Butler*, 131; Hearn, *When the Devil Came Down to Dixie*, 205–12; Teters, *Practical Liberators*, 41–46.

21. Chase to Butler, June 24, 1862, *OR*, Series 3, 2:173–74; Denison to Chase, September 9, 1862, Chase to Butler, October 29, 1862, and Butler to Chase, November 14, 1862, *Private and Official Correspondence of Gen. Benjamin F. Butler*, 2:271, 422–25. For more on the Butlers' speculations in New Orleans, see Trefousse, *Ben Butler*, 122–24; Hearn, *When the Devil Came Down to Dixie*, 183–96.

22. Denison to Chase, November 14, 1862, and Butler to Lincoln, November 28, 1862, *Private and Official Correspondence of Gen. Benjamin F. Butler*, 2:426–27, 447.

23. Denison to Chase, November 14, 1862, Butler to Lincoln, November 28, 1862, and Chase to Butler, July 31, 1862, *Private and Official Correspondence of Gen. Benjamin F. Butler*, 2:428, 450, 131; "Official memo of Banks's conversation with General Butler," December 18, 1862, box 79, Military Papers, Nathaniel Banks Papers, LOC, cited in Weaver, *Thank God My Regiment an African One*, 159; John A. Nelson, Compiled Service Record, Seventy-Third USCT, https://www-fold3-com.www.libproxy.wvu.edu/image/273/273305195, accessed May 25, 2018; John A. Nelson, Compiled Service Record, Seventy-Fifth USCT, https://www-fold3-com.www.libproxy.wvu.edu/image/273/279929869, accessed May 25, 2018.

24. Brewster to Dear Parry [Mary], January 10, 1863, Brewster to Dear Mother, May 6, 1863, Brewster to Dear Mattie, May 12, 1863, and Brewster to Dear Mary, June 20, 1863, *WTCWIO*, 210, 223, 229, 236.

25. Brewster to Dear Mary, February 12, 1863, *WTCWIO*, 212; *Circular of James B. Fry, Provost Marshal General, 1863*, box 2, folder 6, Alexander Henry Papers, HSP; Lincoln, "Opinion on the Draft," [September 14?], 1863, *CW*, 6:447. For other soldiers who wanted deserters to be executed, see Carmichael, *War for the Common Soldier*, 197.

26. Brewster to Dear Mattie, July 22, 1863, *WTCWIO*, 247; Lincoln, "Opinion on the Draft," *CW*, 6:447–48.

27. Brewster to Dear Mattie, May 12, 1863, *WTCWIO*, 229; "The Destiny of the African Race in the United States," *Continental Monthly* 3, no. 5 (May 1863): 600–610. For other Northerners' assertions that slavery had created a weakened "mulatto" race and that emancipation could provide prosperity for both white and black Americans, see Reidy, *Illusions of Emancipation*, 258–59, 263–64.

28. Henry Walker to Persis Walker, January 4 and 24, February 15, March 12, 1863, Henry Walker Correspondence, LOC.

29. Henry Walker to Persis Walker, January 4, February 6, March 29, 1863, Henry Walker Correspondence, LOC. For the "go-ahead" spirit and "ideology of achieved identity" of this era, see Sandage, *Born Losers*, 18, 22–43.

30. Henry Walker to Persis Walker, March 12, April 5, 1863, Henry Walker Correspondence, LOC.

31. Henry Walker to Persis Walker, July 11, 1863, October 17, 1862, Henry Walker Correspondence, LOC. For scholarship on Northern women and the economy during the Civil War that debates the significance of the gap between what men said and

what women did, see Silber, *Daughters of the Union*, 11, 42–43, 47–49, 54, 64–65, 71; Giesberg, *Army at Home*, 17–44; Attie, *Patriotic Toil*; Paludan, *People's Contest*, 157–58. For examinations of women's work and economic practices and strategies, see Boydston, *Home and Work*; Stanley, "Home Life and the Morality of the Market"; Hartigan-O'Connor, *Ties That Buy*; Benson, *Household Accounts*.

32. Persis Walker to Henry Walker, May 1, 1863, and Henry Walker to Persis Walker, May 8, 1863, Henry Walker Correspondence, LOC.

33. Henry Walker to Persis Walker, July 26, 1863; Henry Walker Correspondence, LOC.

34. "Late News from New Orleans," *PI*, February 18, 1863; "The Negro Soldiers," *The Liberator*, April 3, 1863, 55.

35. Capt. J. A. Gla et al. to Maj. Gen. N. P. Banks, February 19, 1863, in Berlin et al., *Freedom: . . . Series II, The Black Military Experience*, 316–17; Nelson to Banks, February 15, 1863, in Weaver, *Thank God My Regiment an African One*, 34; Reidy, *Illusions of Emancipation*, 55.

36. For more on the role played by the Louisiana Native Guards at Port Hudson, see Hollandsworth, *Louisiana Native Guards*, 53–58; Luke and Smith, *Soldiering for Freedom*, 89–91.

37. "Curious Betting at Port Hudson," *Albany Evening Journal*, July 29, 1863.

38. C. T. Buddeck to Banks, August [5, 1863], Geo. H. Hanks to Banks, August 5, 1863, P. F. Mancosas to Banks, August 7, 1863, and Statement of 'A Colored Man,' [September? 1863], in Berlin et al., *Freedom: . . . Series II, The Black Military Experience*, 150–52, 154–55; Teters, *Practical Liberators*, 122–23.

39. Special Order No. 199, Department of the Gulf, August 14, 1863, Case of John A. Nelson, NA; Assistant Adjutant General to Banks, August 15, 1863, Department of the Gulf, Letters Sent, Volume 5, NA; Banks to Lincoln, August 17, 1863, Lincoln Papers, LOC; Nathan W. Daniels Diary, September 23, 1863, in Weaver, *Thank God My Regiment an African One*, 152; "Personal," *Hartford Daily Courant*, September 11, 1863; "Col. John A. Nelson," *Boston Daily Advertiser*, September 14, 1863.

40. Henry to Wm. D. Whipple, June 15, 1863, E. D. Bassett to Henry, June 16, 1863, Henry to Bassett, June 16, 1863, Henry to Curtin, June 17, 1863, Curtin to Henry, June 18, 1863, and Henry to Curtin, June 19, 1863, box 1, folder 12, Alexander Henry Papers, HSP; Supervisory Committee for Recruiting Colored Enlistments, "Circular for Donations," June 27, 1863, box 1, folder 5, Abraham Barker Collection on the Free Military School for the Command of Colored Regiments, HSP. For the War Department's conferral of authority to Webster to recruit black soldiers in Philadelphia, see Stanton to Webster, June 17, 1863, and C. W. Foster to Webster, June 22, 1863, OR, Series 3, 3:376, 405. See also Luke and Smith, *Soldiering for Freedom*, 39–41.

41. Supervisory Committee for Recruiting Colored Regiments, Circular to "Men of Color," June 27, 1863, box 1, folder 6, Abraham Barker Collection, HSP; H. L. Stephens, "Victory!," *Album Varieties No. 3*, LOC. For more on how *Vanity Fair*'s editors tried to balance their opposition to emancipation with their ridicule of the administration, see Gallman, *Defining Duty in the Civil War*, 18. *Vanity Fair*'s editors stopped publishing the paper early in 1863, though, suggesting that devotees of the war for Union were no longer in a mood to countenance that balancing act.

42. *Addresses of the Hon. W. D. Kelley, Miss Anna E. Dickinson, and Mr. Frederick Douglass*, [1], 4, 7. For more on this mass meeting, see Gallman, *Defining Duty in the Civil War*, 242–45. For racial segregation in the artisanal trades and factory work, racist violence, and

the economic decline of the African American community in antebellum Philadelphia, see Hershberg, "Free Blacks in Antebellum Philadelphia"; Ignatiev, *How the Irish Became White*, 92–121.

43. *Addresses of the Hon. W. D. Kelley, Miss Anna E. Dickinson, and Mr. Frederick Douglass*, [1].

44. Henry Walker to Persis Walker, August 5 and 22, November 8, 1863, Henry Walker Correspondence, LOC.

45. Gooding to Lincoln, September 28, 1863, in Berlin et al., *Freedom: . . . Series II, The Black Military Experience*, 385–86; Lincoln, "Opinion on the Draft," [September 14?, 1863], *CW*, 6:445.

CHAPTER 5

1. Lincoln to Stanton, September 29, 1863, Case of John A. Nelson, NA.

2. Lincoln, "Memorandum concerning Henry M. Naglee," September 26, 1863, *CW*, 6:483.

3. Butler to Stanton, October 16, 1863 [Draft], box 21, and Butler to Assistant Adjutant General of the State of Massachusetts, February 13, 1862 [Draft], box 10, Butler Papers, LOC.

4. See Endorsement of Stanton, September 29, 1863, and War Department Special Order No. 438, September 30, 1863, Case of John A. Nelson, NA; Wilson to Lincoln, October 25, 1863, Lincoln Papers, LOC; Butler to Chase, October 21, 1863, and E. D. Townsend to Butler, November 2, 1863, *Private and Official Correspondence of Gen. Benjamin F. Butler*, 3:125, 135; Webster to Lincoln, November 5, 1863, Lincoln Papers, LOC; Lincoln, "Proclamation Calling for 300,000 Volunteers," October 17, 1863, *CW*, 6:523–24. For more on white recruiters of black soldiers, see Franklin, "James T. Ayers."

5. Nelson to Townsend, October 15, 1863, Nelson to Lieut. Schroeder, October 25, 1863, and Nelson to Townsend, October 27, 1863, Tenth USCT Infantry, Regimental Letter, Order, & Detail Book, pp. 1–2, NA.

6. Nelson to Lieut. Col. Hoffman, October 28, 1863, Nelson to R. S. Davis, November 15, 1863, Nelson to Davis, December 6, 1864[3], Nelson to H. W. Allen, December 24, 1863, and E. H. Powell to Butler, January 3, 1864, Tenth USCT Infantry, Regimental Letter, Order, & Detail Book, pp. 3, 6, 7, 9, 14, NA.

7. Nelson to Hoffman, October 28, 1863, Nelson to Foster, November 3, 1863, Nelson to Townsend, November 5 and 10, 1863, and Nelson to Davis, December 27, 1863, Tenth USCT Infantry, Regimental Letter, Order, & Detail Book, pp. 3–5, 12–13, NA.

8. Butler to Barnes, December 14, 1863, F. Morton to Butler, December 4, 1863, and Butler to F. Morton, December 6, 1863, *Private and Official Correspondence of Gen. Benjamin F. Butler*, 3:156, 181–82.

9. "Copy of an order drafted by Genl. [sic] Wilder for issue by Genl. Butler relating to enlisting Africans," KL, NA. For more on Wilder's management of African Americans' labor on Tidewater farms confiscated by the government, see Berlin et al., *Freedom: . . . Series I*, vol. 2, *The Wartime Genesis of Free Labor*, 96–97; Gerteis, *From Contraband to Freedman*, 37.

10. Butler, General Order 46, December 5, 1863, *Private and Official Correspondence of Gen. Benjamin F. Butler*, 3:183–84; Ervin L. Jordan, *Black Confederates and Afro-Yankees*, 267.

11. Butler, General Order 46, *Private and Official Correspondence of Gen. Benjamin F. Butler*, 3:184–85. See also Berlin et al., *Freedom: . . . Series II, The Black Military Experience*, 13, 115; Berlin et al., *Freedom: . . . Series I*, vol. 2, *The Wartime Genesis of Free Labor*, 100–101.

12. Butler, General Order 46, *Private and Official Correspondence of Gen. Benjamin F. Butler*, 3:183, 185–86. For antebellum social policy on vagrants, see O'Brassill-Kulfan, *Vagrants and Vagabonds*.

13. Butler, General Order 46, *Private and Official Correspondence of Gen. Benjamin F. Butler*, 3:186–87.

14. Stewart to Joseph G. Totten, December 11, 1863, in Berlin et al., *Freedom: . . . Series I*, vol. 2, *The Wartime Genesis of Free Labor*, 175–76.

15. Berlin et al., *Freedom: . . . Series I*, vol. 2, *The Wartime Genesis of Free Labor*, 175–76; Butler to Stanton, December 23, 1863, *Private and Official Correspondence of Gen. Benjamin F. Butler*, 3:246–47.

16. Lincoln, Annual Message to Congress, December 8, 1863, *CW*, 7:55; H. S. Olcott to Butler, December 10, 1863, Butler to Phillips, December 11, 1863, and Phillips to Butler, December 13, 1863, *Private and Official Correspondence of Gen. Benjamin F. Butler*, 3:198, 204, 206–7. For Butler as a potential challenger to Lincoln, see Trefousse, *Ben Butler*, 138–39.

17. Butler, "Order to Investigate Alleged Cases of Impressment of Colored Men by Col. J. A. Nelson," December 11, 1863, KL, NA.

18. Kinsman to Butler, December 12, 1863, KL, NA. For more on Craney Island as a refugee camp, see Berlin et al., *Freedom: . . . Series I*, vol. 2, *The Wartime Genesis of Free Labor*, 94–96; Manning, *Troubled Refuge*, 57–60; Taylor, *Embattled Freedom*, 87, 89–91; Ervin L. Jordan, *Black Confederates and Afro-Yankees*, 85–86.

19. Jane Wallis to Sir, December 10, 1863, and Testimony of Phillis Bess, undated, KL, NA; Hartigan-O'Connor, *Ties That Buy*.

20. Testimony of David Owens, undated, KL, NA.

21. Testimony of America Nash, undated, KL, NA. While Abram (or Abraham) Nash "never came back" to work for David Owens, neither he nor America served in the Tenth USCT. They were listed in the 1870 census as heads of adjacent households in Portsmouth, both draymen with $300 and $400 worth of real estate, respectively. See 1870 Federal Census Manuscripts, Portsmouth, Jefferson Ward, Norfolk, Virginia, roll M593_1667, p. 469A, Family History Library Film 553166, ancestry.com, accessed June 20, 2018.

22. For men working on area farms, see Testimony of William Edward Smith, December 17, 1863, KL, NA. For men who appear to be employed for themselves, see America Nash ("driving my own horse and truck"), Frank Shepard ("I must go to my shop"), undated, KL, NA; Statement of John Banks ("I was cutting wood . . . about a mile from my house . . . and obliged to do the work for my family"), January 2, 1864, and Testimony of John Banks (quotation in text), February 24, 1864, "Proceedings on a Board of Examination of John A. Nelson," Case of John A. Nelson, NA.

23. Testimony of James Thoroughgood, Mrs. John Pugh, Frank Shepard, and Moses Reddick, undated, and Testimony of Beverly Smith and William Carney, December 17, 1863, KL, NA; Testimony of John Banks, February 24, 1864, "Proceedings on a Board of Examination of John A. Nelson," Case of John A. Nelson, NA.

24. Testimony of George Colden, December 10, 1863, KL, NA; George Colden, Compiled Service Record, Tenth USCT, https://www-fold3-com.www.libproxy.wvu.edu/image/273/113369348, accessed July 25, 2018. For African Americans' attempts to

claim the rights and obligations inherent in citizenship for themselves in the Civil War, see Manning, *Troubled Refuge*, 201–31; Samito, *Becoming American*, 77–102; Mathisen, *Loyal Republic*, 105–13; Kantrowitz, *More Than Freedom*; Diemer, *Politics of Black Citizenship*.

25. Testimony of William Carney, February 26, 1864, Case of John A. Nelson, NA. On the various punishments levied by officers against enlisted men, see Ramold, *Baring the Iron Hand*.

26. Testimony of William Carney, February 26, 1864, Case of John A. Nelson, NA. William Carney, Compiled Service Record, Tenth USCT, http://www.footnotelibrary.com/image/163/113368043/, accessed March 15, 2015. Carney's inner conflict suggests that Chandra Manning's argument about African American notions of citizenship as "a mutually beneficial alliance with the national government" is correct, even if Carney also recognized the challenges in cementing that alliance. See Manning, *Troubled Refuge*, 14.

27. William Carney, Compiled Service Record; Mary Carney, Widow's Pension Application, Tenth USCT, http://www.footnotelibrary.com/image/296307534/, accessed March 15, 2015. For the docking of soldiers' pay for a variety of infractions, see Foote, *Gentlemen and the Roughs*, 11–12, 24, 49–50, 134; Carmichael, *War for the Common Soldier*, 53. For the ways slavery and emancipation shaped African Americans' marriages and married women's claims to freedom, see Hunter, *Bound in Wedlock*; Stanley, "Instead of Waiting."

28. E. A. Wild to J. B. Kinsman, December 25, 1863, and Testimony of Mills Benton and William Carney, December 17, 1863, KL, NA. See also Furstenberg, "Beyond Freedom and Slavery."

29. Testimony of John H. Holman, "Report of Lieut. Col. Kinsman," December 12, 1863, Case of John A. Nelson, NA; Holman to Kinsman, December 25, 1863, KL, NA; Testimony of Henry Williams, January 5, 1864, "Report of Lieut. Col. Kinsman," Testimony of Henry Williams, February 26, 1864, "Proceedings on a Board of Examination of John A. Nelson," 41, and Volunteer Enlistment of Henry Williams, November 28, 1863, Case of John A. Nelson, NA; Nelson to Holman, November 23, 186[3], Tenth USCT Infantry, Regimental Letter, Order, & Detail Book, p. 7, NA; Henry Williams, Compiled Service Record, Tenth USCT, https://www-fold3-com.www.libproxy.wvu.edu/image/273/113400526, accessed February 25, 2019. For an instance of Nelson taking recruits away from a different regiment, see Testimony of C. H. C. Brown, November 9, 1863, Case of John A. Nelson, NA.

30. For more on the ways consent and coercion shaped the experience of African American soldiers, see Glatthaar, *Forged in Battle*, 108–20; Foote, *Gentlemen and the Roughs*, 162–63; Luke and Smith, *Soldiering for Freedom*, 15–16, 18, 21–23, 36–37, 44–47; Oakes, *Freedom National*, 381–89; Lande, "Trials of Freedom."

31. Butler, General Order 4, January 9, 1864, Lincoln to Butler, January 14, 1864 (endorsement on General Order 4), and Nelson to Lincoln, January 27, 1864, Case of John A. Nelson, NA. For the ways men who participated in markets deemed illegitimate by their contemporaries tried to illuminate their good character, see Hollander, "Underground on the High Seas."

32. Sprague, *History of the 13th Infantry Regiment of Connecticut Volunteers*, 27, 297; Thompson to Butler, November 4, 1863, box 21, Butler Papers, LOC; Butler to Lincoln, February 24, 1864, and Testimony of Jared D. Thompson, February 23, 1864, *Private and Official Correspondence of Gen. Benjamin F. Butler*, 3:464–65; Testimony of J. W. [sic] Thompson, February 24, 1864, "Proceedings on a Board of Examination of John A.

Nelson," General Order 33, Department of Virginia and North Carolina, March 17, 1864, and Special Order 122, War Department, March 19, 1864, Case of John A. Nelson, NA. For more on Draper's recruitment of African American soldiers, see Lause, *Free Labor*, 63.

33. Colonel Nelson's Statement, February 27, 1864, Case of John A. Nelson, NA.

34. Colonel Nelson's Statement, February 27, 1864, and "Detective" to Butler, December 27, 1863, Case of John A. Nelson, NA.

35. Butler, Response to Nelson's Court Martial, March 15, 1864, Case of John A. Nelson, NA.

36. Wilson to Butler, December 18, 1863, *Private and Official Correspondence of Gen. Benjamin F. Butler*, 3:227; Amos A. Lawrence et al. to Stanton, December 10, 1863, in Berlin et al., *Freedom: . . . Series II, The Black Military Experience*, 108–9.

37. Butler to Forbes, December 18, 1863, *Private and Official Correspondence of Gen. Benjamin F. Butler*, 3:222–23.

38. Forbes to Andrew, November 18, 21 and 24, 1863, box 12, folder 12, and Forbes to Andrew, November 29, 1863, box 12, folder 13, Andrew Papers, MHS. As John Larson and Richard Abbott have shown, Forbes also recruited soldiers in the loyal states and Europe to serve in Massachusetts regiments. See Larson, *Bonds of Enterprise*, 98; Abbott, *Cotton and Capital*, 114–16, 130. As Scott Reynolds Nelson and Andrew Urban have argued, the movement of immigrants to the United States during the war, encouraged by an 1864 act passed by Congress, often served the interests of a variety of employers from the army to railroad men like Forbes and household mistresses. See Nelson, "After Slavery"; Urban, *Brokering Servitude*, 76.

39. Butler to Forbes, December 19, 1863, Fry to Butler, December 19, 1863, and Forbes to Butler, December 22, 1863, box 22, Butler Papers, LOC.

40. Forbes to Butler, December 22, 1863, Butler Papers, LOC; Butler to [Forbes], December 25, 1863, *Private and Official Correspondence of Gen. Benjamin F. Butler*, 3:245.

41. Hill to Whelden, December 12, 1863, "Advantages to the Black Soldier," undated memorandum in Hill's handwriting, Charles M. Whelden Papers, reel 12, Civil War Correspondence, Diaries, and Journals Collection, MHS.

42. Andrew to Lincoln, February 12, 1864, Lincoln Papers, LOC.

43. Lincoln to Andrew, February 18, 1864, *CW*, 7:191.

44. Lincoln to Andrew, February 18, 1864, *CW*, 7:191; Affidavit of Aaron Willett, June 8, 1864, Case File of Benjamin S. Pardee, box 4, Reports and Papers Relating to Fraudulent Activities in Various Districts of the Several States, NA. For the lack of clarity in the conscription law concerning who could serve as substitutes for whom, see Murdock, *One Million Men*, 180. For other examples of brokers who sought to enlist black men cheaply, see Marvel, *Lincoln's Mercenaries*, 219–20.

45. Affidavit of Aaron Willett, June 8, 1864, and Affidavit of John H. Swears, June 17, 1864, Case File of Benjamin S. Pardee, NA.

46. General Order 23, Department of the East, March 25, 1864, Dix to Stanton, June 22, 1864, and Examination of Lieut. Col. B. S. Pardee, June 18, 1864, Case File of Benjamin S. Pardee, NA; Fry to Stanton, June 20, 1864, E. D. Townsend to Dix, June 21, 1864, and Buckingham to Dix, June 13, 1864, *OR*, Series 3, 3:439–40, 444–45; Aaron Willett, Compiled Service Record, Twenty-Ninth Connecticut (Colored) Infantry, https://www-fold3-com.www.libproxy.wvu.edu/image/273/264938078, accessed June 18, 2018. For other examples of fraud in the recruitment of black soldiers, see Glatthaar, *Forged in Battle*, 65–68.

47. *Norwich Morning Bulletin*, March 28, 1864; Nelson to Mr. Read [sic], April 16, [1864], box 28, Butler Papers, LOC.

48. Nelson to Butler, February 10, 1864, box 25, Butler Papers, LOC; B. C. Ludlow to R. S. Davis, February 9, 1864, Case of John A. Nelson, NA.

49. M. H. Kimball, *Emancipated Slaves*, LCP; Webster to Phelps, undated letter labeled "No. 2" [December 1863], and Webster to Phelps, December 21, 1863, box 37, folder 59, Henry P. Slaughter Collection, Robert W. Woodruff Library, Atlanta University Center. For more on the enlistment and training of black soldiers in Philadelphia, see Tremel, "Union League, Black Leaders." For more on Bacon's photographs and antislavery consumption, see Mary Niall Mitchell, *Raising Freedom's Child*, 1–10; Reidy, *Illusions of Emancipation*, 102–3; Glickman, *Buying Power*, 61–90; *Harper's Weekly*, January 30, 1864.

50. Webster to C. W. Foster, December 12, 1863, Webster to Foster, December 17, 1863, Webster to Foster, December 21, 1863, Webster to Foster, December 29, 1863, Webster to Foster, January 6, 1864, Webster to Foster, February 18, 1864, and Webster to Foster, February 22, 1864, Colored Troops Division, Letters Received, NA; P. S. Duval & Son, *United States Soldiers at Camp "William Penn" Philadelphia, Pa.*, LCP; Hall, "To Render the Private Public," 46. As Mark Neely has shown, Webster arranged in 1864 for large "transparencies and gas-jet lettering" to adorn the edifice of the Supervisory Committee's building on Chestnut Street to celebrate emancipation in Maryland. See Neely, *Boundaries of American Political Culture*, 79.

51. Webster to Phelps, December 28, 1863, January 15, 1864, box 37, folder 59, Henry P. Slaughter Collection; Webster to Foster, January 15, 1864, Colored Troops Division, Letters Received, NA; "Circular for the Free Military School of Philadelphia's Supervisory Committee for Recruiting Colored Regiments," Miscellaneous Folder, 1863, box 23, Butler Papers, LOC. Webster sent Lincoln the circular, too, of course. See Webster to Lincoln, April 9, 1864, Lincoln Papers, LOC. For more on Webster's school, see Glatthaar, *Forged in Battle*, 45–47; Luke and Smith, *Soldiering for Freedom*, 60–62; Wilson, "Thomas Webster and the 'Free Military School for Applicants for Commands of Colored Troops.'"

52. "Report of the Special Committee appointed to visit Washington in reference to the subject of pay, Substitution, and other matters affecting the interests of the Colored troops," April 1864, box 1, folder 18, Webster to the Supervisory Committee for Recruiting Colored Regiments, April 25, 1864, box 1, folder 20, Forbes to Butler, April 11, 1864, and Pass from Butler to Webster and Son, April 15, 1864, box 1, folder 17, Abraham Barker Collection, HSP.

53. See Webster to Stanton, April 27, 1864, Forney to Butler, May 14, 1864, box 1, folder 21, Wade to Butler, May 18, 1864, Samuel Wilkeson to Butler, May 19, 1864, and Henry Wilson to Butler, May 18, 1864, box 1, folder 22, Abraham Barker Collection, HSP. For commercial corruption in Butler's Department of Virginia and North Carolina, see Ludwell H. Johnson, "Contraband Trade," 641–52.

CHAPTER 6

1. Lincoln, "Proclamation Calling for 500,000 Volunteers," July 18, 1864, *CW*, 7:448–49; Stephens, *Idol of Abolitionism*, LCP.

2. Lincoln to Isaac M. Schermerhorn, September 12, 1864, *CW*, 8:2. Michael Johnson has estimated that some eighty thousand enslaved people moved to the Union states (mainly to the Northwest) during the war. See Michael P. Johnson, "Out of Egypt,"

239–40. It is difficult to determine how many white and black refugees from the South found their way to Philadelphia during the conflict. The records kept by the Pennsylvania Abolition Society and Union Volunteer Refreshment Saloon (UVRS) that will provide the evidence for conclusions in this chapter are incomplete and often illegible, as the agents of these institutions admitted and lamented. The book kept by PAS's employment agents lists the names of perhaps four hundred workers, but some of them were from Philadelphia, as I will explain below. The UVRS employment ledger includes the names of some nine hundred refugees passing through the Saloon during the war. The leaders of the organization, however, boasted that by the end of the war their organization had "secured" some seventeen thousand "Rebel Deserters, Refugees & Freedm[e]n" by arranging work "for a large portion of them." See Pennsylvania Abolition Society Employment Agency Book, 1862–1865, AmS 138, HSP; "Notes on Refugees, Deserters, and Employment, 1864–1865," Series 6, vol. 11, and "Statement about UVRS and Rebel Deserters," undated, box 12, folder 1, Samuel Fales Collection, HSP.

3. For the Eighteenth Corps attack on June 15, 1864, see Rhea, *On to Petersburg*, 251–303 (quotation on 301).

4. Brown to Kinsman, May 12, 1864, KL, NA.

5. Brown to Kinsman, May 12, 1864, KL, NA.

6. Brown to Kinsman, May 12, June 15, July 14, 1864, KL, NA. For the vital "usefulness" of African Americans' labor for the U.S. Army that "created plenty of room for exploitation," see Manning, *Troubled Refuge*, 213, 230; Urban, *Brokering Servitude*, 73; Carmichael, *War for the Common Soldier*, 58.

7. Kinsman to Butler, July 15, 1864 (with Butler's endorsement, dated July 18, 1864), and Butler to Wilder, April 13, 1864 (with Wilder's endorsement, dated April 29, 1864), KL, NA.

8. Henry Walker to Persis Walker, January 10 and 12, 1864, Henry Walker Correspondence, LOC. For more on William Paasch, whose name Henry Walker and the census taker spelled "Pash," see the unit's roster at https://dmna.ny.gov/historic/reghist/civil/infantry/117thInf/117thInfMain.htm, accessed June 20, 2018; 1860 Federal Census Manuscripts, Remsen, Oneida County, New York, roll M653_825, p. 759, Family History Library Film 803825, ancestry.com, accessed June 20, 2018; Mowris, *History of the One Hundred and Seventeenth Regiment, N.Y. Volunteers*, 281.

9. Henry Walker to Persis Walker, January 14 and 31, March 17 and 31, 1864, Henry Walker Correspondence, LOC. For Weeks, see 1860 Federal Census Manuscripts, Remsen, Oneida County, New York, roll M653_825, p. 774, Family History Library Film 803825, ancestry.com, accessed June 20, 2018. For the importance of accounting practices—what Caitlin Rosenthal has termed "highly calculating modes of management"—for establishing cultures of control and legitimacy, see Rosenthal, "From Memory to Mastery," 735; Zakim, "Bookkeeping as Ideology"; Ryan, *Cradle of the Middle Class*, 202.

10. Henry Walker to Persis Walker, March 6, April 25, 1864, and Chaplain James Shrigley to Mrs. Mary [sic] Walker, July 24, 1864, Henry Walker Correspondence, LOC; Persis D. Walker, Application WC52101, Case Files of Approved Pension Applications of Widows and Other Dependents of Civil War Veterans, https://www-fold3-com.www.libproxy.wvu.edu/image/271008499?terms=Henry%20Walker&pqsid=MGlBB-5erkwz7KU1lICLaA:506000:488028296, accessed June 20, 2018; Henry Walker, New York Civil War Muster Roll Abstracts, New York State Archives, https://www-fold3-com.www.libproxy.wvu.edu/image/315855515?terms=Henry%20Walker&pqsid=MGlBB-5erkwz7KU1lICLaA

Notes to Pages 179–84

:555000:1905168872, accessed June 20, 2018; https://www.findagrave.com/memorial/2548788/henry-walker, accessed June 25, 2018.

11. Brewster to Dear Mary, June 15, April 3, 1864, *WTCWIO*, 317, 319, 281.

12. Brewster to Dear Mother, July 30, 1864, Brewster to Dear Mary, August 4, 1864, and Brewster to Dear Mattie, August 30, 1864, *WTCWIO*, 320–22, 328. For the recruiting of African American substitutes in the concluding months of the war, see Murdock, *One Million Men*, 180; Shannon, *Organization and Administration*, 2:76.

13. Brewster to Dear Mary, August 21, 1864, *WTCWIO*, 326–27. See also Ervin L. Jordan, *Black Confederates and Afro-Yankees*, 270–71.

14. Brewster to Dear Mary, August 21, 1864, Brewster to Dear Mattie, August 30, 1864, and Brewster to Dear Mother, October 27, 1864, *WTCWIO*, 327–29, 336.

15. "Our Domestic Affairs," *Continental Monthly* 6, no. 3 (September 1864): 241, 243; "A Great Social Problem," *Continental Monthly* 6, no. 4 (October 1864): 441; Luskey, "Houses Divided," 637–38.

16. "Our Domestic Affairs," 248–49, 252; "A Great Social Problem," 441–42; Luskey, "Houses Divided," 638.

17. "Our Domestic Affairs," 245, 252, 253; "A Great Social Problem," 444. For the *Continental*'s antislavery ideology, see Fahs, *Imagined Civil War*, 159, 345n14; "Our War and Our Want," *Continental Monthly* 1, no. 2 (February 1862): 113–17; "Among the Pines," *Continental Monthly* 1, no. 1 (January 1862): 35–46; "The True Basis," *Continental Monthly* 1, no. 2 (February 1862): 136–38; Luskey, "Houses Divided," 638–39. Andrew Urban has shown that organizations such as PAS advocated for the northward movement of formerly enslaved laborers to combat the dangers that Irish draft rioters as well as domestic servants allegedly posed. See Urban, *Brokering Servitude*, 76.

18. J. Wistar Evans to Respected Friend, November 3, 1864, Board of Education: Committee on Employment, Series 1, folder 28, Minutes and Reports, 1864–1865 and undated, and Joseph Truman to Hannibal Hamlin, June 10, 1862, Correspondence Outgoing, Series 2, folder 25, 1862, PAS Papers, HSP; Oakes, *Freedom National*, 97; Luskey, "Houses Divided," 639–40. For the efforts of Philadelphia benevolent societies to care for poor people, soldiers, and their families during the war, see Gallman, *Mastering Wartime*, 117–45.

19. Mitchell to Truman, 2nd mo. 20th, 1862, Incoming Correspondence, Series 2, folder 19, 1862, PAS Papers, HSP; "The Aid of Friends and Others," *Friends' Intelligencer*, 7th mo. 23, 1864, 320; Luskey, "Houses Divided," 642.

20. Cary to Truman, 7th mo. 30th, 1864, Correspondence Incoming, Series 2, folder 1, January–August, 1864, PAS Papers, HSP. For the Cary (sometimes spelled "Carey") household, see 1850 Federal Census, Albany Ward 4, Albany, New York, roll M432_471, p. 169A, image 340, 1855 New York State Census, Albany City Ward 4, Albany, New York, Enumeration District 2, p. 22, 1860 Federal Census, Albany Ward 3, Albany, New York, roll M653_719, p. 455, image 464, and 1865 New York State Census, Ward 3, Albany, New York, p. 24, ancestry.com, accessed June 22, 2015; Luskey, "Houses Divided," 643.

21. Naval Transport Diary Typescript, July 30–August 7, 1864, Rubenstein Library, Duke University; Luskey, "Houses Divided," 652. For the correspondence about this shipment of people aboard the *George Leary*, see Kinsman to Butler, July 15, 1864, "List of Colored People taken North on the Stmr Geo. Leary by Lt. Col. J. B. Kinsman," August 2, 1864, Truman to Respected Friend, 8th mo. 11, 1864, and Truman to Respected Friend, 8th mo. 31, 1864, KL, NA. For the kidnapping of Southern freedpeople to Cuba during the war,

see Rothman, *Beyond Freedom's Reach*. See also Baptist, "'Cuffy,' 'Fancy Maids,' and 'One-Eyed Men'"; Morgan, *Laboring Women*, 12–49.

22. Jenkins to Truman, July 27, 1864, Correspondence Incoming, Series 2, folder 1, January–August 1864, PAS Papers, HSP; Luskey, "Houses Divided," 653. Truman and other benevolent society agents tried not to separate families, but such separations clearly occurred and would have been reminders of the slave trade's consequences. See Daniel Breed to Truman, January 17, 1865, Correspondence Incoming, Series 2, folder 3, January–April 1865, and E. Matlack letter, unaddressed and undated [c. 1864], Correspondence Incoming, Series 2, folder 2, September–December 1864, PAS Employment Agency Book, 1862–1865, p. 41, PAS Papers, HSP. For the language of the slave market and the social types most desired by consumers of slaves, see Walter Johnson, *Soul by Soul*, 57–59, 78–116.

23. Elisha Bassett to Truman, November 22, 1864, Correspondence Incoming, Series 2, folder 2, September–December 1864, PAS Papers, HSP; Luskey, "Houses Divided," 653–54. For New Jersey's 1846 abolition law, see Gigantino, *Ragged Road to Abolition*, 234–38. For this practice elsewhere in the early Republic, see Rockman, *Scraping By*, 107–8. For the wages of domestic servants in Northern cities, see Geo. M. Tatum to Truman, October 23, 1864, and John Collins to Truman, October 24, 1864, Correspondence Incoming, Series 2, folder 2, September–December 1864, PAS Papers, HSP; Stansell, *City of Women*, 272n9. For PAS's role in placing African Americans in apprenticeships, see John Milliway & Son to Dear Sir, April 24, 1860, Thomas Garrett to Truman, 4th mo. 16th 1860, and Garrett to Truman, 4th mo. 25th 1860, Incoming Correspondence, Series 2, folder 17, 1860, PAS Papers, HSP.

24. Shannon, *Organization and Administration*, 1:246; Gallman, *Mastering Wartime*, 224; Lause, *Free Labor*, 30; Hershberg, "Free Blacks in Antebellum Philadelphia"; Ignatiev, *How the Irish Became White*, 92–121. African American women in Philadelphia accounted for 11 percent of domestic servants in the city in 1860 and over 16 percent in 1870. See Brown, "Migrants and Workers in Philadelphia," 157.

25. B. Chase to J. M. Truman, 8th mo. 2nd, 1864, and H. Bancroft Letter, August 4, 1864, Correspondence Incoming, Series 2, folder 1, January–August 1864, PAS Employment Agency Book, 1862–1865, pp. 15, 17, PAS Papers, HSP; Silber, *Daughters of the Union*, 231–32; Luskey, "Houses Divided," 655. For more on Chase's household after the war, see 1870 Federal Census, Macedon, Wayne County, New York, roll M593_1112, p. 271A, image 548, ancestry.com, accessed July 9, 2015.

26. Mary A. Smith to Esteemed Friend, 8th mo. 8th, 1864, Gideon Frost to Truman, 8th mo. 6, 1864, Eliza H. Bell to Truman, July 2, 1864, Lydia C. Garrett to Truman, 7th mo. 28th, 1864, and Lydia C. Alston to Respected Friend, 7th mo. 28th, 1864, Correspondence Incoming, Series 2, folder 1, January–August 1864, PAS Papers, HSP. Andrew Urban shows how the labor market was conspicuously international in *Brokering Servitude*.

27. Hartigan-O'Connor, "Gender's Value in the History of Capitalism," 616–17, 628–31; *PL*, September 7, 1843, February 26, 1847, October 11, 1848, March 1, 1850, May 27, 1850, August 10, 1853, February 22, 1854, September 14, 1854, February 20, 1856, September 29, 1857, February 16 and 24, 1859, June 28, 1859, July 6, 1859, October 26, 1859, April 24 and 30, 1860, May 24 and 30, 1860; Chas. M. Greene to whom it may concern, July 26, 1864, Correspondence Incoming, Series 2, folder 1, January–August 1864, PAS Employment Agency Book, 1862–1865, pp. 16, 18 1/2, PAS Papers, HSP; Leslie, *Mr. and Mrs. Woodbridge*, 102; Margaret B. Harvey, "The Story of a Dollar," *Godey's Lady's Book and Magazine* (November 1884): 485; "Rewarding the Army," *Continental Monthly* 2, no. 2 (August 1862):

163. As noted above, the typical wage of a domestic servant in the North during this period was $1.00 to $1.25 per week. When newspaper advertisements cited wages for half-grown girls, they typically offered fifty cents per week.

28. Mary A. Smith to Respected Friend, 10th mo. 16, 1864, Correspondence Incoming, Series 2, folder 2, September–December 1864, PAS Papers, HSP.

29. Ann Cope to Jane Boustead, May 1865, Correspondence Incoming, Series 2, folder 4, May–December 1865, PAS Employment Agency Book, 1862–1865, p. 41, PAS Papers, HSP; Luskey, "Houses Divided," 656. The PAS employment ledger lists only fourteen-year-old Lydia Berry, but not her sister Matilda. For more on the liberating potential of mobility for African Americans during the war, see Sternhell, *Routes of War*, 152. For more on the conflict between white and black Southern women about the power dynamics of their households after emancipation, see Glymph, *Out of the House of Bondage*.

30. Cope to Boustead, May 1865; Luskey, "Houses Divided," 657.

31. J. H. Johnson, Minutes for April 27, 1865, Board of Education, Committee on Employment, Minutes, 1864–1865 and undated, folder 28, Minutes and Reports, Series 1, PAS Papers, HSP. See also Bourque, "Women and Work in the Philadelphia Almshouse, 1790–1840"; Hartigan-O'Connor, "Gender's Value in the History of Capitalism," 628–29; Rockman, *Scraping By*.

32. Lincoln, "Speech at the Great Central Sanitary Fair, Philadelphia, Pennsylvania," June 16, 1864, *CW*, 7:394; Webster to Lincoln, June 15, 1864, Lincoln Papers, LOC; "Circular to the Contributors to 'The Association to Procure Employment for Rebel Deserters, who have taken the Oath of Allegiance to the United States,' May 17, 1865," Civil War Volunteer Saloons and Hospitals Ephemera, John A. McAllister Collection, box 1, folder 9, LCP; General Order 64, War Department, February 18, 1864, *OR*, Series 3, 4:118; Jno. W. R. Cato to J. B. Wade, November 1, 1864, box 11, folder 7, and "Notes on Refugees, Deserters, and Employment, 1864–1865," 64, Series 6, vol. 11, Samuel Fales Collection, HSP; Luskey, "Special Marts," 361, 373–74.

33. Edward Shoemaker to Wade, June 24, 1864, box 2, folder 3, Jacob Rupp to Dear Sir, [blank] 5, 1864, box 2, folder 1, Letter from Reuben Foster (for Anthony Reybuhl) to Mr. Cooper, May 17, 1864, box 2, folder 2, Wm. H. Ruddach to Wade, 1864, box 2, folder 1, and "Notes on Refugees, Deserters, and Employment," 113, Samuel Fales Collection, HSP; Luskey, "Special Marts," 374.

34. E. Burket to Geo. H. Stewart, March 28, 1865, box 2, folder 1, Maxwell S. Rowland to Wade, October 2, 1864, box 2, folder 4, Edward Shoemaker to Wade, May 9, 1864, box 2, folder 2, Shoemaker to Wade, June 24, 1864, box 2, folder 3, "Notes on Refugees, Deserters, and Employment," 54, and Joseph Garrett to Wade, January 17, 1865, box 2, folder 5, Samuel Fales Collection, HSP; Luskey, "Special Marts," 375.

35. C. Soest to Mr. Cooper, April 25, 1864, box 2, folder 2, Wade to Provost Marshal, June 17, 1864, box 2, folder 3, and "Notes on Refugees, Deserters, and Employment," 3, 13–14, Samuel Fales Collection, HSP; 1860 Federal Census Manuscripts, Criglersville, Madison County, Virginia, roll M653_1360, p. 81, Family History Library Film 805360, ancestry.com, accessed June 27, 2018; William A. Rosson, Compiled Service Record, https://www-fold3-com.www.libproxy.wvu.edu/image/9741878, accessed June 27, 2018; 1870 Federal Census Manuscripts, Philadelphia Ward 21 District 70, Philadelphia, Pennsylvania, roll M593_1409, p. 412A, Family History Library Film 552908, ancestry.com, accessed June

27, 2018. Back returned with his family to Madison County after the war, while Weakley moved with his family to Lexington, Illinois. See 1870 Federal Census Manuscripts, Locustdale, Madison County, Virginia; roll M593_1662, p. 42B, Family History Library Film 553161, and 1880 Federal Census Manuscripts, Lexington, McLean County, Illinois, roll 230, Family History Film 1254230, p. 513D, Enumeration District 177, image 0719, ancestry.com, accessed June 27, 2018.

36. Alex Cabaniss and J. J. Nabors [Neighbors] to Wade, August 28, 1864, box 11, folder 7, J. J. Nabors to Wade, September 17, 1864, Alex Cabaniss to Wade, September 18, 1864, December 1, 1864, box 2, folder 4, and "Notes on Refugees, Deserters, and Employment," 31, 33, Samuel Fales Collection, HSP; Luskey, "Special Marts," 374–75. For information on the Alabamians' military service, see the National Park Service's Civil War Soldiers and Sailors Database, http://www.nps.gov/civilwar/soldiers-and-sailors-database.htm, accessed June 14, 2012; Alex. C. Cabaniss, Compiled Service Record, Forty-First Alabama, https://www-fold3-com.www.libproxy.wvu.edu/image/11981083, accessed June 27, 2018.

37. Anna Shippen to Edward Shippen, August 25, 1864, box 4, Shippen Family Papers, HSP.

38. Edward Shoemaker to Wade, May 9, 1864, box 2, folder 2, Price to Wade, July 30, August 29, 1864, box 2, folder 3, Price to J. B. Wade, August 23, 1864, box 1, folder 3, Wade to Price, September 15, 1864, box 2, folder 4, Pembroke Scott to Wade, January 6, 1865, box 2, folder 5, and Price to Wade, undated, box 3, folder 7, Samuel Fales Collection, HSP. On the contest for the labor of enslaved and deserting runaways in the Confederate South, see Sternhell, *Routes of War*, 124.

39. "Rough Memorandum," undated [possibly August 28, 1865], box 2, folder 7, Samuel Fales Collection, HSP; "Circular to the Contributors," McAllister Collection, LCP; Luskey, "Special Marts," 375–76.

40. Letter of Introduction from James R. Ross on behalf of Mrs. Garvin, October 29, 1864 (with endorsement of Clement Soest to Wade, October 31, 1864), box 2, folder 4, Samuel Fales Collection, HSP; "Astounding Frauds on Government," *New York Times*, February 8, 1865.

41. For other works that frame the brokerage of bounties and substitutes around the narrative of the unscrupulous middleman, see Murdock, *One Million Men*, 255–304; Murdock, *Patriotism Limited*, 107–48; Michael Thomas Smith, *Enemy Within*, 127–53.

42. Testimony of Isaac M. Twitchings, April 8, 1865, box 1, Papers of Lafayette C. Baker, NA. For draft insurance, see Gallman, *Mastering Wartime*, 39.

43. Micheal [sic] Lawrance to Baker, March 19, 1865, Testimony of James J. Powers, April 22, 1865, and Testimony of Thomas Patterson, April 22, 1865, box 1, Baker Papers, NA; Shannon, *Organization and Administration*, 2:69–70.

44. Testimony of Christian Sorenson, January 17, 1865, Testimony of Nicholas Welter, March 29, 1865, Joseph Krapp to My Dear Ernest, February 8, 1865, and Testimony of Margaret Bennett, Edward H. Dingley, Patrick Murphy, and John Furey, January 28, 1865, box 1, Baker Papers, NA. For the enlistment of minors and its corresponding threat to family economies, see Clarke and Plant, "No Minor Matter."

45. J. B. Auld to Baker, March 27, 1865, Testimony of Bridget Lehey, March 27, 1865, Testimony of Mary Vogeltest, March 21, 1865, Testimony of Pauline Steinberger, March 8, 1865, Handwritten Note in regard to William White, May 9 [no year], Testimony of

Henrietta Theileman, April 21, 1865, Testimony of Sarah C. Waters, March 23, 1865, Testimony of Mary Shea, April 3, 1865, Testimony of Ann Lamey, March 27, 1865, and Testimony of Julia Sullivan, March 3, 1865, box 1, Baker Papers, NA.

46. Testimony of Jane Wilsey, March 13, 1865, box 1, Baker Papers, NA.

47. Captain John Duffy to Baker, April 7, 1865, Testimony of Julia Sullivan, March 3, 1865, Petition on Behalf of John Shay to Baker, March 16, 1865, Testimony of Thomas Sitman, March 24, 1865, and Testimony of John G. Williams, April 21, 1865, box 1, Baker Papers, NA.

48. For the application—and the midcentury easing—of the legal doctrine of "entirety," which stated that workers were not owed monthly payments in annual contracts unless explicitly stipulated, see Montgomery, *Citizen Worker*, 39–42; Steinfeld, *Coercion, Contract, and Free Labor*, 291–92. For a discussion of the ways "assymetrical information" tends to reward dishonesty in market exchanges, see Akerlof, "Market for 'Lemons.'" For an examination of wages and the labor market in antebellum New York, see Stott, *Workers in the Metropolis*. Gregory P. Downs and Kate Masur suggest in "Echoes of War," 6–11, that the power of the federal state in the Civil War era has been overemphasized.

CONCLUSION

1. "Abraham Lincoln. Oration by R. W. Emerson," *Littell's Living Age*, May 13, 1865, 282. See also Fox, *Lincoln's Body*, 105; Luskey, "Ambiguities of Class."

2. *Montana Post*, October 8 and 22, November 19, 1864; Safford, *Mechanics of Optimism*, 38–43, 55–56; 1870 Federal Census Manuscripts, Cedar Creek Mines, Missoula, Montana Territory, roll M593_827, p. 317A, image 639, Family History Library Film 552326, 1880 Federal Census Manuscripts, Park City, Summit County, Utah, roll 1338, Family History Film 1255338, p. 38B, Enumeration District 074, and John A. Nelson Death Certificate, *Utah Veterans with Federal Service Buried in Utah, Territorial to 1866*, ancestry.com, accessed June 25, 2018; *Salt Lake Herald*, October 28, 1880.

3. Blight, introduction to *WTCWIO*, 22–23; Augusta to Samuel B. Fales, December 24, 1865, box 2, folder 8, and Wade to Ould Friend John [B. S. Brown?], May 19, 1865, box 2, folder 6, Samuel Fales Collection, HSP; *McElroy's Philadelphia City Directory* for 1866; *Age*, June 12, 1866.

4. "Disabled Soldiers," *Army and Navy Journal*, January 28, 1865, 356, container 26, vol. 1, Bound Volumes of Correspondence of Department of Special Relief, U.S. Sanitary Commission, Cleveland Branch, WRHS. The members of the society who pasted newspaper columns in these volumes gave their own title to the essay—"Four Rules for Discharged Soldiers"—suggesting its broader applicability for all veterans. For the origin of Taylorist time studies in Southern slaveholders' management, see Rosenthal, "Slavery's Scientific Management," 73; Rodgers, *Work Ethic in Industrial America*, 53. Frances Clarke describes how wounded veterans attempted to demonstrate "willpower" and "character" as well as highlight their "redemptive sacrifice" on the battlefield in order to establish themselves in postbellum society in *War Stories*, 144–74. For the efforts of the U.S. Sanitary Commission and other organizations to broker employment for Union veterans who could not find work, see Marten, *Sing Not War*, 52, 56–58, 236–40; Brian Matthew Jordan, *Marching Home*, 55–56, 80.

5. Entry 146, September 25, 1865, and Entry 120, September 12, 1865, vol. 2: Employer's Register, Bureau of Information and Employment, Entry 144, July 24, 1865, vol. 3:

Applicant's Register, Bureau of Information and Employment, J. T. Briggs to Miss Maggie, September 5, 1865, and L. H. Severance to Miss Ellen F. Terry, October 23, 1865, container 26, vol. 3, U.S. Sanitary Commission, Cleveland Branch, WRHS.

6. "Chief of Freedmen's Bureau," *New-York Tribune*, March 6, 1865, 4. For more on the creation of the bureau, see Hahn et al., *Freedom: . . . Series 3*, vol. 1, *Land and Labor, 1865*, 17.

7. Thomas Webster, Shipping Agent, Pennsylvania, vol. 144, p. 208, R. G. Dun & Co. Credit Report Volumes, BL; *McElroy's Philadelphia City Directory* for 1866 and 1867; McCorison, "Impressions of the President Elect," 296. See also Hahn, *Making Tobacco Bright*, 72.

8. Ludwell H. Johnson, "Contraband Trade," 641–52; Trefousse, *Ben Butler*, 170–77; *Speech of Maj.-Gen. Benj. F. Butler*, 4–5.

9. *Speech of Maj.-Gen. Benj. F. Butler*, 30, 32. Butler's correspondence with radical Republicans like Charles Sumner shows that he wanted to head the Bureau. See Trefousse, *Ben Butler*, 303n79.

10. *Speech of Maj.-Gen. Benj. F. Butler*, 86. See also Powell, *New Masters*; Trefousse, *Ben Butler*, 178–256.

11. S. N. Clark to William H. De Councey, September 21, 1865, roll 1: Letters Sent, vol. 1, BRFAL-DC; Luskey, "Special Marts," 376.

12. N. A. M. Dudley to W. J. Clark, September 29, 1865, roll 27, Letters Sent, vol. 1, Records of the Subassistant Commissioner at Memphis, NA; Luskey, "Special Marts," 376. For more on Dudley's and other Bureau officials' efforts to return freedpeople from cities to farms, see Hahn et al., *Freedom: . . . Series 3*, vol. 1, *Land and Labor, 1865*, 186, 266–69, 272–74. For the congressional debate about whether the Bureau should help place former slaves in Northern households in order to protect them from "harpies" who would exploit them in the labor market, see Richardson, *Greatest Nation on Earth*, 231–36.

13. John Eaton to George B. Carse, June 16, 1865, Charles H. Howard to Max Woodhull, February 16, 1866, and Charles H. Howard to Lyman Abbott, March 6, 1866, roll 1: Letters Sent, vol. 1, Charles H. Howard to Lyman Abbott, April 6, 1866, and Charles H. Howard to Henry Livingston, July 5, 1866, roll 1: Letters Sent, vol. 2, and Annual Report of Charles H. Howard to Oliver O. Howard, October 1, 1867, roll 1: Letters Sent, vol. 3, BRFAL-DC; Luskey, "Special Marts," 376–77. Kate Masur argues that the bureau's intervention in the labor market "did little to alleviate crowding and unemployment in the city." See Masur, *Example for All the Land*, 69. For the numbers of freedpeople the bureau transported, see Harrison, *Washington during Civil War and Reconstruction*, 89.

14. Charles H. Howard to G. A. Wadsworth, November 1, 1866, William W. Rogers to S. A. Tillman, January 20, 1867, and Charles H. Howard to R. A. Haskins, January 31, 1867, roll 1: Letters Sent, vol. 2, Charles H. Howard to H. A. Kingsbury, May 13, 1867, roll 1: Letters Sent, vol. 3, and Deposition of James Gray, April 10, 1866, roll 5: Letters Received, BRFAL-DC; Luskey, "Special Marts," 377. For employers who failed to abide by the contracts they made through the Freedmen's Bureau, see Urban, *Brokering Servitude*, 84–85.

15. Charles H. Howard to Henry Livingston, July 5, 1866, roll 1: Letters Sent, vol. 2, L. Riley to Oliver O. Howard, February 19, 1867, and J. V. M. Vandenburgh to W. W. Rogers, July 16, 1867, roll 8, Letters Received, BRFAL-DC; Luskey, "Special Marts," 377–78; "Interview with *The Times* [London] Correspondent, April 12, 1866," *Papers of Andrew Johnson*, 10:407; *Evening Star*, March 1, 1866; Harrison, *Washington during Civil War and Reconstruction*, 88; Urban, *Brokering Servitude*, 87.

16. G. A. Wadsworth to Genl. Howard, October 13, 1866, Howard C. Dunham to R. M. Howard, January 16, 1867, and F. A. Tschiffely to M. H. Doolittle, February 5, 1867 (and endorsement of R. G. Rutherford, March 15, 1867), roll 7, Letters Received, Josiah Crawford to Dear sur, January 23, 1867, Jno. C. Holbrook to S. N. Clark, March 28, 1867, Roll 8, Letters Received, BRFAL-DC; Luskey, "Special Marts," 378. My argument about Tschiffely's gambit corresponds with Barbara Fields's contention that white Marylanders often complained about a "shortage of labor" when they were really frustrated about their inability to hire free blacks to lengthy contracts at low wages. See Fields, *Slavery and Freedom on the Middle Ground*, 70–71. See also Urban, *Brokering Servitude*, 64–67. For the conflict among states, parents, former slaveholders, Northern employers, and agents of the Freedmen's Bureau over the apprenticeship and wage labor of children during Reconstruction, see Manning, *Troubled Refuge*, 257, 269; Mary Niall Mitchell, *Raising Freedom's Child*, 143–87; Jones, *Intimate Reconstructions*, 103–32.

17. C. L. Woodworth to O. O. Howard, July 25, 1866, roll 6, Letters Received, BRFAL-DC; Luskey, "Special Marts," 379. Harrison discusses the Woodworth letter, Republicans' "sympathy" for former slaves, and their animosity to Irish immigrants in *Washington during Civil War and Reconstruction*, 94.

18. Charles H. Howard to William M. Beebe, April 29, 1867, roll 1: Letters Sent, vol. 3, and J. O. Bloss to S. N. Clark, March 12, 1867, roll 8, Letters Received, BRFAL-DC; Luskey, "Special Marts," 379. For more on Bloss, see Urban, *Brokering Servitude*, 90.

19. Hahn et al., *Freedom: . . . Series 3*, vol. 1, *Land and Labor, 1865*, 535–37; Oliver Wood to Charles H. Howard, March 26, 1866, Deposition of Wm. Washington Banks, May 11, 1866, and W. F. Spurgin to W. W. Rogers, May 11, 1866, roll 6, Letters Received, BRFAL-DC; Hayden et al., *Freedom: . . . Series 3*, vol. 2, *Land and Labor, 1866–1867*, 816–19; Luskey, "Special Marts," 379–80.

20. Oliver Wood to Gen. Stannard, May 22, 1866, roll 6, Letters Received, BRFAL-DC; Fields, *Slavery and Freedom on the Middle Ground*, 160; *Baltimore Sun*, August 9, 1864; Luskey, "Special Marts," 380. For the ambitions of the labor agents who worked for and with the Freedmen's Bureau after the war, see Faulkner, *Women's Radical Reconstruction*, 123–26.

21. Still, *Brief Narrative of the Struggle for the Rights of the Colored People of Philadelphia*, 8–9; Hall, "To Render the Private Public," 37–38, 46–55; Reidy, *Illusions of Emancipation*, 320–22, 326.

22. Luskey, "Special Marts," 380–81.

23. "A Great Social Problem," 441–44; Luskey, "Special Marts," 383. The desire for machines that would replace workers echoes Herman Melville's dialogue between the proprietor of an intelligence office and a prospective employer of labor in his 1857 novel, *The Confidence Man*. See Dudden, *Serving Women*, 86–87.

24. Luskey, "Special Marts," 383; Eric Foner, *Reconstruction*, 582–85; Montgomery, *Beyond Equality*; Beckert, *Monied Metropolis*, 176–77, 280–81; Richardson, *Death of Reconstruction*.

BIBLIOGRAPHY

PRIMARY SOURCES

Manuscript Collections

Baker Library, Harvard Business School, Cambridge, Massachusetts
    R. G. Dun & Co. Credit Report Volumes
Historical Society of Pennsylvania, Philadelphia, Pennsylvania
    Abraham Barker Collection on the Free Military School
        for the Command of Colored Regiments
    Alexander Henry Papers
    Citizens' Bounty Fund Committee Records
    Pennsylvania Abolition Society Papers
    Samuel Fales Collection
    Shippen Family Papers
Library Company of Philadelphia, Philadelphia, Pennsylvania
    Duval, P. S. & Son. *United States Soldiers at Camp "William
        Penn" Philadelphia, Pa*. Philadelphia: Supervisory Committee
        for Recruiting Colored Regiments, [1863].
    Espy, S. Barlow. *Another War Declared*. Philadelphia: Duross Bros., 1861.
    Fox, S. C. & L. *Attention Union Men!* Philadelphia: Duross Bros., 1861.
    Gray Reserves! Philadelphia, [1862].
    John A. McAllister Collection.
    Kimball, M. H. *Emancipated Slaves*. New York, 1863.
    Leadbeater's Renowned Stove Polish. Philadelphia, 1861.
    *March On, Brave Volunteers, Head Quarters, Company H, 66th
        Regiment, P. V.* Philadelphia: Duross Bros., 1861.
    Ramage, Benjamin. *Attention Volunteers!* Philadelphia:
        Duross Bros., May [1861].
    Sinclair, Thomas. *Wootten's Excelsior Stove Lustre or Pure
        Black Lead*. Philadelphia: Thomas Sinclair, 1859.
    Spruance & Megear. *Secession Has Produced a Wonderful Change
        in the Price of Goods*. Philadelphia: Duross Bros., 1861.
    Stephens, Henry Louis. *Idol of Abolitionism*.
        Philadelphia, L. H. Stephens, [1864].
    Templeton, P. & C. *Attention Union Men!* Philadelphia: Duross Bros., 1861.
    Volunteers Wanted! Company C, Col. Chantry's Regiment.
        Philadelphia: Duross Bros., 1861.
Library of Congress, Washington, D.C.
    Abraham Lincoln Papers

Benjamin F. Butler Papers
Henry Walker Correspondence
John Sherman Papers
Stephens, H. L. "VICTORY!" In *Album Varieties No. 3; The Slave in 1863*. Philadelphia: William A. Stephens, 1863.
War views. No. 2041, Bounty brokers looking out for substitutes. New York: E. & H. T. Anthony, c. 1865–69.
War views. No. 2042, Bounty brokers looking out for substitutes. New York: E. & H. T. Anthony, c. 1865–69.

Massachusetts Historical Society, Boston, Massachusetts
Charles M. Whelden Papers
John A. Andrew Papers

National Archives, Washington, D.C.
Colored Troops Division, Letters Received, 1863–1864, RG 94, Records of the Adjutant General's Office.
Court Martial of J. A. Nelson, July 3, 1861, Box 281, II-389, RG 153, Records of the Office of the Judge Advocate General.
Department of the Gulf, Letters Sent. Part I, Entry 1738, RG 393, Records of U.S. Army Continental Commands.
Lafayette C. Baker Papers, 1863–1866, RG 110, Records of the Provost Marshal General's Bureau.
Letters, Orders, and Telegrams Received by Lt. Col. J. B. Kinsman, Subordinate Field Offices, Fort Monroe (Department of Negro Affairs, 1863–1865), RG 105, Roll 114, Records of the Field Offices for the State of Virginia, Bureau of Refugees, Freedmen, and Abandoned Lands.
Records of the Assistant Commissioner for the District of Columbia, RG 105, Bureau of Refugees, Freedmen, and Abandoned Lands, 1865–1869.
Records of the Subassistant Commissioner at Memphis, RG 105, Records of the Bureau of Refugees, Freedmen, and Abandoned Lands, Tennessee, 1865–1872.
Reports and Papers Relating to Fraudulent Activities in Various Districts of the Several States, RG 110, Records of the Provost Marshal General's Bureau.
Tenth USCT Infantry, Regimental Letter, Order, & Detail Book, RG 94, Records of the Adjutant General's Office.

Robert W. Woodruff Library, Atlanta University Center, Atlanta, Georgia
Henry P. Slaughter Collection

Rubenstein Library, Duke University, Durham, North Carolina
Naval Transport Diary Typescript, 1864–1865

Western Reserve Historical Society, Cleveland, Ohio
Records of the U.S. Sanitary Commission, Cleveland Branch (Soldier's Aid Society of Northern Ohio), 1861–1869

Newspapers and Periodicals

Age (Philadelphia)
Albany Evening Journal (New York)
Baltimore Sun
Continental Monthly (New York)
Daily Evening Traveller (Boston)
Evening Star (Washington, D.C.)

Farmer's Cabinet (Amherst, New Hampshire)
Frank Leslie's Illustrated Newspaper (New York)
Friends' Intelligencer (Philadelphia)
Godey's Lady's Book and Magazine (Philadelphia)
Harper's Weekly (New York)
Hartford Daily Courant
Keowee Courier (South Carolina)
Liberator (Boston)
Littell's Living Age (Boston)
Lowell Daily Citizen and News
Memphis Daily Appeal
Montana Post (Virginia City)
National Police Gazette (New York)
New York Herald
New York Times
New-York Tribune
Norwich Morning Bulletin (Connecticut)
Philadelphia Inquirer
Press (Philadelphia)
Public Ledger (Philadelphia)
Richmond Daily Dispatch
Salt Lake Herald
Vanity Fair (New York)
Wilmington Journal (North Carolina)

Census Data and Online Resources

117th New York Infantry Unit History Project, New York State Military Museum and Veterans Research Center. dmna.ny.gov.

117th New York State Volunteer Infantry Regiment, Digital Collections, Hamilton College Library. https://elib.hamilton.edu/117th.

1850 United States Federal Census [database online]. Provo, Utah: Ancestry.com Operations, 2009.

1860 United States Federal Census [database online]. Provo, Utah: Ancestry.com Operations, 2009.

1860 United States Federal Census — Slave Schedules [database online]. Provo, Utah: Ancestry.com Operations, 2010.

1870 United States Federal Census [database online]. Provo, Utah: Ancestry.com Operations, 2009.

1880 United States Federal Census [database online]. Provo, Utah: Ancestry.com Operations, 2010.

"The American Presidency Project." https://www.presidency.ucsb.edu/.

Applications for Appointments as Customs Service Officers, Records of the Division of Appointments, Records Relating to Customs Service Appointments. RG 56, Entry 247, NA. http://papersofabrahamlincoln.dataformat.com/.

Appointment Records, Applications and Recommendations for Office, Applications and Recommendations for Public Office, 1797–1901. RG 59, Entry 760, NA. http://papersofabrahamlincoln.dataformat.com/.

Civil War Soldiers and Sailors Database. www.nps.gov/civilwar/soldiers-and-sailors-database.htm.

Civil War Soldiers Compiled Service Records. fold3.com.

Civil War Widows Pension Applications. fold3.com.

Find a Grave. www.findagrave.com.

Geer's Hartford City Directory for 1860–61. Hartford: Elihu Geer, 1860. ancestry.com.

New York Civil War Muster Roll Abstracts, New York State Archives. fold3.com.

Books

Acts of the General Assembly of Virginia, Passed in 1855–6, in the Eightieth Year of the Commonwealth. Richmond: William F. Ritchie, 1856.

Addresses of the Hon. W. D. Kelley, Miss Anna E. Dickinson, and Mr. Frederick Douglass, at a Mass Meeting, Held at National Hall, Philadelphia, July 6, 1863, for the Promotion of Colored Enlistments. [Philadelphia, 1863.]

Basler, Roy P., ed. *Collected Works of Abraham Lincoln.* 8 vols. New Brunswick, N.J.: Rutgers University Press, 1953.

Bergeron, Paul H., ed. *The Papers of Andrew Johnson.* Vol. 10, *February–July 1866.* Knoxville: University of Tennessee Press, 1992.

Blight, David W., ed. *When This Cruel War Is Over: The Civil War Letters of Charles Harvey Brewster.* Amherst: University of Massachusetts Press, 1992.

Butler, Benjamin F. *Autobiography and Personal Reminiscences of Major-General Benj. F. Butler.* Boston: A. M. Thayer & Co., 1892.

———. *Private and Official Correspondence of Gen. Benjamin F. Butler during the Period of the Civil War.* 5 vols. Norwood, Mass.: Plimpton Press, 1917.

———. *Speech of Maj.-Gen. Benj. F. Butler, upon the Campaign before Richmond, 1864. Delivered at Lowell, Mass., January 29, 1865.* Boston: Wright & Potter, 1865.

Hammond, James Henry. *Selections from the Letters and Speeches of the Hon. James H. Hammond, of South Carolina.* New York: John F. Trow & Co., 1866.

House of Representatives. *Report on William B. Thomas, February 26, 1874, 43d Congress, 1st Session, Report No. 190.* Washington: Government Printing Office, 1874.

Ingersoll, C. M. *Catalogue of Connecticut Volunteer Organizations.* Hartford: Brown & Gross, 1869.

Keating, Ryan W., ed. *The Greatest Trials I Ever Had: The Civil War Letters of Margaret and Thomas Cahill.* Athens: University of Georgia Press, 2017.

Leland, Charles Godfrey. *Memoirs.* London: William Heinemann, 1893.

Leslie, Miss E. *Mr. and Mrs. Woodbridge, with Other Tales, Representing Life as It Is: And Intended to Show What It Should Be.* Providence: Isaac H. Cady, 1841.

McElroy's Philadelphia City Directory. A. McElroy and other publishers, 1839–67.

Mowris, J. A. *A History of the One Hundred and Seventeenth Regiment, N.Y. Volunteers.* Hartford: Case, Lockwood & Co., 1866.

Murray, Thomas Hamilton. *History of the Ninth Regiment, Connecticut Volunteer Infantry.* New Haven: Price, Lee & Adkins Co., 1903.

Newell, Joseph Keith, ed. *"Ours": Annals of the 10th Regiment, Massachusetts Volunteers, in the Rebellion.* Springfield, Mass.: C. A. Nichols & Co., 1875.

Proceedings of the Board of Councilmen of the City of New York from October 5th to December 31st, 1857. Vol. 68. New York: Charles W. Baker, 1857.

Sears, David. *Contrabands and Vagrants.* [Newport, R.I.], 1861[?].

Sprague, Homer B. *History of the 13th Infantry Regiment of Connecticut Volunteers, during the Great Rebellion.* Hartford: Case, Lockwood & Co., 1867.

Still, William. *A Brief Narrative of the Struggle for the Rights of the Colored People of Philadelphia in the City Railway Cars; and a Defence of William Still, Relating to His Agency Touching the Passage of the Late Bill, &c.* Philadelphia, 1867; repr., Philadelphia: Rhistoric Publications, 1969.

———. *The Underground Railroad.* Philadelphia: Porter & Coates, 1872.

Turner, Justin G., and Linda Levitt Turner. *Mary Todd Lincoln: Her Life and Letters.* New York: Alfred A. Knopf, 1972.
War of the Rebellion: A Compilation of the Official Records of the Union and Confederate Armies. Washington: Government Printing Office, 1880–1901.
Weaver, C. P., ed. *Thank God My Regiment an African One: The Civil War Diary of Colonel Nathan W. Daniels.* Baton Rouge: Louisiana State University Press, 1998.
Wilson, Douglas L., and Rodney O. Davis, eds. *Herndon's Informants: Letters, Interviews, and Statements about Abraham Lincoln.* Urbana: University of Illinois Press, 1998.
Winthrop, Robert C., Jr. *Memoir of the Hon. David Sears.* Cambridge, Mass.: John Wilson & Son, 1886.

SECONDARY SOURCES

Books

Abbott, Richard H. *Cotton and Capital: Boston Businessmen and Antislavery Reform, 1854–1868.* Amherst: University of Massachusetts Press, 1991.
Anbinder, Tyler. *Five Points: The 19th-Century New York City Neighborhood That Invented Tap Dance, Stole Elections, and Became the World's Most Notorious Slum.* New York: Free Press, 2001.
Attie, Jeanie. *Patriotic Toil: Northern Women and the American Civil War.* Ithaca, N.Y.: Cornell University Press, 1998.
Baker, Jean. *Mary Todd Lincoln: A Biography.* New York: W. W. Norton, 1987.
Balleisen, Edward J. *Fraud: An American History from Barnum to Madoff.* Princeton, N.J.: Princeton University Press, 2017.
———. *Navigating Failure: Bankruptcy and Commercial Society in Antebellum America.* Chapel Hill: University of North Carolina Press, 2001.
Beckert, Sven. *The Monied Metropolis: New York City and the Consolidation of the American Bourgeoisie, 1850–1896.* New York: Cambridge University Press, 2001.
Benson, Susan Porter. *Household Accounts: Working-Class Family Economies in the Interwar United States.* Ithaca, N.Y.: Cornell University Press, 2007.
Berlin, Ira, Steven F. Miller, Joseph P. Reidy, and Leslie Rowland, eds. *Freedom: A Documentary History of Emancipation, 1861–1867, Series I.* Vol. 2, *The Wartime Genesis of Free Labor: The Upper South.* New York: Cambridge University Press, 1993.
Berlin, Ira, Joseph P. Reidy, and Leslie Rowland, eds. *Freedom: A Documentary History of Emancipation, 1861–1867, Series II, The Black Military Experience.* New York: Cambridge University Press, 1982.
Bernstein, Iver C. *The New York City Draft Riots: Their Significance for American Society and Politics in the Age of the Civil War.* New York: Oxford University Press, 1990.
Berry, Daina Ramey. *The Price for Their Pound of Flesh: The Value of the Enslaved, from Womb to Grave, in the Building of a Nation.* Boston: Beacon Press, 2017.
Blackett, R. J. M. *Making Freedom: The Underground Railroad and the Politics of Slavery.* Chapel Hill: University of North Carolina Press, 2013.
Bledsoe, Andrew S. *Citizen-Officers: The Union and Confederate Volunteer Junior Officer Corps in the American Civil War.* Baton Rouge: Louisiana State University Press, 2015.
Blewett, Mary H. *Men, Women, and Work: Class, Gender, and Protest in the New England Shoe Industry, 1780–1910.* Urbana: University of Illinois Press, 1988.

Boritt, Gabor S. *Lincoln and the Economics of the American Dream*. Urbana: University of Illinois Press, 1978.

Boydston, Jeanne. *Home and Work: Housework, Wages, and the Ideology of Labor in the Early Republic*. New York: Oxford University Press, 1990.

Brasher, Glenn David. *The Peninsula Campaign and the Necessity of Emancipation: African Americans and the Fight for Freedom*. Chapel Hill: University of North Carolina Press, 2012.

Broadwater, Robert P. *The Battle of Fair Oaks: Turning Point of McClellan's Peninsula Campaign*. Jefferson, N.C.: McFarland & Co., 2011.

Bruegel, Martin. *Farm, Shop, Landing: The Rise of a Market Society in the Hudson Valley, 1780–1860*. Durham, N.C.: Duke University Press, 2002.

Bunker, Gary L. *From Rail-Splitter to Icon: Lincoln's Image in Illustrated Periodicals, 1860–1865*. Kent, Ohio: Kent State University Press, 2001.

Burke, Martin J. *The Conundrum of Class: Public Discourse on the Social Order in America*. Chicago: University of Chicago Press, 1995.

Bushman, Richard L. *The Refinement of America: Persons, Houses, Cities*. New York: Vintage, 1992.

Carman, Harry J., and Reinhard H. Luthin. *Lincoln and the Patronage*. New York: Columbia University Press, 1943.

Carmichael, Peter S. *The War for the Common Soldier: How Men Thought, Fought, and Survived in Civil War Armies*. Chapel Hill: University of North Carolina Press, 2018.

Cicero, Frank, Jr. *Creating the Land of Lincoln: The History and Constitutions of Illinois, 1778–1870*. Urbana: University of Illinois Press, 2018.

Clark, Christopher. *The Roots of Rural Capitalism: Western Massachusetts, 1780–1860*. Ithaca, N.Y.: Cornell University Press, 1990.

Clarke, Frances M. *War Stories: Suffering and Sacrifice in the Civil War North*. Chicago: University of Chicago Press, 2011.

Cohen, Andrew Wender. *Contraband: Smuggling and the Birth of the American Century*. New York: W. W. Norton, 2015.

Cohen, Joanna. *Luxurious Citizens: The Politics of Consumption in Nineteenth-Century America*. Philadelphia: University of Pennsylvania Press, 2017.

Cohen, Patricia Cline, Timothy Gilfoyle, and Helen Lefkowitz Horowitz. *The Flash Press: Sporting Male Weeklies in 1840s New York*. Chicago: University of Chicago Press, 2008.

Cohen, William. *At Freedom's Edge: Black Mobility and the Southern White Quest for Racial Control, 1861–1915*. Baton Rouge: Louisiana State University Press, 1991.

Cook, James W. *The Arts of Deception: Playing with Fraud in the Age of Barnum*. Cambridge, Mass.: Harvard University Press, 2001.

Diemer, Andrew K. *The Politics of Black Citizenship: Free African Americans in the Mid-Atlantic Borderland, 1817–1863*. Athens: University of Georgia Press, 2016.

Diner, Hasia R. *Erin's Daughters in America: Irish Immigrant Women in the Nineteenth Century*. Baltimore: Johns Hopkins University Press, 1983.

Donald, David. *Lincoln*. New York: Simon and Schuster, 1995.

Downs, Jim. *Sick from Freedom: African-American Illness and Suffering during Civil War and Reconstruction*. New York: Oxford University Press, 2012.

Dudden, Faye E. *Serving Women: Household Service in Nineteenth-Century America*. Middletown, Conn.: Wesleyan University Press, 1983.

Dunbar, Erica Armstrong. *A Fragile Freedom: African American Women and Emancipation in the Antebellum City*. New Haven, Conn.: Yale University Press, 2008.

Dusinberre, William. *Civil War Issues in Philadelphia, 1856–1865*. Philadelphia: University of Pennsylvania Press, 1965.

Engle, Stephen D. *Gathering to Save a Nation: Lincoln and the Union's War Governors*. Chapel Hill: University of North Carolina Press, 2016.

Engs, Robert F. *Freedom's First Generation: Black Hampton, Virginia, 1861–1890*. 1979; repr., New York: Fordham University Press, 2004.

Enstad, Nan. *Ladies of Labor, Girls of Adventure: Working Women, Popular Culture, and Labor Politics at the Turn of the Twentieth Century*. New York: Columbia University Press, 1999.

Fahs, Alice. *The Imagined Civil War: Popular Literature of the North and South, 1861–1865*. Chapel Hill: University of North Carolina Press, 2001.

Faulkner, Carol. *Women's Radical Reconstruction: The Freedmen's Aid Movement*. Philadelphia: University of Pennsylvania Press, 2004.

Fields, Barbara Jeanne. *Slavery and Freedom on the Middle Ground: Maryland during the Nineteenth Century*. New Haven, Conn.: Yale University Press, 1985.

Fleischner, Jennifer. *Mrs. Lincoln and Mrs. Keckly: The Remarkable Story of the Friendship between a First Lady and a Former Slave*. New York: Broadway Books, 2003.

Foner, Eric. *The Fiery Trial: Abraham Lincoln and American Slavery*. New York: W. W. Norton & Co., 2010.

———. *Free Soil, Free Labor, Free Men: The Ideology of the Republican Party before the Civil War*. 1970; repr., New York: Oxford University Press, 1995.

———. *Gateway to Freedom: The Hidden History of the Underground Railroad*. New York: W. W. Norton, 2015.

———. *Reconstruction: America's Unfinished Revolution, 1863–1877*. New York: Harper & Row, 1988.

Foner, Philip S. *Business and Slavery: The New York Merchants and the Irrepressible Conflict*. Chapel Hill: University of North Carolina Press, 1941.

Foote, Lorien. *The Gentlemen and the Roughs: Violence, Honor, and Manhood in the Union Army*. New York: New York University Press, 2010.

———. *The Yankee Plague: Escaped Union Prisoners and the Collapse of the Confederacy*. Chapel Hill: University of North Carolina, 2016.

Fox, Richard Wightman. *Lincoln's Body: A Cultural History*. New York: W. W. Norton, 2015.

Gallagher, Gary. *The Union War*. Cambridge, Mass.: Harvard University Press, 2011.

Gallman, Matthew. *Defining Duty in the Civil War: Personal Choice, Popular Culture, and the Union Home Front*. Chapel Hill: University of North Carolina Press, 2015.

———. *Mastering Wartime: A Social History of Philadelphia during the Civil War*. New York: Cambridge University Press, 1990.

Gerteis, Louis S. *From Contraband to Freedman: Federal Policy toward Southern Blacks, 1861–1865*. Westport, Conn.: Greenwood, 1973.

Giesberg, Judith. *Army at Home: Women and the Civil War on the Northern Home Front*. Chapel Hill: University of North Carolina Press, 2009.

Gigantino, James J., II. *The Ragged Road to Abolition: Slavery and Freedom in New Jersey, 1775–1865*. Philadelphia: University of Pennsylvania Press, 2015.

Glatthaar, Joseph T. *Forged in Battle: The Civil War Alliance of Black Soldiers and White Officers*. New York: Free Press, 1990.

Glickman, Lawrence B. *Buying Power: A History of Consumer Activism in America*. Chicago: University of Chicago Press, 2009.

Glickstein, Jonathan A. *Concepts of Free Labor in Antebellum America*. New Haven: Yale University Press, 1991.

Glymph, Thavolia. *Out of the House of Bondage: The Transformation of the Plantation Household*. New York: Cambridge University Press, 2008.

Gorn, Elliott J. *The Manly Art: Bare-Knuckle Prize Fighting in America*. Ithaca, N.Y.: Cornell University Press, 1986.

Greenwood, Janette Thomas. *First Fruits of Freedom: The Migration of Former Slaves and Their Search for Equality in Worcester, Massachusetts, 1862–1900*. Chapel Hill: University of North Carolina Press, 2009.

Hahn, Barbara. *Making Tobacco Bright: Creating an American Commodity, 1617–1937*. Baltimore: Johns Hopkins University Press, 2011.

Hahn, Steven, Steven F. Miller, Susan E. O'Donovan, John C. Rodrigue, and Leslie S. Rowland, eds. *Freedom: A Documentary History of Emancipation, 1861–1867, Series 3*. Vol. 1, *Land and Labor, 1865*. Chapel Hill: University of North Carolina Press, 2008.

Halttunen, Karen. *Confidence Men and Painted Women: A Study of Middle-Class Culture in America, 1830–1870*. New Haven, Conn.: Yale University Press, 1982.

Harris, Leslie M. *In the Shadow of Slavery: African Americans in New York City, 1626–1863*. Chicago: University of Chicago Press, 2003.

Harrison, Robert. *Washington during Civil War and Reconstruction: Race and Radicalism*. New York: Cambridge University Press, 2008.

Hartigan-O'Connor, Ellen. *The Ties That Buy: Women and Commerce in Revolutionary America*. Philadelphia: University of Pennsylvania Press, 2009.

Hayden, René, Anthony E. Kaye, Kate Masur, Steven F. Miller, Susan E. O'Donovan, Leslie S. Rowland, and Stephen A. West, eds. *Freedom: A Documentary History of Emancipation, 1861–1867, Series 3*. Vol. 2, *Land and Labor, 1866–1867*. Chapel Hill: University of North Carolina Press, 2013.

Hearn, Chester G. *When the Devil Came Down to Dixie: Ben Butler in New Orleans*. Baton Rouge: Louisiana State University Press, 1997.

Hilliard, Kathleen M. *Masters, Slaves, and Exchange: Power's Purchase in the Old South*. New York: Cambridge University Press, 2014.

Hollandsworth, James G., Jr. *The Louisiana Native Guards: The Black Military Experience during the Civil War*. Baton Rouge: Louisiana State University Press, 1998.

Hunter, Tera W. *Bound in Wedlock: Slave and Free Black Marriage in the Nineteenth Century*. Cambridge, Mass.: Belknap Press of Harvard University Press, 2017.

Huston, James L. *Calculating the Value of the Union: Slavery, Property Rights, and the Economic Origins of the Civil War*. Chapel Hill: University of North Carolina Press, 2003.

———. *The Panic of 1857 and the Coming of the Civil War*. Baton Rouge: Louisiana State University Press, 1987.

Ignatiev, Noel. *How the Irish Became White*. New York: Routledge, 1995.

Jaffee, David. *A New Nation of Goods: The Material Culture of Early America*. Philadelphia: University of Pennsylvania Press, 2010.

Johnson, Russell L. *Warriors into Workers: The Civil War and the Formation of Urban-Industrial Society in a Northern City*. New York: Fordham University Press, 2003.

Johnson, Walter. *River of Dark Dreams: Slavery and Empire in the Cotton Kingdom.* Cambridge, Mass.: Belknap Press of Harvard University Press, 2013.

———. *Soul by Soul: Life in the Antebellum Slave Market.* Cambridge, Mass.: Harvard University Press, 1999.

Jones, Catherine A. *Intimate Reconstructions: Children in Postemancipation Virginia.* Charlottesville: University of Virginia Press, 2015.

Jordan, Brian Matthew. *Marching Home: Union Veterans and Their Unending Civil War.* New York: Liveright, 2014.

Jordan, Ervin L. *Black Confederates and Afro-Yankees in Civil War Virginia.* Charlottesville: University of Virginia Press, 1995.

Kamensky, Jane. *The Exchange Artist: A Tale of High-Flying Speculation and America's First Banking Collapse.* New York: Viking, 2008.

Kantrowitz, Stephen. *More than Freedom: Fighting for Black Citizenship in a White Republic, 1829–1889.* New York: Penguin Press, 2012.

Keating, Ryan W. *Shades of Green: Irish Regiments, American Soldiers, and Local Communities in the Civil War Era.* New York: Fordham University Press, 2017.

Lang, Andrew F. *In the Wake of War: Military Occupation, Emancipation, and Civil War America.* Baton Rouge: Louisiana State University Press, 2017.

Larson, John Lauritz. *Bonds of Enterprise: John Murray Forbes and Western Development in America's Railway Age.* Expanded ed. Iowa City: University of Iowa Press, 2001.

Lause, Mark A. *The Antebellum Crisis and America's First Bohemians.* Kent, Ohio: Kent State University Press, 2009.

———. *Free Labor: The Civil War and the Making of an American Working Class.* Urbana: University of Illinois Press, 2015.

Lepler, Jessica M. *The Many Panics of 1837: People, Politics, and the Creation of a Transatlantic Financial Crisis.* New York: Cambridge University Press, 2013.

Levy, Jonathan. *Freaks of Fortune: The Emerging World of Capitalism and Risk in America.* Cambridge, Mass.: Harvard University Press, 2012.

Licht, Walter. *Getting Work: Philadelphia, 1840–1950.* Cambridge, Mass.: Harvard University Press, 1992.

Lott, Eric. *Love and Theft: Blackface Minstrelsy and the American Working Class.* New York: Oxford University Press, 1993.

Luke, Bob, and John David Smith. *Soldiering for Freedom: How the Union Army Recruited, Trained, and Deployed the U.S. Colored Troops.* Baltimore: Johns Hopkins University Press, 2014.

Luskey, Brian P. *On the Make: Clerks and the Quest for Capital in Nineteenth-Century America.* New York: New York University Press, 2010.

Luskey, Brian P., and Wendy A. Woloson, eds. *Capitalism by Gaslight: Illuminating the Economy of Nineteenth-Century America.* Philadelphia: University of Pennsylvania Press, 2015.

Magness, Phillip W., and Sebastian N. Page. *Colonization after Emancipation: Lincoln and the Movement for Black Resettlement.* Columbia: University of Missouri Press, 2011.

Mahoney, Timothy R. *From Hometown to Battlefield in the Civil War Era: Middle Class Life in Midwest America.* New York: Cambridge University Press, 2016.

Manning, Chandra. *Troubled Refuge: Struggling for Freedom in the Civil War.* New York: Alfred A. Knopf, 2016.

———. *What This Cruel War Was Over: Soldiers, Slavery, and the Civil War.* New York: Alfred A. Knopf, 2007.
Marten, James. *Sing Not War: The Lives of Union and Confederate Veterans in Gilded Age America.* Chapel Hill: University of North Carolina Press, 2011.
Martinez, Jaime Amanda. *Confederate Slave Impressment in the Upper South.* Chapel Hill: University of North Carolina Press, 2013.
Marvel, William. *Lincoln's Mercenaries: Economic Motivation among Union Soldiers during the Civil War.* Baton Rouge: Louisiana State University Press, 2018.
Masur, Kate. *An Example for All the Land: Emancipation and the Struggle over Equality in Washington, D.C.* Chapel Hill: University of North Carolina Press, 2010.
Mathisen, Erik. *The Loyal Republic: Traitors, Slaves, and the Remaking of Citizenship in Civil War America.* Chapel Hill: University of North Carolina Press, 2018.
May, Robert E. *Slavery, Race, and Conquest in the Tropics: Lincoln, Douglas, and the Future of Latin America.* New York: Cambridge University Press, 2013.
McInnis, Maurie. *Slaves Waiting for Sale: Abolitionist Art and the American Slave Trade.* Chicago: University of Chicago Press, 2011.
McPherson, James M. *For Cause and Comrades: Why Men Fought in the Civil War.* New York: Oxford University Press, 1997.
Mihm, Stephen. *A Nation of Counterfeiters: Capitalists, Con Men, and the Making of the United States.* Cambridge, Mass.: Harvard University Press, 2007.
Mitchell, Mary Niall. *Raising Freedom's Child: Black Children and the Vision of the Future after Slavery.* New York: New York University Press, 2010.
Mitchell, Reid. *The Vacant Chair: The Northern Soldier Leaves Home.* New York: Oxford University Press, 1993.
Montgomery, David. *Beyond Equality: Labor and the Radical Republicans, 1862–1872.* 1967; repr., Urbana: University of Illinois Press, 1981.
———. *Citizen Worker: The Experience of Workers in the United States with Democracy and the Free Market during the Nineteenth Century.* New York: Cambridge University Press, 1993.
Morgan, Jennifer L. *Laboring Women: Reproduction and Gender in New World Slavery.* Philadelphia: University of Pennsylvania Press, 2004.
Murdock, Eugene C. *One Million Men: The Civil War Draft in the North.* Madison: State Historical Society of Wisconsin, 1971.
———. *Patriotism Limited, 1862–1865: The Civil War Draft and the Bounty System.* Kent, Ohio: Kent State University Press, 1967.
Murphy, Sharon Ann. *Investing in Life: Insurance in Antebellum America.* Baltimore: Johns Hopkins University Press, 2010.
Nash, Gary B. *Forging Freedom: The Formation of Philadelphia's Black Community, 1720–1840.* Cambridge, Mass.: Harvard University Press, 1988.
Neely, Mark E., Jr. *The Boundaries of American Political Culture in the Civil War Era.* Chapel Hill: University of North Carolina Press, 2005.
Nelson, Scott Reynolds. *A Nation of Deadbeats: An Uncommon History of America's Financial Disasters.* New York: Alfred A. Knopf, 2012.
Newby-Alexander, Cassandra L. *An African American History of the Civil War in Hampton Roads.* Charleston, S.C.: History Press, 2010.
Oakes, James. *Freedom National: The Destruction of Slavery in the United States, 1861–1865.* New York: W. W. Norton, 2013.

O'Brassill-Kulfan, Kristin. *Vagrants and Vagabonds: Poverty and Mobility in the Early American Republic*. New York: New York University Press, 2019.

O'Malley, Michael. *Face Value: The Entwined Histories of Money and Race in America*. Chicago: University of Chicago Press, 2012.

Osterud, Nancy Grey. *Bonds of Community: The Lives of Farm Women in Nineteenth-Century New York*. Ithaca, N.Y.: Cornell University Press, 1991.

Paludan, Phillip Shaw. *A People's Contest: The Union and Civil War, 1861–1865*. 2nd ed. Lawrence: University Press of Kansas, 1996.

Phillips, Jason. *Looming Civil War: How Nineteenth-Century Americans Imagined the Future*. New York: Oxford University Press, 2018.

Pierson, Michael D. *Free Hearts and Free Homes: Gender and American Antislavery Politics*. Chapel Hill: University of North Carolina Press, 2003.

Powell, Lawrence N. *New Masters: Northern Planters during the Civil War and Reconstruction*. New York: Fordham University Press, 1998.

Pryor, Elizabeth Stordeur. *Colored Travelers: Mobility and the Fight for Citizenship before the Civil War*. Chapel Hill: University of North Carolina Press, 2016.

Ramold, Steven J. *Baring the Iron Hand: Discipline in the Union Army*. Dekalb: Northern Illinois University Press, 2010.

Reidy, Joseph P. *The Illusions of Emancipation: The Pursuit of Freedom and Equality in the Twilight of Slavery*. Chapel Hill: University of North Carolina Press, 2019.

Rhea, Gordon C. *On to Petersburg: Grant and Lee, June 4–15, 1864*. Baton Rouge: Louisiana State University Press, 2017.

Richardson, Heather Cox. *The Death of Reconstruction: Race, Labor, and Politics in the Post-Civil War North, 1865–1901*. Cambridge, Mass. Harvard University Press, 2001.

———. *The Greatest Nation on Earth: Republican Economic Policy during the Civil War*. Cambridge, Mass.: Harvard University Press, 1997.

Roberts, Brian. *American Alchemy: The California Gold Rush and Middle-Class Culture*. Chapel Hill: University of North Carolina Press, 2000.

Rockman, Seth. *Scraping By: Wage Labor, Slavery, and Survival in Early Baltimore*. Baltimore: Johns Hopkins University Press, 2009.

Rodgers, Daniel T. *The Work Ethic in Industrial America, 1850–1920*. Chicago: University of Chicago Press, 1978.

Roediger, David R. *The Wages of Whiteness: Race and the Making of the American Working Class*. New York: Verso, 1991.

Rose, Willie Lee. *Rehearsal for Reconstruction: The Port Royal Experiment*. Indianapolis: Bobbs-Merrill, 1964.

Rosenthal, Caitlin. *Accounting for Slavery: Masters and Management*. Cambridge, Mass.: Harvard University Press, 2018.

Rothman, Adam. *Beyond Freedom's Reach: A Kidnapping in the Twilight of Slavery*. Cambridge, Mass.: Harvard University Press, 2015.

Ryan, Mary P. *The Cradle of the Middle Class: The Family in Oneida County, New York, 1790–1865*. New York: Cambridge University Press, 1981.

Safford, Jeffrey J. *The Mechanics of Optimism: Mining Companies, Technology, and the Hot Springs Gold Rush, Montana Territory, 1864–1868*. Boulder: University Press of Colorado, 2004.

Samito, Christian G. *Becoming American under Fire: Irish Americans, African Americans, and *the Politics of Citizenship during the Civil War Era*. Ithaca, N.Y.: Cornell University Press, 2009.

Sandage, Scott A. *Born Losers: A History of Failure in America*. Cambridge, Mass.: Harvard University Press, 2005.

Schermerhorn, Calvin. *The Business of Slavery and the Rise of American Capitalism, 1815–1860*. New Haven, Conn.: Yale University Press, 2015.

Schwalm, Leslie A. *Emancipation's Diaspora: Race and Reconstruction in the Upper Midwest*. Chapel Hill: University of North Carolina Press, 2009.

Schwarz, Philip. *Slave Laws of Virginia*. Athens: University of Georgia Press, 2010.

Sentilles, Renée M. *Performing Menken: Adah Isaacs Menken and the Birth of American Celebrity*. New York: Cambridge University Press, 2003.

Shannon, Fred Albert. *The Organization and Administration of the Union Army, 1861–1865*. 2 vols. Cleveland: Arthur H. Clark, 1928.

Siddali, Silvana. *From Property to Person: Slavery and the Confiscation Acts, 1861–1862*. Baton Rouge: Louisiana State University Press, 2005.

Silber, Nina. *Daughters of the Union: Northern Women Fight the Civil War*. Cambridge, Mass.: Harvard University Press, 2005.

Silkenat, David. *Driven from Home: North Carolina's Civil War Refugee Crisis*. Athens: University of Georgia Press, 2016.

Sklansky, Jeffrey. *Sovereign of the Market: The Money Question in Early America*. Chicago: University of Chicago Press, 2017.

Smith, Michael Thomas. *The Enemy Within: Fears of Corruption in the Civil War North*. Charlottesville: University of Virginia Press, 2011.

Smith, Stacey L. *Freedom's Frontier: California and the Struggle over Unfree Labor, Emancipation, and Reconstruction*. Chapel Hill: University of North Carolina Press, 2013.

Stanley, Amy Dru. *From Bondage to Contract: Wage Labor, Marriage, and the Market in the Age of Slave Emancipation*. New York: Cambridge University Press, 1998.

Stansell, Christine. *City of Women: Sex and Class in New York, 1789–1860*. New York: Alfred A. Knopf, 1986.

Steinfeld, Robert J. *Coercion, Contract, and Free Labor in the Nineteenth Century*. New York: Cambridge University Press, 2001.

Sternhell, Yael. *Routes of War: The World of Movement in the Confederate South*. Cambridge, Mass.: Harvard University Press, 2012.

Stott, Richard B. *Workers in the Metropolis: Class, Ethnicity, and Youth in Antebellum New York City*. Ithaca, N.Y.: Cornell University Press, 1990.

Taylor, Amy Murrell. *Embattled Freedom: Journeys through the Civil War's Slave Refugee Camps*. Chapel Hill: University of North Carolina Press, 2018.

Teters, Kristopher A. *Practical Liberators: Union Officers in the Western Theater during the Civil War*. Chapel Hill: University of North Carolina Press, 2018.

Trefousse, Hans. *Ben Butler: The South Called Him Beast!* New York: Twayne, 1957.

Tuchinsky, Adam. *Horace Greeley's* New-York Tribune: *Civil War–Era Socialism and the Crisis of Free Labor*. Ithaca, N.Y.: Cornell University Press, 2009.

Urban, Andrew. *Brokering Servitude: Migration and the Politics of Domestic Labor during the Long Nineteenth Century*. New York: New York University Press, 2018.

Wilson, Mark R. *The Business of Civil War: Military Mobilization and the State, 1861–1865*. Baltimore: Johns Hopkins University Press, 2006.

Woloson, Wendy A. *In Hock: Pawning in America from Independence through the Great Depression.* Chicago: University of Chicago Press, 2009.

Woods, Michael E. *Emotional and Sectional Conflict in the Antebellum United States.* New York: Cambridge University Press, 2014.

Articles, Book Chapters, Dissertations, Presentations, and Theses

Adams, Sean Patrick. "Soulless Monsters and Iron Horses: The Civil War, Institutional Change, and American Capitalism." In *Capitalism Takes Command: The Social Transformation of Nineteenth-Century America*, edited by Michael Zakim and Gary J. Kornblith, 249–76. Chicago: University of Chicago Press, 2012.

Agnew, Jean-Christophe. "Afterword: Anonymous History." In *Capitalism Takes Command: The Social Transformation of Nineteenth-Century America*, edited by Michael Zakim and Gary J. Kornblith, 277–84. Chicago: University of Chicago Press, 2012.

Akerlof, George A. "The Market for 'Lemons': Quality Uncertainty and the Market Mechanism." *Quarterly Journal of Economics* 84, no. 3 (August 1970): 488–500.

Anbinder, Tyler. "Moving beyond 'Rags to Riches': New York's Irish Famine Immigrants and Their Surprising Savings Accounts." *Journal of American History* 99, no. 3 (December 2012): 741–70.

Ayers, Edward L., and Scott Nesbit. "Seeing Emancipation: Scale and Freedom in the American South." *Journal of the Civil War Era* 1, no. 1 (March 2011): 3–24.

Baptist, Edward E. "'Cuffy,' 'Fancy Maids,' and 'One-Eyed Men': Rape, Commodification, and the Domestic Slave Trade in the United States." *American Historical Review* 106, no. 5 (December 2001): 1619–50.

———. "Toxic Debt, Liar Loans, Collateralized and Securitized Human Beings, and the Panic of 1837." In *Capitalism Takes Command: The Social Transformation of Nineteenth-Century America*, edited by Michael Zakim and Gary J. Kornblith, 69–92. Chicago: University of Chicago Press, 2012.

Beckert, Sven, and Seth Rockman. "Introduction: Slavery's Capitalism." In *Slavery's Capitalism: A New History of American Economic Development*, edited by Sven Beckert and Seth Rockman, 1–27. Philadelphia: University of Pennsylvania Press, 2016.

Bell, Richard. "Counterfeit Kin: Kidnappers of Color, the Reverse Underground Railroad, and the Origins of Practical Abolition." *Journal of the Early Republic* 38, no. 2 (Summer 2018): 199–230.

Blair, William. "We Are Coming, Father Abraham—Eventually: The Problem of Northern Nationalism in the Pennsylvania Recruiting Drives of 1862." In *The War Was You and Me: Civilians in the American Civil War*, edited by Joan E. Cashin, 183–208. Princeton, N.J.: Princeton University Press, 2002.

Boodry, Kathryn. "August Belmont and the World the Slaves Made." In *Slavery's Capitalism: A New History of American Economic Development*, edited by Sven Beckert and Seth Rockman, 163–78. Philadelphia: University of Pennsylvania Press, 2016.

Bourque, Monique. "Women and Work in the Philadelphia Almshouse, 1790–1840." *Journal of the Early Republic* 32, no. 3 (Fall 2012): 383–413.

Brown, Scott Campbell. "Migrants and Workers in Philadelphia, 1850–1880." Ph.D. diss., University of Pennsylvania, 1981.

Carmichael, Peter S. "Soldier-Speak." In *Weirding the War: Stories from the Civil War's*

Ragged Edges, edited by Stephen Berry, 272–81. Athens: University of Georgia Press, 2011.

Cecere, David A. "Carrying the Home Front to War: Soldiers, Race, and New England Culture during the Civil War." In *Union Soldiers and the Northern Home Front: Wartime Experiences, Postwar Adjustments*, edited by Paul A. Cimbala and Randall M. Miller, 293–323. New York: Fordham University Press, 2002.

Clarke, Frances, and Rebecca Jo Plant. "No Minor Matter: Underage Soldiers, Parents, and the Nationalization of Habeas Corpus in Civil War America." *Law and History Review* 35, no. 4 (November 2017): 881–927.

Clegg, John J. "Capitalism and Slavery." *Critical Historical Studies* 2, no. 2 (Fall 2015): 281–304.

Cornelius, James M. "Introduction." In *Gettysburg Replies: The World Responds to Abraham Lincoln's Gettysburg Address*, edited by Carla Knorowski, xii–xix. Guilford, Conn.: Rowman & Littlefield, 2015.

Currarino, Rosanne. "Toward a History of Cultural Economy." *Journal of the Civil War Era* 2, no. 4 (December 2012): 564–85.

Downs, Gregory P., and Kate Masur. "Echoes of War: Rethinking Post–Civil War Governance and Politics." In *The World the Civil War Made*, edited by Gregory P. Downs and Kate Masur, 1–21. Chapel Hill: University of North Carolina Press, 2015.

Emberton, Carole. "Unwriting the Freedom Narrative: A Review Essay." *Journal of Southern History* 82, no. 2 (May 2016): 377–94.

Erickson, Paul. "Economies of Print in the Nineteenth-Century City." In *Capitalism by Gaslight: Illuminating the Economy of Nineteenth-Century America*, edited by Brian P. Luskey and Wendy A. Woloson, 190–214. Philadelphia: University of Pennsylvania Press, 2015.

Formisano, Ronald P. "The 'Party Period' Revisited." *Journal of American History* 86, no. 1 (June 1999): 93–120.

Franklin, John Hope. "James T. Ayers, Civil War Recruiter." *Journal of the Illinois State Historical Society* 40, no. 3 (September 1947): 267–97.

Furstenberg, François. "Beyond Freedom and Slavery: Autonomy, Virtue, and Resistance in Early American Political Discourse." *Journal of American History* 89, no. 4 (March 2003): 1295–1330.

Gamble, Robert J. "The Promiscuous Economy: Cultural and Commercial Geographies of Secondhand in the Antebellum City." In *Capitalism by Gaslight: Illuminating the Economy of Nineteenth-Century America*, edited by Brian P. Luskey and Wendy A. Woloson, 31–52. Philadelphia: University of Pennsylvania Press, 2015.

Garvey, Ellen Gruber. "Back Number Budd: An African American Pioneer in the Old Newspaper and Information Management Business." In *Capitalism by Gaslight: Illuminating the Economy of Nineteenth-Century America*, edited by Brian P. Luskey and Wendy A. Woloson, 215–32. Philadelphia: University of Pennsylvania Press, 2015.

Glatthaar, Joseph T. "A Tale of Two Armies: The Confederate Army of Northern Virginia and the Union Army of the Potomac and Their Cultures." *Journal of the Civil War Era* 6, no. 3 (September 2016): 315–46.

Goettsch, Corey. "'The World Is But One Vast Mock Auction': Fraud and Capitalism in Nineteenth-Century America." In *Capitalism by Gaslight: Illuminating the Economy of Nineteenth-Century America*, edited by Brian P. Luskey and Wendy A. Woloson, 109–26. Philadelphia: University of Pennsylvania Press, 2015.

Greenberg, Joshua R. "The Era of Shinplasters: Making Sense of Unregulated Paper Money." In *Capitalism by Gaslight: Illuminating the Economy of Nineteenth-Century America*, edited by Brian P. Luskey and Wendy A. Woloson, 53–75. Philadelphia: University of Pennsylvania Press, 2015.

Hall, Stephen G. "To Render the Private Public: William Still and the Selling of *The Underground Railroad*." *Pennsylvania Magazine of History and Biography* 127, no. 1 (January 2003): 35–55.

Hartigan-O'Connor, Ellen. "Gender's Value in the History of Capitalism." *Journal of the Early Republic* 36, no. 4 (Winter 2016): 613–35.

Heerman, M. Scott. "'Reducing Free Men to Slavery': Black Kidnapping, the 'Slave Power,' and the Politics of Abolition in Antebellum Illinois, 1830–1860." *Journal of the Early Republic* 38, no. 2 (Summer 2018): 261–91.

Hemphill, Katie M. "Selling Sex and Intimacy in the City: The Changing Business of Prostitution in Nineteenth-Century Baltimore." In *Capitalism by Gaslight: Illuminating the Economy of Nineteenth-Century America*, edited by Brian P. Luskey and Wendy A. Woloson, 168–89. Philadelphia: University of Pennsylvania Press, 2015.

Hershberg, Theodore. "Free Blacks in Antebellum Philadelphia." In *The Peoples of Philadelphia: A History of Ethnic Groups and Lower-Class Life, 1790–1940*, edited by Allen F. Davis and Mark H. Haller, 111–33. Philadelphia: Temple University Press, 1973.

Hilliard, Kathleen M. "Bonds Burst Asunder: The Transformation of the Internal Economy in Confederate Richmond." In *New Directions in Slavery Studies: Commodification, Community, and Comparison*, edited by Jeff Forret and Christine E. Sears, 130–49. Baton Rouge: Louisiana State University Press, 2015.

Hollander, Craig B. "Underground on the High Seas: Commerce, Character, and Complicity in the Illegal Slave Trade." In *Capitalism by Gaslight: Illuminating the Economy of Nineteenth-Century America*, edited by Brian P. Luskey and Wendy A. Woloson, 127–49. Philadelphia: University of Pennsylvania Press, 2015.

Johnson, Ludwell H. "Contraband Trade during the Last Year of the Civil War." *Mississippi Valley Historical Review* 49, no. 4 (March 1963): 635–52.

Johnson, Michael P. "Out of Egypt: The Migration of Former Slaves to the Midwest during the 1860s in Comparative Perspective." In *Crossing Boundaries: Comparative History of Black People in Diaspora*, edited by Darlene Clark Hine and Jacqueline McLeod, 223–45. Bloomington: Indiana University Press, 1999.

Johnson, Walter. "The Pedestal and the Veil: Rethinking the Capitalism/Slavery Question." *Journal of the Early Republic* 24, no. 2 (Summer 2004): 299–308.

Lande, Jonathan. "Trials of Freedom: African American Deserters during the U.S. Civil War." *Journal of Social History* 49, no. 3 (Spring 2016): 693–709.

Lasser, Carol. "Conscience and Contradiction: The Moral Ambiguities of Antebellum Reformers Marcus and Rebecca Buffum Spring." *Journal of the Early Republic* 38, no. 1 (Spring 2018): 1–35.

Lears, T. J. Jackson. "The Concept of Cultural Hegemony: Problems and Possibilities." *American Historical Review* 90, no. 3 (June 1985): 567–93.

Levine-Gronningsater, Sarah. "Delivering Freedom: Gradual Emancipation, Black Legal Culture, and the Origins of Sectional Crisis in New York, 1759–1870." Ph.D. diss., University of Chicago, 2014.

Lipartito, Kenneth. "Reassembling the Economic: New Departures in Historical Materialism." *American Historical Review* 121, no. 1 (February 2016): 101–39.

Luskey, Brian P. "The Ambiguities of Class in Antebellum America." In *A Companion to the Era of Andrew Jackson*, edited by Sean Patrick Adams, 194–212. New York: Wiley-Blackwell, 2013.

———. "Dishonest Clerks and the Culture of Capitalism." *Common-place: The Interactive Journal of Early American Life* 10, no. 4 (July 2010). http://www.common-place-archives.org/vol-10/no-04/author/.

———. "Houses Divided: The Cultural Economy of Emancipation in the Civil War North." *Journal of the Early Republic* 36, no. 4 (Winter 2016): 637–57.

———. "Men Is Cheap." *New York Times' Disunion Blog* (February 4, 2015). http://opinionator.blogs.nytimes.com/2015/02/04/men-is-cheap/.

———. "Special Marts: Intelligence Offices, Labor Commodification, and Emancipation in Nineteenth-Century America." *Journal of the Civil War Era* 3, no. 3 (September 2013): 360–91.

Lynn, Joshua A. "Half-Baked Men: Doughface Masculinity and the Antebellum Politics of the Household." M.A. thesis, University of North Carolina at Chapel Hill, 2010.

Mackintosh, Will B. "The Loomis Gang's Market Revolution." In *Capitalism by Gaslight: Illuminating the Economy of Nineteenth-Century America*, edited by Brian P. Luskey and Wendy A. Woloson, 10–30. Philadelphia: University of Pennsylvania Press, 2015.

Martin, Bonnie. "Neighbor-to-Neighbor Capitalism: Local Credit Networks and the Mortgaging of Slaves." In *Slavery's Capitalism: A New History of American Economic Development*, edited by Sven Beckert and Seth Rockman, 107–21. Philadelphia: University of Pennsylvania Press, 2016.

Masur, Kate. "'A Rare Phenomenon of Philological Vegetation': The Word 'Contraband' and the Meanings of Emancipation in the United States." *Journal of American History* 93, no. 4 (March 2007): 1050–84.

McCorison, J. L, Jr. "Impressions of the President Elect, 1860: A Letter of Thomas Webster, Jr." *Abraham Lincoln Quarterly* 3, no. 6 (June 1945): 291–301.

McGrath, A. Hope. "'A Slave in Uncle Sam's Service': Labor and Resistance in the US Army." *Labor* 13, nos. 3/4 (December 2016): 37–56.

Mendelsohn, Adam. "The Rag Race: Jewish Secondhand Clothing Dealers in England and America." In *Capitalism by Gaslight: Illuminating the Economy of Nineteenth-Century America*, edited by Brian P. Luskey and Wendy A. Woloson, 76–92. Philadelphia: University of Pennsylvania Press, 2015.

Mishler, Max. "The Myth of Modern Slavery: Coercion in the Age of Freedom." Paper presented at the Global Nineteenth Century Workshop, University of Pennsylvania, Philadelphia, Pa., December 2015.

Nelson, Scott Reynolds. "After Slavery: Forced Drafts of Irish and Chinese Labor in the American Civil War, or the Search for Liquid Labor." In *Many Middle Passages: Forced Migration and the Making of the Modern World*, edited by Emma Christopher, Cassandra Pybus, and Marcus Rediker, 150–65. Berkeley: University of California Press, 2007.

Newman, Richard. "The Pennsylvania Abolition Society and the Struggle for Racial Justice." In *Antislavery and Abolition in Philadelphia: Emancipation and the Long Struggle for Racial Justice in the City of Brotherly Love*, edited by Richard Newman and James Mueller, 117–46. Baton Rouge: Louisiana State University Press, 2011.

O'Malley, Brendan P. "Lickspittles and Land Sharks: The Immigrant Exploitation Business in Antebellum New York." In *Capitalism by Gaslight: Illuminating the Economy* of Nineteenth-Century America, edited by Brian P. Luskey and Wendy A. Woloson, 93–108. Philadelphia: University of Pennsylvania Press, 2015.

Orr, Timothy J. "'We Are No Grumblers': Negotiating State and Federal Military Service in the Pennsylvania Reserve Division." *Pennsylvania Magazine of History and Biography* 135, no. 4 (October 2011): 447–80.

Pierson, Michael D. "'He Helped the Poor and Snubbed the Rich': Benjamin F. Butler and Class Politics in Lowell and New Orleans." *Massachusetts Historical Review* 7 (2005): 36–68.

Rael, Patrick. "African Americans, Slavery, and Thrift from the Revolution to the Civil War." In *Thrift and Thriving in America: Capitalism and Moral Order from the Puritans to the Present*, edited by Joshua J. Yates and James Davison Hunter, 183–206. New York: Oxford University Press, 2011.

Robertson, John Gordon. "Rich Man's War, Poor Man's Opportunity? Civil War Reenlistment and the Right to Rise." Ph.D. diss., Carnegie Mellon University, 2009.

Rockman, Seth. "Northern Manufacturers, Southern Slavery, and the Antebellum Origins of American Business Ethics." Paper presented at the American Origins Seminar, University of Southern California, Los Angeles, Calif., March 2011.

Rosenthal, Caitlin. "From Memory to Mastery: Accounting for Control in America, 1750–1880." *Enterprise and Society* 14, no. 4 (December 2013): 732–48.

———. "Slavery's Scientific Management: Masters and Managers." In *Slavery's Capitalism: A New History of American Economic Development*, edited Sven Beckert and Seth Rockman, 62–86. Philadelphia: University of Pennsylvania Press, 2016.

Rothman, Joshua D. "The Contours of Cotton Capitalism: Speculation, Slavery, and the Economic Panic in Mississippi, 1832–1841." In *Slavery's Capitalism: A New History of American Economic Development*, edited by Sven Beckert and Seth Rockman, 122–45. Philadelphia: University of Pennsylvania Press, 2016.

Sklansky, Jeffrey. "The Elusive Sovereign: New Intellectual and Social Histories of Capitalism." *Modern Intellectual History* 9, no. 1 (April 2012): 233–48.

———. "Labor, Money, and the Financial Turn in the History of Capitalism." *Labor* 11, no. 1 (2014): 23–46.

Smallwood, Stephanie. "Commodified Freedom: Interrogating the Limits of Anti-Slavery Ideology in the Early Republic." *Journal of the Early Republic* 24, no. 2 (Summer 2004): 289–98.

Stanley, Amy Dru. "Home Life and the Morality of the Market." In *The Market Revolution in America: Social, Political, and Religious Expressions, 1800–1880*, edited by Melvin Stokes and Stephen Conway, 74–96. Charlottesville: University of Virginia Press, 1996.

———. "Instead of Waiting for the Thirteenth Amendment: The War Power, Slave Marriage, and Inviolate Human Rights." *American Historical Review* 115, no. 3 (June 2010): 732–65.

———. "Slave Breeding and Free Love: An Antebellum Argument over Slavery, Capitalism, and Personhood." In *Capitalism Takes Command: The Social Transformation of Nineteenth-Century America*, edited by Michael Zakim and Gary J. Kornblith, 119–44. Chicago: University of Chicago Press, 2012.

———. "Wages, Sin, and Slavery: Some Thoughts on Free Will and Commodity Relations." *Journal of the Early Republic* 24, no. 2 (Summer 2004): 279–88.

Stansell, Christine. "Whitman at Pfaff's: Commercial Culture, Literary Life and New York

Bohemia at Mid-Century." *Walt Whitman Quarterly Review* 10, no. 3 (Winter 1993): 107–26.

Thompson, Michael D. "'Some Rascally Business': Thieving Slaves, Unscrupulous Whites, and Charleston's Illicit Waterfront Trade." In *Capitalism by Gaslight: Illuminating the Economy of Nineteenth-Century America*, edited by Brian P. Luskey and Wendy A. Woloson, 150–67. Philadelphia: University of Pennsylvania Press, 2015.

Thomson, David K. "'Like a Cord through the Whole Country': Union Bonds and Financial Mobilization for Victory." *Journal of the Civil War Era* 6, no. 3 (September 2016): 347–75.

Tremel, Andrew T. "The Union League, Black Leaders, and the Recruitment of Philadelphia's African American Civil War Regiments." *Pennsylvania History* 80, no. 1 (Winter 2013): 13–36.

Varon, Elizabeth. "'Beautiful Providences': William Still, the Vigilance Committee, and Abolitionists in the Age of Sectionalism." In *Antislavery and Abolition in Philadelphia: Emancipation and the Long Struggle for Racial Justice in the City of Brotherly Love*, edited by Richard Newman and James Mueller, 229–45. Baton Rouge: Louisiana State University Press, 2011.

Voegeli, V. Jacque. "A Rejected Alternative: Union Policy and the Relocation of Southern 'Contrabands' at the Dawn of Emancipation." *Journal of Southern History* 69 (2003): 765–90.

Way, Peter. "Class and the Common Soldier in the Seven Years' War." *Labor History* 44, no. 4 (November 2003): 455–81.

Weicksel, Sarah Jones. "The Dress of the Enemy: Clothing and Disease in the Civil War Era." *Civil War History* 63, no. 2 (June 2017): 133–50.

Wilson, Keith. "Thomas Webster and the 'Free Military School for Applicants for Commands of Colored Troops.'" *Civil War History* 29, no. 2 (June 1983): 101–22.

Winch, Julie. "Philadelphia and the Other Underground Railroad." *Pennsylvania Magazine of History and Biography* 111, no. 1 (January 1987): 3–25.

Woloson, Wendy A. "The Rise of the Consumer in the Age of Jackson." In *A Companion to the Era of Andrew Jackson*, edited by Sean Patrick Adams, 489–508. Malden, Mass.: Wiley-Blackwell, 2013.

———. "Wishful Thinking: Retail Premiums in Mid-Nineteenth-Century America." *Enterprise and Society* 13, no. 4 (December 2012): 790–831.

Woods, Michael E. "Tracing the 'Sacred Relicts': The Strange Career of Preston Brooks's Cane." *Civil War History* 63, no. 2 (June 2017): 113–32.

Zakim, Michael. "Bookkeeping as Ideology." *Common-place: The Interactive Journal of Early American Life* 6, no. 3 (April 2006). http://www.common-place.org/vol-06/no-03/zakim/.

———. "The Dialectics of Merchant Capital: New York City Businessmen and the Secession Crisis of 1860–61." *New York History* 87, no. 1 (Winter 2006): 67–87.

Zakim, Michael, and Gary J. Kornblith. "Introduction: An American Revolutionary Tradition." In *Capitalism Takes Command: The Social Transformation of Nineteenth-Century America*, edited by Michael Zakim and Gary J. Kornblith, 1–12. Chicago: University of Chicago Press, 2012.

INDEX

abolitionists, 15, 29, 54, 66, 103–5, 136, 140–41, 144. *See also* Pennsylvania Abolition Society (PAS)

advertisements, 13, 29; for black recruits, 139–40, 172–74; featuring and for black servants, 33–34, 190, 193–94; and fraud, 68–71; for household products, 31–33; recruitment posters, 71–73, 80, 86, 109–11; for runaway slaves, 13–14; wartime shifts in language and images, 67–68, 71–72, 173; for workers, 44–45

African Americans, 29, 155, 212–13; in advertisements, 33–34; domestic servants, 29, 33–35, 94–95, 189, 190–95, 216, 247nn22, 27; education, 171–72; free people in the North, 48, 140–41, 217–18; laborers migrating to the North, 101–5, 108, 120–22, 190–92; servants in Union armies, 91–93, 96–101, 131; transition from slaves to wage laborers in Union armies, 50–52, 123–25, 126, 128, 146, 152, 159–60; women and their households, 153, 157–58, 180–81. *See also* apprenticeship; contraband; emancipation; Freedmen's Bureau; refugees; slavery

African American soldiers, 123, 125; in combat, 136, 179; impressed and coerced into military service, 137, 152–60, 179–81; inequality of pay, 139–40, 142, 145, 148, 166, 174; as manual laborers, 135, 142, 147–48, 150–51; recruitment fraud, 167–69; recruitment of, 138–41, 170–75; Southerners recruited to fill Northern quotas, 139, 163–64, 165–66, 184–85; wage labor, 147–51, 163–64, 165; and white officers, 135–36, 145. *See also* Butler, Benjamin; General Order 46; Louisiana; Nelson, John; United States Colored Troops (USCT)

agricultural labor, 14, 127, 149; cotton, 125–26, 137, 162; sugar, 127–28, 135

Alabama soldiers, 198–99

amnesty, 151, 152, 196

Andrew, John: and former slaves as Union laborers, 122; Massachusetts soldier recruitment, 80–84, 86–88, 109, 166–67, 184–85; requests for work, 44–46, 48; USCTs, 164

antislavery ideology: and Northern tobacco merchants, 22–23; in Union armies, 97–101; and white Southerners, 24

apprenticeship: for African Americans in the North, 34, 54, 65, 103; as proposal for gradual emancipation during the Civil War, 125–26, 191

Ashley, James, 166

Bacon, Philip, 171
Baker, Lafayette, 3–5, 201–5
Baker, Michael, 113–14
Banks, Nathaniel, 128, 135–38, 143
Barnum, P. T., 29
benevolence, 20–21, 55, 63–64, 104, 189
benevolent associations, 17–18, 66; for all soldiers, 112, 117, 164; as labor brokers for refugees, 54–55, 104; as labor brokers for veterans, 209–10; as labor brokers for women, 63–68. *See also* Freedmen's Bureau; Pennsylvania Abolition Society (PAS); Union Volunteer Refreshment Saloon (UVRS)
Bennett, James Gordon, 55–59, 64, 77, 122
Bermuda Hundred campaign, 179–80
Birney, William, 210–11
black republican, 12–13, 23, 24. *See also* Webster, Thomas
Blair, Montgomery, 52–55, 67

271

border states, 53, 119, 120, 145. *See also* Maryland
bounty brokers. *See* substitute brokers
bounty jumping, 113, 129–30, 202–3
bounty men, 78, 80, 129
bounty payments, 73, 86–87, 89, 236n2; federal, 80, 109, 113; fraud within the system, 112–14, 116, 157; local, 109–10; as a means to financial independence, 116–17, 133, 183; state, 82–83, 116–17, 164–66, 169, 184; USCT, 138–41, 145, 148, 165. *See also* General Order 46
Breckinridge, John, 22, 35–36
Brewster, Charles: black refugees and servants in camp, 91–92, 94, 96–101, 131–32, 181, 234n35; the draft and commutation, 130; economics of soldiering, 89–91, 95, 105, 107, 117–18; entrepreneurship, 118, 208; home front finances, 106–8; rations and food, 105, 128–29; as a recruiter, 108, 114, recruiting black soldiers as substitutes, 184–86, 201; on refugees and slavery, 92–94, 108; uniform and equipment, 95–96, 107–8
Briggs, Henry, 92, 99, 100–101, 107
Brown, Orlando, 179–81
Buchanan, James, 35, 38, 61
Buckingham, William, 85, 87–88, 169
Burr, William Henry, 56
Butler, Andrew, 127
Butler, Benjamin, 137–38, 174–76, 211–13; African American recruitment, 123–28, 144–45, 153, 157, 163–66, 180; contraband policy, 48–55, 67; dry goods speculation in Louisiana, 127–28; General Order 46, 145, 147–52, 163–65; and impressment claims in Virginia, 152, 153, 160–63; Massachusetts recruitment efforts, 80–89; regulating black wage labor in Union armies, 163–64, 165; sending black laborers North, 180–82
Butt, Bob, 20–21

Cabaniss, Alex, 198–200, 201
Cahill, Thomas, 87–89
Cameron, Simon, 40–42, 50–52, 82
Camp Parapet, 123, 126

Canada, 15–16, 101
capital, 2; of former slaves for the North, 106, 122–23; and kinship, 11; and labor, 28, 40, 61, 77, 93–94, 103, 114, 122, 125, 148, 216; link to power and independence, 13, 40, 45, 77, 94, 96, 101, 104, 118, 141; and material goods, 118; for Northern war effort, 79, 120, 142, 179; and patronage, 24–26; "in self," 99, 103, 108, 122–23; of slavery, 15, 16–17, 45, 52, 96, 97, 106; and soldier recruitment, 80–82; for workers, 56, 96
capitalism, 5, 30, 63, 65, 80, 90, 96, 111
Carey, Henry C., 25
Chase, Salmon, 41–42, 83, 127–28, 145, 161
Citizens' Bounty Fund (Philadelphia), 109–10, 112–13, 138
class: and appearance, 26–27, 95–96, 192, 207; and the draft, 130, 167; and labor options, 27, 30–31, 84, 186–87, 216; and the promise of free labor, 91–92, 106
clerks, 4, 8; in the military, 51, 157, 203; in shops, 30, 31, 46, 58, 67, 89, 90, 95
colonization, 52–53, 94, 119, 120, 125
commerce. *See* trade
Commissioners of Emigration (N.Y.), 56–57, 64
commutation, 1, 4, 130, 200, 202, 205. *See also* draft; substitutes
Confederate States of America, 45, 48–49, 120
confiscation, 106, 212
Confiscation Act, 67, 123–24
Connecticut: Ninth Infantry, 85–89; soldier recruitment, 86–89, 166, 168–69; Third Infantry, 84
conscription. *See* draft
consumerism, 31–33, 95–96
consumers, 6, 40, 53, 77, 125, 217; and clerks, 30; and credit, 70–71; and demand, 60; soldiers as, 80, 91, 105; and want advertisements, 13, 31, 67–69
Continental Monthly, 101–3, 106, 108, 131, 186–87, 218–19
contraband: Benjamin Butler's policy on, 48–55, 67, 147; economics of, 49–52, 122; as labor assets to Union armies,

48–49, 53; in Union armies, 96–101. *See also* fugitive slaves; General Order 46; refugees
contractors, 73–76, 90–91
Couch, Darius, 138
courts-martial, 85, 129, 138, 169, 198
credit (financial), 3; agencies, 11; benefit of, 70; criticism of, 68–70; on the home front, 132–35, 183; reports, 11–12, 20, 22, 40, 59, 211; soldiers' access to and use of, 7, 79–80, 116–18, 122, 132
credits, paper. *See* substitute brokers
Curtin, Andrew, 40, 73, 77, 138

Dalton, Richard, 2–5, 8
Davis, Benjamin, 13–16
Davis, Clarissa, 17
Davis, Jefferson, 45–47, 52, 142
Delaware, 94, 172, 190, 197–99
Denison, George, 127–28
Department of New England, 81
Department of the Gulf, 123–28, 138, 144, 160, 171. *See also* Butler, Benjamin; Nelson, John
Department of Virginia and North Carolina, 144–45, 147, 160, 165, 174, 212. *See also* Butler, Benjamin; Nelson, John; Webster, Thomas
deserters: Confederate, 7, 176, 187, 196–201; Union, 129–30, 131, 169
Dickinson, Anna, 140–41
disabilities, 209
disease, 17–18, 115
Dix, John, 52, 122, 169
domesticity. *See* households
domestic necessity, doctrine of, 8, 54, 182
domestic servants, 186–95, 216, 218–19; in advertisements, 31–33; African American, 33–34, 62, 94–95, 190, 192; independence and authority due to wage labor, 29, 32, 56–60, 63; Irish, 29–31, 61–62, 186–87, 188–89; labor market for, 63–65, 181–82, 197; and the Lincoln family, 61–63, 65; relationship with mistresses, 29–33, 57–60. *See also* households
Douglas, Stephen, 22, 35–36
Douglass, Frederick, 140–41

draft, 108–10, 130; and black soldiers to fill the ranks, 139, 163–64, 165–66, 184; calls, 3, 145; and men as capital, 142; opposition to, 143; quotas, 3, 139, 202. *See also* commutation; Enrollment Act; recruitment; substitutes
Draper, Alonzo, 60, 161
dry goods: antebellum trade of, 11–12, 67–71; wartime speculation in, 90–91, 127–28, 137
Dudley, Nathan, 88, 213–14
Duross Brothers, 68–72, 172

economics, national, 13; antislavery ideology as economic principle, 23–24, 40; cost of war, 79, 119–20, 177, 202, 212; disease, impact on, 17–18; of emancipation, 16, 20, 94, 119–20, 125–26; of fugitive slave capture, 18–19; Northern industrial production, 163, 167; and secession, 24–25, 38–40, 44–46, 67; war, impact on Northern households, 78, 106–8, 129, 197. *See also* agricultural labor and speculation; labor markets
economics, of soldiering: black servants, 97–99; entrepreneurship, 116, 118; greater opportunities for officers, 92, 95–98, 105, 118; paymasters, 86, 87, 90, 117–18, 130, 135, 142, 146; pensions, 107, 132–34, 141, 157–58, 183–84; promotions, 89, 92, 93, 95–96, 118, 129; state aid, 83–84, 87, 88–89, 109; theft in camp, 107–8, 115, 182; wages, 83, 87, 89–90, 96, 105, 115, 117–18, 129, 132. *See also* bounty payments; emancipation; recruitment; soldiers; sutlers; uniforms and equipment
Ellmaker, Peter C., 109–10
emancipation, 103, 154, 190, 214; compensation for, 20–21, 94, 119–20; and confiscation of Southern land, 106; effects on labor in the North, 114, 120–22, 131, 187–88; gradual, proposals for, 53–55, 64, 119–20, 125; labor costs of, 16, 20; as military necessity, 53–54, 147; in the North, 52, 103, 125, 235n45. *See also* apprenticeship
Emancipation Proclamation, 118–20, 130,

139, 147–48, 154, 156, 176–77. *See also* General Order 46
Emerson, Ralph Waldo, 207
employers, 2, 6, 55, 154, 197–98; benefits of free labor for, 2, 52, 63, 103, 150–51; control over employees, 29, 187–88, 190–91, 218–19; dependence on workers, 5, 65, 194–95; opportunities provided by war, 7, 187, 205–6; and refugee labor, 53–54, 187–88, 193, 214; and social mobility, 6, 96. *See also* households; intelligence offices
employment agencies. *See* intelligence offices
employment agents, 6, 44, 55, 193, 197, 215–16
Enrollment Act of 1863, 1, 123, 130–31, 139, 156, 167, 176, 200
entrepreneurs, 116, 118
Espy, Barlow, 67–70
Eustis, Henry, 118

Fair Oaks, battle of, 107
Farnham, Eliza, 63–64
fashion, 26–27, 30–32, 38, 68
Fay, John, 2–5, 8
Fillmore, Millard, 61
financial markets, 3, 40, 46, 67, 78. *See also* economics, national; economics, of soldiering
Forbes, John Murray, 48, 144, 163–67, 174–76
Fort Monroe, Va., 14, 48–51, 54, 122, 146, 150, 160
Foster, John, 144–45
fraud: against employers, 6; in free labor ideology, 2, 28, 51, 77, 92, 167; in intelligence offices, 55–59, 216–17; in manufacturing and distribution of soldier uniforms, 73–76; in military promotion system, 92; objections to, 51; in recruiting soldiers, 3–4, 87–89, 112–14, 159, 167–69; shifting boundaries of in wartime, 76–77; against slaveholders, 18, 39, 93; slavery as an act of, 15, 45–46, 48, 92; and substitutes, 3–5, 201–6; unpaid wages as a form of, 51, 90; in

want advertisements for and sale of goods, 68–71; and white complicity, 2; against workers, 6, 29, 50–51, 63. *See also* recruitment; substitutes
Freedmen's Bureau, 210–14, 218
free labor ideology, 2, 5, 7–8, 218–19; and Abraham Lincoln, 27–28, 60–61, 79, 93–94, 122–23, 167, 177; and antislavery principles, 12–14, 106, 124–25; character traits associated with, 44, 50, 52, 116, 132, 207, 209; and competition between black and white laborers, 131–32; disillusionment with and unfulfilled promise of, 7, 39–40, 59, 91–92, 94, 108, 133; and military necessity, 51–53, 149–51; and the promise of success and mobility, 2, 5, 28–29, 31, 60, 93–94, 96, 106, 115–16, 128, 199; promise of in Union armies, 79, 96, 98, 128, 130, 141; Southern criticism of, 27, 28, 66; and the work of soldiering, 78–80, 92, 122, 157. *See also* fraud; intelligence offices; labor markets; substitutes; wage labor
Frémont, Jessie, 62
Frémont, John, 61
French, Jonas, 84
Fry, James, 130, 165, 169
Fugitive Slave Act, 16, 49
fugitive slaves, 13–17, 18–19, 30, 96–101, 158–59. *See also* contraband; refugees; Underground Railroad
Funk, Peter, 45–47, 77

Garrison, William Lloyd, 135
General Order 46, 147–54, 158, 163–66, 180–81. *See also* African American soldiers; refugees; United States Colored Troops (USCT)
General Order 64, 196
Gilbert, Charles, 13–15
Girard House (Philadelphia), 73–76
Gooding, James Henry, 142
government posts, 44, 46; agents, 74; port collectorships, 23–26, 40–42
Grant, Ulysses, 125–26, 211
Greeley, Horace, 36, 64

Hammond, James Henry, 27–28, 38–39, 61, 66, 93, 97, 131
Helper, Hinton, 37–38, 227n40
Henry, Alexander, 112, 138
Hickman, John, 22, 25, 40, 41, 171
Hill, Moses, 166
Holman, John, 146, 158–59
households, 45, 155, 187–89; advertisements for, 30–35; gender and class power in, 29–33, 35, 57–60, 62–63, 94–95, 133–34, 193–95; impact of war on, 106–8, 109, 112–13, 115; interdependence with soldier economies, 83, 114–17, 132–35, 153, 182–83, 203–4; and promise of black labor, 53–54, 80, 134–35; and respectability, 29, 32, 56, 60, 63, 192, 218–19; role in Northern economy, 31, 66, 78; in the South, 61–62. See also domestic servants; labor markets
Howard, Charles, 214–16
Howard, Oliver, 213–14
Howe, Frank, 81
humor. See political cartoons
Hygeia Hotel (Old Point Comfort, Va.), 14, 160, 170

Illinois, 61–62, 65–68, 70
immigrants, 57, 150, 243n38. See also Irish servants
impressment, 137, 150, 152–63, 179–80
independence, 5, 92, 212–13, 218; connected to capital, 2, 13, 40, 79–80, 114, 169; economic, 5, 13, 42, 63, 117, 141–42; in the household, 30, 35, 57, 62–63, 134–35, 153; by owning land, 141–42, 152; and personal freedom, 16, 99, 101, 104, 154, 158, 217; through wartime opportunity, 114, 117, 129; for workers, 60–61, 63, 78
Indiana, 64–65
intelligence offices, 83, 111, 205, 218–19; and benevolent associations, 103, 193, 209; for black laborers and refugees, 103–5, 213–14, 216–17; definition and purpose of, 2, 4, 6–7, 44–45, 54–55, 104, 105, 229n21; fees, 193; fraud in, 55–59, 216–17; and women, 63–64, 67. See also Pennsylvania

Abolition Society (PAS); Union Volunteer Refreshment Saloon (UVRS)
Irish servants, 29–31, 34–35, 57, 61–62, 186–87, 188–89, 216
Irish soldiers, 82, 84–86

Johnson, Andrew, 123, 215
journalism, 29–30, 36, 55, 64, 101–3, 201. See also *Continental Monthly*; political cartoons

Kelley, William, 140–41
Kinsman, J. B., 152–53, 156, 158–60, 163, 180–83, 188

labor: as commodity, 40, 77, 115, 122, 185, 218; as a form of credit, 132–35; in relation to capital, 28, 40, 61, 77, 93–94, 103, 114, 122, 125, 148, 167. See also free labor ideology; wage labor
labor markets, 1–2, 40, 180, 193; competition, 56, 108, 146, 149, 150, 164, 191; Confederate deserters and white refugees, 187, 196–201; fraud and speculations in, 4, 6, 8, 13, 58, 201; in the Midwest, 63–65; postwar, 209–10, 213–17; for Southern white labor in the North, 197–201; and "want," 52–53, 67. See also domestic servants; intelligence offices; movement of people; refugees; substitutes
labor strikes, 60–61, 90–91, 150, 167, 219
Leland, Charles Godfrey, 29, 103
Lewis, George, 85
Lincoln, Abraham, 177, 196, 207; appearance, 26–27, 38; and black soldiers, 142, 143–45, 167, 177; commutation, 1, 160; in the domestic sphere, 62–63, 65; and the draft, 130; and emancipation, 118–21; on free labor, 27–28, 60, 79, 93, 122–23; patronage requests, 21, 25–27, 40–42; in political cartoons, 35–36, 38; reconstruction plans, 151–52; on secession, 41; on slavery, 59–61, 66, 94; and soldier labor, 79; and soldier recruitment, 79, 81

Lincoln, Mary Todd, 26–27, 38, 61–63, 65
liquor, 4, 86, 129, 207
Louisiana: black wage labor on plantations, 127–28; First and Third Native Guards (black units), 127–28, 135–39, 143, 146, 160–61; refugees in the Union military in, 123–28. *See also* Butler, Benjamin; Nelson, John

Malvern Hill, battle of, 107
manufacturing, 11, 17, 46–48, 53, 76, 91, 96, 111, 208. *See also* uniforms and equipment
Marsh, William, 100–101
Maryland: refugees from, 92, 195; slaveholders, 98–99; soldiers, 101
Massachusetts, 44; Eastern Bay State Regiment (Thirtieth Massachusetts Infantry), 83–84, 87–88, 144, 233n19; Fifty-Fourth Massachusetts Infantry, 142, 164; recruiting Southern black soldiers to fill quotas, 163–67, 185; recruiting white soldiers, 80–89; Tenth Massachusetts Infantry, 89–91, 99–100, 107, 130; Twenty-Sixth Infantry, 82. *See also* Brewster, Charles
Meigs, Montgomery, 126
mercenaries, 48, 78, 82, 83
merchants, 8; antebellum, 42, 58, 67–70; of dry goods, 68–70, 77; of military uniforms and equipment, 75–77, 90–91. *See also* sutlers; Webster, Thomas
middlemen, 19–20, 43, 56, 77, 185, 193, 217
military necessity, doctrine of: and emancipation, 53–54, 147; and free labor, 52–53; and labor of black recruits in the military, 147–52; and recruitment of Southern black soldiers, 166, 176; and slave refugee labor, 49, 51–52, 179–81
Militia Acts of 1792 and 1862, 48, 123, 126, 139, 142
mobility, social and economic, 28–29, 31–32, 60, 93–94, 96, 96, 106, 115–16, 128
Montana territory, 207–8
Morgan, Edwin, 81
movement of goods. *See* trade
movement of people, 7, 9, 43, 66, 176, 179, 186–87; black refugees, 54–55, 101–5, 108, 181–82, 189–90; Confederate deserters, 196–201; emancipated slaves, 120–22; opportunities created by war, 4, 45; slaves, 15, 65–66, 92–93, 98; soldiers, 147, 166–67, 176; working women, 63–68. *See also* benevolent associations; intelligence offices; labor markets; recruitment; refugees
mudsills and mudsill theory, 27–28, 93, 97, 107, 131

Naglee, Henry, 144
Nelson, John, 8, 170, 207–8; early recruitment irregularities in New England, 84–89, 168; impressment of black recruits in Tidewater Virginia, 152–63, 180; military discharge in Louisiana, 137–38; as officer of black Louisiana Native Guards, 128, 135–37; recruiting for Tenth USCT, 143–47, 170, 176, 179; speculations in soldiers' goods, 162–63
New York: 117th Infantry, 112; recruitment, 3, 81, 112; soldiers, 115. *See also* Walker, Henry
Northrup, George, 2–3, 8

old fogeyism, 31–32
Old Point Comfort, Va., 14, 18, 160

Panic, financial, of 1857, 13, 19, 27, 60
Pardee, Benjamin, 168–69
Parmelee, Lewis, 81–82
patriotism, 5, 76, 78, 83, 93, 95, 109
patronage, 13, 44; and character and kinship, 23, 35, 67–68; economics of, 13, 42; and partisanship, 23–24, 40, 211
Peck, Joseph, 168–69
Pennsylvania Abolition Society (PAS), 103–5, 187, 191–96
Pennsylvania soldiers: Gray Reserves (119th Infantry), 109; recruitment, 71–76, 108–13; Sixty-Sixth Infantry, 72–73
pensions, 107, 132–34, 141, 157–58, 183–84
People's Party, 21, 38, 40
Petersburg campaign, 179, 182–83, 196, 201
Pettifoot, Jack, 16–17
Phelps, Elizabeth, 63

Phelps, John, 50, 123–27, 171, 173
Philadelphia: fugitive and refugee slaves, 15–17, 101, 181, 190–91; intelligence offices, 103–5; labor market, 197–99; politics, 21–23, 25–26, 41; soldier recruitment, 71–76, 108–13; trade, 11–12, 68
Philadelphia Supervisory Committee for Recruiting Colored Regiments, 138–40, 170–75, 179
Phillips, Wendell, 152
political cartoons: Abraham Lincoln and emancipation, 120, 177; African American servants and laborers, 33–34, 101; Confederacy, 45–46; fraud in the military, 73–74, 122; household affairs, 29–35; Irish servants, 29–32; secession crisis, 35–38
popular culture, 29, 35–36, 55, 140, 171–72. *See also* advertisements; political cartoons
Portsmouth Relief Association, 20
Portsmouth, Va., 17, 20–21, 147, 154
presidential elections: of 1856, 61; of 1860, 21, 22, 27, 35–36
print culture. See *Continental Monthly*; journalism; political cartoons

quartermasters, 50–51, 73, 75, 95, 126, 147, 151, 170, 180

radical Republicans, 82, 151–52, 164, 167, 212–13, 219
railroads, 19, 163, 223n14
Ramage, Benjamin, 71
reconstruction plans, 151–52
recruiters, 4, 6, 111, 144; and African American soldiers, 8, 48; and bounty jumping, 113–14; fees and wages, 71–72, 86–87, 130; motivation, 73, 78; subscriptions, 109–10, 112–13. *See also* Brewster, Charles; Nelson, John; Webster, Thomas
recruitment, 1; authority over, 80–84, 86; blame for breakdowns in system, 113–14; and class of men, 83, 114, 167; and commercial culture, 68, 171, 176; financial logistics of, 81–84, 86–87, 109–11, 130; for the labor of war, 78–80; partisanship in, 80–81; quotas, 3, 109–10, 113, 168–69; of Southern black soldiers to fill Northern quotas, 139, 163–64, 165–67, 184–85; speculation in, 87–89, 123; and subsistence funds, 163–64, 165; of USCT, 138–41; want advertisements, 71–73, 80, 109–11. *See also* bounty payments; draft; economics, of soldiering; impressment; soldiers; substitutes
recruitment agents and brokers, 4, 81, 83, 166, 167–69
Redpath, W. J., 58–59
refugees: economics of, for Union armies, 49–50, 181; as labor for Northern households, 54–55, 103–5, 108; official status of, 51–53, 123–26; wage laborers in the South for Union armies, 126, 128, 179–81; women and children in Northern households, 181–82, 187–95. *See also* African Americans; African American soldiers; contraband; emancipation; Pennsylvania Abolition Society (PAS); Union Volunteer Refreshment Saloon (UVRS)
Republican Party, 21–22, 25, 27, 36–37, 62
respectability, 27, 29–32, 36, 56, 57, 60, 62, 63, 74, 135
Richmond, Va., 11–12, 17, 19, 217

Scott, Winfield, 49
Sears, David, 53–55
secession: economic impact of, 24–25, 38–40, 44–46, 67; in political cartoons, 35–39
servants. See domestic servants
Seward, William, 21, 38
Shepley, George, 179–80
Sherman, John: political satire of, 36–38; and Thomas Webster, 21–26, 38, 41–42
shipping. See trade
slaveholders, 17, 98–99, 123, 126
Slave Power, 29, 35
slavery, 5, 189–90, 218; as act of Southern fraud, 15, 45–46, 48, 92; antislavery ideology, 20, 23–24, 40, 124–25, 134; antislavery white Southerners, 24;

auctions, 12, 14, 16, 45–46, 48, 66, 92, 190, 218; proslavery ideology, 25, 27–28; traders, 12–15, 137, 190, 193; and transition to free labor in the South, 125–26, 128, violence of, 171. *See also* emancipation; white Southerners

slaves: as commodities and valuation of, 16, 20, 51–52, 92, 96, 98; as Confederate laborers during the war, 48; labor costs of runaways, 13–17. *See also* African Americans; African American soldiers; contraband; fugitive slaves; refugees

soldiers, 2; on black refugees, 92–93, 98–101; dependence on government, 117–18, 122, 132; dependence on wives, 133; as employers of black laborers, 80, 91–93, 97–99, 131–32; as entrepreneurs in camp, 91, 132; food and rations, 115, 129–30; gambling, 136–37; misbehavior, 99–100, 204; motivation, 78–79, 133, 177; physical condition and suffering, 117, 122; and the politics of emancipation, 98–101; recruitment, economics of, 71–73, 79–83, 112–14; uniforms and cost of, 73–77, 90–91, 96, 107, 118; as wage laborers, 72, 83, 89–90. *See also* bounty payments; economics, of soldiering; households; recruitment; substitutes

Soldiers Aid Society (Ohio), 209–10

speculations, 2, 6, 13, 123, 173; clothing and dry goods, 76–77, 93, 127–28, 137, 162–63; connected to independence, 80; land, 19, 48; opportunities created by war, 111, 205; recruitment, 87–89, 138, 166; and substitutes, 201–3

speculators, 8, 40, 42–43, 78, 111, 130

sporting activities, 84, 208

Spurgin, W. F., 217, 218

Stafford, S. H., 144

Stanton, Edwin, 82, 109, 113, 125–27, 144, 151, 163–66, 169, 174

Stephens, Henry Louis, 29, 35–38, 45–46, 73–74, 77, 101, 120, 122, 140, 177

Stewart, Seaforth, 150–51

Still, William, 15–17, 103–5, 108, 120, 173, 191–92, 217–18. *See also* Pennsylvania Abolition Society (PAS)

substitute brokers, 1–5, 7–8, 185, 200–206. *See also* recruitment agents and brokers

substitutes, 3–4, 185, 201–6; black soldiers for white recruits, 139, 165–67, 184; and Southern deserters, 198, 200–201. *See also* Enrollment Act; recruitment

Sullivan & Hyatt (firm), 31–32

sutlers, 90–91, 105, 117, 122, 162, 173

Tappan, Lewis, 54–55, 58, 63–64, 101, 121

Taylor, Frederick Winslow, 209

Thompson, Jared, 160–63

tobacco economy, 11–12, 16–18, 20, 23–24, 211

trade, 11–13, 15, 17–19, 46, 67–68, 128

Truman, Joseph, 188–93

Underground Railroad, 15–16, 18, 23, 49, 52, 218. *See also* contraband; fugitive slaves; refugees

uniforms and equipment, 118; cost of, 90–91, 107; fraud in the production of, 73–76; materials and quality, 74–75, 95–96; as recruitment tool, 71–73, 146; and soldier entrepreneurship, 116, 118, 132

Union Steamship Company, 12, 15, 18–19, 25, 52, 76

Union Volunteer Refreshment Saloon (UVRS), 112, 187, 196–201, 208

United States Colored Troops (USCT), 138–39; First USCT, 146, 158–59; Sixth USCT, 171, 174, 179; Tenth USCT, 144, 146–47, 152–62, 170, 179; Twenty-Second USCT, 171, 174, 179, 210–11; Twenty-Fifth USCT, 171; recruitment, 138–40, 145, 146–48, 170–73; training, 173–74. *See also* African American soldiers; General Order 46; impressment

U.S. Treasury Department, 41, 83, 127, 133, 161

U.S. War Department, 53, 81, 138, 143–44, 146, 164, 166–67, 173, 179, 196, 201

Vanity Fair, 103, 140; African Americans, satire of, 101; Confederacy, 45–46; critiques of domestic affairs, 29–35; Lincoln, satire of, 120–21; military fraud,

73–74, 122; secession, 35–38. *See also Continental Monthly*, journalism veterans, 209–10, 250n4

Virginia: fugitive slaves, 18–19, 52; impressment of black soldiers, 152–63, 179–81; recruitment of black soldiers, 167; USCT, 144–46. *See also* Fort Monroe; General Order 46

Wade, Joseph, 197–201, 208
wage labor, 5–8; allowing for social mobility, 28–29, 31–32, 60, 93–94, 96, 155, 198; challenging traditional household relationships, 31–32, 56–60; and coercion, 2, 9, 31, 34, 60, 65, 77, 114, 123, 145, 149, 153, 155, 158, 176, 194, 198; and concept of progress, 27, 28, 32–33; and consent, 9, 28, 54, 114, 145, 147, 153–56, 159, 160, 176, 177, 180, 182; and contraband during the Civil War, 50–52, 54, 96–101; creating options for lower-class women, 31–32, 63; criticism of and disillusionment with, 59, 60–61, 64, 93–95, 219; dependence on the system, 78–79; impact of secession and Civil War, 45; soldiering as a form of, 78–80, 83, 115, 123, 142, 146–47; in the South, 126–28, 213; and Southern deserters in the North, 196–201; and Southern refugee women, 187–90, 198; and substitutes, 202, 204–5; and white women, 60–61, 63–67

Walker, Albert, 115, 132–33
Walker, Henry, 112, 122, 196; link between household and soldier economies, 114–18, 132–34, 141–42, 182–83; as soldier entrepreneur, 116, 118, 132, 182–83; trying to find black laborer for wife, 134–35
Walker, Persis, 115–17, 132–35, 141–42, 182–84
Washington, D.C., 214–16
Webster, Eliza Ann Richardson, 11, 22–23, 26, 211
Webster, Thomas, 11–13, 38, 111, 210–11; and Abraham Lincoln, 24–27, 40–42; antislavery ideology (black Republican),

16–17, 20, 23–24; benevolence for moral capital, 17–18, 21; commercial affairs, 20, 22–23, 175–76; commissary during the Civil War, 76–77; family, 22–23; and John Sherman, 21–26, 38, 41–42; political affairs, 21–24, 40–42; recruitment efforts, 109–10; recruitment for USCT, 138–40, 145, 170–76; and runaway slaves, 20–21; Southern tobacco business interests, 12, 16, 20–21, 25, 76

Whelden, Charles, 166
white Southerners, 17, 24, 27, 37, 98–99, 123, 126; deserters seeking labor in the North, 196–201; refugees, 187, 196–201; women, 61–62, 187
Wild, Edward, 158–59
Wilder, Charles, 147–49, 150, 152, 180, 181
Willett, Aaron, 168–69
Wilson, Henry, 53, 82, 144–45, 163–64, 167, 171
Woman's Protective Emigration Society (WPES), 63–68
women, Northern: class power and authority, 29–35, 58, 62–63, 188–89; and household responsibilities, 29, 58, 62, 133–34, 194; refinement and respectability, 29, 30, 32, 56, 57, 60; as wage earners, 44, 60–61, 63–67; and war economy, 113, 133, 141, 153, 182–83, 203–4. *See also* households
Wool, John, 50–51, 165
workers, white, 5, 7–8, 55, 150; benefits of wage labor for, 27, 28, 56; coercive arrangements for in the North, 34, 50; fears of black refugees and former slaves competing for jobs, 103, 104, 120–22, 131, 187, 191; fraud against, 6, 29, 50–51, 56, 58, 63; and gender roles, 29–31; important personality characteristics of, 44; limited choices of, 7, 9, 45; postwar, 209–10; in print culture, 29–35. *See also* domestic servants; intelligence offices; labor markets

Zouaves, 152–56

www.ingramcontent.com/pod-product-compliance
Lightning Source LLC
Chambersburg PA
CBHW021851230426
43671CB00006B/347